ASIA ANNUAL 2008

ASIA ANNUAL 2008

UNDERSTANDING POPULAR CULTURE

Editor-in-Chief
H.S. Vasudevan, Director, MAKAIAS

Issue Editor
Kausik Bandyopadhyay, Fellow, MAKAIAS

Associate Editors
Rakhee Bhattacharya, Fellow, MAKAIAS
Swarupa Gupta, Fellow, MAKAIAS
Kingshuk Chatterjee, Fellow, MAKAIAS

MANOHAR
2010

First published 2010

© Maulana Abul Kalam Azad Institute of Asian Studies, 2010

ISBN 978-81-7304-844-9

Published by
Ajay Kumar Jain *for*
Manohar Publishers & Distributors
4753/23 Ansari Road, Daryaganj,
New Delhi 110 002

Printed at
Salasar Imaging Systems
Delhi 110 035

Contents

REVIEW ARTICLE

RESEARCH NOTES

Contributors

Kausik Bandyopadhyay, former Fellow of the Maulana Abul Kalam Azad Institute of Asian Studies, is Reader in History, West Bengal State University, Barasat.

Rakhee Bhattacharya is Fellow, Maulana Abul Kalam Azad Institute of Asian Studies, Kolkata.

Susmita Bhattacharya is Fellow, Maulana Abul Kalam Azad Institute of Asian Studies, Kolkata.

Swapna Bhattacharya (Chakraborti) is Professor in the Department of South and Southeast Asian Studies, University of Calcutta.

Arpita Basu Roy is Fellow, Maulana Abul Kalam Azad Institute of Asian Studies, Kolkata.

Sabyasachi Chatterjee is Senior Lecturer in History, New Alipore College, Kolkata

Suchandana Chatterjee is Fellow, Maulana Abul Kalam Azad Institute of Asian Studies, Kolkata.

Amiya K. Chaudhuri is Fellow, Maulana Abul Kalam Azad Institute of Asian Studies, Kolkata.

Sreemati Ganguli is Fellow, Maulana Abul Kalam Azad Institute of Asian Studies, Kolkata.

Suparna Ghosh (Bhattacharya) is Senior Lecturer in History, Loreto College, Kolkata.

Sharmishtha Gooptu is Founding Trustee of the South Asia Research Foundation and Joint Editor of *South Asian History and Culture* (Routledge)

Charu Gupta is Fellow, Nehru Memorial Museum and Library, New Delhi.

Boria Majumdar is Senior Research Fellow, University of Central Lancashire, UK.

Monika Mandal is Fellow, Maulana Abul Kalam Azad Institute of Asian Studies, Kolkata.

Nalin Mehta is Honorary Research Fellow, La Trobe University, Melbourne.

Nabanita Mitra is Senior Lecturer in History, Women's Christian College, Kolkata.

Sunetra Mitra is Senior Lecturer in History, RKSM Vivekananda Vidyabhavan, Kolkata.

Anita Sengupta is Fellow, Maulana Abul Kalam Azad Institute of Asian Studies, Kolkata.

Jawahar Singh is Fellow, Maulana Abul Kalam Azad Institute of Asian Studies, Kolkata.

Priya Singh is Fellow, Maulana Abul Kalam Azad Institute of Asian Studies, Kolkata.

Krishnan Srinivasan, former Foreign Secretary, Government of India, is Fellow, Maulana Abul Kalam Azad Institute of Asian Studies, Kolkata.

Anuradha Roy is Professor of History, Jadavpur University, Kolkata.

Kaushik Roy is Lecturer in History, Presidency College, Kolkata.

1

Introduction
Understanding Popular Culture

KAUSIK BANDYOPADHYAY

For history is not simply an academic subject: the knowledge of the history of mankind should be a common property of humanity and should above all benefit our nation, without which our work could not have been accomplished.[1]

Thus commented Leopold von Ranke, the architect of 'scientific history'. Although committed to the scientific, source-critical, empiricist and professionalized brand of history, Ranke was aware of 'the danger of losing sight of the universal, of the type of *knowledge everyone desires*'.[2] He acknowledged that, 'history is indeed a social necessity, the property of all humanity'.[3] The remark, moreover, by implication opened up a field in which history moved beyond disciplinary, academic/professionalized limits. Viewed through this prism, history becomes a space studying the 'popular'—alongside, and even in contrast to histories of nationalist movements, famous personalities, dynasties and the high politics of states.[4]

The present volume *Understanding Popular Culture* drew initial inspiration from Ranke. Academic research on the central role of popular culture in the everyday life of a nation in modern society requires an eclectic approach that seriously reconsiders the long-lived dichotomy of the *intellectual* and the *popular* in the study of history and other social sciences. As the great Indian poet Rabindranath Tagore lamented a century ago:

A careful thought reveals that the difference between the educated and uneducated in our country lies in their knowledge of history. Common people have no idea of how men have grown strong, got together and achieved what they have; they fail to comprehend the flow of the thoughts and ideas of the educated and cannot join their activities. It's pathetic on the part of humans not to know what man has achieved and has been capable of achieving in this world.[5]

Understanding Popular Culture is an attempt to reflect upon, and bridge the intellectual gap, that still persists between the two poles.

Popular culture affords a domain where the social scientist can honestly blend the *intellectual* with the *popular* without really disturbing their respective sanctities. The way the contributors in the present volume have approached the intellectual representations of popular culture intends to make the point that intellectualizing the popular and popularizing the intellectual can go hand in hand and generate a synthetic genre of scholarship. While the former trend is well established in Indian academia, the latter, I am afraid, still lacks adequate emphasis. In making this assertion, the present work shares the concern emphasized by S.N. Mukherjee in the 1970s, again, with reference to the writing of history as an intellectual discipline:

> We must recognise that historians are made for history and the reverse cannot be true. We should not only concern ourselves with the problems which the man in the street faced in the past, but make them entertaining and instructive for the man in the street today.[6]

In Asia, popular culture has long been a site which articulates the complexities and diversities of the everyday life of the nation. In view of the complexities of popular culture in different parts of this vast continent, it is easy to comprehend that a single volume can only scratch the surface. Moreover, given the availability and quality of expertise on the subject, the volume has a preponderantly Indian orientation in terms of its contents. *Understanding Popular Culture* therefore attempts to reveal at least part, if not the whole, of the processes of how significant variegated aspects of popular culture was/has become for parts of Asia and particularly for India— politically, socially, economically, culturally and emotionally.

Raymond Betts has recently argued, 'contemporary popular culture is almost without definition; so all-embracing are its subjects, so far its effects'.[7] What sets it apart from anything preceding it is the mass-produced means of pleasure and entertainment that are now being enjoyed by multitudes never reached before. As the architect Frank Gehry argued, 'The modern age is an avalanche of stuff coming at you.'[8] This 'avalanche of stuff', among others, consists of variegated and nuanced forms of popular culture coming at us swiftly, inexorably, and overwhelmingly. People, society, nation—all confront, negotiate and internalize or exclude this phenomenon in their own ways from time to time. Popular culture thus represents people, redefines society, and, to be bold, reconditions humanity.[9] It is the *one* cultural form that engages so many diverse groups and classes of people so widely in a common environment: in front of the television screen, at the sports stadium, in the cinema or music hall, on the computer. These are the corners—all within easy reach, not scattered years and cultures apart—which pertain intense effect to all. The two most distinctive characteristics of this development are the proliferation of images and stuff, and the intensification of the means of communication and diffusion through distributive mechanisms. However, the focal point of interrogating, understanding and analysing popular culture is entertainment or pleasure, because it is this virtue that ensures popular culture its global effects. As Biswarup Sen aptly remarks:

A more productive way to interrogate the texts of popular culture is to analyze them through the category of *pleasure*. Whatever else the popular is, it is that which elicits intense positive affect. . . . The series of likes and dislikes that make up the fortunes of the popular also provide us with a perspective into its meaning.[10]

To put it more succinctly, as Richard Dyer and Ginette Vincendeau sum up in their work on popular European cinema, 'There is a sense in which "the popular" is what it is most popularly assumed to be: what people like.'[11]

As early as 1982, the Open University of Great Britain introduced a course on popular culture for its students. The course was divided into seven parts, which were sub-divided into 32 units. The titles of the parts deserve mention here: (1) Popular culture: themes and issues, (2) The historical development of popular culture in Britain, (3) Popular culture and everyday life, (4) Form and meaning, (5) Politics, ideology and popular culture, (6) Science, technology and popular culture, and (7) The state and popular culture.[12] Researches on popular culture since then have engaged scholars into the apparent dichotomies of high/low or elite/popular cultures.[13] More importantly, the growing self-consciousness about the politics of the term *popular culture* has linked it to the problematics of the public sphere[14] and raised a further debate regarding the viability of alternative terms such as *mass* or *public* to understand the tensions and contradictions between national sites and transnational cultural processes.[15] As Christopher Pinney has argued, 'conventional notions of "popular culture" have little analytical use in the context of a global modernity, and in the context of South Asia's position within that modernity'.[16] In the context of the present volume, however, I would argue that the *popular* in Asian countries bears little resemblance to that in the West. Contributions herein refer to culture that tends to exceed the nation and become global. Hence I prefer to use the term 'popular' to understand the wider reach of its suffix, 'culture'.

The present volume, as has already been mentioned, is an inter-disciplinary effort designed to respond to the growing interest in popular culture in parts of Asia. While some scholars like John Storey would argue that the idea of popular culture is an invention of the intellectuals,[17] this volume does not try to explore the conceptual or intellectual discourses on popular culture; neither does it examine how these intellectual discourses articulate questions of power and culture. Rather, it intends to address the changing intellectual ways of constructing, reconstructing or deconstructing texts and activities as popular culture. Popular culture, in such context, is defined in a broad and inclusive way to incorporate lived and textual cultures, the mass media, ways of life, and discursive modes of representation.[18] Central to the formation of these popular cultures are articulations of the economic, social and political spheres, and the volume offers contributions that highlight these issues. Asian popular culture is of interest to cultural, media, film, and sports studies, as well as social geography, history, business management, international relations, area and diaspora studies, and post-modern and post-colonial theoretical formulations. The volume therefore intends to bring together scholars who will offer critical appreciation, from theoretical and empirical perspectives, the production, distribution, and consumption of popular cultural forms within Asia and across the international borders. It thus seeks to serve as an innovative and informative effort to discuss and debate the emergence and vibrancy of new forms of social, cultural and political strategies and representations of popular culture in art, film, music, theatre, sport, media, advertisement, science, politics and visual cultures.

The volume unfolds with the most familiar theme of colonial cultural histories—nationalism, albeit conceived in a nuanced context of understanding nationalism as popular culture. Anuradha Roy's essay 'The Poet's Swadeshi Movement', in an attempt to explore the poetical underpinnings of the anti-Partition movement of 1905 in Bengal, argues after Sumit Sarkar, the greatest living historian of the movement, that 'the Swadeshi Movement's greatest claim to immortality' lies perhaps in the realm of patriotic poetry and songs'.[19] Emphasizing at the outset that the movement was largely a creation of poets, it shows how a galaxy of people, including the great Rabindranath Tagore, chose to respond to the call of the movement through poems and songs. This poetical representation of the movement needs to be understood in the wider perspective of a freedom movement, which was more than just a medley of some activities, organizations and events, a process related to mentality.

From this perspective, Roy argues, the movement appears necessarily and primarily a movement of, and by the poets.

The story of colonial Indian literature, however, had never been a monotonous tryst with nationalism. It had its *own* aura of versatility. Guru Dutt's novels bear testimony to this. A legendary Hindi litterateur of the nineteenth century, Guru Dutt gave serious thoughts to religion and culture of man and society in writing his novels. Jawahar Singh tries to analyse these representations of religion and culture in Dutt's most popular social novels. Singh shows how Guru Dutt, an ardent champion of traditional Indian culture, severely criticized social vices such as drinking, prostitution, treason and communalism that posed a threat to the everyday life of a society already suffering from colonial exploitation, and emphasized the importance of humanism, nationalism and unity in Indian psyche. According to Singh, Guru Dutt valued culture as an active philosophy of life and believed in the complementarity of religion and culture. This complementarity, which is the focal theme of the essay, becomes apparent in Dutt's treatment of the tension between Indian and Western or between rural and urban cultures, his understanding of humanism in the context of a perceived *purity* of Indian culture, and his lamentation on the loss of so-called *authenticity* in Indian culture during his time.

Recent researches on popular medical practices and medicinal systems in colonial societies emphasize mostly on dichotomies between traditional and modern or indigenous and Western notions of public health and healing culture. Charu Gupta, in her essay, treats some wider debates on gender hierarchies, questions of health and medicine and their relationship to women in colonial India, and the perceived boundaries between indigenous therapies and modern medical practices through an analysis of the writings of Yashoda Devi, a famous woman ayurvedic practitioner in north India in the beginning of the twentieth century, who negotiated and reinvented the terrain of tradition and modernity in her discourse on women's health, often with contradictory and ambivalent implications. The essay also inquires into the dichotomies between subaltern/hegemonic and feminine/masculine while examining the interrelationship between traditional, indigenous medical practices in colonial societies and the impact of modern, Western, biomedical systems on them. Yashoda Devi's medical discourses reflect an attempt to popularize and commercialize Ayurveda, an indigenous system of medicine.

Central to the conceptualization and understanding of modern popular culture is the representations of everyday life of national and international communities in media. The radio, in this context, argues Nabanita Mitra, serves as an indispensable medium of mass communication, having the potential of facilitating planned development and fostering socio-cultural harmony in the life of any nation. In tracing the origins and evolution of All India Radio (AIR), Mitra highlights the untiring efforts of Sir Lionel Fielden and others, coupled with enthusiastic public response, in the face of initial obstacles it encountered, and the survival strategies it adopted to nullify the imperial government's attempts to appropriate it as a propaganda device. The AIR, particularly its Calcutta chapter, as the author rightly claims, made an enduring contribution to address the need-based requirements of various segments of the populace (farmers, tribals, women, youth and children) through a wide variety of programmes, facilitating India's transformation into a welfare state. More importantly, the pioneers of radio brought about a cultural efflorescence that transformed it into a self-reliant and viable medium of mass communication.

The 1990s constituted a crucial era for Indian television as it could free itself from the clutches of state monopoly with the onset of private satellite television. In an attempt to explore the links between democratic culture and television in terms of the social sources of news television, Nalin Mehta's chapter argues that the emergence of television news networks has greatly enhanced and strengthened deliberative Indian democracy. Going beyond the political-economy equation and developing on Amartya Sen's argument on the argumentative tradition of India, Mehta analyses the rise of Indian news television in the context of a society with a strong argumentative tradition of public reasoning. However, Indian television, according to Mehta, thrives on programming genres that marry older argumentative traditions with new technology and notions of liberal democracy to create new hybrid forms that strengthen democratic culture. The essay also provides a genealogy of Indian politics on satellite television that focuses on the specific ways in which the new medium affected the daily spectacle of Indian politics. Satellite television emerged as a new factor in the Indian political matrix in the mid-1990s and, as Mehta shows, political leaders and parties adapted their daily practices of politics to the 24-hour publicity it provided.

How the satellite television has done wonders to transform societies and cultures across the states in India becomes apparent in Rakhee Bhattacharya's study of the impact of musical reality shows on the mindset of the people of north-east India. According to her, the growth of satellite television, sponsorship and communication network along with the euphoria of the people have made this wonder to happen. In the backdrop of an age-old cultural distance of the north-east from mainland India, the musical reality shows of the satellite television have dramatically transformed the image of north-east India's isolationist cultural identity and have brought the region closer to the mainland. Bhattacharya also explores the significance of sponsorship, consumerism and communication network that lay behind this cultural transformation. She also believes that with the emergence of new patterns of expenditure in urban India, a modern *Indian* identity based on a new professional culture is steadily over-powering the traditional barriers of region, ethnicity or religion to give Indians a more viable sense of unity.

The volume deals specifically with two most important forms of performing arts in modern India—theatre and cinema. Sunetra Mitra, in her essay 'Nationalism and Entertainment: A Study of Colonial Bengali and Gujarati Theatres', examines the interconnectedness between colonial theatre, nationalism and entertainment in colonial Bengal and Gujarat. She highlights the process of appropriation of nationalism as an ideology for the development of native theatre as well as for its commercial viability. The public theatre in both the regions evolved from assimilation of local theatrical forms and practices which had been in vogue for long to novel organizational and theatrical features borrowed from the English play houses. However, as Mitra rightly points out, its adoption of the modes of thought characteristic of rational knowledge in the post-Enlightenment age was mostly limited in nature because of the native theatre's avowed objective of playing a strong nationalist discourse. The professional commercial theatres of the late nineteenth- and early twentieth-century Gujarat and Bengal thus, concludes Mitra, enacted the crisis of colonialism and by extension the power of nationalism.

The 1980s witnessed a radical transformation in Bengali regional language cinema, which most scholars on film history fail to understand and address. Sharmishtha Gooptu analyses the impact of this transformation on the fortunes of the Bengali film industry. She attributes this transformation partly to the creation of a Bengali television watching public in the same period as well as to mainstream Bengali cinema's increasing adaptation of what are commonly known as the 'masala' or 'formula' elements of Bombay cinema. In fact, the effort to alleviate the pecuniary distress of the Bengali film industry went hand in hand with a conceptual and strategic altering of the dominant aesthetic of Bengali cinema till the mid-1970s. Gooptu's essay emphasizes that the growing affinity with the dominant paradigm of Bengali cinema never led the medium to become a purely emulative enterprise. Rather, there was a very structured move towards evolving what Gooptu calls 'a very distinctive product that could appeal to very specific sensibilities among the regional film-going public'. Hence the transformation of Bengali cinema during the 1980s, rather than being an aberration of sorts, may be meaningfully explained in terms of a mutation of the regional film industry's existing paradigm of product differentiation, and its need of securing a niche market against more dominant visual cultures.

Academic enquiry into the experience and memory of Partition in West Bengal after 1947 has more or less concentrated on the politics of refugee rehabilitation and the socio-economic implications of immigration from East Bengal to West Bengal till date. However, there remains a whole domain of cultural activities where the interaction between the immigrants and the hosts took place, leading to a continuous process of cultural confrontation, social negotiation and gradual assimilation. Monika Mandal's essay dwells on the representations of refugee experience and crisis in post-Partition West Bengal through the lens of vernacular literature and cinema. According to Mandal, refugee colonies and refugee existence became the backdrop for narrating other stories—stories of women's struggle, of the poor, of family life, of interpersonal relations, and many other aspects of everyday life. While admitting that artistic works produced as a result of the Partition have not been adequate to the occasion, she highlights the most enduring representations of the event as reflected in contemporary and later Bengali literature as also through the cinematic creations of Ritwik Ghatak.

Like Partition of India, the Holocaust, which refers to the 1933-45 war against the Jews—a war that began with book burnings and culminated in the burning of human beings in the crematoria and lime pits of Nazi occupied Europe—has become *one* event with immense global significance. As an area of study, the Holocaust thrives on controversy. The term, used alternatively with the Hebrew word *Shoah*, continues to be the single-most significant factor in the life of the Jews, and has assumed the character of what Singh calls 'a national trauma'. As the essay shows, the event finds a myriad of voices in the form of varied reflections and multiple analyses in newspaper articles and contemporary writings, both fictional and non-fictional. Moreover, theatrical and cinematic depictions of the ghastly event continue to dominate the Jewish cultural arena. It thus provides a concise insight into the metaphorical representation of the memory of the Holocaust in cinema and literature.

Similarly, the Armenian Genocide, which refers to the atrocities and mass extermination committed against the Armenian people of the Ottoman Empire by the Young Turks in the late 1910s and early 1920s, became an omnipresent source of collective pain and historical consciousness for the Armenians across the globe. It was, however, only in the 1960s, argues Susmita Bhattacharya in her essay 'Representation of the Armenian Genocide in Popular Culture', that the movement for national and international recognition of the Armenian Genocide started to gain in momentum. The politics of genocide recognition began to affect the political identity of the diaspora from the 1970s with increasing attempts to mobilize governments and human rights associations in Europe. These political attempts to gain recognition for the 'Genocide' went hand in hand with serious academic and cultural efforts to garner support from the intelligentsia and the masses for that cause. Bhattacharya's essay tries to understand the appropriation of popular cultural forms, particularly literature and cinema, for the cause of genocide recognition, and analyses the representations of the event through novels and films.

The construction of 'martial race' was a significant theme in the formulation and dispensation of British imperial ideology in colonial India. Kaushik Roy, in his discussion on the construction of martial race culture in British India and its legacies in post-colonial South Asia, brings into focus the importance of the making of 'martial races' out of Afro-Asian demographic resources in the military history of British colonial empire. By an analysis of the organization of the Sepoy Army, he shows how it came to constitute a crucial interface between the British colonizers and the colonized in the subcontinent. However, as the legacies of the martial culture suggest, the post-colonial armies of India and Pakistan absorbed the martial race cultural artefacts. In fact, Roy argues, what started as an elite culture introduced by a colonial institution became part of the popular culture among the inhabitants of modern South Asia, receiving ample reflection in the increasing communal consciousness in the post-colonial Indian society.

In the modern world, sport is one of the most significant social practices. An integral part of popular culture, it has a significant place in public life. Sports and clubs came to colonial societies like India with the British, who always followed a policy of exclusion in those clubs. In such context, Suparna Ghosh (Bhattacharya)'s essay explores the possibility of cultural integration in women's sports in colonial Bengal. She traces the process of Bengali women's absorption, adoption and transmutation of the games played by the Anglo-Indian women in the British-run Anglo-Indian schools and colleges in face of contemporary social taboos and conservatism. Emphasizing the limits of women's participation in sports in colonial Bengal, she investigates the unfulfilled desires and emotions of some women along with the factors that facilitated the sporting activities among Bengali women in the twentieth century. Her essay also focuses on the social stratification in sports based on gender and race through the examples of Parsi and Jews as also the Anglo-Indian women.

Cricket's popularity in contemporary world goes hand in hand with the boom in satellite television. In the Indian context, the complementarity of cricket and satellite television is very well known. Boria Majumdar offers a nuanced understanding of the changing relationship of interdependence between cricket and satellite television in contemporary India. He shows how the Board of Control for Cricket in India (BCCI), has appropriated satellite cricket to become a hugely cash-rich body. Majumdar also interrogates the local/regional dimensions of this relationship by referring to a regional cricket body election in West Bengal. Using two distinct case studies—the implications of the tri-nation one-day series played in Malaysia in September 2006 involving Australia, West Indies and India, and television coverage of the Cricket Association of Bengal elections in July 2006, Majumdar comments on the complex and ever changing relationship between cricket and television in India and examines its impact on the everyday life of the nation.

Popularization of science and technology has been central to the process of development in post-colonial societies. Sabyasachi Chatterjee attempts to explore the popular perceptions of science and addresses the politics of science movements with special reference to post-colonial Bengal. Reminding his readers of conventional representations of science in Bengali society, particularly in literature, he emphasized upon three major ways through which science movements work: popularization of science, spread of scientific temper and the use of science and technology for the welfare of the common people. His essay also focuses on the role of individuals and organizations in the popularization of science. As he argues, science movement in West Bengal in the last three decades was mostly dominated by the political ideologies of the left and with the main aim of opposing the hierarchical Union Government. Finally,

Chatterjee critically examines the role of Paschimbanga Bijnan Mancha in the process, bringing into light the complex equation between science and politics in post-colonial Bengal.

The last essay of the volume considers the significance of political processes in the everyday life of a nation. Apparently, it might seem to be little difficult to integrate hardcore political affairs such as Constituent Assembly elections into the fold of popular culture. However, in a country like Nepal infested with political turmoil for nearly two decades, the process of political transition from monarchy to republic has become so central to the sensibilities of the Nepali masses that the election as a road to the abolition of monarchy and foundation of democracy has come to occupy a reflective place in popular cultural life in contemporary Nepal. It is in this context that Amiya Chaudhuri regards the overthrow of the monarchy and the Constituent Assembly election of April 2008 as a landmark in its contemporary history. At the vortex of an irreversible process of globalization, the new political system evolving in Nepal since the elections has to negotiate with the new realities of liberalization, privatization and global forms of popular culture. Chaudhuri's essay, in the light of the popular euphoria over the last election, enquires whether the state and the civil society in Nepal, languishing from the want of good governance for long, would be able to reprioritize its democratic institutions and adapt the challenges of global commercial culture into its traditional cultural milieu. It also suggests that political transition and electoral politics in a conflict-ridden country like Nepal is frequently embedded with the suppressed or entangled ethos and practices of popular culture.

The study of popular culture is a fast-developing branch of knowledge in social science research. To make it qualitatively viable, it is important to approach the subject with two complementary methods: interdisciplinary perspective and comparative study. Basing on this premise, the present volume seeks to explore some aspects of the variety of representations and dispensations in the field of popular culture. More importantly, the essays concentrate on exploring the relationships between the national, regional and local in the history of popular culture in the countries studied. This is expected to generate future forays into more specialized regional and local studies.

As I have already mentioned, no single volume can cover every inch of ground in its defined field of interest—there is never enough space. However, we have tried to do the next best thing. We have tried to pave the way for further and fuller coverage of the significant issues revealed through attitudes to popular culture in the polity and society of some relevant Asian nations. Among these are: cultural nationalism, identity politics, the increasing importance of commerce and its interaction with nationalism, mediatization of politics and culture, gender relations, and the cultural politics of entertainment and pleasure in an age of globalization. While this volume has raised a few issues and addressed a few questions with regard to popular culture in parts of Asia, more studies, we expect, will follow to supplement this humble effort.

NOTES

1. Quoted in Arthur Marwick, *The Nature of History*, London: Macmillan, 1970, p. 44.
2. Ibid. Emphasis added.
3. Ibid.
4. Cf. Sumit Sarkar, *Writing Social History*, Delhi: Oxford University Press, 1997; Eric Hobsbawm's definition of social history in *On History*, London: Weidenfeld and Nicholson, 1997; and in the context of Bengal: Niharranjan Ray, *Bangalir Itihas*, 2 vols., Calcutta, reprinted by Dey's Publishers, 2005; and Dineshchandra Sen, *Brihat Banga*, Calcutta, 1935.
5. Rabindranath Tagore, 'Shikhsha', in *Rabindra Rachanabali*, vol. 10, Calcutta: Government of West Bengal, 1992, p. 453. Translation mine.
6. S.N. Mukherjee, 'The Citizen Historian', in S.N. Mukherjee, *Citizen Historian: Explorations in Historiography*, Delhi: Manohar, 1996, p. 8.
7. Raymond F. Betts, *A History of Popular Culture: More of Everything, Faster and Brighter*, New York & London: Routledge, 2004, p. 1.
8. Quoted in ibid., p. 6.
9. For the most insightful and elaborate discussions on the concept, subjects and effects of popular culture, see Tom Pendergast and Sara Pendergast (eds.), *St. James Encyclopaedia of Popular Culture*, vols. 1-5, London: St. James Press, 2000; Milton Keynes, *Popular Culture*, 7 vols., UK: Open University Press, 1982; Betts, *A History of Popular Culture*; John Storey, *Inventing Popular Culture: From Folklore to Globalization*, Malden: Blackwell, 2003; C. Lee Harrington and D.D. Bielby (eds.), *Popular Culture: Production and Consumption*, Malden: Blackwell Publishers, 2001.
10. Biswarup Sen, *Of the People: Essays on Indian Popular Culture*, Delhi: Chronicle Books, 2006, p. 4.
11. Richard Dyer and Ginette Vincendeau, *Popular European Cinema*, New York: Routledge, 1992, p. 5, cited in ibid., p. 4.
12. Keynes, *Popular Culture*.
13. For a study on these dichotomies in the Indian context, see Sumanta Banerjee, *The Parlour and the Streets: Elite and Popular Culture in Nineteenth Century Calcutta*, Calcutta: Seagull Books, 1989.
14. The most inspirational and influential study of public sphere as a historical phenomenon dates back to Jurgen Habermas who analysed the structural transformation of the public sphere in the course of the nineteenth and twentieth centuries in terms of a move 'from a public critically reflecting on its culture to one that merely consumes it'. Habermas, *The Structural Transformation of*

the Public Sphere: An Inquiry into a Category of Bourgeois Society, originally in German, 1962, Cambridge, Mass.: MIT Press, 1989, p. 175.

15. For example, Arjun Appadurai and Carol Breckenridge have preferred *public* as an alternative to *popular* on the ground that 'it appears to be less embedded in such highly specific western dichotomies and debates as high versus low culture'. Arjun Appadurai and Carol A. Breckenridge, 'Why Public Culture?', *Public Culture* 1, no. 1, p. 6. Also see Carol A. Breckenridge (ed.), *Consuming Modernity: Public Culture in Contemporary India*, Delhi: Oxford University Press, 1996, pp. 1-20.

16. Christopher Pinney, 'Introduction', in Rachel Dwyer and Christopher Pinney (eds.), *Pleasure and the Nation: The History, Politics, and Consumption of Public Culture in India*, Delhi: Oxford University Press, 2001, pp. 6-7.

17. Storey, *Inventing Popular Culture*.

18. Asha Kasbekar, in her recent work on Indian pop culture, includes the following as integral components of Indian popular culture industry that has begun to flourish inexorably since the 1990s: music, theatre, Indian literature in English, print media (newspapers and magazines), radio, television (and satellite television), cinema, cricket, and various aspects of consumer culture (malls, cafes and pubs, restaurants, high fashion, e-commerce and new age spirituality). Asha Kasbekar, *Pop Culture India! Media, Arts, and Lifestyle*, Santa Barbara: ABC-CLIO, 2006.

19. Sumit Sarkar, *The Swadeshi Movement in Bengal 1903-1908*, Delhi: People's Publishing House, 1974, p. 289.

2

The Poet's Swadeshi Movement— Nationalism as Popular Culture: A Study of the Poetry of the Swadeshi Movement

ANURADHA ROY

INTRODUCTION

I want to emphasize at the outset that the Swadeshi Movement was largely a creation of poets. If the Swadeshi Movement means boycott of foreign goods, if it means establishment of institutions for national education, if it means meetings, processions, speeches, and somewhat later ascending the gallows by killing white people, it also means penning poetry. Poems were not merely incidental to the movement. They constituted an integral part of it. Hundreds of people wrote thousands of poems as their contribution to the Swadeshi Movement. If we treat songs as poems, the size of the Swadeshi poetry would appear all the more formidable. It was a movement that prompted no less a poet than Rabindranath Tagore to compose numerous songs. And there were many more poets and composers: some of them talented, some not so talented, who nevertheless felt compelled to respond to the movement. The principal historian of the Swadeshi Movement, Sumit Sarkar, has indeed recognized the importance of poems and songs in the movement: 'The Swadeshi Movement's greatest claim to immortality lies perhaps in the realm of patriotic poetry and song.'[1]

But I want to say something more about the songs and poems of the Swadeshi Movement. To my mind, not only the Swadeshi Movement but the entire freedom movement of India was not just a medley of some activities, organizations and events, but a process related to mentality. It was a long process of ideological operation that slowly and gradually made a nation, gave it self-esteem and self-confidence. Its importance and effectuality lie in the mental development of a people. And from this perspective it appears necessarily and primarily a movement of and by the poets. A nationalist movement means a lot of poetry because it involves much idealist romanticism, and is basically a process of imagination, as even realist sociological studies are prone to viewing it nowadays.[2] And between prose and poetry, idealism and imagination are generally taken to be functions of the latter. As we would see, in the Swadeshi Movement, the political leaders took up the tune sung by the poets. Alternatively, it may be said that the movement made a poet of every nationalist. And herein perhaps lies the movement's greatest claim to be a popular movement too.[3] Hence in this essay I propose to reconstruct the history of the Swadeshi Movement through a study of its poetry.

THE NINETEENTH-CENTURY BACKGROUND[4]

Nationalism had flourished in Bengal since the nineteenth century among the literati heavily dependent upon their British masters. British rule was like the sky above their head. Loyalty to the British was an essential component of their nationalism. They simultaneously belonged to two nations—Bengali and Indian. Bengali language and culture formed the basis of their Bengali nationality, while their Indian nation drew upon two myths of an immemorially old 'we'—namely Hindu and Aryan. The nineteenth-century Indian nation was Hindu and Aryan in character. In specific contexts, the main enemy of this nation was regarded not as the British, but the *Yavanas* or Muslims. Rather, the British were supposed to have delivered this nation from Muslim tyranny. As is well known, the heroic annals of this incipient nation had as its abiding theme the medieval Hindu chiefs' resistance to Muslim aggressors.

Of course, the nineteenth-century nationalists also felt the agony of subjection and detested many aspects of British rule. Yet they had to accept this rule. This was an anomalous situation, which they rationalized by creating a set of myths. These were: (1) The British royal family was something divine and capable of correcting all wrongs of British rule. (2) The British were materially superior and greater in physical prowess, while the Indians were hopelessly weak; and this was the prescript of providence. (3) British rule was doing much good to India and above all had brought her the gift of modern Western civilization, ethically and epistemologically much superior to that of India. (4) If the regenerative possibilities of British rule were not being realized in India, that was due to some bad Englishmen who subverted the good intentions of the good Englishmen. Together, these myths gave structure to the ideology of colonialism in the minds of the nationalist intelligentsia by imputing to their own nation an inescapable inferiority, and to the British a sort of omnipotence and a magic ability to help. So what the nationalists did most of the time, at least so far as our literary evidence goes, was extolling a glorious Hindu-Aryan past, bemoaning the present plight and begging the kindness of the British. It was a very passive cultural nationalism in the nineteenth century which involved assertion of autonomy only in certain cultural matters such as virtues of women, food habits, sartorial practices, and so on. We must also add that sometimes the nationalists criticized the economic exploitation of the foreigners, called it 'un-British' and intended to correct it within the framework of British rule.

THE PREPARATION FOR THE SWADESHI MOVEMENT

The nationalist preoccupation of sitting and whining about the lost glory of the nation gradually made some nationalists impatient. They wanted a nation active in the present and oriented to the future. Thus an increasing number of awakening calls were heard as the nineteenth century drew to a close. The passive cultural nationalism was becoming an active political one. The birth of the Indian National Congress was a milestone in the process. It articulated a number of political demands, though not yet that of political sovereignty. At first its method consisted of mere prayers and petitions to the colonial masters. But soon, in the flush of awakening and activism, this method came to be criticized.

With this came some more changes in the nationalist consciousness. In the atmosphere of forward-looking nationalist awakening at the turn of the century, Bengali nationalism vied for ascendancy over Indian nationalism. After all, being Bengali was a shared experience, and anchored the nationalists to the present-day reality. The root-myths of the Indian nation, that is, Hindu and Aryan, on the other hand, took shape and colour only in the context of the past and thus inspired more awe and reverence than intimacy and activism. We may recall that even in the nineteenth century the nation of seven crore that in Bankimchandra's imagination would rise with a thundering roar and with sharp swords flashing in their hands had been the Bengali nation. Furthermore, political nationalism involves a strong sense of territoriality and this opened the eyes of the Hindu nationalists to the fact that the Muslims were mixed up with them all over the place in such a way that any attempt at unscrambling would be impractical. So even the *Yavan*-baiters now gave out calls for Hindu-Muslim unity.

Above all, this forward-looking nationalism worked out a programme for the nation which involved forging national unity, practising national culture and much more. It involved founding indigenous industries to replace foreign goods (an extension of 'economic nationalism' that had flourished earlier). It involved cultivating physical prowess intending it to reach a political fulfilment sooner or later (as evident in the activities of revolutionary terrorists in particular). It also involved cultivation of *atma-shakti* (self-prowess) as advocated by Rabindranath Tagore to build the character and uplift the soul of every countryman and thus to counter the West's 'endless vanity', 'pompous luxury', 'oppression of the poor' and warmongering. The ideal of *atma-shakti* thus rejected the myth of the superiority of Western civilization quite categorically.

And all this was reflected in songs and poems from the end of the nineteenth century. Sumit Sarkar has marked the year 1903 as the beginning of the Swadeshi Movement. But we might even go back a few more years to trace the beginning of the movement. The Swadeshi mood was definitely building up from the 1890s. In 1896, at Aswini Kumar Datta's school Brajamohan Bidyalay in Barishal, a student named Jajneshwar led a chorus singing a song that must have sounded quite militant—*Chal re, chal re, chal re, o bhai, jiban ahabe chal* (Come, come brothers, let's go and sacrifice our lives). This Jajneshwar turned out to be the celebrated bard Mukunda Das ('the notorious jatrawalla' in police reports)[5] during the Swadeshi Movement. Such militancy often used the trope of the crematorium-residing Goddess Kali asking of her sons warm blood from their gashed chests, that is, insisting on their martyrdom in the process of taking revenge. Sometimes it used the metaphor of brandishing of the sword against the enemy. The urge to cultivate physical prowess was registered in verses looking up to heroes from the history of the nation and celebrating its valour of the olden days. Some of these verses were about the good old medieval Hindu heroes fighting the Muslims, such as Shivaji and Rana Pratap. But some Muslim heroes too became popular about this time, such as Mir Qasim and Sirajuddaulah. The triumph of Japan over Russia in 1904 greatly helped the Bengali intelligentsia to overcome their inferiority complex with regard to physical prowess, by revealing that an Asian power could after all successfully challenge a Western power in an armed conflict. The harassment of the English at the hands of the Boers had also been a source of inspiration. All this was reflected in a good many number of poems written in the late nineteenth and early twentieth centuries. But more importantly, Sayiid Abu Mohammad Ismail Hossain Siraji worshipped 'freedom' in his poem 'Swadhinata Bandana' (Worship of Freedom) included in his book of poems *Anal Prabaha* (The Flow of Fire) published in 1901, soon to be banned by the government. This was the first time that the urge for freedom was articulated so unambiguously in Bengali literature. Here are a few lines from the poem:

> Come, you sacred mother!
> You who have always provided salvation to the sinner and the destitute.
> Let your sharp scimitar shine like lightening
> Let it thunder terribly.
> Let the fallen lives seek salvation after ages.
> Let us once again stand in Bengal and in the world with our heads held high.[6]

Also, calls for Hindu-Muslim unity multiplied and Bengali nationalism flourished. The idea of partition was already floating in the air and this being an issue concerning Bengal, was a boost to Bengali nationalism. There appeared poems protesting the proposal of partition. Bijaychandra Majumdar wrote his satirical poem 'Bangamangal' in 1903:

> The Governor General came with a sharp sword in his hand
> To dissect the body of Banga.
> And who could dare to prevent his judicious act? . . .
> When the head was cut off, the body turned cold.
> Some even took Banga to be dead.
> The head of Orissa was attached to the body.
> Yet it did not move.
> Assam donated its nice long nose
> Yet it refused to breathe.[7]

The partition came into effect on 16 October 1905, as the last straw on the camel's back. From then on a huge stream of poetry inundated the collective mind of the Bengali literati to create the history of the Swadeshi Movement, to which we will now turn our attention.[8]

'A NEW AGE ARRIVES'

The first impression that we get from the poetry of the Swadeshi Movement is a sense of awakening all around, a sense of richness and promise. So far the Bengalis had tried the method of prayers and petitions to prevent the partition. A few days before the partition they launched an angry agitation. Even a moderate leader like Surendranath Banerjee dared to declare that the settled fact of partition would be unsettled. The morning of the partition day saw observation of the ritual of *rakhi-bandhan* (a religious rite thus being secularized and used as a symbol of fraternity), procession and bathing in the river Ganga under the leadership of Rabindranath. We also know that the poet tied *rakhis* on the hands of some Muslim coachmen and mullahs on his way to the Ganga.[9] The partition was perceived as a conspiracy of the British to drive a wedge between the two communities of Bengal. Rabindranth's song 'Banglar mati Banglar jal' was sung in the procession:

> The earth of Bengal, the water of Bengal
> The wind of Bengal, the fruits of Bengal
> May they all become sacred, o God!
> The hearts of the Bengalis
> The souls of the Bengalis
> All brothers and sisters of Bengali homes
> May they remain united, o God!

Another procession in the afternoon sang Rabindranth's *Oder bandhan jatoi shakto habe, moder bandhan tatoi tutbe* (The tighter their bondage is, the looser will be ours), which was found highly seditious by the government.[10] We may also recall his *Amar sonar Bangla, ami tomay bhalobasi* (My golden Bengal, I love you), which had been sung in a huge meeting at the Town Hall a few days before the partition. This was the first and the last time in his life that Rabindranath got involved in active politics. But the greatest contribution to the movement were his songs, which constitute a permanent treasure for Bengalis—*O amar desher mati, tomar pare thekai matha* (O the soil of my country, I bow to thee), *Jadi tor dak shune keu na ase tabe ekala chalo re* (If no one responds to your call, go alone), *Je tomay chhare chharuk, ami tomay chharbo na ma* (Whoever deserts you, mother, I will cling to you forever).[11] And most of his Swadeshi songs adapted folk tunes of Bengal in search for an indigenous musical tradition.

This emotional situation was intense enough as to make even a political leader like Bipin Chandra Pal write a number of poems. One of them ran thus:

> The cruel axe of the king cannot divide you, my country
> It has only awakened us from our sleep.[12]

And how right Pal was! This awakening was the most important feature of the Swadeshi Movement. Everything else can be attributed to it. Seeing this awakening all around, the poet Satyendranath

Datta exclaimed: 'It is a juncture of history, a new age has arrived in Bengal.'

The awakening was evident in the rejection of the method of prayers and petitions. Kartik Chandra Dasgupta, a prolific poet of the Swadeshi era, captured the mood of the moment thus:

> What is the point of further flattery?
> Those who do not respond even when we prostrate at their feet,
> Cannot be our friends.
> Don't you have any self-respect?[13]

Calls for resistance were heard everywhere. And unity among countrymen was considered the primary mode of resistance. Amritalal Basu said:

> Let them sacrifice Bengal by force.
> We shall remain close–heart to heart in one body.

Also, calls were given to cast off hesitation, fear and laziness and thus to take the nation along the path of progress. And it is in this way that the silted river was inundated ('*mara gange ban*' in the words of Rabindranath), the life was flooded ('Jibanbanya', title of a poem by Satyendranath Datta) and a new enthusiasm (*Naba-Uddipana*, title of a book of poems by Siraji) dawned. The verses were both reflections and inspirations of this awakening.

BOYCOTT AND SWADESHI

Boycott of foreign goods was the main item on the Swadeshi agenda. And poetry was a major means of propagating it. Quite a few poets were involved in Swadeshi industries, such as Karunanidhan Bandyopadhyay who sold his wife's ornaments and set up factories to manufacture matchsticks and aerated water, though none of these enterprises met with success.[14] Calls to boycott foreign goods were numerous. Rabindranath pledged: 'No longer shall I buy hanging ropes from foreigners taking them for nice clothes'[15]; Swarnakumari Devi called dressing up like foreigners *Matridroha* (rebellion against one's own mother).[16] Mukunda Das castigated the *babus* fascinated with foreign goods:

> Babu, are you not going to come to your senses before your death?
> Do you not realise that a white ghost is haunting you and that it will ruin you totally?
> You used to eat from plates of gold
> Now you are satisfied with plates of steel.
> Your foolishness is unparalleled.

You have taken to pomatum abandoning your indigenous *attar*.
It is not for nothing that they call you 'brute', 'nonsense' and 'foolish'.
You had a barnful of paddy, but let it all destroyed by white rats.
Take off your spectacles and look at the ruins.[17]

This song caused Mukunda Das three years' rigorous imprisonment
and a fine of three hundred rupees.

Pramathanath Raychaudhuri's book of poems *Deshbhakti* (Devotion
to One's Country) contained some narrative poems describing the
refusal of a coachman to give a ride to a *babu* who smokes a foreign-
made cheroot, the refusal of a shoeshine boy to brush a *babu's* foreign
boots, the pride of a wife on her husband's resignation from his
job as his white employer asks him to wear foreign clothes in the
office, and even the patriotic zeal of a little girl who throws away
her imported doll. Chandicharan Bandyopadhyay's book of poems
Swadeshrenu (Some Pollens of the Country) written for children tried
to invoke the spirit of Swadeshi and boycott in young minds. There
were also calls to give up foreign manners and customs, foreign titles
as well as lowly jobs under foreigners (*chakuri kukuri*). Manomohan
Chakrabarty's song *Chhere dao kacher churi Banganari* (Throw away
your glass bangles, o women of Bengal) was popularized by Mukunda
Das. Another very popular song was Rajanikanta Sen's *Mayer deoya
mota kapor mathay tule ne re bhai* (Brother, respectfully take upon
your head the coarse cloth given by your mother), probably written
to promote the textiles of Bangalakshmi Cotton Mill, a Swadeshi
enterprise. It is said that the young members of the Anti-Circular
Society used to hawk Swadeshi cloth on Calcutta streets singing this
song.[18]

AN INCREASINGLY MILITANT MOOD

As the British went all out to crush the movement, the militancy of
the agitators increased proportionately. In Barishal alone, the atrocity
of Lt.-Governor Bamfield Fuller gave birth to a number of songs. It
was Barishal that earned the epithet 'Banglar Boston' and where
Fuller with all his efforts failed to stop the slogan 'Bande Mataram'.[19]
In 1906, the police brutality perpetrated at the provincial conference
in Barishal prompted Kaliprasanna Kabyabisharad to compose at
least three songs, one of them being the famous *Mago jay jeno jiban
chale/shudhu jagat majhe tomar kaje Bande Mataram bale* (Mother,
let my life perish in your service, I will die with 'Bande Mataram'
on my lips), which fell under the purview of Section 124A of Indian
Penal Code.[20] One of the stanzas of the poem ran thus:

Red hats and black suits—
How long will these continue to scare us?
I will keep on serving my mother,
Despite all brutal forces applied to arrest me.
They cannot make me forget mother by caning me—
I am not that kind of a son of the mother!

On the first day of the conference, a local boy named Chittaranjan Guha Thakurta raised the slogan 'Bande Mataram' and was ruthlessly beaten by the police as a result. He was ultimately pushed to a pond nearby with blood all over his body. It is said that every time he was beaten with the staff, he shouted 'Bande Mataram'. We may read this incident side by side with the song above.

The savage brutality on teenagers and youths all around, facilitated by the Carlyle Circular, provoked many poets to protest. Kartikchandra Dasgupta thus challenged the British:

They want blood of children, do they?
Sacrifice one boy
And a hundred will come to life.
Let's see how much blood is required to satisfy them.
Mother, don't you worry.
You know we are descendents of *Raktabija*
One drop of blood gives birth to a hundred thousand of us.
Let's see how much blood they need to be satisfied.[21]

In a number of songs the Motherland was addressed as crematorium-residing Kali or warring Durga and pledges were made to worship her in her terms and using her modes, that is through blood and death. Metaphors like *Rudra* (God of destruction), *bahni* (fire), *ranabheri* (war-trumpet) and *kripan* (sword) were used very often. Calls were given out to seek regeneration by sacrificing one's life. It is true that only a few revolutionaries put this ideal into practice. But the poets did not lag behind in its articulation. Bijaychandra Majumdar said: 'Today you will be tested as to whether you have been initiated by the *mantra* of fire.'[22] He also wrote:

Come, those who want to die today.
The ghouls are impatient to break your bones and suck your blood.
If you are initiated in *tantra* and know the *mantra* of *sadhana*, why do you fear the ghouls?
Die like a *sadhak* and not like an already dead man.[23]

We may also recall Mukunda Das' 'Bhay ki Marane' (one of the songs which formed the charge of sedition against him):

Why fear death?
To save her children Matangi herself is engaged in a war-dance today.
Ta thoi ta thoi thoi drimi drimi drang drang—
Ghosts and ghouls are dancing along with Jogini.[24]

SEEKING INSPIRATION FROM HEROES

The militant Swadeshi agitators sought inspiration from patriotic heroes of history, both from India and abroad. Let me mention the foreign heroes first. There were ancient heroes like Leonidas and Hannibal, the English barons initiating the parliamentary system of government, Cromwell and his likes who fought to curtail monarchic despotism, the heroes of the American War of Independence fighting the British (Boston in particular fascinated the Bengalis preaching boycott), the French heroes fighting the Germans, and also the heroes of the struggle for unification of Italy, such as Mazzini and Garibaldi. Siraji, in his poem titled 'Misharer Abhyutthan' (The Rise of Egypt), expressed the hope that the Egyptians would teach the Indian Muslims the theory that 'freedom cannot be achieved without struggle'. Two very contemporary sources of inspiration were the Japanese and the Boers. Mukunda Das, in one of his songs, called his countrymen to wake up and emulate the above two:

The Boers have awakened to a new dawn
Japan has awakened in a great mirth
If India awakens too in this new age
She can conquer the world in a moment.[25]

Now let us come to the Indian heroes. Among them Shivaji remained the most popular. The Shivaji Festival, first introduced in Maharashtra by Tilak in 1897, soon spread to Calcutta. In 1902, Rabindranath wrote his poem 'Shivaji Utsav' by way of an introduction to Sakharam Ganesh Deuskar's booklet *Sivajir Diksha* (The Initiation of Shivaji).[26] In most of the poems on Shivaji, the focus was on the awakening of India and not that of the Hindus alone. In a song written on the occasion of Shivaji Festival, Ashwini Kumar Datta called both Hindus and Muslims to build a new India in the name of Shivaji.[27] But the Hindu leader Shivaji was not entirely forgotten. Indeed a dilemma is noticed regarding the perceived character of Shivaji's leadership (Hindu or Indian). But we will go into this later.

Amongst the Bengali heroes revered about that time, the most popular were Pratapaditya, the Raja of Jessore, and Sitaram of the same region. Both had fought against the Mughals. But many of the Swadeshi heroes had nothing to do with Hindu-Muslim hostility.

Girish Ghosh's play *Basar* was about the defeat of the Sakas at the hands of Vikramaditya, though the play ends with a song singing the glory of the Aryans—'Glory to Mother India/The Aryan Raj is once again restored to the Aryan throne.' There are quite a few instances of poems glorifying Muslim heroes fighting Muslims, e.g. Chandbibi against Akbar. Anti-British Muslim heroes in the persons of Siraj and Mir Qasim were often venerated. So were the leaders of the Revolt of 1857 such as Nana Sahib, Kunwar Singh and the Rani of Jhansi, something almost unthinkable a few years back. Tributes were paid to heroines too, mostly mythical figures from the Puranas, those who had goaded their husbands and sons to go to war and defeat the enemy.[28]

THOUGHTS ABOUT DRAWING WOMEN INTO THE MOVEMENT

In poem after poem men and women, brothers and sisters were called together to support the movement. Sometimes women were called separately, both by male and female poets. Women were expected to play an important role in the movement mainly by boycotting foreign goods and also urging their family members to do the same. But this limited role was indeed important, for boycott was the principal weapon of the Swadeshi agitation. And of course women were considered a noble source of inspiration for men. A handful of women went beyond this limited role, the most notable among them being Sarala Devi, who took the initiative in the cultivation of physical prowess among the militant nationalists and was involved in many other activities. However, Sarala knew that she was an exception. This is evident in the following lines penned by her:

> All other women are homely and protected by their families.
> You aspire after something greater.
> And dedicate yourself to the cause
> With firmness, diligence and austerity.[29]

Everyone wanted women to participate in the movement under the guardianship of men—as mothers, wives, daughters or sisters. Anything else was quite unthinkable. Even women poets like Mankumari Basu, Ambujasundari Das and Girindramohini Dasi were no exception. The ideal of Indian womanhood preached during the Swadeshi age with much enthusiasm was that of the self-sacrificing 'Grihalakshmi' loyal to her male guardian. Chandicharan Sen, in his book of verses for children, tried to inspire the *Khoka* (a boy child) to go abroad for higher studies and then return to serve the countrymen, to earn a lot of money and spend it for the good of villages, and so on, while for the *Khuku* (a girl child) his advice was to learn household work in order to become a good housewife later in life. If a *Khuku* disregarded this advice, she deserved scolding: 'Shame on *Khuku*/she has not learnt cooking/she asks her aunt what spices to use to make *jhol* (a kind of gravy).' Women who served their husbands despite being oppressed by them were upheld as ideal. Women of the past, who had sacrificed their lives in fire in order to save their own honour and that of their country, were venerated.

THOUGHTS ABOUT DRAWING THE MASSES INTO THE MOVEMENT

In Pramathanath Raychaudhuri's book of narrative poems, *Desh-bhakti*, we find a number of stories telling how cobblers, coachmen and vendors identified themselves with the spirit of the movement. We may also mention his long narrative poem 'Pratishodh' about the poor but spirited Bhimdas Karmakar, an ironsmith, who participates in the movement despite the opposition of the powerful *daroga* (inspector) of the local police station and the latter's zamindar friend.[30] Rajanikanta Sen in one of his songs called the weaver and his wife to weave more cloth, because in this way they would not only serve the country but also make profit for themselves. Girindramohini Dasi wrote *Bangabhange Krishaker Gan* (The Peasant's Song on the Partition of Bengal). Kartikchandra Dasgupta dedicated his book of poems *Amar Desh* (My Country) to the weavers and the peasants of the country.[31] There dawned an awareness that people 'lower' in the social scale were important part of the nation and that their participation in the national movement was essential.

The movement involved efforts at mass mobilization, more so in the countryside. Mukunda Das, the Swadeshi bard, used to tour East Bengal villages, rowing the boat himself and taking along with him a couple of *dohars* (associate singers). He earned great popularity by singing Swadeshi songs in the style of *jatra*. The keenness of Ashwini Kumar Datta in Barishal to make the Swadeshi agitation a mass move-ment was responsible for many more musical experimentations of a similar nature. In Sumit Sarkar's book[32] we find many such examples not only from Barishal but from many other places. It is evident that the agitators were trying to reach out to the masses through songs and for this purpose adapted their music to popular elements, both tonal and linguistic.

Such efforts naturally bore some fruits. Some peasants and workers did participate in the movement. But it is well known that failure in drawing the masses was the Achilles' heel of the Swadeshi Movement. Those who tried to preach Swadeshi to the peasants did it from their own point of view and did not bother about the economic interests of the peasantry. Many of these leaders had vested interest in land, which prevented them from taking up a radical programme in the agrarian field and thus from attracting the peasantry.

THOUGHTS ABOUT HINDU-MUSLIM UNITY

The urge for Hindu-Muslim unity was clearly manifest in the poetry of the movement. The partition was considered as an attempt of the British to spoil the relations between the two communities. So the nationalists stressed on unity. Many poems addressed Hindus and Muslims together. 'Ram and Rahim, don't you quarrel/Keep your minds pure' was an anonymous folk song that was older than the Swadeshi Movement, but popularized by Mukunda Das about this time. Kabyabisharad specially called the Muslims to join the movement, reminding them of their proud past and present plight:

> Those who were *badshahs*
> Are now servants, and oh so obstinate!
> What tempts them to kill their brothers!
> What can they hope to become but mere *khansamas* [table servants]
> Or at best sub-registrars.[33]

However, the pull of Hindu nationalism of the nineteenth century remained. We have already seen that it had been gradually giving way to a secular pan-Indian nationalism. But it was not easy to get rid of the illusion of Hindu-Aryan glory altogether. Many a poem of the Swadeshi period took pride in Aryan glory. Some of them clearly showed a tension between the Hindu and the secular nationalist ideologies, but consciously encouraged the latter. For example, Narendranath Majumdar in his poem 'Bangabhumi',[34] having described in detail the glory of the Aryans and particularly their achievement of suppressing the *Yavanas* (with special reference to Pratapaditya), appealed to the reader—'Yavan and Brahman, do embrace each other.'

Nationalism since the nineteenth century had been glorifying Hindu heroes as adversaries of Muslims. During the Swadeshi era the urge for hero-worship increased, but the proportion of such instances decreased. Shivaji was still considered a great hero. As already pointed out, he was venerated as a symbol of Hindu nationalism on the one hand and that of secular pan-Indian nationalism on the other. A dilemma in this regard can be noticed in the play *Chhatrapati Sivaji* by Girish Ghosh. Here Shivaji is presented as a deadly enemy of the temple-breaking and cow-killing *Yavana*, as a pious man who would restore the Aryan faith and freedom. In the same play, however, Shivaji is also supposed to build up an independent kingdom where there would be no religious animosities. *Sitaram,* another play by Girish Ghosh, expressed the hope—'The Hindus will set up their capital once again in India. Glory to Mother Bhavani!', while in two other plays he established Siraj and Mir Qasim as great heroes.[35]

D.L. Ray's communal inclination had been manifest for some time. Immediately before the partition he wrote his play *Pratap Singha.*[36] The title-hero had been a favourite of the Bengalis since the nineteenth century as a rival of the infidel Mughal emperor. Moreover, the song *Dhao dhao samarakshetre* (Run to the battle-field) featured in the play, though set in the background of Mewar, thrives on the refrain *Jay ma Bharat, jay ma Kali*, making it quite clear that it is actually Indian nationalism that the composer has in his mind and that furthermore this Indian nationalism is nothing but Hindu nationalism. Then in 1908 Ray published his play *Mebar Patan* (The Fall of Mewar), in the beginning of which Hindu nationalism appears quite strong. However, gradually this gives way to another tune. The Mughal crown prince Khurram's address to the Rajput bard Satyabati shows a very secular and liberal attitude:

The Mughal emperor shall never obstruct righteous mother-worship sanctified by devotion. Sing, mother, don't you fear. I would listen to you. I know how to cry mingling my tears with your mother's past glory.

Thus Mughal rule becomes part of Indian tradition. And in the last scene, Rana Amar Singha and the Mughal general Mohabbat Khan (a converted Muslim), though at one point about to engage in a duel, ultimately embrace and ask forgiveness of each other. The song that is responsible for this change of their hearts is—*Kiser shok koris bhai, abar tora manush ha/Giyachhe desh duhkha nai, abar tora manush ha* (Why do you grieve? Be proper men once again/Let's not regret the loss of our country/Only become proper men once again). And in the play *Shah Jehan* written in 1909, Mughal rule became all the more acceptable. The song *Dhanadhanyapushpabhara* (Filled with wealth, grains and flowers) in this play does not grudge any enemy and only expresses a deep love for the motherland.[37]

The Muslim poets tried to promote fraternity too. Sayiid Abu Mohammad Ismail Hossain Siraji was foremost among them. His book of poems *Anal Prabaha* was full of the spirit of awakening and the dream of freedom, common during the Swadeshi period. In some of the poems he especially called upon his coreligionists, but there was no separatism in this. He simply wanted them to take part in the freedom movement of the country along with their Hindu brethren. We may consider his 'Misharer Abhyutthan' looking up to Salahuddin, the hero of Egypt, as a parallel to his deriving inspiration from the Boers or the Japanese. Nur Rahman Eusufji wrote poems of patriotic enthusiasm too. And to him, his country was the mother. Muslim poets were yet to reject the cult of worshipping the motherland as a Hindu religious practice.[38]

I would not deny that there was separatism too. Was not even Siraji a bit too concerned about the progress of Muslims alone? It is well known that several incidents of Hindu-Muslim conflict gradually overshadowed the Swadeshi enthusiasm. Of course, there were zealous Muslim individuals, but Muslims on the whole seemed indifferent and even hostile to the movement. One of the reasons for this is perhaps the failure of the leaders to organize an agrarian movement, because the majority of the agriculturists of Bengal were Muslim. Furthermore, there was the separatist leadership of the nawab of Dhaka. Some Muslims took the initiative to form the Muslim League. The British masters encouraged all this on account of their 'divide and rule' policy. Fuller openly said that Muslims were his dear queen (*suyorani*) and Hindus the wretched one (*duyorani*). Many subtle and gross methods were used to create communal divides.

DOUBTS IN THE MOVEMENT

No wonder, gradually the Swadeshi enthusiasm gave way to doubts about the movement. Many words (including poetry) were being heard, but how much work was being done? Was it not mainly prayers and petitions still? Verbal radicalism combined with cowardice and incompetence in practice provoked D.L. Ray and Bijaychandra Majumdar to write satirical poems. These are poems of the movement, but do not conform to its general tone. For instance, D.L. Ray's 'Neta' (The Leader) ran thus:

> Words are generating more words
> Songs are sweeping the country
> Still we cannot say what will happen ultimately.
> Meetings are being held all over the place,
> Lectures are piercing the sky and the earth
> Those who had earlier found it difficult to pass their time
> Seem quite happy now.[39]

Aryanism or pride in the supposed Aryan glory was a major prop of this hollow verbalism. And this was a target of ridicule by both Dwijendralal and Bijaychandra. Thus runs the latter's poem 'Kheyalpanchak' (Five Whims):

> Oh, of course I can kill the enemies in the meeting.
> But bother! The police come running.
> However, if we beat the drum of our voices together
> The enemy would immediately board the ship and take their leave.
> The poet says—'This time round we are sure to triumph.
> The Japanese on our behalf will scare our enemy to flight.
> If the disciples had reduced Russia to nothing
> The masters are sure to devastate Europe.'
> We need not go to war ourselves,
> Our fame is enough to drive away the ghost.
> Now, you son of Aryan, sleep peacefully.[40]

Since the nineteenth century, satirical humour had been an alternative to political activism. But naturally, such writings numbered much more in the nineteenth century than in the twentieth. However, their very existence, even though in a small number, proves that the Swadeshi Movement started experiencing an ebb-tide too.

Rabindranath, whose participation enriched the movement from the very beginning, got disillusioned very soon. And he articulated this disillusionment not in poetry but in two novels: *Gora*[41] and *Ghare-Baire*[42]. What repulsed him particularly was the Hindu character of Swadeshi. He had sometimes hoisted the flag of Hindu nationalism himself (his poem 'Shivaji Utsav' is an example), but in his case the number and fierceness of such examples was very limited. And he retraced his steps very soon. Gora's patriotism transcended Hinduism to become liberal humanitarianism. In *Ghare-Baire* the Swadeshi Movement was criticized on many counts. First, Rabindranath found it a passing madness and hence ineffectual. Second, he saw a lot of greed, falsehood, deception and nihilistic tendency in the movement. Third, he found, and this was his major objection, that this movement was not concerned with the poor countrymen. Buying and selling of foreign goods were essential to the living of many poor villagers. So the high-handed application of the Swadeshi ideal brought about conflicts in rural markets over a wide area. It was in this context that the revered *mastermoshai* (teacher) of the novel rebuked the Swadeshis:

After all, the country is not just soil, it is these people. Have you ever cast so much as a sidelong glance at them? Today, you intervene in their life all of a sudden trying to dictate what clothes they would wear and what salt they would consume. Why should they tolerate this?

And needless to say, in the East Bengal countryside, many of these poor people were Muslim and this easily led to communal conflicts.

Rabindranath's observation and analysis hit the bull's eye. We can corroborate it by comparing it with the following poem by an ordinary Muslim poet (calling himself *Garib shayer-praneta*, that is, a poor poet) and published as a book entitled *Krishak-Bandhu* (Friend of the Peasant) in 1910. Here a long description of the misery of the peasants was followed by an equation of the oppressed peasants with the Muslims on the one hand and the oppressors with the Hindu *babus* on the other. In the end the poet wants the Muslims to follow a path of separatism and conform to the politics of the Muslim League:

> The *babus* do *babugiri* on the strength of your money.
> If you refuse to grow crops
> They will simply die.
> What fun the *babus* have been creating by running the Congress
> And thus by shaking India!
> However, almost all the peasants of Bengal are Muslim,
> Hindus are only a small fraction.
> Don't forget that Muslims are all brothers to each other.
> Never ever forget this.
> Never consider yourselves inferior.
> Remember that the Muslims are the highest *jati* in the world.[43]

REVOLUTIONARY TERRORISM

It is not just that a few men like Rabindranath became disillusioned and withdrew from the movement. The movement as a whole became weaker by 1907-8. And then revolutionary terrorism raised its head. Verses directly linked with the activities of the revolutionaries—songs composed or sung by them or poems addressing them—may be discussed separately.

The conceptualization of a revolutionary ideal is different from revolutionary activities. Only a handful of young men were involved in revolutionary activities. But the revolutionary mood and ideal had been present in the Swadeshi Movement from the very beginning and on a large scale too. In fact, it is difficult to distinguish it from what is regarded as the 'extremist' trend within the movement, and it was registered in poetry very widely. All the verses that sounded the 'war-trumpet' or sang the praise of the 'sword', or worshipped the goddess of power by pledging self-sacrifice, may be considered associated with revolutionary terrorism in a way. I have already cited some such verses. On the one hand, we can say that such poems gave a cathartic outlet to the militant mood and thus returned the Bengali intelligentsia to passivity. On the other hand, it can be claimed that such revolutionary volubility mentally prepared some people to take part in revolutionary activities. And it must also be remembered that there were many more people who were not directly involved in revolutionary activities but helped the lawful and open activities of the revolutionaries and also sympathized with their illegal and secret activities.

Here I will just mention some poems directly related to the narrow stream of armed activism. For example, this secret *Ramayana* song of the Anushilan Party expressed:

> Patriotism makes a person noble,
> Even if he is a terrible sinner otherwise.
> One who easily sacrifices his life for the motherland
> Gets admission into heaven straightaway.[44]

The periodical *Jugantar* published an article and a poem in the context of the Maniktala Bomb case. This led to the imprisonment of its editor Birendra Bandyopadhyay and the banning of the periodical itself. Thus ran the poem:

> Mother, even before your *bodhan* [ceremonial awakening of a goddess]
> The *rakshasa* [demon] has broken the *mangalghat* [a consecrated pitcher to win divine favour]
> Wake up, *Ranachandi* [the warrior goddess], wake up.
> We will make a wreath of human skulls to adorn you,
> We will churn the ocean of blood to retrieve the gem of freedom.[45]

Hemchandra Kanungo, a militant nationalist, on being imprisoned, noticed the following lines addressed to the motherland carved on the floor of the Alipore cellular jail by some predecessor:

> Had you been a desert
> Or a gravelled barren land infested with barbarians,
> Even then you would have been the ultimate pilgrimage of my life.
> Just as a baby knows its mother from the moment of its birth
> I have known you, mother.
> And also known that my fate is bound with yours.
> You are the mother of my present life and of many more.[46]

Quite a few songs were composed to immortalize the martyr Khudiram who was hanged for his attempt to kill Kingsford, the erstwhile Chief Presidency Magistrate of Calcutta. The most famous of them is of course—'Ekbar biday de ma ghure asi':

> O ma, for once bid farewell to me;
> Now smilingly I'll adorn the hangman's noose
> For all my countrymen to see.

An indigenous bomb I had made
And waited by the roadside, o ma!
To kill the viceroy, but instead
Missed and killed another Englishman.
A vast crowd on Saturday morning ten o'clock,
Gathered by the High Court criminal dock, o ma!
Came the verdict of life transport for Abhiram
And for me—hang till death.

But worry not. After ten months and ten days
I'll surely incarnate in your sister's house, o ma!
If you fail to recognize me on that day
Look and you'll find the mark of noose on my throat.

The song is full of factual errors. Khudiram's target was Kingsford and not the Viceroy. The death sentence on him was not pronounced on a Saturday. And there was no 'Abhiram' given a life-sentence in this case. The knowledge of the rural poet about the incident was evidently incomplete and erroneous. But this facilitated his reconstruction of the story in the mould of universally popular myths of young heroes fighting against terrible tyrants (like Krishna against Kamsa in the *Mahabharata* and David against Goliath in the Bible). The poet made Khudiram take on an enemy no less formidable than the Viceroy. He also inserted a number of indigenous cultural elements in his narrative. Saturday is popularly considered as inauspicious in our country and so is the time after 10 a.m. in the morning (*barbela*). So the sentence had to be pronounced on Saturday, after 10 a.m. Abhiram, the most strikingly imaginary element in the song, is evidently a hero whose name rhymes with Khudiram and who together with the latter creates an archetypal image of twin heroes standing for righteousness (matching other such pairs traditionally venerated in Bengali culture, for example, Kanai-Balai and Nimai-Nitai).

To complete the cycle of the myth, the poet predicts the hero's reincarnation. Khudiram would have to return, as his mission remains incomplete. In the Indian belief-system reincarnation usually takes the form of rebirth. So Khudiram would be born of an ordinary Bengali woman—a sister of his present mother in whose image his motherland is cast. He would have the mark of noose on his throat— the identification mark that the leader of a religious struggle is often believed to bear. In religious-cum-millenarian movements across the world, we have had such saviour-leaders, who even though defeated and killed, leave behind a hope for the future in the popular mind—a hope of reincarnation of the leader himself and of a fresh opportunity to fight back. Thus the story of Khudiram transcends the realm of reality, acquires a religious flavour and rouses a millenarian hope among the common people. And therein lies the significance of the very small, stray and mostly unsuccessful efforts of our revolutionary terrorists.[47]

A MOTHER CULT

The country was addressed as mother in most of the poems. We have already quoted a number of instances so far. But there are many more, some of them written with the sole purpose of worshipping mother in the forms of the soil or other natural features of the country. These were poems apparently unconnected with the Swadeshi agitation. However, even these perhaps involved a sort of anti-colonial resistance. Edward Said argues that 'the history of colonial servitude is inaugurated by the loss of the locality to the outsider', that is, colonialism is primarily a geographical dispossession, and hence the first and foremost task of cultural anti-colonialism is to recover the locality in one's own terms, to retrieve the geography of one's country inch by inch, to stamp one's own identity on the rivers, mountains, flora and fauna of the country.[48] The worship of the country or its nature indeed serves this purpose, even if it does not protest against colonialism in a loud voice. It is perhaps because of this that the young revolutionary Ullaskar Datta, on hearing his death sentence pronounced by the judge, sang out the following song of Rabindranath in the courtroom itself—a song with no hatred for the colonists, with no awakening call to countrymen, but a very private love-offering to one's motherland. It is an exquisitely beautiful song expressing one's absorption in the physical richness of the land and of an ethereal tenderness for it:

> I'm gratified mother that I have been born in this country
> I'm gratified by loving you.
> I don't know if flowers are so overwhelmed with their own fragrance in any other forest
> Or if the moon smiles so beautifully in any other sky.
> Your light soothed my eyes when I first opened them
> I shall shut these eyes for good, looking at that light.[49]

There were two images of the motherland.[50] One was the mother goddess imagined as a source of *shakti* or prowess in the religious tradition of this country. This mother was either Durga or Kali. The other image was that of one's own mother—an ordinary woman perhaps, yet very special—who gives birth, protects and nurtures, whose 'words sound like nectar to my ears'.[51] However, in the popular religious tradition of *bhakti* in Bengal, which imagines a humane and personal relationship between man and his god/goddess, these two mothers are not opposed to each other. So the goddess of power can also become a homely mother (or daughter) to the *bhakta* (devotee). It is because of this human character of mother goddess that even many Muslims participated in her worship.

Since the late nineteenth century in most such patriotic songs it was Mother Bengal who was addressed. The poets were better acquainted with, and felt closer to the natural features of Bengal than those of the rest of India. The Bengali language was deeply loved and the Bengalis were looked upon as close kindred. It is true that Mother India was held in high esteem too. But she evoked more reverence than intimacy. It is to be noticed in this connection that Mother Bengal was often addressed with the pronoun *tui*, while Mother India was almost always addressed with *tumi*. The former denotes a profounder intimacy. But of course, as said before, there was no rivalry between Mother Bengal and Mother India, that is, between Bengali nationalism and Indian nationalism; and the two were often combined or mentioned interchangeably. Dwijendralal's song *Dhanadhanyapushpabhara* (Filled with Wealth, Paddy and Flowers) is a well-known description of the beautiful and affectionate mother. Though it is sung in praise of Mewar in his play *Shah Jehan*, actually the song invokes none other than Mother Bengal. The poet gives himself away in the line—'In what country does the wind play in the paddy field making such waves?'—a scene quite unthinkable in Rajasthan and rather typical of the Bengal countryside.

The motherland, be it Bengal or India, was idealized as both beautiful and bountiful. But often this mother was presented as a sorrowful woman too. For example, D.L. Ray expressed: *Banga amar, janani amar, dhatri amar, amar desh/Keno go ma tor malin badan, keno go ma tor ruksha kesh?* (My Banga, my mother, my nurse, my country,/Why does your face look so sad and why is your hair so dishevelled?). In this song, an interesting thing to be noted is that the poet unknowingly mentions thirty crore of children while talking about *Bangamata*, that is his Indian nationalism overlaps his Bengali nationalism.

DAWNING OF THE DESIRE FOR FREEDOM

The Swadeshi Movement aimed merely at the revocation of partition and not at freedom. Its weapons were not very sharp either. The Swadeshis mostly wanted to trouble the British a bit by boycotting foreign goods. But the greatest success of their movement lay in bringing about a very fundamental change in the nationalist consciousness. It made the nationalists long for freedom for the first time. It exploded the myths that had supported the supremacy of the British masters during the nineteenth century. Regarding the most powerful of these myths, that is the *mantra* of a superior Western civilization, which according to the nationalists, the British had imparted to the Indians, Pyarishankar Sengupta said:

> Deceive us no more with your *mantra*
> And corrupt us no more with your modernism
> As you did in the nineteenth century
> When we thought that everything related to Gora (the white man) was nothing but good.
> But today we know better.
> A religious and peace-loving people have been taken unfair advantage of
> By some murderous and alcoholic brutes,
> Who having been rejected by the whole world
> Came here to loot this country.[52]

The myth of physical prowess of British along with the infirmity of Indians exploded too. Amritalal Basu protested—'Even today if we smear ourselves with earth and take up *lathis* (sticks), we can shake the world.' There is only one obstacle on the way—an unreasonable fear—'Only a ghost haunts us—a ghost named Fear/But it is nothing but a mere obsession.'

That the British had taken away the freedom of India and that British rule was in no way desirable was at last realized. The agony of subservience became acute and a desire for freedom was strongly felt. We have already mentioned Siraji's 'Swadhinata Bandana' (Worship of Freedom). Gobindachanda Das's craving for freedom is clear in quite a few of his poems—for example when he castigated his countrymen saying 'What is this thing you call your own country?/This country is not yours!/If the rivers Jamuna or Ganga had been yours,/How could white soldiers carry foreign merchandise on them?' A similar tone is present in his attempts to hearten them with the examples of the Swedish, the French, the Portuguese and other peoples who practised 'free will and free thought—the inalienable rights of men'. (Poems entitled 'Swadesh' and 'Tomrao Manush' respectively).[53]

But the nineteenth-century myths did not wholly disappear. The devotion to the royal family in particular remained strong in many minds. Pramathanath Chaudhury in his poem 'Je Deshbhakta Sei Rajbhakta' (He who loves his country, loves his king too) tried to combine the anti-British movement with devotion to the British king.[54] And needless to say, the allegiance to the king was a major pillar of allegiance to British rule. It is true that such myths took a back seat in the flush of Swadeshi excitement. But they surfaced soon. In 1911, the royal visit swept India with a tide of encomiums. Relevant in this context is a song by Rajanikanta Sen—'What kind of a justice is Gora (the white man) doing to us!/Having taught us how to walk, he is now maiming us by breaking our legs.'[55] This was an acknowledgement that the British had after all taught the Indians to walk, that is civilized them. And sometimes this acknowledgment came with an even more grateful tone. This myth of receiving civilization from the British proved tenacious indeed. It has even survived the demise of the formal empire.

NOTES

1. Sumit Sarkar, *The Swadeshi Movement in Bengal, 1903-1908*, Delhi: Peoples' Publishing House, 1974, p. 289.
2. I obviously have in my mind Benedict Anderson's seminal work *Imagined Communities: Reflections on the Origin and Spread of Nationalism*, London: Verso, 1983.
3. I am not really sure whether my essay fits into a volume on popular culture. But I can say this much that when the Swadeshi phase of our national movement took off, the elitism of the earlier mainstream nationalists largely gave way to an urge to establish contact with the living culture of the masses, which made the respectable and refined *bhadralok* come out of their exclusive domains. Rabindranath's adaptation of folk tunes for his Swadeshi songs is a well-known example. Among efforts from below, the most famous are those of the Swadeshi bard Mukunda Das, who used to tour East Bengal villages, rowing the boat himself and taking along with him a couple of *dohars* (associate singers). He earned great popularity by singing Swadeshi songs in the style of *jatra*. Nationalism indeed became very pervasive during those days. Books of Swadeshi poems and songs, small in size and quite cheap too, flooded Bengal and their readership net was cast vary far, even to illiterate audiences. More often than not the anonymity of these works foregrounded popular expectations. Nationalism was no longer the preoccupation of an exclusivist group of intelligentsia. The intense patriotic emotion of the moment largely narrowed down the gulf between the elite and the popular. But of course, we know that there had never been any strictly binary distinction between elite and popular cultures and that dialogues between the two cultures had also been very true, which seemed all the more natural when both confronted a common enemy, viz., the foreign masters.

   When I say that the national movement turned from an elitist to a popular one during the Swadeshi Movement, I do not use the word 'popular' in a reductive sociological sense. I just mean to say that the movement got remarkably broadened at that time. It broadened first of all in a spatial sense. While the Swadeshis tried hard to conquer the urban space as well as spread their movement to mofussil and even rural areas that had not been very prominent in the national movement before. Teenagers and youths, mostly students, became involved in the movement on an unprecedented scale. The number of Muslim poets increased remarkably too. There were more and more women joining the movement and making poetic contributions to it. The lesser social orders (lesser in terms of class and caste) were also getting involved, as indicated by a number of folk poets' participation in the movement.

But of course, it is well known that the popular character of the movement had serious limitations. The failure in drawing in the masses is considered the Achilles' heel of the movement by historians. Most of the Muslims remained alienated from it too. Gradually there appeared critics to whom the very popular character of the movement stood for a sort of cheapness. Even Rabindranath very soon found it full of pettiness, cowardice and insincerity. Even if we call the Swadeshi Movement a popular culture, we cannot expect any uniformity or consistency of it. This popular culture was not free from societal fears and prejudices. It suffered from many paradoxes and ambiguities. It veered between conflicting trends; for example, between an urge for Hindu-Muslim unity and communal separatism, or between the visions of the motherland as a Hindu goddess and as a human mother. Above all, the popular culture during the Swadeshi Movement was marked by both support and hostility to the movement itself.

But I think, through all this, our nationalism emerged fundamentally transformed. What I would stress most in this essay is that this quantitative expansion came hand in hand with some significant qualitative changes in the nationalist consciousness. I do not claim any causal relationship between the two. But perhaps the two had some connection. The way people lower down the social scale tried to make sense of colonialism had always been quite different from the intelligentsia's way of organizing and rationalizing colonial experience. During the Swadeshi Movement, the two perceptions came rather close to each other.

When I talk of fundamental qualitative changes in the nationalist consciousness brought about by the Swadeshi Movement, I do not mean that the new trends became absolute or even dominant characteristics of our national movement from then on. Even after the Swadeshi Movement there remained much hesitation and many ambiguities in the nationalist mind, and back-and-forth movements were common. But the new trends certainly marked off the period from the earlier one.

4. For a more detailed and nuanced discussion, see Anuradha Roy, *Nationalism as Poetic Discourse in Nineteenth Century Bengal*, Kolkata: Papyrus, 2003.

5. For Mukunda Das' life and songs, see Jayguru Goswami's *Charankabi Mukunda Das* and Pulak Chanda's *Jagaraner Kabi Mukunda Das*.

6. The edition I have seen was published from East Pakistan some time in the early 1950s.

7. *Bangadarshan*, Phalgun 1310 (1904).

8. The poems I cite in this essay and many more are included (wholly or partly) in the volume *Swadhinata Sangramer Gan o Kabita: Bingsha Shatabdi* that I compiled and edited for Sahitya Akademi, New Delhi (published in 2000). There I mentioned all my sources, which are not always given in the present essay. Two secondary sources need to be mentioned too: Soumendra Gangopadhyay, *Swadeshi Andolan o Bangla Sahitya* and Geeta Chattopadhyay, *Bangla Swadeshi Gan*. In this connection, I may also refer to my Bengali article 'Kabider Swadesi Andolan' in Pabitra Sarkar (ed.), *Shraddhanjali: Sukumar Sen Shatabarsha Smarak Samkalan*, Kolkata: Paschim Banga Bangla Akademi, 2003, which is an enlarged version of the present essay.

9. Abanindranath Thakur's reminiscences in *Gharoya*.

10. Ashok Kumar Mukhopadhyay, 'Pulish Reporte Swadeshi Gan', *Sharadiya Anandabajar Patrika*, 1412 (2005).
11. All the patriotic songs of Rabindranath are available in *Geetabitan* published by Visva-Bharati.
12. 'Banga Bibhage', *Bangadarshan*, Kartik 1312 (1905).
13. *Nabyabharat*, Asharh 1313 (1906).
14. See Karunanidhan's biography by Madanmohan Kumar, *Karunanidhan: Jeeban o Kabya*, Kolkata: Bangiya Sahitya Parishat, 1974.
15. A line in his song *Amar sonar Bangla, ami tomay bhalobasi*.
16. 'Matridrohir Prati', *Bharati*, Shraban, 1313 (1906).
17. Included in his *jatra*-play *Matripuja* (Worship of Mother).
18. Krishnakumar Mitra, *Atmacharit* (autobiography), Kolkata: Sadharan Brahmo Samaj, 2nd edn., 1381 (1974), p. 195.
19. For a portrayal of Barishal during the Swadeshi age, see Hiralal Dasgupta, *Swadhinata Sangrame Barishal*, vol. 1, Kolkata: Sahitya Samsad, 1972; Surendranath Sen, *Ashwinikumar Datta*, published on the birth centenary of Ashwinikumar; and Mitra, *Atmacharit*.
20. Mukhopadhyay, 'Pulish Reporte Swadeshi Gan'.
21. *Raktabija* implied a mythical demon, each drop of whose blood, as soon as it falls to the ground, instantly creates a new demon equal in prowess to him. *Nabyabharat*, Asharh, 1313 (1906).
22. *Prabasi*, Shraban, 1314 (1907).
23. *Tantra* is an esoteric cult of religious worship invoking prowess, often taking the form of *sabasadhana*, that is sitting upon a corpse. *Mantra* implies sacred hymns recited in prayer to a deity. *Sadhana* means an austere endeavour, particularly by way of worshipping a god. *Sadhak* refers to one who practices this. *Prabasi*, Jyaishtha, 1313 (1906).
24. Matangi and Jogini are both incarnations of Mother Goddess.
25. The first line of the song is *Jagore bhai sabe smariye Keshabe*.
26. Rabindranath Tagore, 'Sivaji Utsab', included in the anthology *Sanchayita* published by Visva-Bharati.
27. Included in Durgadas Lahiri (comp. and ed.), *Bangalir Gan*, Kolkata, 1312 (1905).
28. For concrete examples of all this, see Roy, *Swadhinta Sangramer Gan o Kabita*, and Roy, 'Kabider Swadeshi Andolan'.
29. 'Ahitagnika', *Bharati*, Asharh 1306 (1899).
30. *Sahitya*, Kartik, 1312 (1905).
31. For sources, see Roy, *Swadhinata Sangramer Gan o Kabita*.
32. The chapter entitled 'Techniques of Mass Contact'.
33. The first line of the song was *Ekhan Musalmaner Iman kotha*.
34. *Nabyabharat*, Ashwin, 1314 (1907).
35. See different volumes of *Girish Rachanabali* published by Sahitya Samsad.
36. *Pratap Singha* and *Mebar Patan* are included in vol. 3 and *Sajahan* in vol. 1 of *Dwijendralal Granthabali* (Granthabali series of Basumati Sahitya Mandir). For other writings of D.L. Ray, *Dwijendra Rachanabali* published by Sahitya Samsad (vols. I & II) proves useful. How Dwijendralal got disillusioned with the Swadeshi Movement despite his initial enthusiasm has been described by Balaichand Mukhopadhyay in his *Dwijendra Darpan*, Kolkata: Bookland, and by Sudhir Chakrabarty in *Dwijendralal Ray: Smarane Bismarane*, Kolkata: Pustak Bipani.

37. Partha Sarathi Gupta in his comparative study of the patriotic songs of Dwijendralal Ray and Kazi Nazrul Islam pointed out this evolution in Ray's attitude to Muslims. See Partha Sarathi Gupta, 'Music and Political Consciousness (Regional, Pan-Indian and Communal): A Critical Study of D.L. Roy and Nazrul Islam', Occasional Paper, No. XV on History and Society, New Delhi: Nehru Memorial Museum & Library (December 1988).

38. See my *Swadhinata Sangramer Gan o Kabita* for quite a few poems written by Muslims during the Swadeshi age, including those referred to here.

39. Included in his book of poems *Alekhya*.

40. *Bharati*, Bhadra 1312 (1905).

41. Serialized in *Prabasi* during 1314-16 (1907-8).

42. First published in *Sabujpatra* in 1322 (1915).

43. Quoted by Sumit Sarkar in his *The Swadeshi Movement in Bengal*, pp. 462-3.

44. Quoted in Prabhat Chandra Gangopadhyay, *Biplabi Juger Katha*.

45. Ibid.

46. Quoted in Kshirod Kumar Datta, *Biplabi Barindrakumar*.

47. For the discussion of this song I have derived insights from the remarkable essay 'Dwipantari Abhram' by Arun Nag, *Jogsutra*, July-September 1995, later included in his book *Galpa o Tar Goru*, Kolkata: Subarnarekha, 2005.

48. Edward Said, 'Yeats and Decolonization', in *Culture and Imperialism*, London: Vintage, 1994, p. 271.

49. Sumit Sarkar has referred to this incident in his *The Swadeshi Movement in Bengal*, p. 293.

50. See Sugata Bose, 'Nation as Mother: Representation and Contestations of "India" in Bengali Literature and Culture', in Sugata Bose and Ayesha Jalal (eds.), *Nationalism, Democracy and Development: State and Politics in India*, Delhi: Oxford University Press, 1997.

51. A line in Rabindranath's 'Amar sonar Bangla'.

52. 'Clive-er Smriti', *Nabyabharat*, Baisakh 1314 (1907).

53. Both were published in the periodical *Nabyabharat* during the Swadeshi era.

54. Included in his book of poems *Deshbhakti*.

55. This song is included in Chattopadhyay, *Bangla Swadeshi Gan. Kantabani* by Dipti Tripathi contains many *swadeshi* songs of Rajanikanta.

3

गुरुदत्त के सामाजिक उपन्यासों में सांस्कृतिक चित्रण

जवाहर सिंह

प्रस्तावना

हम सभी के मन में एक प्रश्न यह अवश्य ही पैदा होता है कि 'संस्कृति' क्या है हम इसके बारे में क्या सोचते हैं, समझते हैं ।

संस्कृति क्या है ?

'सम् उपसर्ग पूर्व कृ धातूपरान्त क्तिन प्रत्यय लगाकर सुट् के आगम से संस्कृति शब्द बनता है ।" (*मानक हिन्दी कोश*, पांचवा खण्ड, पृ. 243)

'कल्चर इज़ द वे व्ही थिंक' अर्थात् जैसा हम सोचते हैं वह संस्कृति है । 'संस्कृति' एक अमूर्त अवधारणा है और अपनी अमूर्त व्यापकता में इसे परिभाषित नहीं किया जा सकता । संस्कृति एक उधार ली हुई पश्चिमी अवधारणा है और 'कल्चर' का पर्याय । जबकि सच यह है कि संस्कृति का सही पर्याय 'कल्चर' नहीं है । 'संस्कृति' में संस्कार का तत्त्व प्रबल होने के कारण वह एक संस्कारात्मक परिणति है । 'कल्चर' में संस्कार-परिष्कार का भाव न होकर अभ्यास से उत्पन्न परिणाम का बोध प्रमुख है । लेकिन संस्कृति न आर्थिक-भौतिक-आध्यात्मिक होती है, वह एक समग्र प्रक्रिया है ।

कैसे ?

जैसे, हम भारतीय हैं । सभी भारतीयों का सोचने का तरीका, परिस्थिति विशेष में उनकी क्रियाएं-प्रतिक्रियाएं लगभग एक समान ही होंगी, चाहे वे भारत में हैं अथवा भारत से सुदूर सात समुद्र पार हैं । प्रत्येक देश का मिजाज उसकी अपनी संस्कृति है । हमारी बहु-सांस्कृति भारतीयता ही हमारी संस्कृति है ।

फिर सभ्यता क्या है ?

संस्कृति सोच है, अत: सूक्ष्म है 'इंटेंजीबल' (intangible) है, किन्तु इसी सूक्ष्म का बाह्य और स्थूल रूप सभ्यता है और वह 'टेंजीबल' (tangible) है । हमारा रहन-सहन, खान-पान, कलाएं, प्रार्थना आदि करने

की पद्धति सभ्यता है । किन्तु इसमें मौजूद विचार संस्कृति है । इस दृष्टि से सभ्यता और संस्कृति घुली-मिली हैं ।[2]

रामधारी सिंह दिनकर (संस्कृति के चार अध्याय) के अनुसार—

संस्कृति सभ्यता की अपेक्षा महीन चीज़ होती है । यह सभ्यता के भीतर उसी तरह व्याप्त होती है जैसे दूध में मक्खन या फूलों में सुगंध । और सभ्यता की अपेक्षा यह टिकाऊ भी अधिक है, क्योंकि सभ्यता की सामग्रियाँ टूट–फूटकर विनष्ट हो सकती हैं, लेकिन संस्कृति का विनाश उतनी आसानी से नहीं किया जा सकता ।

अंग्रेज़ी की एक कहावत में संस्कृति को स्पष्ट करते हुए कहा है कि—

सभ्यता वह वस्तु है जो हमारे पास है किन्तु संस्कृति वह चेतना है जो हममें व्याप्त है । किसी समाज में व्यष्टि की चिन्तन प्रक्रिया पर आधारित उसके कर्म, प्रतिक्रियाएं और उनकी भौतिक परिणति मिलकर समष्टि की संस्कृति और सभ्यता का निर्माण करते हैं ।

आचार्य नरेन्द्र देव ने मानव और प्रकृति, मिथक और धर्म, दर्शन और आध्यात्म को एक संश्लिष्टता में गूंथकर कहा है—'संस्कृति चित्त की खेती है ।' खेती की तरह चित्त को जोतना-बोना-निराना-सींचना-रखवाली करना, खर-पतवार निकालकर फेंकना, उसे निरंतर माँजते-सँवारते रहना ही संस्कृति है ।

मुंशी प्रेमचन्द, राहुल सांकृत्यायन आदि ने एवं गुरुदत्त ने संस्कृति शब्द को अलग-अलग ढंग से परिभाषित किया है । मुंशीजी ने संस्कृति को शिष्टजनों के जन-हितकारी प्रयासों का समुच्चय माना है, राहुलजी का मानना है कि संस्कृति पीढ़ियों के प्रभाव व संस्कार का प्रवाह है, इसलिए यह अचल नहीं है । वहीं गुरुदत्त ने 'भारतीयता' शब्द को ही संस्कृति की पूर्ण परिभाषा से नमाजा है । उन्होंने भारतीय संस्कृति को सात्विक, योग-प्रधान तथा लोक-कल्याणकारी माना है । क्योंकि यह शब्द सम्पूर्ण भारतीय समाज को एक सूत्र में बांधे रखने में समर्थ है । और इसी भारतीयता के भाव को अपने साहित्य के माध्यम से जन-जन तक पहुँचाने का अथक प्रयास किया है, गुरु दत्त जी ने ।

1. उपन्यासकार गुरुदत्त : एक सामान्य परिचय

हिन्दी साहित्य की साधना भूमि पर अनवरत साधनारत एक सुपरिचित साहित्यकार हैं जिनका नाम है - 'गुरुदत्त' । गुरुदत्त का व्यक्तित्व बहुआयामी है—उपन्यासकार, कहानीकार, निबंधकार, ज्योतिषशास्त्री, निष्णातवैद्य, समाजसेवी एवं सरल मानवीय गुणों से ओत-प्रोत एक विचारक ।

श्री गुरुदत्त जी के बहुआयामी व्यक्तित्व के बारे में डॉ० विजेन्द्र स्नातक, भूतपूर्व अध्यक्ष, हिन्दी विभाग, दिल्ली विश्वविद्यालय ने एक अभिनंदन समारोह में अपने श्रद्धा-सुमन अर्पित करते हुए ठीक ही कहा था—'कोई भी उनके दैदीप्यमान मुखाकृति को देखे तो यही अनुभव करेगा मानो मार्ग-निर्देश करता हुआ कोई तपस्वी बैठा है ।'[3]

'परिवर्तिनि संसारे मृत: को वा न जायते ।
स जातो येन जातेन याति वंश: समुन्नतिम् ।।'

अर्थात् इस परिवर्तनशील संसार में कौन नहीं मरता और कौन नहीं जन्म लेता । किन्तु उसका ही जन्म लेना सार्थक है जिसके जन्म लेने से वंश की उन्नति होती हो ।

गुरुदत्त भी उसी श्रेणी में आते हैं । उनके जन्म से न केवल उनका वंश समुन्नत हुआ है, न केवल हिन्दी साहित्य समुन्नत हुआ है, न केवल हिन्दी भाषा समृद्ध हुई है अपितु उनके साहित्य से समस्त राष्ट्र समुन्नत हुआ है, मानवता समुन्नत हुई है ।

गुरुदत्त का जन्म लाहौर (वर्तमान में पाकिस्तान) के निम्न मध्यमवर्गीय पंजाबी अरोड़ा परिवार में 8 दिसम्बर 1894 में हुआ था, तब लाहौर भारत का ही अंग था । पिता श्री कर्मचन्द जी निम्न मध्य वित्तीय अवस्था के व्यक्ति थे । इनके यहाँ अनेक पीढ़ियों से वैद्य का व्यवसाय होता था । वे कट्टर आर्य समाजी थे । माता सुहावी वैष्णवी आस्थाओं के प्रति नितान्त श्रद्धालु थी । परिणामस्वरूप गुरुदत्त में सहिष्णुता, आतिथ्य भाव और समन्वय की भावना बचपन से ही परिपक्व हो गई थी । अभाव-ग्रस्त परिवार में गुरुदत्त का जन्म हुआ था । अत: उनका बचपन और किशोरावस्था सर्वसामान्य की भाँति ही व्यतीत हुआ । बाल्यकाल से ही उन्हें पढ़ने-लिखने में विशेष रूचि थी । यही कारण था कि विशेष साधनों के अभाव के होते हुए भी उन्होंने एम.एससी. तक अध्ययन किया । सन् 1919 में रसायन विज्ञान में एम.एससी. करने के बाद वे सन् 1920 में गवर्नमेंट कॉलेज, लाहौर के विज्ञान विभाग में डिमांस्ट्रेटर (demonstrator) के पद पर आसीन हुए । इन दिनों लोगों में सरकार के साथ असहयोग की भावना पनप रही थी । लाहौर में लाला लाजपतराय के उद्यम से राष्ट्रीय संस्थाओं की स्थापना की गई थी । स्कूल, कॉलेज के विद्यार्थी पढ़ाई को एक ओर छोड़ राष्ट्रीय संस्थाओं में शामिल होने लगे । विदेशी चीज़ों का खूब विरोध हुआ । ऐसी राजनीतिक उथल-पुथल ने युवक गुरुदत्त के मानस-पटल पर गहरी छाप छोड़ दी । उनका युवा मन इस परिस्थिति का विद्रोह कर उठा । इसलिए सन् 1921 में असहयोग आंदोलन में रूचि लेने के कारण नौकरी छोड़ दी । 1 अक्टूबर 1921 में गुरुदत्त नेशनल स्कूल के मुख्याध्यापक पद पर अधिष्ठित हुए । परन्तु मन राजनीति में इतना लगा कि सन् 1926 तक ही इस पद पर रहे । भाग्यचक्र श्री गुरुदत्त को 7 सितम्बर 1927 में उत्तर प्रदेश में अमेठी ले गया, और चार वर्ष तक कुँवर रणजय सिंह के निजी सचिव के रूप में कार्य किया । जहाँ राजनैतिक स्थिति, स्वार्थ, राजकीय भ्रष्टाचार आदि हथकंडों का पर्याप्त परिचय प्राप्त हुआ । सन् 1931 तक वे अमेठी में रहे । सन् 1932 तक लखनऊ में एवं फिर लखनऊ छोड़ वे लाहौर चले गये । लाहौर में अक्टूबर 1933 से 6 मार्च 1937 तक वैद्य का काम किया । वहाँ भी वैद्य के व्यवसाय में ठीक निर्वाह न होने के कारण 7 मार्च 1937 को दिल्ली आ गये । यहाँ आकर आजीविका धीरे-धीरे पटरी पर आई । सन्तोषजनक स्थिति बनते ही उन्होंने एक ओर सामाजिक कार्य में रूचि लेनी आरम्भ की तो दूसरी ओर साहित्य-सृजन आरम्भ किया । उनका यही सिलसिला लगभग सन् 1975 तक अनवरत रूप से चलता रहा लेकिन इन सबके मध्य साहित्य-सृजन का कार्य निरंतर जारी रहा । उन्होंने अमेठी में सन् 1927 में प्रथम कहानी 'अदृश्य व्यक्ति' लिखी थी । लखनऊ की *माधुरी* पत्रिका में इस कहानी का प्रकाशन हुआ । इन्हीं दिनों में एक दो कहानियाँ और लिखी गयी थी परंतु उनका प्रकाशन किसी कारणवश नहीं हो पाया । उनमें से 'प्रेम का अभिशाप' कहानी किसी पत्रिका में छपी थी एवं प्रथम उपन्यास *मेरे भगवान* सन् 1929 में लिखा गया था, परंतु इस उपन्यास का प्रकाशित भी नहीं हो सका था । इसके प्रकाशित न होने के विषय में गुरुदत्त स्वयं कहते हैं —

मुंशी प्रेमचन्द जी ने, जो उन दिनों माधुरी कार्यालय में काम करते थे, इसको पसन्द किया प्रतीत होता था । इनसे एक दिन कार्यालय में मिला भी था और उन्होंने पुस्तक प्रकाशित करने का आश्वासन भी दिया था, परन्तु वह स्वयं माधुरी कार्यालय से चले गये और पुस्तक नहीं छप सकी । उसकी पाण्डुलिपि भी नहीं मिली । सम्भवतया कहीं खो गई थी ।[4]

परन्तु उनका *स्वाधीनता के पथ पर* उपन्यास सन् 1940–41 में लिखा गया एवं सन्
1942 में विद्या मंदिर लिमिटेड से प्रकाशित हुआ था । इस उपन्यास की सफलता ने उन्हें
प्रौढ़ उपन्यासकार की श्रेणी में खड़ा कर दिया । और मृत्युपर्यंत अनेक सफल उपन्यास
लिखे । उपन्यासों के अतिरिक्त चिन्तनपरक रचनाएँ—वेद, गीता, उपनिषद् एवं दर्शनशास्त्रों
की व्याख्या व समीक्षा भी की, एवं *Cultural State in Bharatvarsh* आदि अंग्रेज़ी
पुस्तकों की भी रचना की थी । आजीवन साधनारत रहते हुए 8 अप्रैल 1989 को दिल्ली में
इन्होंने शरीर त्यागा और अपना अमूल्य साहित्य भारत-भू को समर्पित कर दिया ।

वे उपन्यास, संस्मरण और जीवन साहित्य के महान् सृजक बने । ज्ञान, राग और शब्द-
शिल्प के संगम के साथ-साथ विज्ञान और साहित्य के सेतु थे । सदाचार, संकल्प, निर्मल
मैत्री और पारस्परिक समझदारी उनके अलंकरण थे । हिन्दुत्व के दृढ़ स्तम्भ थे तो रग-रग
हिन्दु उनका परिचय तथा आर्य समाज उनका पुराण था ।

गुरुदत्त का यहाँ हिन्दुत्व अर्थात् हिन्दु से तात्पर्य किसी सम्प्रदाय विशेष से न लेकर
समूचे भारतीय समाज से लिया है जो भारतवर्ष में सभी वर्गों के साथ शान्ति व सौहार्द्र के
वातावरण में एक साथ रह रहे हैं—

हिन्दुओं में एक ही समान चीज़ है, वह है भारतवर्ष में रहने तथा भारतीयता की परम्पराओं से सम्बद्ध होने
की । भारतीयता न तो कोई धर्म है, और न ही कोई सामाजिक या नागरिक नियम कही जा सकती है ।
इसमें प्रादेशिकता या विशिष्ट राजनीतिक सैद्धान्तिकता को कोई स्थान नहीं । भारतीयता जीवन-यापन का
एक ढ़ंग है; इसलिए वे सब लोग जो भारतवर्ष के वफ़ादार और भारतीय जीवन-दृष्टिकोण के पोषक हैं,
हिन्दु कहला सकते हैं । अत: 'हिन्दु' एक ऐसा शब्द है जो भारतवर्ष की भौगोलिक सीमाओं में बसे राष्ट्र
तथा देश के पुरातन ऋषियों-मुनियों एवं शास्त्रों द्वारा निर्दिष्ट जीवन-संस्कारों को अपनाने वाली समूची
जनता के लिए प्रयोग होता है ।[5]

गुरुदत्त ने सामाजिक-पारिवारिक, ऐतिहासिक, राजनीतिक और सांस्कृतिक आदि वर्ग के
उपन्यासों पर लेखनी चलाकर यह सिद्ध कर दिया कि उपन्यास-जगत् के वे बेताज बादशाह
थे ।

स्वाधीनता के पथ पर से आरम्भ हुआ उनका उपन्यास-जगत् का सफर लगभग 200
उपन्यासों से *माँ भारती* के अंक को सुशोभित-सुगंधित करते हुए *अस्ताचल की ओर* पर
समाप्त होने से पूर्व सिद्ध कर गया कि वे हिन्दी साहित्य के एक देदीप्यमान नक्षत्र थे ।

2. गुरुदत्त के सामाजिक उपन्यासों में सांस्कृतिक तत्त्व

(1) *पाश्चात्य संस्कृति बनाम भारतीय संस्कृति*

विदेशी सरकार, औद्योगिक सभ्यता और पाश्चात्य शिक्षा के परिणामस्वरूप भारत में पाश्चात्य
संस्कृति का प्रचार-प्रसार हुआ । नव-चेतना के फलस्वरूप भारत की गौरवमयी संस्कृति के प्रति
आकर्षण तथा राष्ट्रीय भावना के कारण भारतीय संस्कृति का महत्त्व भी बढ़ने लगा । दो
विशिष्ट प्रकार की संस्कृतियों में संघर्ष होना अनिवार्य था । दोनों के जीवन मूल्य भिन्न
थे । यह अलग बात है कि सामाजिक और राजनैतिक क्षेत्र में हिन्दी के उपन्यासकारों ने जहाँ
पाश्चात्य मानदण्ड स्वीकार किया है वहीं सांस्कृतिक धरातल पर भारतीय संस्कृति के प्रति
भी उनका विचार है कि पाश्चात्य देशों ने भले ही सामाजिक, आर्थिक और राजनैतिक क्षेत्र

में कितनी ही उन्नति कर ली है लेकिन सांस्कृतिक दृष्टि से भारत के पास अपनी गौरवशाली परम्परा है और वह विश्व की अन्य संस्कृतियों से कहीं अधिक श्रेष्ठ है । जयशंकर प्रसाद के अनुसार –

हिमालय के आँगन में प्रथम किरणों का दे उपहार ।
उषा ने हँस अभिनंदन किया और पहनाया हीरक हार ।
जगे हम, लगे जगाने विश्व लोक में फैला फिर आलोक ।
व्योम तम पुंज हुआ तब नष्ट, अखिल संसृति हो उठी अशोक ॥

गुरुदत्त के अनुसार भारतीय और पाश्चात्य संस्कृतियों के मूल बिन्दु भिन्न-भिन्न हैं—पाश्चात्य संस्कृति व्यक्तिपरक है । व्यक्ति का दृष्टिकोण केवल अपने हित-अहित तक सीमित रहता है, लेकिन भारतीय संस्कृति की विशेषता यह है कि व्यक्ति सामूहिक कल्याण, लोक दृष्टि तथा निष्काम कर्म भाव से जीवन को देखता है । पाश्चात्य संस्कृति में व्यक्ति अन्त तक व्यक्तिपरक स्वार्थों के लिए संघर्ष करता है, लेकिन भारतीय संस्कृति में व्यक्ति नि:स्वार्थ भाव से परोपकार के लिए साधना करता है ।

वे भारतीय संस्कृति को सात्विक, योग-प्रधान तथा श्रेष्ठ समझते हैं तथा पाश्चात्य संस्कृति को तामसिक, भौतिक प्रधान तथा हेय बताते हैं । *न्यायाधिकरण* उपन्यास में भारतीय संस्कृति का निष्कर्ष प्रस्तुत करते हुए लेखक कहता है—'शरीर से शरीर का विरोध तो हो सकता है । कभी मन और मन का विरोध होना भी सम्भव है, परन्तु आत्मा से विरोध नहीं होता ।'[6]

भारतीय संस्कृति और पाश्चात्य संस्कृति के स्वरूप को स्पष्ट करते हुए विभिन्न विद्वानों की राय ।

डॉ. कृष्णदत्त पालीवाल, प्रोफ़ेसर, हिन्दी विभाग, दिल्ली विश्वविद्यालय, दिल्ली के अनुसार—

अनेक तरह के कर्मकांड, यज्ञ-देवता, भक्ति, धर्म, अध्यात्म, सदाचार, राम-कृष्ण-शिव से अभिभूत भारतीय संस्कृति आध्यात्मिक संस्कृति है जिसमें मुक्त भोग की मनाही है । अनेक प्रकार के संस्कारों और वर्जनशीलताओं पर टिकी है भारतीय संस्कृति । जबकि पश्चिम की संस्कृति भौतिकवादी है, भोगवादी है और वर्जनशीलता को भंग करने में विश्वास करती है ।[7]

योगी अरविन्द जी ने भारतीय संस्कृति और पश्चिमी संस्कृति की तुलना करते हुए कहा है कि 'यूरोप अपनी भोगवादी-आधुनिकतावादी संस्कृति को भारतीय संस्कृति पर धूर्ततापूर्वक लादना चाहता है—यह अनुचित है ।' (*भारतीय संस्कृति के आधार*, पृ. 213)[8]

गुरुदत्त भारतीय संस्कृति के पक्षधर हैं । उनके उपन्यासों के पात्र विभिन्न संस्कृतियों के भाव रूप हैं । पाश्चात्य संस्कृति के अनुरागी पात्रों से उन्हें मोह नहीं है । उनके पात्र विभिन्न मार्गों का अनुसरण करते हुए अंत में भारतीय संस्कृति का वरण करते हैं । *विवेक* उपन्यास में लेखक कहता है –

भावनाओं को उत्पन्न करने में काम, क्रोध, मोह, लोभ, अहंकार आदि मन के विकार प्रमुख भाग लेते हैं । अत: प्रत्येक भावना के बनते समय यह समझ लेना आवश्यक है कि वह युक्ति-युक्त भी है अथवा नहीं । युक्ति करते समय मन के उक्त पाँच विकारों से रहित होकर विचार करना चाहिए। ऐसा करने पर ऐसी भावना का निर्माण होगा जिसका आधार विवेक युक्त होगा और उसके परिणाम भी अनुचित अथवा अनर्थकारी नहीं हो सकते ।[9]

परन्तु आधुनिक समय में गुरुदत्त भारतीय संस्कृति पर दिनोंदिन बढ़ रहे पाश्चात्य प्रभाव से खिन्न हैं । उनकी मान्यता है कि वर्तमान समाज में युवक-युवतियों की उच्छृंखलता, बढ़ती हुई वासना, मिथ्याचरण और अयुक्तिपूर्ण व्यवहार सब पाश्चात्य प्रभाव के ही कारण हैं । हमारे देश का दुर्भाग्य है कि लगभग दो सौ वर्षों तक राज्य कर लेने मात्र से ही यूरोपियन-साम्राज्यवाद ने हमारी संस्कृति और इतिहास का इतना विनाश किया है कि हम लोग अपनेपन को सदा के लिए भूलकर यूरोपीय-सभ्यता का अंधानुकरण करने लगे हैं और हम अपनी नीति और संस्कृति की उपेक्षा और उपहास कर रहे हैं । इसमें सबसे बड़ा दोष शिक्षा प्रणाली व हमारी मानसिक-दासता का है जिसका सीधा-सीधा प्रभाव नारी पर पड़ा है क्योंकि पाश्चात्य नारी शासक वर्ग की संस्कृति से समझौता कर अपने जीवन मूल्य खो चुकी है । जिसका स्पष्ट प्रभाव *विकृत छाया* उपन्यास की पात्रा छाया पर देखा जा सकता है । एवं इसी उपन्यास का प्रमुख पात्र बलवीर, जो लंदन से एम.डी. किये हुए था । फिर भी उसके विचारों में हिन्दुस्तानी संस्कृति के लक्षण प्रत्यक्ष रूप से विद्यमान थे । दूसरी ओर छाया और भृगुदत्त का विद्याभ्यास हिन्दुस्तान में हुआ फिर भी उनके चरित्रों पर पाश्चात्य शिक्षा का दूषित प्रभाव अत्यधिक दिखाई पड़ता है । छाया जो हिन्दु नारी होते हुए भी अपने को पाश्चात्य सभ्यता की देन समझती है । उसके भाई भृगुदत्त पर भी पूँजीवाद का गहरा प्रभाव है । वह नारी को खिलौना समझता है । इसलिए तो माया के सच्चे प्रेम को समझ नहीं पाता है वह और गर्भावस्था में ही उसे छोड़ देता है । सभ्य समाज में माया को आश्रय मिलता है तो सिर्फ कमल के आश्रम में ही । भारतीय संस्कारों में अटूट प्रेम एवं श्रद्धा रखने वाला बलवीर पाश्चात्य शिक्षा से तरबतर छाया से विवाह नहीं करना चाहता है । बाद में छाया ने बलवीर के दोस्त कमल पर डोरे डालना शुरू किया । ग्रामोद्धार में लगे हुए कमल पर छाया का मायाजाल निरर्थक साबित होता है । स्वभाव की चंचलता उसे अनेक पुरुषों की अंकशायिनी बना देता है । इसी बीच वकील रामलुभाया सेठ से उसका परिचय होता है । वह सेठ के साथ क्लब में जाने लगती है । शराब के नशे में चूर रहने लगती है । क्लब में मणीन्द्र कुमार चौधरी से भी उसका परिचय होता है । चौधरी के संसर्ग से वह अविवाहित गर्भवती बन जाती है । उसकी हालत देख नवल रामलुभाया सेठ से कहता है कि छाया को तुमने ही खराब किया है अतएव उसकी रक्षा का फर्ज़ तुम्हारा है । उस समय रामलुभाया सेठ छाया के चरित्र के विषय में कहता है—'मैंने उसे बिल्कुल खराब नहीं किया । वह तो स्वयं ही पके आम की भांति मेरी झोली में आ गिरी थी । बस मैंने उसे उठाकर चूसने का कष्ट किया । यदि मैं ऐसा नहीं करता तो कोई दूसरा उसे चूस जाता । मैंने तो केवल अवसर से ही लाभ उठाया ।'

'भाई सेठ ! मुझे तो उस पर दया आती है । यह ठीक है कि उसकी शिक्षा में ही दोष था । परन्तु तुमने उसे सीधे मार्ग पर लाने के स्थान पर उल्टा ही मार्ग दिखाया । उसका जीवन बर्बाद करने के वास्तव में दोषी तुम ही हो ।'[10]

आधुनिकता की चकाचौंध में बिगड़े हुए भारतीय नारी जीवन का सच्चा चिट्ठा यहाँ छाया के चरित्र से मिलता है ।

गुरुदत्त ने सभी जगह अपने उपन्यासों में भारतीय संस्कृति पर पाश्चात्य संस्कृति को हावी नहीं होने दिया है । बल्कि उल्टे भारतीय नारी जो अपनी संस्कृति व धर्म के प्रति अगाध आस्था व विश्वास रखती है, को भी अपने उपन्यासों में स्थान दिया है । जो जीवनपर्यन्त इसके लिए संघर्ष करती है और भारतीय संस्कृति को कायम रखने का प्रयत्न करती है । *विडम्बना* उपन्यास की नूरी इसकी प्रत्यक्ष उदाहरण है । नूरी का विवाह बचपन में ही प्रभूदयाल से तय हो जाता है । बाद में वह मेडिकल की शिक्षा के लिए लंदन चला जाता है वहाँ से लुइसी

नामक युवती से विवाह कर लौटता है । लेकिन नूरी उसे भारतीय संस्कृति के अनुसार अपना आराध्य देव मानती है और अपना सारा जीवन उसकी सेवा, सुरक्षा में लगाना चाहती है और लुइसी से कहती है यदि उसे अपने यहाँ नौकरानी बनकर रहने दे तो भी वह अपने आपको धन्य मानेगी । लेकिन लुइसी इसके लिए तैयार नहीं होती है और उससे कहती है—

'तुम हमारे यहाँ नौकरानी ? असम्भव है । जहाँ तुम रहोगी, वहाँ मैं तुम्हारी नौकरानी प्रतीत हूँगी, और तुम घर की मालकिन ।'

'क्या प्रतीत होगा और दूसरे क्या समझेंगे, इससे मेरा कोई सरोकार नहीं । मैं तो तुमको वचन देती हूँ कि मैं तुम्हारे अधिकार पर डाका नहीं डालूंगी । यह एक हिन्दुस्तानी औरत का वचन समझो ।'

'तो तुम उनसे और मुझसे क्या चाहती हो'

'केवल मात्र यह कि मुझको उनके दर्शन मिलते रहें और उनकी सेवा करने का अवसर मिल सके।'

'इससे क्या होगा ?'

'तुम यह नहीं समझ सकती । इस बात को समझने के लिए हिन्दुस्तान में किसी माँ के पेट से जन्म लेने की आवश्यकता है और हिन्दु धर्मशास्त्र अथवा भारतीय साहित्य पढ़ने और समझने की आवश्यकता है । एक यूरोप की महिला इस बात को समझ नहीं सकती ।'[11]

यहाँ गुरुदत्त ने नूरी के चरित्र को भारतीय नारी के लिए एक प्रेरणा रूप में प्रस्तुत करने की कोशिश की है जो अपने नारीत्व व संस्कृति को हर हाल में बचाती है ।

आज भारतीय संस्कृति पर पश्चिमी संस्कृति तथा सभ्यता का गहरा रंग चढ़ गया है । अपने मूल सिद्धांत एवं आदर्श को छोड़ जनता ने पाश्चात्य सिद्धांत और आदर्श अपनाने शुरू कर दिए हैं । जिसका सीधा-सीधा प्रभाव विवाह और पति-पत्नी के संबंधों पर भी देखा जा रहा है । विवाह जिसे भावनात्मक, पवित्र एवम् जन्म-जन्मान्तर का बंधन माना जाता है वे विवाह को मात्र काम-क्रीड़ा की वस्तु ही समझते हैं । गुरुदत्त का मानना है कि समाज में पति-पत्नी का दर्जा एक भावनात्मक व सम्मानजनक होता है । जिसे मृत्युपर्यंत कायम रखना विशेष रूप से भारतीय समाज में, हिन्दु समाज में, उन दोनों की पूर्ण जिम्मेदारी होती है । उपन्यासकार ने *पाणिग्रहण* में अपने विचार व्यक्त करते हुए कहा है कि—

विवाह में केवल शारीरिक सौन्दर्य ही एकमात्र विचार की वस्तु मानना वेश्यावृत्ति को सुलभ करना तथा विस्तार कर देना है । वे लोग, जो विवाह संबंध में शारीरिक सौन्दर्य को एकमात्र कारण मानते हैं और विवाहित जीवन में यौन क्रिया को ही उद्देश्य समझते हैं । विवाह को वेश्यावृत्ति का सत्ता रूप कहने लगते हैं ।[12]

गुरुदत्त ने विवाह संबंध में मात्र बाहरी गुण को ही सर्वोपरि नहीं माना है बाहरी रूप रंग से विवाह कर लेना वेश्यावृत्ति करने जैसा है । शारीरिक सौन्दर्य को सर्वोच्च स्थान देकर विवाह करना मूर्खता है । कभी-कभी बहुत सुन्दर लड़की भी गुणों से गिरी हुई हो सकती है । चमड़ी के काले और गोरे से विवाह का संबंध होना मूर्खता है । पारिवारिक-जीवन में विवाह तो एक सहायक-कृत्य है, सम्भोग मात्र इसका लक्ष्य नहीं । यह तो पाश्चात्य-भौतिकवादी पृष्ठभूमि है कि जितने दिन एक से मन मिला, रह लिया; अन्यथा तलाक़ देकर किसी दूसरे की सेज गर्माने लगे । यह वृत्ति भारतीय पारिवारिक धारणा पर बड़ा आघात पहुँचा रही है । लेखक का विश्वास है कि—

साधारण रूप में विवाह-सम्बन्ध अटूट होना चाहिए । जहाँ गृहस्थ-जीवन का अर्थ प्राय: कर्त्तव्य-पालन हो, वहाँ तलाक़ की स्वीकृति नहीं होनी चाहिए । तलाक़ वहीं क्षम्य हो सकता है, जहाँ पति-पत्नी परस्पर इकट्ठे रहते हुए अपने वर्णाश्रम-संबंधी कर्मों का पालन करने में असुविधा मानते हों ।[13]

हिन्दुस्तानी सभ्यता व समाज में पति-पत्नी में धर्म का संबंध है अर्थात् इस संसार में होने वाले कर्म के पीछे पति-पत्नी का परस्पर सहयोग अपेक्षित है ! गृहस्थाश्रम में पुरुष-स्त्री इकट्ठे रहकर समाज में कुछ आवश्यक कार्य करते हैं । जिसमें धनोपार्जन कर उसका सदुपयोग, सन्तानोत्पत्ति कर उसका पालन-पोषण और शिक्षा-दीक्षा का प्रबन्ध करना गृहस्थाश्रम में सम्मिलित हैं । भारतीय संस्कृति में एक पुरुष एक ही स्त्री को विवाहित बना सकता है । यद्यपि गृहस्थ के अनेकानेक कर्त्तव्यों की पूर्ति करने के लिए ऐकाधिक स्त्री की आवश्यकता पड़ती है तो उसको ठुकराया नहीं गया है । इस गृहस्थ कार्य के लिए यह उचित माना जाता है कि एक पुरुष का एक ही स्त्री से संबंध बने । परन्तु यदि किसी अवस्था विशेष में किसी घर-गृहस्थी के कर्त्तव्य पालन में स्त्री समर्थन हो तो दो की सहायता भी सम्भव है अर्थात् दूसरा विवाह भी मान्य हो सकता है । *न्यायाधिकरण* में लेखक ने इसे स्पष्ट करते हुए कहा है—

यह है हिन्दुस्तानी सभ्यता का सार । एक स्त्री से विवाह अथवा एक पुरुष से विवाह नियम है । इस पर भी यह उद्देश्य है गृहस्थ धर्म का पालन । विवाह के नियम साधन हैं । उद्देश्य की प्राप्ति के लिए साधन होते हैं न कि साधन की रक्षा के लिए उद्देश्य की हत्या क्षम्य ।[14]

ऐसा नहीं है कि गुरुदत्त ने अपने उपन्यासों में भारतीय नारी को पाश्चात्य संस्कृति के रंग में ही रंगा है वरन् पाश्चात्य सभ्यता व संस्कृति को भारतीय संस्कृति का जामा भी पहनाया है । अमेरिका में जन्म, शिक्षा, रहन-सहन, आचार-विचार रखने वाली लिसा, भारत में आकर भारतीय सभ्यता व संस्कृति के रंग में ऐसी डूब जाती है कि वह विदेशी खान-पान, संस्कृति, विदेशी भाषा आदि को छोड़ हिन्दी भाषा के प्रति लगाव भारतीय संस्कृति के प्रति श्रद्धा एवं गाँधीवादी जीवन-दर्शन के लिए अपने आपको पूर्णत: समर्पित कर देती है । *अन्तरिक्ष में* उपन्यास की लिसा जो अमेरिका मूल की है, सोम (भारतीय) से शादी करती है । सोम लिसा को वहीं भारतीय संस्कृति से परिचित कराता है। जब वे भारत वापिस आते हैं तो सोम के साथ-साथ उसकी पत्नी लिसा भी आती है । लिसा को भारतीय संस्कृति और भाषा के प्रति इतनी आस्थावान देखकर सोम की भाभी सावित्री जब इस लगाव के बारे में पूछती है, तब लिसा कहती है -

जी, वह सब आपके देवर की कृपा का फल है । विवाहोपरांत इन्होंने मेरे मस्तिष्क में यह बैठाने का प्रयत्न किया कि हिन्दी भाषा और उसकी देवनागरी लिपि नितान्त वैज्ञानिक भाषा और लिपि हैं । मैंने दोनों को सीखना आरम्भ कर दिया है । दो वर्ष की अवधि में मैंने इस पर अच्छी प्रगति की है । अब ये मुझे एक अन्य भाषा पढ़ा रहे हैं ।

वह है वेद की भाषा । इतना कहना है कि दो वर्ष की अवधि में उसको भी मैं भलीभांति हृदयागम कर लूंगीं ।[15]

लिसा भारतीय समाज, धर्म और संस्कृति से इतनी अधिक प्रभावित होती है कि वह नाम ही परिवर्तित कर सरस्वती रख लेती है जो कि पूर्णत: भारतीयता का परिचायक है । इतना ही नहीं भारतीयता को सर्वश्रेष्ठ जाति की संज्ञा देते हुए कहती है—

जी नहीं, जन्म से तो सभी मनुष्य ही होते हैं । इसमें देश का संबंध क्या कर सकता है ? देश से तो राष्ट्रीयता का संबंध होता है । सभी मनुष्यों और राष्ट्रों में भले-बुरे कर्मों के आधार पर श्रेष्ठ अथवा नीच मनुष्य अर्थात् जातियाँ होती हैं । मैं स्वयं को मनुष्य जाति की मानती हुई, भारतीय मनुष्यों में अपनी गणना करती हूँ । इसी को मैं भारतीय जाति मानती हूँ ।[16]

महत्त्वपूर्ण बात यह है कि सरस्वती गाँधीवादी-दर्शन और भारतीय संस्कृति के लिए समर्पित है । वह एक भारतीय पुरुष के लिए अपनी माँग में सिन्दूर भरती है । उसके लिए अहिंसा, गाँधीवादी-दर्शन केवल उद्घोष न होकर जीवन और उसके आचरण के अंग हैं ।

गुरुदत्त ने यहाँ भारतीय बनाम पाश्चात्य संस्कृति के माध्यम से समाज फैली उन कुत्सित प्रवृत्तियों—वेश्यावृत्ति और पाश्चात्य शिक्षा का अंधानुकरण आदि सामाजिक बुराइयों को जिनसे भारतीय समाज और संस्कृति को खतरा है स्पष्ट करने का प्रयत्न किया ।

(2) अभिजात्य वर्ग की संस्कृति

प्रत्येक युग की अपनी भाव-धारा होती है । उसी के आधार पर विभिन्न संस्कृतियों का अध्ययन किया जाता है । भारत के मध्ययुग का सामाजिक दृष्टिकोण धर्म था, अत: धर्म के आधार पर भारतीय संस्कृति का विवेचन करना उपयुक्त था । आधुनिक युग भारतीय और पाश्चात्य संस्कृति के संघर्ष का युग है । इन संस्कृतियों के तनाव में ही भारतीय व्यक्ति के जीवन संबंधी दृष्टिकोण का निर्धारण कर सकते हैं । बीसवीं शताब्दी में यह वर्गीकरण ग्राम्य और शहरी संस्कृति के रूप में विकसित हुआ। आज़ादी के बाद औद्योगीकरण के विकास तथा विज्ञान की सुविधाओं के कारण नगरों का स्वरूप बिल्कुल बदल गया और ग्राम्य और शहर की संस्कृति में बड़ा अंतर आया । इनके निवासियों की परिस्थितियों और जीवन दृष्टिकोण भी एक दूसरे से भिन्न थे । इन सब परिस्थितियों का मूल कारण था गांव में पर्याप्त शिक्षा का अभाव । जो किसी मानव जाति के विकास का प्रथम चरण है, क्योंकि शिक्षा से बुद्धि और धन दोनों की प्राप्ति सहज है । *नगर-परिमोहन* के मास्टर जगतराम गाँव में ऐसी शिक्षा के पक्षधर हैं तथा वह ऐसी शिक्षा देना चाहते हैं, जिससे गाँवों में अधिक-से-अधिक धन प्राप्त हो, ताकि यहाँ के लोगों का जीवन-स्तर सुधर सके । वे कहते हैं—

नगरों में सुख-सुविधाएं अधिक हैं । वे सुख-सुविधाएं धन से प्राप्त होती हैं । वहाँ देहात में उतना धन नहीं है । धन उत्पन्न करने के लिए तीन वस्तुएं चाहिए—परिश्रम, पूँजी और बुद्धि । देहात में पहली दो बातें हैं, लेकिन उनके प्रयोग का ढ़ंग नहीं आता । इसका कारण यह है कि तीसरी वस्तु अर्थात् बुद्धि का अभाव है । बुद्धि चाहिए । यह स्कूलों में नहीं बिकती । स्कूलों में तो अक्षर-ज्ञान ही हो सकता है । अक्षर-ज्ञान आवश्यक और अनिवार्य होते हुए भी समस्या का समाधान नहीं है । बुद्धि प्राप्त करने के लिए शिक्षण की आवश्यकता है, मैं विचार यह करता हूँ कि शिक्षा किस प्रकार दूँ ।[17]

आधुनिक युग के उपन्यासों में अधिकांश रूप से अभिजात्य वर्ग के लोगों का चित्रण हुआ है। इन तथाकथित अभिजात्य (कुलीन) वर्ग की प्रमुख समस्या है काम समस्या । इस वर्ग के पात्रों का कोई रचनात्मक दृष्टिकोण तो है नहीं, समाज की समस्याओं से वे अनभिज्ञ हैं । केवल काम-तृप्ति में ही संलग्न दिखाई देते हैं । इनका अपना पारिवारिक जीवन भी स्वस्थ एवं सुखी नहीं है। कस्तूरी के हिरन के समान इनका पूरा जीवन सांसारिक चमक-दमक और काम वासनाओं की पूर्ति में ही व्यतीत हो गया है । लेकिन खेद की बात यह भी है कि इस युग के उपन्यासकारों ने तटस्थ होकर इस वर्ग के पात्रों का चित्रण नहीं किया । लेकिन अमृतलाल नागर और रांगेय राघव की भांति गुरुदत्त ने इस वर्ग के पात्रों की मनोवृत्ति, संस्कृति और जीवन-मूल्यों का तटस्थता के साथ वर्णन किया है । *विडम्बना* उपन्यास में रानी का चरित्र-चित्रण एक चरित्रहीन नारी के रूप में किया गया है, जो अपनी सुख-सुविधाओं के लिए सोहन के हाथों अपना शरीर तक बेच देती है । इतना सब कुछ होते हुए भी वह सम्मानित है क्योंकि उसका संबंध और संपर्क समाज के अभिजात्य वर्ग से है । उसके पास सोहन से

प्राप्त आर्थिक साधन हैं । आज का अभिजात्य वर्ग सबसे अधिक मूल्यहीन और असांस्कृतिक सा हो गया है । अंग्रेज़ों के सम्पर्क में आकर इस वर्ग ने अपने सांस्कृतिक मूल्यों को ठुकरा दिया और पश्चिम के मूल्यों को वह आत्मसात नहीं कर सका । सुविधा के अनुसार कुलीन वर्ग के मूल्य बनते और टूटते जाते हैं । अभिजात्य वर्ग न संस्कारों से नैतिकतावादी है और न व्यवहार में उसका प्रयोग करता है । सांस्कृतिक और चारित्रिक दृष्टि से यह वर्ग अत्यन्त पतित है । कुलीन वर्ग की संस्कृति निरुद्देश्य, अकर्मण्य और काम-पीड़ा से ग्रसित है । अगर इस वर्ग को अर्थ-सत्ता से अलग कर दिया जाए तो समाज में इसका कोई स्तर नहीं रहेगा और स्तरहीन व समाज से पृथक् मानव चाहे वह धनी (कुलीन) वर्ग हो या फिर निर्धन वर्ग का, मरे हुए के समान होता है । *पड़ोसी* की राजरानी इन मनोवृत्तियों और स्वार्थ-लोलुपता पर कटाक्ष करते हुए अपने बेटे कर्मजीत सिंह को अभिजात्य वर्ग की मूल्यहीन संस्कृति से दूर रहने का उपदेश देते हुए कहती है - 'देखो बेटा ! यह संसार बहुत ही गंदा स्थान है । हम अपने भाग्य से इसमें आये हैं तो हमको कमल के समान इस कीचड़ से अलिप्त होकर रहना पड़ेगा, नहीं तो इस गंदगी में हम भी कीड़ों के समान दूषित हो जायेंगे ।'[18]

अभिजात्य वर्ग की संस्कृति का एक कड़वा व कटु सत्य *विडम्बना* उपन्यास में भी देखने को मिलता है । मुहम्मद कुलीन संस्कृति का पोषक है, काम-वासना की तृप्ति उसका मुख्य लक्ष्य है । प्रेम जैसे शब्द उसे वाग्जाल के अतिरिक्त कुछ और अर्थ नहीं देते । कमलाबाई एक सच्चे प्रेमी की तरह सच्चे मन से उसे प्रेम करती है, उसके जीवन का एक अभिन्न अंग बनना चाहती है । लेकिन मुहम्मद चारित्रिक दृष्टि से इतना पतित, हीन व खोखला हो गया है कि अपनी प्रेमिका को 'रंडी' जैसे अपशब्द व असामाजिक शब्द जिसे भारतीय संस्कृति में बिल्कुल हीन समझा जाता है से संबोधित करते हुए कहता है—'जमाना बदल गया है । रंडियां भी भगवान् का भजन करने लगी हैं । तभी तो लोग कहते हैं कि कलियुग आ गया ।'[19]

ऐसा नहीं है कि शहर ही अभिजात्य वर्ग की इस खोखली व काम-तृप्ति की विभीषिका में जल रहे हैं, बल्कि इसका प्रभाव गाँव में भी जहाँ-तहाँ प्रचुर मात्रा में देखने को मिलता है । आजकल हर प्रवृत्ति का मानव हर जगह अपनी पैठ बनाए हुए है, चाहे वह सदाचारी हो या दुराचारी । शहर में इस वर्ग का प्रभाव कुछ अधिक है तो गाँव भी इस समस्या से अछूते नहीं रहे हैं । जहाँ अधिक साधन-सम्पन्नता है वहाँ दुराचारी प्रवृत्ति के भाव कुछ ज्यादा पनपते हैं । गाँव में यह भाव आर्थिक विपन्नता व शिक्षा के अभाव में अंकुरित होते हैं । जिनका धनी वर्ग, महाजन व साहूकार आदि लाभ उठाकर उन गरीबों का न केवल शोषण करते हैं बल्कि अपनी काम-वासना का शिकार भी बनाते हैं। *नगर-परिमोहन* की मंगली पथभ्रष्ट होकर वेश्या बनी तो उसका कारण कुछ सामाजिक परिस्थितियां थी और ये परिस्थितियां पैदा करता है गाँव का धनी वर्ग और जड़ समाज । अन्यथा मंगली भी समाज की अन्य स्त्रियों की भांति सच्चरित्र थी । गाँव में रहकर मेहनत-मजदूरी कर अपना जीवन-यापन करती है । लेकिन मौका देखकर गाँव के धनी वर्ग के व्यक्तियों ने उसे अपनी काम-वासना की पूर्ति का साधन बनाया । इस सबको भुलाकर भी मंगली अपना आगे का जीवन जीना चाहती है । लेकिन यह जड़ समाज उसे सुधरने का मौका देना नहीं चाहता । वह समाज-सुधारक मास्टर जगतराम से अपना दुखड़ा रोती है और सद्मार्ग की याचना करती है । वह उसे सद्मार्ग दिखाता है लेकिन मास्टर जगतराम के इस सुकार्य को गाँव का धनी वर्ग सहन नहीं कर सका और उन्होंने मास्टर जगतराम को ही दुश्चरित्र घोषित कर मंगली के साथ गाँव छोड़ देने

के लिए विवश कर दिया और कहते हैं—'जो औरत एक बार पेशा कर चुकी हो, भला वह उसका मजा कैसे भूल सकती है । जिसको जन-जन की झूठी थाली में खाने की आदत पड़ जाये, वह एक थाली में नहीं खा सकती ।'[20]

मास्टर जगतराम इस बात को सुनकर हतप्रभ रह जाता है कि उसे दुश्चरित्र कहकर गाँव से निकल जाने को विवश कर रहे हैं । वह गाँव के चौधरी से इन गुंडा तत्वों की हठधर्मिता का खुलासा करते हुए कहता है—'ठीक है । जहाँ मान-मर्यादा सुरक्षित नहीं, वहाँ रहने में कुछ लाभ नहीं । हमारी बात तुमसे अधिक कठिन है । एक पेड़ की भांति जड़ उखड़ जाने से हम सूख जाएंगे । इस पर भी विचार करता हूँ कि यहाँ आँधी इतने वेग से चल रही है कि पेड़ भी टूटकर गिर रहा प्रतीत होता है ।'[21]

गुरुदत्त इसे अभिजात्य वर्ग की दूषित मानसिकता व असंस्कृति का ही प्रतीक मानते हैं। जो मास्टर जगतराम के इस सुकार्य को भी दुश्चरित्र मानते हैं और उसे गाँव से पृथक् करना चाहते हैं ।

(3) जन संस्कृति

जनवादी संस्कृति का सटीक व यथार्थ रूप से चित्रण करने वाले उपन्यासकारों में मुंशी प्रेमचंद का कोई सानी नहीं है । उन्होंने अपने साहित्य में ग्रामीण किसानों, श्रमिक वर्ग एवम् शोषित वर्ग की वेदना को जिस तरह से समाज के समक्ष रखा है वह अछूती नहीं है । उनके द्वारा हमें देश के इस विशाल जनसमूह की सरल, स्वाभाविक, सांस्कृतिक एवं सदाचार का परिचय मिलता है। उन्होंने माना कि शोषित वर्ग, किसानों, जमीदारों को लेकर आज सामाजिक उपन्यास विशेष लिखे जाते हैं। चूँकि समाज में दबे हुए लोगों को और गिराने का प्रयास हो रहा है । भारतीय रहन-सहन, खान-पान, रीति-रिवाज, व्यवहार इत्यादि को लेकर भी उपन्यास लिखे जाते हैं। प्रेमचंद के अनुसार—'साहित्य की प्रवृत्ति अहंवाद या व्यक्तिवाद तक परिमित नहीं रही बल्कि वह मनोवैज्ञानिक और सामाजिक होती जाती है । अब वह व्यक्ति को समाज से अलग नहीं देखता, किन्तु समाज के एक अंग के रूप में देखता है ।'[22]

प्रेमचंद ने व्यक्ति की पीड़ा को सामाजिक परिस्थितियों के बीच स्पष्ट किया है । समाज को आधार मान व्यक्ति की समस्याओं पर प्रकाश डाला है । प्रेमचंद सच्चे अर्थों में जनवादी संस्कृति के पुजारी थे । उपन्यासकार गुरुदत्त ने भी काफी हद तक प्रेमचंद की उस भाव-धारा को अपने साहित्य में कायम रखने का प्रयास किया है । गुरुदत्त के उपन्यासों के दो-तिहाई पात्र जनवादी संस्कृति का परिचय देते हैं । जिनमें मजदूर, कृषक और शोषित वर्ग आदि सम्मिलित हैं । उन्होंने अपने उपन्यासों के पात्रों के नाम भी ग्रामीण परिवेश के अनुसार ही रखे हैं जो पाठक को पूर्ण आभासित कराने में सक्षम होते हैं ।

उनका *नगर-परिमोहन* उपन्यास ग्राम्य जीवन की स्वस्थ एवं सुरुचिपूर्ण झांकी प्रस्तुत करता है। रामसिंह और गुणवंती ग्रामीण एवं साधारण वर्ग के पात्र हैं । जो अपनी संस्कृति की अंत तक रक्षा करते हैं । नगर की चकाचौंध भरी जिन्दगी भी रामसिंह को अपनी ओर आकर्षित नहीं कर पाती । वह अन्त में अपनी पत्नी के साथ वापस अपने गाँव में आकर कृषि कार्य करने लगता है। वह फकीरचंद से कहता है—'गाँव में सरल सादा जीवन था । झूठ बोलने का स्वभाव न था और न ही कभी आवश्यकता पड़ी थी । चोरी करने का तो कभी विचार तक नहीं आया था । आवश्यकता ही नहीं थी । न किसी से बैर था और न किसी से ईर्ष्या ।'[23]

रामसिंह अपनी पत्नी गुणवंती के कहने पर शहर जाता है। वे वहाँ जाकर धन कमाना चाहते हैं, बच्चों को अच्छी शिक्षा व जीवन में कुछ विकास करना चाहते हैं लेकिन होता है इसके बिल्कुल विपरीत । रामसिंह अनपढ़ होने के कारण वहाँ की चकाचौंध भरी जिन्दगी में अपना सब कुछ गवाँ देता है अर्थात् आर्थिक, मानसिक रूप से पूरा पतित और गुणवंती अभिजात्य वर्ग की संगति में पड़कर जुआ, शराब आदि के कारण चारित्रिक दृष्टि से व अपनी संस्कृति से बिल्कुल हीन हो जाता है । दूसरी तरफ मोहन सिंह है जो अपनी खेती अर्थात् गाँव छोड़कर शहर जाना ही नहीं चाहता है । खेती की आमदनी से उसने अपने मकान को सुधार लिया है । अर्थात् उसने गाँव में ही रहकर अपना विकास कर लिया है । यहाँ गुरुदत्त ने दोनों पात्रों के द्वारा उस द्वन्द्व को व्यक्त कराने की चेष्टा की है जो उन्होंने गाँव व शहर में रहकर वहाँ की संस्कृति से अनुभव किया है और आज समाज में घटित भी हो रहा है । मोहन सिंह कहता है—

यह ठीक था कि तम्बाकू की खेती की आय पर्याप्त होती थी । साथ ही गन्ने के खेतों में भी आय कम नहीं होती थी । इस बात को जब वह सोचता था तो उसको घर छोड़कर परदेश में आने पर शोक होने लगता था । वह समझता था कि वह व्यर्थ ही पिता से झगड़ा कर यहाँ आया है । . . . इसमें एक भारी बाधा थी । उसके कारण ही रंगा बाबू ने उन खेतों में एक भारी रकम लगा दी थी और ऐसे समय खेतों को छोड़कर चले आना उसको रंगा बाबू के साथ धोखा देना प्रतीत होता था ।[24]

आज भारतीय अभिजात्य वर्ग का जन सामान्य से संबंध टूट सा गया है । जन सामान्य को भारतीय संस्कृति से जितना लगाव है, उतना अभिजात्य वर्ग को नहीं । इसका प्रमुख कारण गुरुदत्त गाँव में शिक्षा व धन का पर्याप्त विकास न होना एवं रोजगार व अन्य आवश्यकता की पूर्ति हेतु गाँव से शहर की ओर पलायन मानते हैं । इस पलायनवादी प्रवृत्ति को *नगर-परिमोहन* के माध्यम से स्पष्ट करते हुए लेखक कहता है—

आधुनिक सभ्यता के विकास के साथ-साथ जनता देहातों से निकलकर नगरों की ओर आ रही है । इसमें कारण है भौतिक विज्ञान में उन्नति । . . . सड़कें, नालियाँ, बिजली, पानी, भव्य भवन तथा अन्य सुख के सामान विज्ञान की उन्नति के साथ-साथ नगरों में उपलब्ध होते जाते हैं । इन सब साधनों की प्राप्ति में धन व्यय होता है । अतएव नगरों में रहने और शारीरिक सुख-सुविधा प्राप्त करने के लिए धन अत्यन्त आवश्यक वस्तु हो गई है । परन्तु जहाँ नगरों में धन व्यय करने के साधन हैं वहाँ धनोपार्जन के स्रोत नहीं हैं । वास्तविक धन उत्पन्न होता है परिश्रम और भूमि से । ये दोनों वस्तुएं नगरों में नहीं हैं, न तो वहाँ भूमि है और न ही वहाँ पर परिश्रम करने वाले लोग हैं ।

इन पर भी धन संचित मिलता है नगरों में । यह धन कैसे नगरों में आता है ? इस प्रश्न का उत्तर ही नगर और गाँव की समस्या को सुलझाने में सहायक हो सकता है । वास्तविक धन (Real Wealth) का स्रोत नगर नहीं हैं । यह देहात अथवा उन साधनों में जो नगर के बाहर हैं, उत्पन्न होता है लहलहाते खेतों में, भूमि के गर्भ में खोदी खानों में तथा सागर तल पर धन के स्रोत हैं । इन स्रोतों से धन निकलता है, मानव परिश्रम से । परिश्रम के फल को बढ़ाकर कई गुणा करने की शक्ति है, मशीनों में ।[25]

गुरुदत्त ने *सभ्यता की ओर* उपन्यास में भी समाज के बदलते हुए इस दृष्टिकोण को चित्रित करने का प्रयास किया है । शहर का कुलीन वर्ग अनुचित साधनों से धन कमा कर सभ्य और सुसंस्कृत बन गया है । वह गाँव के सत्यनिष्ठ एवं सरल हृदय व्यक्ति को असभ्य और असंस्कृत मानता है । गुरुदत्त सभ्यता का मानदण्ड मन और व्यवहार की श्रेष्ठता को मानते हैं । अभिजात्य और जनवादी संस्कृति के अन्तर को स्पष्ट शब्दों में व्यक्त करते हुए वे कहते हैं—

क्षण-क्षण में झूठ का सहारा लेने वाला, अभिमानयुक्त कुटिलता का व्यवहार करने वाला, धोखा-धड़ी करने वाला व्यक्ति सभ्य नहीं कहा जा सकता । भले ही वह महलों में रहता हो, मोटर और हवाई जहाजों में घूमता हो, सभ्य तथा सभ्यता का मानदण्ड मन और व्यवहार की श्रेष्ठता है न कि धन, सम्पदा, सम्पन्नता ।[26]

वास्तव में, गुरुदत्त जनवादी कलाकार हैं उन्होंने अभिजात्य और जनवादी संस्कृति का कलात्मक दृष्टि से विवेचन किया है । उनकी लेखनी जन साधारण के उदात्त एवं मानवीय गुणों का चित्रण करने में समर्थ है ।

3. उपसंहार

उपन्यास मानव-जीवन की सफलतम अभिव्यक्ति है । जीवन के जितने विविध रूपों का निरूपण और सजीव चित्रांकन उपन्यास करता है, उतना साहित्य की अन्य विधाओं द्वारा सम्भव नहीं। उपन्यासकार उस मानव समाज से घटनाओं और चरित्रों का चयन करता है जिसमें वह सांस लेता है मानसिक रूप से विचरण करता है । उपन्यासकार गुरुदत्त जो भारतीय संस्कृति के प्रबल समर्थक व सजग प्रहरी माने गये हैं, ने प्रत्येक उपन्यास कोई न कोई विशेष दृष्टिकोण, समस्या एवं सुझाव को लेकर लिखे हैं और इसी विधा के माध्यम से उन्होंने समाज में फैली उन दुर्बलताओं व हीन प्रवृत्तियों जैसे—वेश्यावृत्ति, उच्छृंखलता, मद्यपान, पाश्चात्य रंग में डूबे युवक-युवतिओं, देशद्रोह, मिथ्याचार व अयुक्तिपूर्ण व्यवहार आदि सामाजिक बुराईयों पर जमकर प्रहार किया है जिनसे मानव समाज व संस्कृति को खतरा है । साथ ही भारतीय जनमानस में मानवतावादी भाव, राष्ट्र-प्रेम, आपसी भाईचारा व एकता तथा हिन्दी भाषा के प्रति लगाव की बात को भी जोर देकर कहा है । संस्कृति चाहे पाश्चात्य वर्ग की हो, अभिजात्य वर्ग की या जनसामान्य वर्ग की यदि वह दूसरी संस्कृति पर हावी होती है तो वहाँ टकराव व विघटन की स्थिति पैदा होती है और यही टकराव एक संस्कृति का दूसरी संस्कृति में पलायन का प्रमुख कारण है जैसे पाश्चात्य संस्कृति का भारतीय संस्कृति में, कुलीन वर्ग का जनसाधारण में, शहरी संस्कृति का ग्रामीण संस्कृति में पलायन हो रहा है । जो मानव की बुद्धि को दूषित व भ्रमित कर अपना साम्राज्य स्थापित कर रही है । गुरुदत्त इस पलायन के प्रति चिन्तित हैं । क्योंकि भारतीय संस्कृति जिसे विश्व की अन्य संस्कृतियों का सिरमौर माना जाता था, पाश्चात्य संस्कृति के आगमन से उसमें कुछ कमी आई है । यह कमी हमारे द्वारा ही हमारी संस्कृति में प्रविष्ट हुई है क्योंकि इसकी चकाचौंध ने हम सभी को चौंधा दिया है । और इसका केन्द्र बनी नारी । नारी जिसे भारतीय संस्कृति में देवी तुल्य माना गया है अर्थात् जहाँ नारी का वास होता है वहाँ देवता निवास करते हैं । लेकिन कुछ काम के पुजारियों ने इसे मात्र 'काम-तृप्ति का साधन', 'अपनी उन्नति की सीढ़ी' व 'बच्चे पैदा करने की मशीन' बनाकर रख दिया है । क्या यही है नारी के प्रति सम्मान, आदर ? *गुण्ठन* उपन्यास में एक पिता अपने बेटे की उन्नति से अत्यन्त चिन्तित रहते थे । वे बेटे की योग्यता-अयोग्यता से अच्छी तरह वाकिफ थे । बेटे की उच्च सरकारी पद पर नियुक्ति व उन्नति का माध्यम अपनी योग्यता नहीं बल्कि अपनी पत्नी के सौन्दर्य का सौदा होता है । पहले पति अपनी स्त्री की मान-मर्यादा की रक्षा के लिए जान की बाजी लगा देता था पर आज वही पति अपने ही हाथों से पत्नी का सतीत्व लुटा रहा है । यही है अभिजात्य वर्ग की संस्कृति । क्योंकि साधारण वर्ग का मनुष्य ऐसी उन्नति व संस्कृति के प्रति कदापि समझौता नहीं कर सकता ।

भाषावाद जो आज की प्रमुख समस्या है ! देश का प्रत्येक वर्ग इस समस्या से ग्रसित है क्योंकि देश के विभिन्न क्षेत्रों ने स्वभाषा की ममता ने ऐसा उग्र रूप धारण किया कि राजभाषा हिन्दी को पीछे धकेल दिया गया है । आज राजनीतिक दाव-पेंच की लपेट के कारण हिन्दी राजभाषा नहीं बन पाई । इन ह्रासशील प्रवृत्तियों की आलोचना करते हुए शशिभूषण सिंहल ने लिखा है—

स्वार्थपटता, संकीर्णता, अकर्मण्यता, शिथिलता हमारे राष्ट्रीय जीवन की क्षमताओं को घुन की भाँति खाये जा रही हैं । हमारा क्या राष्ट्रीय और क्या सांस्कृतिक सम्पूर्ण जीवन थोथे कल्पित आदर्शों और अंतर्विरोध के तनाव को न सह सकने के कारण टूटा जा रहा है । मनुष्य, मनुष्य की तरह नहीं जी पा रहा है । साम्प्रदायिक हित उसके नैसर्गिक कुशलक्षेम को चट कर गए हैं ।

इस तनाव और अंतर्विरोध की स्थिति से छुटकारा पाने के लिए गुरुदत्त प्रत्येक व्यक्ति से धर्म पालन की अपेक्षा रखते हैं । चूंकि वे भारतीय धर्म की छाया में सभी सम्प्रदायों को फलता-फूलता देखना चाहते हैं । समाज के सांस्कृतिक, धार्मिक, सामाजिक और बौद्धिक संघर्ष एवं अन्तर्द्वन्द्व का चित्रण गुरुदत्त ने बखूबी किया है । उन्होंने अपने साहित्य के माध्यम से यह स्पष्ट करने की कोशिश भी की है कि वे वास्तव में भारतीय संस्कृति के प्रबल समर्थक थे । उन्होंने विशेषकर पाश्चात्य शिक्षा व संस्कृति, अतिआधुनिकता, अभिजात्य वर्ग एवं अपने राष्ट्र व भाषा के प्रति सम्मान न करने वालों पर कटाक्ष किया है और भारतीय संस्कृति, धर्म व भाषा के प्रति आदर व सम्मान करने वालों के लिए एक प्रेरणा-स्रोत का कार्य किया है । मुंशी प्रेमचन्द के बाद भारतीय जीवन-पद्धति एवं रीति-रिवाज़ों, भारतीय समाज व उसकी संस्कृति एवं मध्यम वर्ग के जीवन संघर्ष को व्यापकता से चित्रित किया है तो गुरुदत्त ने ही ।

वास्तव में, गुरुदत्त के साहित्य ने पाठकों के ज्ञान को नया आलोक और नयी दिशाएं प्रदान की हैं ।

संदर्भ-सूची

1. डॉ. नंदलाल मेहता 'वागीश', 'संस्कृति और संस्कार', *संस्कृति पत्रिका* 13-14, 2007, पृ. 119।

2. मोहिनी हिंगोरानी, 'बहु-सांस्कृतिक भारतीयता', *संस्कृति पत्रिका* 13-14, 2007, पृ. iv ।

3. अशोक कौशिक, *साहित्यकार गुरुदत्त प्रतिनिधि रचनाएं*, उपन्यास का परिचय, पृ. 9 ।

4. सम्पादक अशोक कौशिक, *गुरुदत्त अभिनन्दन ग्रन्थ*, पृ. 80 ।

5. गुरुदत्त, *Cultural State in Bharatvarsha*, p. 166 ।

6. गुरुदत्त, न्यायाधिकरण, पृ. 275 ।

7. कृष्णदत्त पालीवाल, 'भारतीय संस्कृति और मूल्य बोध', *संस्कृति पत्रिका* 13-14, 2007, पृ. 125।

8. वही ।

9. गुरुदत्त, *विवेक*, 1958, पृ. क. ख ।

10. गुरुदत्त, *विकृत छाया*, 1946, पृ. 143 ।

11. गुरुदत्त, *विडम्बना*, 1952, पृ. 283 ।

12. गुरुदत्त, *पाणिग्रहण*, 1960, भूमिका ।

13. वही ।

14. गुरुदत्त, *न्यायाधिकरण*, पृ. 216 ।

15. गुरुदत्त, *अंतरिक्ष में*, पृ. 11 ।

16. वही, पृ. 90 ।
17. गुरुदत्त, *नगर-परिमोहन*, 1955, पृ. 60 ।
18. गुरुदत्त, *पड़ोसी*, 1967, पृ. 62 ।
19. गुरुदत्त, *विडम्बना*, 1952, पृ. 11 ।
20. गुरुदत्त, *नगर-परिमोहन*, 1955, पृ. 129 ।
21. वही, पृ. 139 ।
22. प्रेमचन्द, *साहित्य का उद्देश्य*, पृ. 16 ।
23. गुरुदत्त, *नगर-परिमोहन*, 1955, पृ. 296 ।
24. वही, पृ. 197-8 ।
25. वही, पृ. भूमिका ।
26. गुरुदत्त, *सभ्यता की ओर*, 1959, भूमिका ।
27. गुरुदत्त, *गुण्ठन*, 1955 ।

सहायक संदर्भ-ग्रन्थों की सूची

आधुनिक उपन्यासों में वस्तु विन्यास – डॉ. सरोजनी त्रिपाठी ।
उपन्यासकार गुरुदत्त : व्यक्तित्व एवं कृतित्व – के. शाह प्रतीक ।
हिन्दी उपन्यास : पृष्ठभूमि और परम्परा – डॉ. बद्रीदास ।
संस्कृति का दार्शनिक विवेचन – डॉ. देवराज ।
हिन्दी उपन्यास का संस्कृति अध्ययन – डॉ. रमेश तिवारी ।
श्री गुरुदत्त अभिनन्दन ग्रन्थ – सं. अशोक कौशिक ।
उपन्यासकार गुरुदत्त व्यक्तित्व विवेचन – मनमोहन सहगल ।
वृन्दावन लाल वर्मा के उपन्यासों का सांस्कृतिक अध्ययन – डॉ. श्रीकृष्ण अवस्थी ।
साहित्य का उद्देश्य और कुछ विचार – मुंशी प्रेमचन्द ।
भारतीय संस्कृति और उसका इतिहास – डॉ. सत्यकेतु विद्यालंकार ।
साहित्यकार गुरुदत्त प्रतिनिधि रचनाएँ – अशोक कौशिक आदि ।

4

Commercializing Tradition: Women, Ayurveda and Healing in Colonial North India

CHARU GUPTA

INTRODUCTION

This essay scrutinizes the extensive writings of Yashoda Devi, one of the most commercially successful and famous woman ayurvedic practitioners at the beginning of the twentieth century in colonial north India. Located in Allahabad, in the state of United Provinces, Yashoda Devi was a Kayastha, upper middle class woman. She was not only a leading Ayurvedic woman doctor of her time, but also a prolific writer. Her writings are representative of some of the women's voices which began appearing in the Hindi print-public sphere in the early twentieth century. Yashoda Devi wrote on a wide range of subjects, with a particular emphasis on women's health, in the process negotiating and reinventing the terrain of tradition and modernity, often with contradictory and ambivalent implications. I use Yashoda Devi's extensive writings here to examine the relationship between women, Ayurveda and healing in colonial north India and also to reveal how women's writings, though severely monitored by women themselves and by the larger public, were also an arena for potential possibilities and instabilities.

Yashoda Devi's writings provide a window to other discourses as well. They highlight on the one hand the relationship and contradictions between Western medicine and Ayurveda, and on the other, they are also critical in examining the correlation between women and medicine. It has been argued that Western medical knowledge became an important instrument to assert disciplinary power over the body of the colonized by the colonial Indian state, and to displace indigenous medical systems.[1] The Ayurvedic practitioners reacted both defensively and offensively to this process, by reconstituting Ayurvedic tradition on the one hand, and on the other arguing its unique connection to Indian cultural identity.[2] Simultaneously, scholars have been sceptical about the actual impact of Western medicine on a large number of indigenous populations, and have questioned the efficacy of its disciplinary power.[3]

The subject of women and medicine in colonial India has engaged feminist writings, which have usually focused on white women medical practitioners who came to India,[4] and the role of medical profession in laying claim to authority over indigenous women's bodies by examining the attack on the traditional midwife. These studies tell us a story familiar to feminist scholars—of tensions between male dominated medical authority and a female sphere of health care, and of inscribing gender differences on the female body.[5] Rarely have middle class indigenous women's writings on the subject of medicine been a subject of study.[6] In this essay, I use the writings of Yashoda Devi to complicate the picture by revealing her understanding of, and relationship to, Western and indigenous medical practices, household, women, men, health, body and the nation. What is the character of medical knowledge upheld in these writings? Were women overwhelmingly victims, patients or healers in them? Was patriarchy challenged or gender stereotypes reconstituted? While studying these questions, the writings of Yashoda Devi can also provide a window for interrogating dichotomies between subaltern/hegemonic and feminine/masculine, often made while examining the interrelationship between traditional and modern medicine.

PRINT CULTURE, WOMEN'S WRITINGS AND AYURVEDA

Language, literature and print have been viewed as significant means for contests over power,[7] propagation of dominant ideas,[8] and fashioning of national,[9] regional and community identities in the modern period. In late colonial north India, as indeed elsewhere, print facilitated new expressions of vernacular literature. An influential section of the Hindu middle-class literati was trying to fashion a new collective identity for itself, and language and print became a means of community creation.[10] The period saw a rapid development of public institutions, libraries, and print culture, with growing number of publishing houses, presses, newspapers and books.[11] Hindi magazines and newspapers like *Saraswati*, *Chand* and *Abhyudaya* became the means of journalistic, literary and linguistic expression for assertions of self-identity by a confident Hindu middle class, and for a growing

Hindi public sphere in the early twentieth century. Allahabad became the centre of Hindi publications,[12] with almost all leading magazines and newspapers coming out from there.[13]

The oral tradition of Ayurveda adapted itself to the new commercial form. Print actually gave Ayurvedic discourse a wider diffusion, facilitating its production as a commodity.[14] By early twentieth century, there was a huge literature around it in Hindi, in the form of remedies offered, instruction manuals, dialogue with Western medicine, cookery books, advertisements and magazines, creating a dynamic 'public sphere'.[15] These writers adapted to shifts in relationship between knowledge and power fostered by print culture, encouraging the codification of Ayurveda as a medical science with ancient Indian roots. It facilitated the emergence of a new type of Ayurveda, a new brand of *vaids* (doctors), and a new discourse.

It was in this period too that Hindu middle class, upper caste women increasingly began to participate and become visible in the public realm of print culture. A considerable amount has been written on the fraught and contradictory nature of this exercise, where their entry was a closely monitored process. Women's writings had to move within narrow margins, with constant negotiation with both traditional and reformist notions of womanhood.[16] Women's magazines, the periodical presses and women writers were moving and negotiating in a public domain, and had to be constrained in the use of language and values propounded. Thus, it has been argued, the representational practices of that culture were cast in a reformist mould. They also operated largely in an urban and 'respectable' public sphere, mirroring the class and caste exclusions of the male sphere. Women's journals and their writings became agents of transmission of a middle-class code of conduct, though under the mantle of a progressive orientation towards women. Literature of, for and by women was thus consciously didactic to a large extent.

However, to stop here would be to emphasize only the limits of women's literary public sphere. A study of women's writings in colonial north India, as indeed elsewhere, would be incomplete without drawing attention to levels other than that of the formal script. Though women writers, editors and publishers accepted some of the structures of male reformers, they also translated and negotiated others in order to argue for a voice of their own in family and educational life, and question their role and norms of society, thereby offering a limited challenge to patriarchy.[17] Scholars have, for example, argued how letters written by women in various women's magazines, especially *Chand*, allowed a space for solidarity in a covert and tentative way, and stressed their right to feel and express individual emotions. Or how some of the women writers used their writings to reject stereotypes of women and to manipulate the *pativrata* or the ascetic model to carve out spaces for themselves.[18]

In the United Provinces, Allahabad pioneered women's journalism and education. Many women's voices began appearing in the Hindi print public sphere of the early twentieth century in this region. Yashoda Devi's writings too are representative of this trend. She too operated in this dynamic sphere of women's public print culture, using Hindi as her language, and adopting its writing styles, images and metaphors. Being a prolific writer, she wrote more than 50 books, running from 20 to 1,000 pages, not only on health and sex, but also on different aspects of women.[19] It is entirely possible that Yashoda Devi herself did not pen all her books, since they were too many, though there were endless repetitions in many of them. She was not just a person, but an enterprise, and must have had others to help her with her writing. Some of these books were popular guides, while others dealt with more intricate questions of Ayurveda and women's health. These texts were produced for use as household advice manuals, as medical recipe books, as prescriptive texts, as Ayurvedic remedies, as case studies of her patients, as promotions for her products and letters of praise. Many of her books went into numerous editions, revealing their popularity.[20] She had her own printing and publishing house, known as Devi Pustakalaya. She carried a widespread ad. campaign of her medicines, clinic and books in leading journals.[21] To make her books more commercially viable, she used pictures and photographs. Her book *Dampatya Prem* had 158 pictures in total.[22] Another book, *Nari Sharir Vigyan* ran into 1,144 pages. *Dampati Arogyata Jivanshastra* and *Dampatya Prem aur Ratikriya ka Gupt Rahasya* were of 324 and 520 pages, respectively. She started occasional magazines like *Kanya Sarvasva, Stridharma Shikshak* and *Stri Chikitsak,* the latter catering solely to Ayurvedic treatment of female diseases.[23] The publication and sale of her books is indeed a commercial success story in the sphere of women's writings. It needs to be emphasized however that her writings were not exceptional, though of course their number and scope was wide. Many books on similar subjects and expressing almost parallel concerns came to be written at this time, especially by women. Thus, while I focus here on Yashoda Devi's writings, they mirror larger social realities, issues and interests of the period regarding women.

PROCREATION AND PLEASURE IN
YASHODA DEVI'S WRITINGS

Yashoda Devi received her education in Ayurveda from her father.[24]
At the young age of 16, she entered into active practice.[25] She established her *Stri Aushadhalaya* (Dispensary for Women) at Allahabad
in 1908, and opened a 'Female Ayurvedic Pharmacy'.[26] Subsequently
her dispensaries were established in many other towns of Bihar and
UP. A huge number of women came to her with their problems, and
she received innumerable letters from all over India. She was so popular that letters reached her, just addressed as 'Devi, Allahabad'.[27]
The stream of letters that she received, and the amount of medicines
sent by her through post, point to a thriving mail order business.
Yashoda Devi enjoyed high local acceptance, with a large clientele.
Her fame spread to far off places like Africa and Fiji.[28] Her simultaneous engagement with print, actual check-ups and physical examination moved her beyond the realm of just 'literate'. Her range was
wide, and she penetrated the everyday lives of women and men, contributing in shaping medical, and to an extent, nationalist identities
(see Figure 1).

Yashoda Devi moved in a relatively new territory, as there was
hardly any indigenous dispensary catering exclusively to women
at this time.[29] It was difficult for women in *purdah* to go to male
practitioners,[30] there were limits to their access to cash, and there was
still much bias against Western medical systems. Thus Yashoda Devi
fulfilled two much-felt needs, being a woman and a practitioner of
an indigenous medical system. Her client base was also protected by
the separation of sexes. Like other practitioners of her time, Yashoda
Devi too improvized Ayurveda and enthused it with new life. In this,
she borrowed heavily from Western medical practices. For example,
there was an endless repetition of anatomical drawings in her
books. She was very much guided in her illustrations by a modernist
impulse, recognizing the context of medical pluralism. However, she
maintained the superiority of Ayurveda. She engaged with what she
saw around her, while preserving her basis, providing a vision of
an alternative modernity. Through her discursive manoeuvres, she
evaded any tidy epistemological frames.[31] To posit modern Ayurveda
as a countercultural system in binary opposition to 'hegemonic' bio-
medicine may not always be fruitful.

In her writings, while accepting that some tenets of Western and
Unani medicine could aid Ayurveda,[32] she offered its clear defence,
particularly in its usefulness for women.[33] She stated that Ayurveda

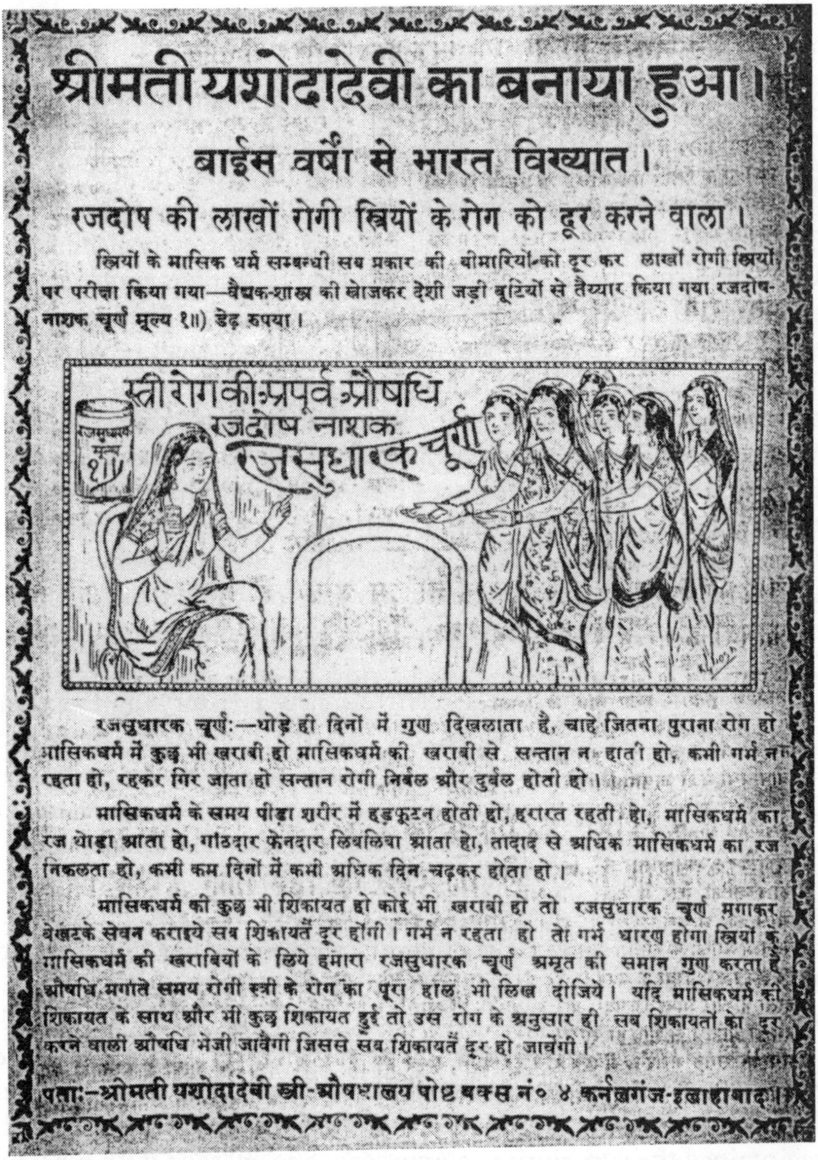

श्रीमती यशोदादेवी का बनाया हुआ ।

बाईस वर्षों से भारत विख्यात ।

रजदोष की लाखों रोगी त्रियों के रोग को दूर करने वाला ।

त्रियों के मासिक धर्म सम्बन्धी सब प्रकार की बीमारियों को दूर कर लाखों रोगी त्रियों पर परीक्षा किया गया—वैद्यक-शास्त्र की खोजकर देशी जड़ी बूटियों से तैय्यार किया गया रजदोष नाशक चूर्ण मूल्य १॥) डेढ़ रुपया ।

स्त्री रोग की अपूर्व औषधि रजदोष नाशक रजसुधाकरचूर्ण

रजसुधारक चूर्ण:—थोड़े ही दिनों में गुण दिखलाता है, चाहे जितना पुराना रोग हो मासिकधर्म में कुछ भी खराबी हो मासिकधर्म की खराबी से सन्तान न होती हो, कमी गर्म न रहता हो, रहकर सिर जाता हो सन्तान रोगी निर्बल और दुर्बल होती हो ।

मासिकधर्म के समय पीड़ा शरीर में दुहकूटन होती हो, हरारत रहती हो, मासिकधर्म का रज थोड़ा आता हो, गाढ़ा लेनदार लिबलिबा आता हो, तादाद से अधिक मासिकधर्म का रज निकलता हो, कमी कम दिनों में कमी अधिक दिन चढ़कर होता हो ।

मासिकधर्म की कुछ भी शिकायत हो कोई भी खराबी हो तो रजसुधारक चूर्ण मुगाकर बेखटके सेवन कराइये सब शिकायतें दूर होंगी । गर्म न रहता हो तो गर्म धारण होगा त्रियों की मासिकधर्म की खराबियों के लिये हमारा रजसुधारक चूर्ण अमृत की समान गुण करता है, औषधि मगाते समय रोगी स्त्री के रोग का पूरा हाल भी लिख दीजिये । यदि मासिकधर्म की शिकायत के साथ और भी कुछ शिकायत हुई तो उस रोग के अनुसार ही सब शिकायतों का दूर करने वाली औषधि भेजी जावेंगी जिससे सब शिकायतें दूर हो जावेंगी ।

पता:—श्रीमती यशोदादेवी स्त्री-औषधालय पोष्ट बक्स नं० ४ कनैखगंज-इलाहाबाद ।

Figure 1: Advertisement in the end pages [not paged] of यशोदा देवी,
नारी धर्मशास्त्र गृह प्रबन्ध शिक्षा, प्रथम भाग, 1931.

was like a huge ocean of nectar, meant to keep the body healthy. It was more suited to Indian conditions as its herbs came from the Indian soil, and was closer to the nature of indigenous people.[34] The body of Indian women was made of this country's atmosphere and climate and thus only wild herbal medicines which had grown in this land were capable of curing women's diseases from its roots.[35]

Male indigenous practitioners were problematic on several counts, she argued. Women would never reveal their true state of disease or show their private parts for examination to them. In any case, male Ayurvedic practitioners had completely ignored questions of women's health. Wives of *vaids* came to her for treatment.[36] Modern medical methods too were inadequate as they were incapable of penetrating the root cause,[37] hence the need of an indigenous woman practitioner.[38] Her medicines and practice also had a huge market because it was much cheaper to allopathic treatment.

Yashoda Devi's discourse was paradoxical. Her concerns overlapped with Hindu reformist rhetoric, assertions of modern nationalism,[39] and biomedical agendas. Her books, like many other science and medical books of the time, placed family, gender and sexuality at their centre.[40] Ayurveda was located in them in the context of middle-class social and domestic life, demonstrating ways in which body processes constructed nationalist identity. Besides offering remedies, they were also prescriptive texts for middle-class Hindu women, and their responsibilities towards maintaining the health of their families and of the Hindu nation, by scientific management within the familial structure.[41] There was a reordering of household and conjugality, alongside images of an idealized *pativrata* imbued with reformist endeavour, and sexual disciplining of the woman's body. The domestic space was regulated by regimens of hygiene, sanitation, cleanliness. Time was rationalized, and thriftiness, budgeting and temperance emphasized.[42] Cooking was an intrinsic part of care of the body and treatment of the ill within the home. Modern and scientific methods of cooking moulded to contemporary indigenous needs were stressed, combining hygiene with ethics. *Grhini Kartavyashastra Arogyashastra Arthat Pakshastra* was directly addressed to the Hindu middle-class housewife, and was a manual on Indian cookery, giving many recipes of healthy food for children, old people and those suffering from various illnesses. Yashoda Devi claimed that her recipes took into account nature, culture, biology, Ayurvedic scriptures and science, making the body healthy and strong.[43] Mothering and childcare became an arena of 'rationality' and constant advice for women. Recommendations on 'scientific' pregnancy, 'correct' neo-natal care, child-birth, care of the new-born, breast-feeding and child-rearing permeated many writings at this time,[44] including those of Yashoda Devi.[45]

Yashoda Devi's forte was in curing women's sexual problems like excessive menstrual bleeding and pains, repeated miscarriages and barrenness.[46] There was an elaborate discourse around menstruation as a bodily marker of female fertility, health and generative power, and her Ayurvedic medicine to cure such disorders seems to have had a huge demand. Using Ayurvedic treatment, she also dealt with vaginal discharges and sexually transmitted diseases in women. Besides having long conversations with her women patients, she had a detailed questionnaire.[47] She herself conducted their physical examination[48] and prepared medicines.[49] The aura of her 'magic hands' and sympathetic listening capabilities were constantly evoked, leading to further commodification and commercialization of her practice and medicines. Further, her clinical encounters and relationships with women patients point out that medical culture was constructed not only in formal literary discourse but also in knowledge-producing practices.

Sexuality engaged her constant attention, and was seen by her in medical-cum-moralistic terms. Her book *Dampatya Prem* was specifically devoted to it. She stressed that sexual science (*kamshastra*) and passionate intercourse were an intrinsic part of Ayurveda.[50] This was a time when printed sex manuals made up a genre that saw substantial growth in UP.[51] In these books the lines between sexual science, eroticism and obscenity were often blurred.[52] Yashoda Devi distanced herself from what she called such 'dirty' works of *kamshastra*, whose purpose was to titillate, and which had increased diseases among women and men.[53] Her books, she argued, presented sexual intercourse on scientific principles of Ayurveda.[54] We see here an excessive preoccupation with reproduction and procreation.[55] This was also reflected in other women's writings of that time, which too talked of the 'scientific' basis for sex, limiting it to procreation.[56] Her writings told women how to recognize 'pure' semen,[57] the ideal time to have sex,[58] how many times to have sex and how to have a healthy child,[59] offering various prescriptions. Her writings point to the inter-action of Ayurveda with sexual diseases of women particularly, which today is largely the domain of obstetrics and gynaecology.

Her years of interaction with female patients made her realize that she would be unable to cure many of them without addressing questions of male illnesses.[60] Her advice and remedies were meant not only to control female bodies but also male ones; sexual mores applied to men as well.[61] It has been emphasized how in the colonial period particularly, there was an attempt to turn away the power of sex from the chaos of passion into disciplined masculine strength.[62] Vivekananda gave a call to sexual abstinence for building a nation of heroes.[63] Gandhi too believed that stored-up semen was the source of splendid energy in the male body, and he linked it to the integrity of the nation. The nation required an end to the wasteful expenditure of time and energy in the pleasures of sex.[64] Many of the Hindu publicists, Sanatan Dharmists and Arya Samajists eulogized semen control. In their arguments and publications, it was no longer just a moral doctrine of self-discipline. Their modern discourse was intertwined with eugenics, childbirth, and a scientific 'rationality'. Healthy bodies ensured strong Hindu men, who in turn were indispensable to a modern, masculine nation. Semen control was a building block for claims to social and political power, cultural identity and a scientific way of life.

Yashoda Devi's writings too endorsed this discourse and argued for restraints on male sexuality. She perceived four main evils in male behaviour: loss of semen, multiple sexual intercourse, homosexuality and masturbation.[65] Masturbation became her chief target of attack. She warned against it on supposedly scientific-cum-moralistic lines.[66] She attributed various 'male' problems like excessive physical weakness, lack of senses, false excitement, semen loss, weak eyesight, enfeeblement of muscles, backaches, mental illness, inability to have a child, urinary diseases and nocturnal emissions chiefly to masturbation.[67] She linked its spread to modern 'vices' like easily availability of dirty books of *kamshastra*, sleazy romantic novels and advertisements of aphrodisiacs, making the heart and mind more fickle and volatile.[68] In her campaign against masturbation, she repeatedly resorted to references from Western doctors.[69] However, she linked it with a nationalist discourse, blaming it for the collapse of Indians and the nation.[70] Further, excessive sex with the wife was a waste of useful energies and time, better utilized in service of the nation.[71] She stated that men wrote to her asking for such medicines by which they could have sex many times a day and still feel energetic.[72] Lamenting this constant demand for aphrodisiacs, she stated that newspapers were constantly filled with such advertisements.[73] She made a case for *brahmacharya*[74] and the preservation of semen, which was being wasted in huge quantities, where 'earning was less than expenditure' (*amdani kam, kharcha zyada*).[75] She asked men to make love sparingly,[76] as semen was power, and the key to a healthy male body.[77] Thus, though commenting on the health of the household, her advice and prescriptions went beyond it, messing the categories of public and private. Her writings were charged with a moral indigenous fervour and codifying behaviour. In effect, the 'inner' and the 'outer' overlapped in her orderings. They cut across the family and extended to the community, concerned with the preservation of ethics of the whole nation.

This, however, is not her full story. Her texts had double-edged implications. They enabled her to participate in a world beyond the household and exercise a degree of autonomy and authority. Through long hours of intimate conversations, she seems to have established a rapport with her women clients, implying both considerable power over and close relationships with them. Unlike white women medical practitioners, the zenana quarters were not so condemned, in spite of the moral edge in her writings. Her case history narratives point to interesting directions. In them she is a sympathetic listener, sharing a common language of the body with those she treated. Her conversations could be 'empowering' for her women patients. Simultaneously, her success story is also a story of women's network, as away from household structures, women could voice their intimate complaints, especially about their male partners.

While women's reproductivity remained the core of Yashoda Devi's writings, she moved beyond it, recognizing women's bodily desires, sexual pleasures and orgasms. She justified expressions of female sexuality as important for a fulfilling sex life. Emphasis was laid on love between husband and wife. Hugs and kisses, sweet talk and foreplay were stressed, to ensure that the woman was ready and sexually aroused. Sex was thus not to be hurried by the male species, as enjoyment of women was as important.[78] Thus she not only talked of women's duties but also their needs, acknowledging feminine subjectivity. She voiced a strong protest against sex without the woman's consent, calling it a grave crime.[79] She referred to such men, and their misplaced sense of masculinity, as worse than that of animals, stating that their number was huge.[80] Here she even made a case for the West, where without the woman's consent, the man could do nothing, and where men were more knowledgeable about women's sexual desires.[81] It seems to be a trope used by her to justify the importance of sexual pleasure and even sexual agency for her women patients. In the process, she offered a scathing critique of Indian male habits and practices. She stressed how various women had confided in her the misdeeds of their husbands.[82] Her books had stories with titles like 'blind lust and tyranny of the husband towards his ailing wife, suffering from vaginal discharge'.[83] Impotent husbands, incapable of giving pleasure to their wife were attacked.[84] Most sexual illnesses of women were attributed to their men.[85] She emphasized that it was a myth that barrenness and infertility was due to some intrinsic defect in women, and here too men were often to be blamed for it.[86] Though infertility could often not be cured without the treatment of men as well, in many such cases they remarried, due to no fault of their wives.[87] Men here were at the mercy of Yashoda Devi, emerging as weak, useless and stupid.[88] Thus her writings at times had the potential of subverting or inverting patriarchy, or at least renegotiating the social and family norms.

While Yashoda Devi may be an exceptional woman, something can be learned of traditional female physicians and their clients by placing her against the stereotype of the *dai* on the one hand and male doctors steeped in bio-medical practices on the other. While her middle-class status gave her more 'respectability', her stories of woman-to-woman interaction suggest a more popular style of medical practice, relying as much on listening as on examination and prescription. Her methods appear to be socially more plebeian and culturally more popular. Perhaps seeing her popularity, and also recognizing the need to focus separately on 'women's diseases', many such writings by women and Ayurvedic clinics exclusively for women appeared,[89] though they could never repeat the success of Yashoda Devi.

Through her writings, we can perhaps also complicate the imagery of women of the household, recognizing the potential of domestic women healers. Yashoda Devi repeatedly urged women to learn some Ayurvedic remedies, take over the agency of health in their own hands, and if possible open many more *stri aushadhalayas*.[90] She wanted them to become a clever *vaid* and a knowledgeable friend.[91] Her prescriptions lead us to the home as the setting of most illness experience, to medicine as a domestic skill, a humble craft largely dominated by women. They were the custodians of a rich fund of knowledge on herbal remedies well into the colonial period.[92] Raising medicinal plants, caring for the sick, and making medicines for their family were mainly female activities, a part of their role as household managers.

These texts perhaps speak something other than the author's intentions, and which also shapes our consciousness. Even if partial and incomplete, they open other avenues of studying women's writings, gender and medicine in a colonial context. They use language in complex ways, where regulation of the body is as much for men as for women, where patriarchal control is intermixed with a scathing critique of men. This points to a dense phenomenology of experience, which allows us to hear the voices of women speaking through Yashoda Devi's narratives. These texts speak in ways that reinforce patriarchal hegemony, but may also allow subversion or transgression.

Yashoda Devi, and maybe other women practitioners of Ayurveda, entered the domain of male practitioners, covertly contesting both their control over the discipline and also offering different arrangements from hospitals. As a moral sexologist, Yashoda Devi moved in a nebulous territory, conforming to new modes of public health and medical science, while successfully moulding modern values to Hindu systems and needs. Her combination of modernity and tradition enabled the enfolding of the bio-body into the traditional body. By addressing critical and 'secret' issues of women's health, Yashoda Devi turned Ayurveda into a commercial success story. Her writings offered indigenous methods for regulating the bodies of Hindu women, and to some extent of men, within the home and the nation. Indigenous healing became another tool in the construction of cultural identity and Indian nationalism. At the same time, while patriarchies were rearticulated and nationalism consolidated through much of her discourse, she was simultaneously critical of male behaviour and occasionally challenged gender hierarchies.

CONCLUSION

The writings of Yashoda Devi are ambiguous and fractured at a number of places, and enframing them in any fixed categories eludes me. They encompass two parallel trends—the disciplining of bodies and households, and simultaneously alternative readings of pleasure and patriarchy. Her writings combined fact with fiction, science with myths, and Ayurvedic tradition with modern commercialization. Once set in motion, the very same vocabulary and processes deployed in her writings to articulate regulated bodies of women, acquired their own dynamic. Her writings thus open out into spaces which cannot be easily categorized, with competing and conflicting models of embodied gender. They simultaneously reiterate and replicate hierarchies of gender and also provide occasions for questioning them. Women's writings in Hindi in colonial north India usually had this ambivalent quality about them. They were largely geared towards making women good wives/good mothers/good Hindus, but had the potential to go beyond its rhetoric and take into account women's feelings, desires and pleasures. They may have reiterated patriarchy but they also placed an obstacle in the assertion of that patriarchal power. Even when writing within set frameworks, women were questioning their pedagogical formation. Finally, Yashoda Devi's writings can provide us with an occasion to examine the broader social historical processes unleashed in colonial India, and to highlight how middle-class formations, patriarchal practices and nationalist identities were consolidated, but also fractured from within by women's writings at this time. These women's spaces could simultaneously have oppressive and liberatory possibilities.

NOTES

1. David Arnold, *Colonizing the Body: State Medicine and Epidemic Disease in Nineteenth-Century India*, Berkeley: University of California Press, 1993 and *Science, Technology and Medicine in Colonial India*, The New Cambridge History of India III.5, Cambridge: Cambridge University Press, 2000; Mark Harrison, *Public Health in British India: Anglo-Indian Preventive Medicine 1859-1914*, Cambridge: Cambridge University Press, 1994; Roy MacLeod and Milton Lewis (eds.), *Disease, Medicine, and Empire: Perspectives on Western Medicine and the Experience of European Expansion*, London: Routledge, 1988; Deepak Kumar (ed.), *Science and Empire: Essays in Indian Context, 1700-1947*, Delhi: Anamika Prakashan, 1991.

2. K.N. Panikkar, 'Indigenous Medicine and Cultural Hegemony: A Study of the Revitalisation Movement in Keralam', *Social History*, 8, no. 2 (1992), pp. 288-95; Brahmananda Gupta, 'Indigenous Medicine in Nineteenth and Twentieth Century Bengal', in Charles Leslie (ed.), *Asian Medical Systems: A Comparative Study*, Berkeley: University of California Press, 1976, pp. 368-78; Paul R. Brass, 'The Politics of Ayurvedic Education: A Case Study of Revivalism and Modernization in India', in Susanne Hoeber Rudolph and Lloyd I. Rudolph (eds.), *Education and Politics in India: Studies in Organisation, Society, and Policy*, Delhi: Oxford University Press, 1972, pp. 342-71.

3. Harrison, *Public Health in British India*, p. 1.

4. These women were guided by combinations of missionary zeal, philanthropic concerns, 'saving' Indian women from the 'unhygienic' zenana, inspiration from a larger women's movement, a promising field of employment, and as a way of asserting professional status denied to them within their own country. See Antoinette Burton, *Burdens of History: British Feminists, Indian Women and Imperial Culture, 1865-1915*, Chapel Hill: University of North Carolina Press, 1994; and 'Contesting the Zenana: The Mission to Make "Lady Doctors for India", 1874-1885', *The Journal of British Studies*, 35, no. 3 (July 1996), pp. 368-97; Geraldine Forbes, 'Medical Careers and Health Care for Indian Women: Patterns of Control', *Women's History Review*, 3, no. 4 (December 1994), pp. 515-30; Rosemary Fitzgerald, 'A "Peculiar and Exceptional, Measure": The Call for Women Medical Missionaries for India in the Later Nineteenth Century', in Robert A. Bickers and Rosemary Seton (eds.), *Missionary Encounters: Sources and Issues*, London: Curzon Press, 1996; Margaret I. Bolfour and Ruth Young, *The Work of Medical Women in India*, London: Humphrey Milford, 1929; Maneesha Lal, 'The Politics of Gender and Medicine in Colonial India: The Countess of Dufferin's Fund, 1885-1888', *Bulletin of the History of Medicine*, 68, no. 1 (March 1994), pp. 29-66.

5. Most of these studies have emphasized the marginalization of the *dai* due to the increasing dominance of bio-medical practices. My own work too has referred to this. See, Charu Gupta, *Sexuality, Obscenity, Community: Women, Muslims and the Hindu Public in Colonial India*, Delhi: Permanent Black, 2001, pp. 177-85.

Also see, Geraldine Forbes, 'Managing Midwifery in India', in Dagmar Engels and Shula Marks (eds.), *Contesting Colonial Hegemony: State and Society in Africa and India,* London: British Academy Press, 1994, pp. 152-74; Kalpana Ram, 'Modernity and the Midwife: Contestations Over a Subaltern Figure, South India', in Linda H. Connor and Geoffrey Samuel (eds.), *Healing Powers and Modernity: Traditional Medicine, Shamanism and Science in Asian Societies,* Westport: Bergin and Garvey, 2001, pp. 64-84; Dagmar Engels, *Beyond Purdah? Women in Bengal 1890-1939,* Delhi: Oxford University Press, 1996, pp. 123-57; Santi Rozario and Geoffrey Samuel (eds.), *The Daughters of Hariti: Childbirth and Female Healers in South and Southeast Asia,* London: Routledge, 2002.

6. An exception is Maneesha Lal, '"The Ignorance of Women is the House of Illness": Gender, Nationalism, and Health Reform in Colonial North India', in Mary P. Sutpen and Bridie Andrews (eds.), *Medicine and Colonial Identity,* London: Routledge, 2003, pp. 14-40.

7. Pierre Bourdieu, *Language and Symbolic'Power,* tr. Gino Raymond and Matthew Adamson, Cambridge, Mass.: Harvard University Press, 1991; and *The Field of Cultural Production: Essays on Art and Literature,* Cambridge: Polity Press, 1993; Michel Foucault, *The Order of Things: An Archaeology of the Indian Human Sciences,* London: Tavistock Publications, 1970; and *The Archaeology of Knowledge,* tr. Alan Sheridan, London: Tavistock Publications, 1972.

8. Elisabeth L. Eisenstein, *The Printing Press as an Agent of Change: Communication and Cultural Transformations in Early-Modern Europe,* 2 vols, Cambridge: Cambridge University Press, 1979; L. Febvre and H.J. Martin, *The Coming of the Book: The Impact of Printing, 1450-1800,* tr. D. Gerard, London and New York: Verso, 1976.

9. Benedict Anderson, *Imagined Communities: Reflections on the Origins and Spread of Nationalism,* London: Verso, 1983.

10. Amrit Rai, *A House Divided: The Origin and Development of Hindi/Hindavi,* Delhi: Oxford University Press, 1984; Christopher R. King, *One Language, Two Scripts: The Hindi Movement in Nineteenth-Century North India,* Bombay: Oxford University Press, 1994; Krishna Kumar, *Political Agenda of Education: A Study of Colonialist and Nationalist Ideas,* New Delhi: Sage Publications, 1991; Mohammad Hasan, *Thought Patterns of Nineteenth Century Literature of North India,* Pakistan: Royal Book Co., 1990; Francesca Orsini, *The Hindi Public Sphere 1920-1940: Language and Literature in the Age of Nationalism,* Delhi: Oxford University Press, 2002; Alok Rai, *Hindi Nationalism,* Delhi: Orient Longman, 2000.

11. For details on the growth of print culture in UP, particularly in Hindi, see Orsini, *Hindi Public Sphere;* Gupta, *Sexuality, Obscenity, Community;* C.A. Bayly, *Empire and Information: Intelligence Gathering and Social Communication in India, 1780-1870,* Cambridge: Cambridge University Press, 1996, p. 338; Kumar, *Political Agenda,* pp. 125-7. By 1925, Hindi newspapers, books and journals far exceeded and surpassed those in Urdu. See *Report on the Administration of UP, 1923-24,* Allahabad, 1924, p. 91.

12. *Statistics of British India for the Judicial and Administrative Departments,* Calcutta, 1879, pp. 48-9; *Judicial and Administrative Statistics of British India for 1901-2 and Preceding Years,* Calcutta, 1903, p. 255; *Statistical Abstracts for British India from 1916-17 to 1925-26,* Calcutta, 1927, p. 323. The number of printing presses in UP had risen from 177 in 1878-9 to 568 in 1901-2 and 743 in 1925-6. By 1925-6, UP had surpassed Bengal in the production of vernacular

books. Lucknow saw the growth of one of the oldest and most reputed press, the Newal Kishore Press, which also went on to publish many books on Ayurveda, both in Urdu and Hindi. See *Uttar Pradesh*, 9, no. 9 (February 1981) [Special issue on Munshi Newal Kishore]; Syed Jalaluddin Haider, 'Munshi Nawal Kishore 1836-95: Mirror of Urdu Printing in British India', *Libri*, 31, no. 3 (1981), pp. 227-37, but Allahabad soon took over.

13. *Report on the Administration of UP, 1907-8*, Allahabad, 1908, p. 52.

14. In the late eighteenth and early nineteenth centuries, a number of British orientalist scholars showed an interest in Ayurveda and wrote a number of treatises and materia medicas based on it. See, Whitelaw Ainslie, *Materia Indica, II*, London: Longman, 1826; T.A. Wise, *Commentary on the Hindu System of Medicine*, London: Trubner and Co., 1860; David C. Muthu, *A Short Account of the Antiquity of Hindu Medicine*, 2nd edn., London: Bailliere, Tindall and Cox, 1927. However, with the decline of British support, a certain amount of defensive Ayurvedic literature was generated, written mostly by Ayurvedic practitioners themselves in the vernacular, and adopting a language of moral self-improvement. For example a book, *Marnonmukhi Arya Chikitsa*, lamented how the old Ayurvedic system was on the verge of extinction, and the urgent need to restore it to its former glory. See Radha Ballabh, *Marnonmukhi Arya Chikitsa* [Treatment of the Dying Ayurvedic System], 2nd edn., Aligarh, 1922.

15. By the early twentieth century, most indigenous writers on Ayurveda in colonial UP inserted themselves in the public domain and chose Hindi and not English or Urdu as their primary medium. In 1934-5, for example, there were at least twelve Hindi journals on Ayurveda coming out from UP alone. *Anubhut Yogmala* was a fortnightly magazine published from Etawah, with a circulation of 1,500. It upheld syncretic indigenous medical practices, dealing with both Ayurvedic and Unani medicines and methods of treatment. *Arogya*, a monthly journal was brought out by the Chikitsak Press based in Kanpur. It was published by Pandit K.D. Vaidya Shastri. Another monthly Ayurvedic journal *Arogyadata*, with 1,000 copies was based in Aligarh and published by Harish Chandra Sharma Vaidya Shastri. *Ayurved Pracharak* and *Vanaushadhi* from Banaras, *Banaspati Vigyan* and *Chikitsak* from Kanpur, *Ban Lakshmi* and *Dhanwantari* from Aligarh, *Grah Chikitsa* from Mathura, *Rakesh* from Etawah and *Vaidya* from Moradabad—all these journals catered solely to the Ayurvedic system of medicine and treatment. And of course, there was *Stri Chikitsak*, the Hindi monthly journal devoted exclusively to Ayurvedic treatment of female diseases that was brought out by Yashoda Devi from Allahabad, with a circulation figure of 5,000 copies per month. See *Statement of Newspapers and Periodicals Published in the United Provinces from 1934-37*, Allahabad, 1935, pp. 152-3. Hindi books on Ayurveda far outnumbered the journals. See for example Hazari Lal comp., *Vaidyak Sar* [The Essence of Ayurvedic Medicine], Banaras, 1910; Jagannath Prasad Shukl, *Ayurveda ka Mahatv* [The Importance of Ayurveda], Allahabad, 1910; Bhaskar Govind Ghanekar, *Aupsargik Rog* [Infectious Diseases], Banaras, 1937. Many of the books used a highly Sanskritized language and ran into numerous pages. At the same time, there were popular, thin, cheap books on Ayurveda, written in colloquial Hindi, popularizing its concepts, methods and sources. This literature circulated among the literate public as much as among professional healers. Most of these works claimed to have been inspired by the most ancient Ayurvedic texts, particularly the *Caraka Samhita*, the *Susrata Samhita*, and the *Ashtanga Samgraha*. It has been pointed out that perhaps the

orientalist valorization of classical Sanskrit texts lead to the emphasis on these in subsequent Ayurvedic literature, which has continued till present. See Jean Langford, 'Ayurvedic Interiors: Person, Space, and Episteme in Three Medical Practices', *Cultural Anthropology*, 10, no. 3 (August 1995), p. 333.

16. Orsini, *Hindi Public Sphere*, pp. 243-308.
17. Vir Bharat Talwar, 'Feminist Consciousness in Women's Journals in Hindi: 1910-1920', in Kumkum Sangari and Sudesh Vaid (eds.), *Recasting Women: Essays in Colonial History*, Delhi: Kali for Women, 1989, pp. 204-32.
18. Nita Kumar, 'Widows, Education and Social Change in Twentieth Century Banaras', *Economic and Political Weekly*, 26, no. 17 (27 April 1991), pp. WS-19-25.
19. For a detailed list of the writings of Yashoda Devi, see Appendix. Henceforth, references to them will be made by just saying Devi, and the first or second word of her book.
20. For example, her book *Garbh Raksha Vidhan* had at least four editions. See the Appendix of her writings for details.
21. I came across many advertisements of her medical dispensary and books in leading journals of UP, like *Chand* and *Madhuri*. Also see here all publications, especially *Nari Sharir*, pp. 48-50, *Kanya*, back page.
22. Devi, *Dampatya Prem*.
23. *Statement of Newspapers and Periodicals Published in the United Provinces from 1934-37*, Allahabad, 1935, pp. 152-3.
24. Most studies on Ayurveda have pointed out that it was totally a male domain. It is true that Ayurvedic training was technically closed to women practitioners as it was largely in Sanskrit. Charles Leslie, 'Introduction', in *Asian Medical Systems: A Comparative Study*, Berkeley and Los Angeles: University of California Press, 1976, p. 3.
25. Gyan Prakash, *Another Reason: Science and the Imagination of Modern India*, Princeton: Princeton University Press, 1999, pp. 148-54.
26. Devi, *Dampati Arogyata*, pp. 1-4; Devi, *Nari Sharir*, p. 48.
27. Devi, *Nari Dharmashastra*, p. last.
28. Devi, *Dampati*, pp. 1-4, 7; Devi, *Adarsh Pati-Patni*, pp. 89-93.
29. Devi, *Adarsh Pati-Patni*, pp. 89-93.
30. 266-67/1872, Public, A, Home Dept, National Archives of India (NAI); Balfour and Young, *Medical*, pp. 34-5.
31. Devi, *Nari Sharir*, p. 2.
32. Ibid., pp. 12-14.
33. Ibid., p. 2.
34. Ibid.
35. Devi, *Dampatya Prem*, p. 337; Devi, *Nari Sharir*, pp. 9-11.
36. Devi, *Nari Sharir*, pp. 18-20.
37. Devi, *Dampatya Prem*, p. 337.
38. Devi, *Adarsh Pati-Patni*, p. 91.
39. The limitations of reform movement and nationalism in colonial India for women have been a subject of much writing. To list a few, see Geraldine Forbes, *Women in Modern India*, Cambridge: Cambridge University Press, 1996; Partha Chatterjee, *The Nation and its Fragments*, Princeton: Princeton University Press, 1993, pp. 116-57; Gail Minault (ed.), *The Extended Family: Women and Political Participation in India and Pakistan*, Delhi: Chanakya, 1981.
40. See for example, Jyotirmayi Thakur, *Gharelu Vigyan* [Domestic Science],

Allahabad, 1932; Chandrikanarayan Sharma, *Manavotpatti Vigyan*, Part I [Science of the Origin of Man], Banaras, 1927.

41. Prakash, *Another Reason*, pp. 148-9.
42. Devi, *Kanya Kartavya*, pp. 8-10, 52-4.
43. Devi, *Grhini Kartavya*, p. 5.
44. See for example, Devi Prasad Dube (ed.), *A Guide to Mothers or, How to Preserve the Health of Children*, Agra, 1899; Sheoji Lal Kala, *Santan Palan* [The Rearing of Children. Hindi translation of Louis Kuhne's work in English entitled 'The Rearing of Children'], Moradabad, 1916; Ganeshdutt Sharma Gaur, *Santan Shastra* [Science of Child Management], 2nd edn., Allahabad, 1928; Hira Lal, *Maa aur Bachcha* [Mother and Child. An Elementary Book Containing Instructions for Indian Women on Maternity, Midwifery and Bringing up of Infants], Allahabad, 1930.
45. Her magazines carried regular columns on these subjects. It has been argued that pregnancy, breast-feeding and early infant care are determined not only by culture but also by power. See Margaret Jolly, 'Introduction', in Kalpana Ram and Margaret Jolly (eds.), *Maternities and Modernities: Colonial and Postcolonial Experiences in Asia and the Pacific*, Cambridge: Cambridge University Press, 1998, pp. 1-2. In UP too, modernizing maternity and disciplining mother love was highlighted, to establish class and caste status of the Hindus.
46. Devi, *Nari Sharir*, pp. 200-1; Devi, *Dampatya Prem*, p. 359; Devi, *Nari Dharmashastra*, last page.
47. Devi, *Dampati Arogyata*, pp. 8-11.
48. Devi, *Nari Sharir*, pp. 218-21; Devi, *Dampatya Prem*, p. 257.
49. Devi, *Dampati Arogyata*, p. 88.
50. Devi, *Dampatya Prem*, pp. 85-149.
51. See for example, Kanhaiya Lal Sharma, *Kok Shastra Athva Yauvan Vilas* [Treatise on Sex or Youthful Pleasure], Moradabad, 1900; Pyarelal Zamindar, *Kok Shastra* [Treatise on Sex], Aligarh, 1905, 7th edn.; Mohan Lal Gupta, *Kok Sagar* [Treatise on Sex], Aligarh, 1908, 2nd edn.; Banarsi Lal Verma, *Kashmiri Kokshastra* [Treatise on Sex], Allahabad, 1928; Jagannath Das, *Kok Chitra Darshan* [The Illustrated Sexual Science], Mathura, 1930; Amarpal Singh 'Visharad', *Kok Shastra* [Sexual Science], Banaras, 1931, 4th edn.; Gopinath Gupta, *Sachitra Kok Shastra* [Illustrated Sexual Science], Etawah, 1931; Ramchandra Vaidya Shastri, *Kamya Yogavali* [A Treatise on Sex], Aligarh, 1939.
52. For details on this, see Gupta, *Sexuality, Obscenity*, pp. 53-4.
53. Devi, *Dampatya Prem*, pp. 11, 60, 181-3.
54. Ibid., pp. 61-4; Devi, *Dampati Arogyata*, p. 3.
55. Devi, *Dampatya Prem*, pp. 152, 223.
56. See for example, Deo Narayan Dube, *Santan Vigyan* [The Science of Procreation], Banaras, 1930; Ram Narayan Vaidya Shastri, *Janan Vigyan ya Garbhadan Rahasya* [The Science of Procreation or the Mystery of Conception], Kanpur, 1931.
57. Devi, *Dampati*, p. 77.
58. Ibid., pp. 149-87.
59. Ibid., pp. 351-6.
60. Devi, *Grhini*, pp. last 4.
61. Gupta, *Sexuality, Obscenity*, pp. 66-83.
62. Joseph S. Alter, *Wrestler's Body: Identity and Ideology in North India*, Delhi: Munshiram Mahoharlal, 1993.

63. Indira Chowdhury Sengupta, *The Frail Hero and Virile History: Gender and the Politics of Culture in Colonial Bengal*, Delhi: Oxford University Press, 1998, pp. 120-49.

64. Bhikhu Parekh, *Colonialism, Tradition and Reform: An Analysis of Gandhi's Political Discourse*, Delhi: Sage, 1989, pp. 172-206.

65. Devi, *Arogya Vidhan*, p. 25; Devi, *Dampatya Prem*, p. 248.

66. She attributed various 'male' problems like excessive physical weakness, lack of senses, false excitement, semen loss, weak eyesight, enfeeblement of muscles, backaches, mental illness, inability to have a child, urinary diseases and nocturnal emissions chiefly to masturbation, Devi, *Arogya Vidhan*, pp. 26-7; Devi, *Dampatya Prem*, p. 224; Devi, *Dampati Arogyata*, pp. 9-10, 19. Stating to have received more than a lakh letters from ill men, she ascribed maximum cases related to masturbation, Devi, *Nari Sharir*, pp. 707-17, p. 992. She linked its spread to modern 'vices' like easily availability of dirty books of *kamshastra*, sleazy romantic novels (*chatpate premwale upanyas*) and advertisements of aphrodisiacs, making the heart fickle and volatile, Devi, *Arogya Vidhan*, p. 1; Devi, *Dampatya Prem*, pp. 210, 221, 302; Devi, *Dampati Arogyata*, p. 5.

67. Devi, *Arogya Vidhan*, pp. 26-7; idem, *Dampatya Prem*, p. 224; idem, *Dampati Arogyata*, pp. 9-10, 19.

68. Ibid., p. 1; and, *Dampatya Prem*, pp. 210, 221, 302; idem, *Dampati Arogyata*, p. 5.

69. Devi, *Arogya Vidhan*, pp. 23-6, 29-30; Devi, *Dampati Arogyata*, p. 26. Thus, I do not agree with Gyan Prakash that her discourse was very different from that perpetuated in the west. Her book *Arogya Vidhan Vidyarthi Jivan* was explicitly against masturbation and pro-*brahmacharya*.

70. Devi, *Dampatya Prem*, p. 210.

71. Devi, *Dampati Arogyata*, p. 25; Devi, *Dampatya Prem*, p. 210.

72. Devi, *Dampatya Prem*, pp. 217-18.

73. Devi, *Arogya Vidhan*, p. 63; Devi, *Dampatya Prem*, pp. 151, 222-3.

74. Devi, *Arogya Vidhan*, pp. 43-52, 85, 134; Devi, *Dampatya Prem*, pp. 150-1.

75. Devi, *Dampatya Prem*, p. 16.

76. Ibid., p. 150.

77. Ibid., p. 225; Devi, *Dampati Arogyata*, p. 3.

78. Ibid., pp. 259-63, 343, 500.

79. Devi, *Nari Sharir*, p. 147; Devi, *Dampatya Prem*, pp. 218-20, 294.

80. Ibid., p. 738; Devi, *Dampatya Prem*, pp. 188, 223.

81. Devi, *Dampatya Prem*, p. 218.

82. Devi, *Nari Sharir*, p. 409; Devi, *Dampatya Prem*, p. 243; Devi, *Dampati Arogyata*, pp. 1-2. Her books had stories with titles like 'blind lust and tyranny of the husband towards his ailing wife, suffering from vaginal discharge', *kamandh aur atyachari pati ki kahani pradar rogi patni ki zubani*, Devi, *Nari Sharir*, p. 654.

83. Devi, *Nari Sharir*, p. 654.

84. Ibid., p. 696, Devi, *Dampatya Prem*, pp. 239-40.

85. Devi, *Dampatya Prem*, pp. 188, 226; Devi, *Dampati Arogyata*, pp. 189-90.

86. Devi, *Dampatya Prem*, pp. 359-60, 439, 475.

87. Ibid., pp. 439, 475.

88. Ibid., pp. 221-2.

89. See for example, Shri Lal Upadhyaya, *Striyon ke Rog Aur Unki Chikitsa* [Female Diseases and their Treatment], Banaras, 1917; Kanhaiya Lal Agarwal, *Grihani*

Chikitsa [Treatment of Feminine Diseases], Allahabad, 1922; Bhadra Gupta, *Yuvati Rog Chikitsa* [Treatment of Female Diseases. An Ayurvedic Publication], Bara Banki, 1925; Bisheshar Dayal, *Stri Rog Chikitsa* [Treatment of Female Diseases. An Ayurvedic Publication], Etawah, 1925; Hanuman Prasad Sharma, *Sukhi Grihani* [A Happy Wife. A Book on Women's Health], Banaras, 1931.

90. Devi, *Nari Sharir*, pp. 169-70, 215.
91. Devi, *Dampati Arogyata*, pp. 3, 372.
92. We get a number of references to this, even in the colonial period. One book on Ayurveda emphasized how women are extremely capable of curing everyday illnesses, Haridas Vaidya, *Chikitsa Chandrodaya: Pehla Bhag*, Agra, 1935, p. 16. Another said that if you wanted your women to be smart housewives, you must ensure that they have some knowledge of Ayurveda, Jagannathprasad Shukl Vaidya, *Arogyavidhan Athva Bharat Mein Mandagni* 2nd edn., Prayag, 1921, last page.

Appendix

SELECT BOOKS BY YASHODA DEVI

1. *Saccha Pati Prem* [A Story of a True Wifely Love and Devotion], Allahabad, 1910, pp. 78.
2. *Nari-Niti Shiksha* [Teachings on Ethics for Women], Allahabad, 1910.
3. *Garbh Raksha Vidhan* [The way to Self-protection during Pregnancy], Allahabad, 1911, 2nd edn. 1912, 3rd edn. 1916, 4th edn. 1927, pp. 106 with illustrations.
4. *Ghar ka Vaid* [The Household Doctor. A medical tract intended for Indian Housewives], Allahabad, 1912, 2nd edn. 1913, 3rd edn. 1917, pp. 24, 1,000 copies each edn.
5. *Adarsh Hindu Vidhva* [Ideal Hindu Widow], Allahabad, 1912, 3,000 copies.
6. *Shishu Raksha Vidhan Arthat Bal Rog Chikitsa: Pratham Bhag* [The Protection of Children or the Treatment of Juvenile Diseases: Part I], Allahabad, 1912, 2nd edn. 1924, pp. 88; pp. 98.
7. *Mahila Jivan Sarvasva* [All about the Life of Females. A Hand-Book on Diseases Peculiar to Women], Allahabad, 1912, pp. 131, 3,000 copies.
8. *Pran Vallabh: Purushatva Vikas* [The Friend of Life. An Ayurvedic Medical Handbook on the Sexual Diseases of Males and how to Build Masculinity], Allahabad, 1923, 2nd edn. 1926, pp. 352, 1,000 copies each edn.
9. *Grhini Kartavya Shastra Arogyashastra Arthat Pakshastra* [Manual for Housewife on Cookery, for a Healthy Family], Allahabad, 1924, 3rd edn., 5th edn. 1932, pp. 384, 2,000 copies each edn.
10. *Adarsh Pati-Patni aur Santati Sudhar* [Ideal Husband-Wife and Child Reform], Allahabad, 1924, 2nd edn., 1,000 copies.
11. *Nari Sangit Ratnmala* [A Collection of Devotional Songs], Allahabad, 1924, 2nd edn., 1,000 copies.
12. *Jivan Shastra* [The Science of Life. An Ayurvedic Book showing how Women should live a Healthy and Happy Life], Allahabad, 1924, pp. 352, 4,000 copies.
13. *Pati Prem Patrika Arthat Pati-Patni ka Patra Vyavahar* [Manual for the Love of Husband, Meaning Letter Correspondence between Husband and Wife], Allahabad, 1925, 3rd edn., 2,000 copies.
14. *Kanya Kartavya* [Duties of Girls], Allahabad, 1925, 1,000 copies.
15. *Pati Bhakti ki Shakti Arthat Pati ki Maryada* [Power of Devotion to Husband, Meaning Husband's Honour], Allahabad, 1925, 1,000 copies.
16. *Nari Svasthya Raksha: Arogya Vidhan Arthat Stri Rog Chikitsa* [Protection of Women's Health, meaning Treatment of Feminine Diseases], Allahabad, 1926, pp. 207, 2,000 copies.
17. *Pativrat Dharma Mala* [Duties of a Wife], Allahabad, 1926, 1,000 copies.
18. *Dampati Arogyata Jivanshastra Arthat Ratishastra Santati Shastra* [The Science of Healthy Conjugal Life or the Science of Sexual Intercourse and Procreation], Allahabad, 1927, 2nd edn. 1931, pp. 324, 4,000 copies each edn.
19. *Arogya Vidhan Vidyarthi Jivan* [Student Life. A Handbook especially intended for Students, treated from a Medical and Hygienic point of view], Allahabad, 1929, pp. 136, 1,000 copies.

20. *Vaidyak Ratn Sangrah Arthat Devi Anubhav Prakash* [A Collection of Ayurvedic Medical Gems or the Illustration of Yashoda Devi's Medical Experience], Allahabad, 1930, pp. 728 with illustrations, 4,000 copies.
21. *Nari Dharmashastra Grh-Prabandh Shiksha* [Education on Home Management for Women], Allahabad, 1931, 1,000 copies.
22. *Adarsh Balika-Bhai Bahina* [Ideal Girl-Brother Sister], Allahabad, 1932, pp. 26.
23. *Dampatya Prem aur Ratikriya ka Gupt Rahasya* [Secret of Love and Sex between the Married Couple], Allahabad, 1933, pp. 510 with illustrations.
24. *Nari Sharir Vigyan Stri Chikitsa Sagar: Sambhog Vigyan* [Women's Physiology and Women's Medical Treatment: Science of Intercourse], Allahabad, 1938, pp. 1144 with illustrations.

5

All India Radio:
Politics and Culture

NABANITA MITRA

INTRODUCTION

The radio serves as an indispensable medium of mass communication, having the potential of facilitating planned development and fostering socio-cultural harmony in the life of any nation. It also serves as one of the primary fountainheads of infotainment and works in a spirit of public service. The All India Radio (AIR) completed 80 years of its glorious existence in 2007. The first part of this essay focuses on the genesis and gradual evolution of radio broadcasting in India, outlines the initial obstacles that it had to encounter, along with the survival strategies that it adopted. The second part deals with how AIR in general and Calcutta Radio Station in particular, was becoming the pivot of myriad socio-cultural activities, leading to a qualitative enrichment of Indian society on the whole. By moulding and elevating public tastes and preferences through its plentiful fare of music, drama, talks, news and special features, the Calcutta chapter of AIR sought to address the need-based requirements of various segments of the populace (farmers, tribals, women, youth and children), facilitating India's transformation into a welfare state.

EARLY HISTORY: GENESIS AND
EVOLUTION OF ALL INDIA RADIO

The year 1895 constituted a landmark event in the history of wireless communication, owing to Sir J.C. Bose's spectacular breakthrough in carrying out wireless transmissions from Calcutta. His pioneering achievement was successfully emulated by Marconi in the 1920s before the British public.[1] In India, amateur radio clubs (set up in Bombay, Calcutta and Madras) started broadcasting 'talks and music' daily in their private capacities. It was from the Physics Department (of the Calcutta Science College) that Dr. Sisir Kumar Mitra set up the first radio transmitter in 1925, which operated for almost a year before attracting the attention of the British Broadcasting Corporation (BBC). The BBC then tried to gauge the commercial viability of wireless propagation in India by setting up a radio transmission studio at Temple Chambers (which shifted first to 1 Garstin Place and finally to the present Akashvani Bhavan besides Eden Gardens).[2] Meanwhile 'organized' broadcasting actually took off with the formation of the Indian Broadcasting Company (IBC) with stations at Bombay and Calcutta (which were established on 23 July and 26 August 1927 respectively).

Although India's burgeoning demography and lingua-cultural diversity posed initial problems for the nascent wireless system, it was actually fiscal constraints from the early 1930s that compelled the IBC to seek governmental intervention, with the result that the IBC was incorporated within the government's Department of Industries and Labour, and renamed thenceforth as the Indian Broadcasting Service (IBS). Furthermore, severe retrenchment drives and stringent economizing measures in the post-Depression years resulted in the qualitative degeneration in the programme standards of the IBS, compelling the government to terminate its broadcasting service by October 1931. The government, however, was to revoke its decision shortly after (following a massive public outcry) whereupon the IBS was again renewed in 1932, albeit under state management, with a strict licensing system.

The steady increase in the number of radio licenses induced the government to set up new stations, appoint Sir Lionel Fielden as the new Controller of Broadcasting in 1935, and to import technical expertise from the BBC. Lord Linlithgow was personally persuaded by Fielden to adopt the name All India Radio in 1936. Yet, despite all the odds which plagued him in the form of vehement Imperial hostility, World War exigencies, pecuniary crunches, staff problems, and dilemma over foreign broadcasts, Fielden strove tirelessly in wresting autonomy and financial viability for AIR. By 1941, AIR came to be integrated within the folds of the Ministry of Information, and Fielden came to be succeeded by Prof. A.S. Bokhari (1943-7).

ALL INDIA RADIO: POLITICS

It is interesting to note how the history of wireless broadcasts in India in the post-First World War period came to be inextricably linked to the struggle for Indian Independence. One of the primary motives of the colonial rulers in reviving and promoting the Indian broadcasting system was to manoeuvre the same for its own vested interests. Yet, during the course of the Second World War, the Imperial Government was placed in the throes of a twofold dilemma—on the one hand, it faced anti-imperial, totalitarian, Nazi and Communist propaganda from Radio Berlin and Radio Moscow, respectively, while at the same time, encountering 'subversive and seditious' nationalist propaganda (that went on clandestinely from the Bombay station in particular, thanks to the heroic efforts of people like Usha Ben Mehta and others).

Faced with the twin menace, both from within and from without, AIR made futile attempts to present balanced 'political talk' (in keeping with the BBC model), while official recommendations compelled it to present 'apolitical' programmes alone (like music, news bulletins, and running commentaries in English and Urdu). British belligerence expressed itself by coming down heavily on detractors, both foreign and indigenous, by 'censoring' all news broadcasts (that were not approved by the 'loyalist' Associated Press), jamming foreign radio stations, banning broadcasts by all Indian political parties by 1937 and penalizing private license holders responsible for pro-Axis, anti-Raj transmissions.[3] AIR failed to serve the Raj as an effective propaganda device, thanks to the innumerable constraints under which it had to function. It could neither become a private concern, nor could it assume the mantle of a governmental mouthpiece. Moreover, by abstaining from all issues that were 'politically sensitive' in nature, AIR began jeopardising its own future in the process.

Given the conditions prevalent in India, the radio should have been the chosen medium for India to build a new social order and should have contributed substantially to the process of planned development in the country. However, the myopic policies of the Imperial Government, which sought to use the radio to achieve its own narrow ends, prevented AIR from fully realizing its potential role in the progress of the nation.

ALL INDIA RADIO: CULTURE

That the Calcutta station of All India Radio was soon becoming a veritable mecca of Bengali cultural efflorescence can be gauged from the vast array of 'infotainment' programmes in its agenda constituting music, drama, talks, news and the like (targeting various audience groups in particular).

Music

Music of different genres, ranging from *Dwijendrageeti, Nazrulgeeti, Rajanikanter gaan* to *Puratani* and *Rabibabur gaan* constituted a major segment of the programme schedule.[4] Shedding off their initial reservations, the early (mostly aristocratic) musicians and established artists started vying with their aspiring counterparts for the coveted title of *betar shilpi* (Radio artist).

Pankaj Kumar Mullick, who had been with AIR right from its formative years, imparted weekly musical training to youngsters, many of whom went on to become established singers in future, through his much-acclaimed *Sangeet Sikshar Ashor*, which he single-handedly nurtured for 46 years (from 1929 to 1975). Although he chose to sing various genres of music, yet his forte remained *Rabindrasangeet*, which he managed to free from the ivory towers to which it was hitherto confined, thereby disseminating and popularizing it among the masses.[5] Suprobha Sarkar, on the other hand, conducted *Nazrulgeetir Sikshar Ashor* while the hour-long bi-weekly *Anurodher Ashor* were followed by *Rabindrasangeeter Anurodher Ashor* and *Nazrulgeetir Anurodher Ashor* respectively. The Akashvani Studios were moreover graced by the presence of men of the stature of Rabindranath, Nazrul and others. And on the midnight of 15 August 1947 (following Nehru's 'Tryst With Destiny' speech), the Calcutta Radio Station presented *Banikumar's Bichitra* which presented a variety of musical and poetical performances and went down well with the masses.

The post-Independence period ushered in 'the golden period of radio music', wherein film songs and *adhunik gaan* (modern song) came to be presented through such programmes like *Rodon Bhora Gaan, Kahini Gaan, Metho Sure, Giti Masiki, Brindaboner Maya, Prabhuj Tum, Hey Nataraj, Giti Orchestra* and *Giti Alekhyas*—covering as it were folk songs, *kirtans* and *bhajans* (devotional songs), dance compositions and orchestral music. Moreover, the musical productions presented through the first National Programme of 1954 became extremely popular.[6] Mention should be made in this regard of *Mahishasur Mardini,* the brainchild of the triumvirate Banikumar (who scripted it), Pankaj Mullick (who set it to music) and Biren Bhadra (who rendered it in his sonorous voice). It created a landmark in the annals of radio history. By rendering a novel musical on *Chandipat* (recital of the Chandi, a Hindu scriptural book narrating the activities and glory of the Goddess Chandi), on the auspicious occasion of *Mahalaya* (the first day on which the worship of Goddess Durga, a Hindu deity, is initiated every year), they had created a place of immortality for this perennially-loved Bengali programme.[7]

The Calcutta radio station presented a rich repertoire of Indian classical music programmes (both Hindustani and Carnatic), like *Bharat Gaurav, Bichitra, Raag Baichitra* and *Sur o Chhanda,* where eminent maestros, both male and female, regaled discerning listeners. Moreover, by introducing programmes like *Jatiya Karyakram, Sursabha* and *Radio Sangeet Sammelan* in the 1950s, classical music was made much more comprehensible and appealing to the masses. Western music too, both of the classical and light varieties, were presented through programmes like *Studio Concerts, Indian Band Box, Lunch Time Variety, Dance Time Folk* and *Country Music.*

It was in his role of a staunch classical music aficionado that B.V. Keskar, the then Director General of AIR, tried to ban Hindi film music from Akashvani's list of programmes. The aggrieved listeners responded to such highhandedness by severing ties with AIR only to switch over to Radio Ceylon. Thus, in a bid to wean away the Indian audience from the latter's stranglehold, AIR sought to launch its own counter offensive through the 'All India Variety Programme' from 1957. It was heralded as bringing in instant welcome relief to the hitherto entertainment-starved public! Ten years thence this was to take the shape of *Vividh Bharati*, which came to be established in Bombay in 1967 from where tapes were borrowed and relayed to other radio stations.[8] Thanks to the new channel, the popularity of Calcutta station increased manifold, since it brought to air numerous plays, songs, film music, humorous skits, mini-dramas and features through programmes such as *Patralekha, Bhule Bisre Geet, Jaymala, Hawa Mahal, Sangeet Sarita, Chayan* and *Bisesh Chayan.*

Radio Dramas

On the basis of audio-visual standards, plays can broadly be classified into two varieties: stage plays and radio dramas, with the latter 'addressing the ear and not the eye'. A radio play depends on four primary ingredients, namely dialogue, sound, music and of course silence, thereby making it the 'Theatre of Imagination'. The initial practice of presenting live relays of dramas and plays (held outside the AIR studios) soon came to be replaced by radio plays proper, i.e. plays written, directed and enacted exclusively for the wireless medium.

The first English plays, presented by the Calcutta station around 1927, were a part of the 'European' programme schedule. They were produced along the BBC model by Calcutta Amateur Theatrical Society (CATS). While English plays regaled the affluent, Western-educated urbanite classes, it was on 5 December 1927 that the first Bengali play (Manilal Gangopadhyay's *Basantalila*) was broadcast. It had in its cast the pioneers of Calcutta Radio Station like Rai Chand Boral, Pankaj Kumar Mullick, Banikumar, Sitangshujyoti Mazumdar (alias Bokubabu), Hiren Basu, with B.K. Bhadra and Rajen Sen as joint associate programme directors. This group called themselves the Betar Natuke Dal (BND). While Hiren Basu was instrumental in creating a number of operas, skits and radio plays, Nripendranath Mazumdar, B.K. Bhadra, Banikumar and Bokubabu formed the main quartet in the drama section.

Meanwhile various theatre groups like Natyamandir Theatre, Chitra Samsad, Listeners' Club and others started relaying their theatrical productions, which perhaps took off with Khirod Prasad's *Nara Narayan* (relayed on 16 December 1927) with actors of the stature of Sisir Kumar Bhaduri. It was therefore becoming increasingly clear that the tryst with this newly found wireless medium had just begun for the theatre-lovers of Bengal. Even Rabindranath Tagore, who liked experimenting with different dramatic genres, had his *Tapati* relayed live from the Jorasanko stage on 28 September 1929. Yet, with live relays from the stages becoming increasingly flawed, a shift in the realm of dramatic content seemed quite inevitable. This, however, irked the listeners who kept clamouring for the erstwhile mythological-cum-socio-historical themes as had been displayed through plays like *Radhakrishna*, *Savitri*, *Alamgir*, *Sita*, *Prafulla*, *Chandragupta* and *Shahjahan*. In keeping with popular demand, therefore, the radio authorities tried to transform these historical plays into suitable radio dramas. This in turn induced leading theatre groups to turn to literary texts.[9]

That modern literature got a chance to be portrayed through the radio can be attested from the way later-day novels and short stories came to be transformed into radio plays. In fact, it was Ashamanja Mukhopadhya's short story 'Jama Kharach' which created history as the first true Bengali if not Indian play to have been broadcast on 17 January 1928 under the name of *Jagadisher Digdari*. This was followed by the relay of Saratchandra's *Dena Paona*, Bankimchandra's *Krishnakanter Will*, Bokubabu's *Jamai Shashthi*, Tagore's *Baikunther Khata*, Jyotirindranath Tagore's *Alikbabu*, Parashuram's *Chikitsa Sankat* and a few other Bengali radio versions of English and foreign skits as well.

While Baidyanath Bhattacharya (alias Banikumar) was a multi-faceted literary genius whose numerous short plays and musicals (*gitinatya*) bear out his immense potential as a dramatist, lyricist and producer *par excellence*, the dramatist Sachindranath Sengupta's *Praloy* (directed and produced by B.K. Bhadra), aired on 5 June 1959, perhaps remains as the first preserved radio (*betar*) drama. Among Sachindranath's other plays were *Raktakamal* and *Tatinir Bichar*, as well as the radio-version of Tagore's *Khudito Pashan*. Ritwik Ghatak too presented such powerful plays as *Kalo Sayor* and *Jwala*.

Another milestone in the history of radio plays was reached on 14 July 1954 with the inauguration of National Programme of Plays or *Akhil Bharatiya Natyanushthan*, which perhaps ushered in the first phase of modernization into radio dramatic productions. Its inaugural session began with the Hindi adaptation of *Chandalika*, followed by *Pathanirdesh, Devi Chaudhurani, Bicharak, Ebong Indrajit*, as well as others.

Among B.K. Bhadra's successors, Ajitbaran Mukhopadhaya displayed a penchant for famous dramatists and music directors, well-known novels and stories, glamorous artists and highly ornate productions. Some of his plays include *Srikanta, Suno Baranari, Tahar Namti Ranjana*, and others. In some of his prize-winning productions like *Timi Timingil, Mrityuhin Pran, Fossil*, etc., Samaresh Ghosh, another renowned dramatist, tried to portray the inherent character-conflicts poignantly with minimal sound additions. Jagannath Basu also won accolades for plays like *Sarisrip, Koni, Septopasher Khide* and *Kalpurush*, while Sukhla Bandopadhya proved her versatility as an actress *par excellence.*

Jatras

Although the post-Independence scenario started threatening the very existence of Bengali *jatra* plays, it was rejuvenated around the 1950s and 1960s through *jatra* festivals. It was from here that the Delhi station began relaying select scenes from *Chandimangal*, thereby inspiring other professional *jatra* groups to do the same. Strangely enough, although *jatras* were largely derided by most educated Bengalis in colonial times, the leading personalities of the day including Rabindranath were unequivocal in its praise. *Betar jatras* have indeed been a source of psychological sustenance for rural listeners in particular.

Jatras, which had always been a part of *Pallimangal Ashor*, came to be included within *Krishibibhag* and *Krishi Kathar Ashor* in the 1960s. Many leading professional *jatra* groups of Calcutta began relaying their plays through the *jatra utsav* in 1972, as well as through the new programme of *Bichitra*. An informative programme named *Jatragaan* was organized in 1999 wherein interviews of eminent *jatra* personalities like Bina Dasgupta, Srila Majumdar, and Swapan Kumar were relayed.[10] Sudhir Sarkar, who spearheaded the *Pallimangal Ashor*, was so enamoured by this medium that he wrote and directed a number of innovative and humorous *jatra palas* (plays). Many amateur groups belonging both to the city and its outskirts, received considerable support from the AIR, which enabled them to vie with their professional counterparts in relaying the plays through a parallel system.

It was from around May 1970 that the *jatra dals* began relaying 'sponsored programmes' through *Vividh Bharati*. The immense popularity of these (24-hour) sponsored programmes soon made the radio an all-time favourite with the masses. This was particularly true in case of the toiling farmers who would put their radio sets on the *aals* (dividers between plots of farmland) in a bid to ameliorate the tedium of their work. The subsequent decline in the flow of advertisements from the 1990s has somewhat jeopardized the marketability and consequent popularity of radio *jatras*.

Radio *jatras* have indeed gone a long way in upholding the tradition of presenting myriad mythological, historical and social subjects (through songs, concerts and dramatics), thereby evoking the interest of the rural laity at large. There is no mistaking the fact that despite all the unwelcome odds facing it, radio *jatras* have become an integral and wholesome part of rural popular culture.

NEWS

The radio was to the audience what perhaps Sanjay was to Dhritarashtra in the *Mahabharata*. This was all the more true in case of transmission of news, which formed the mainstay of AIR programmes. Radio news in particular has been serving as the primary source of information to countless millions across the globe, making them instantaneously aware of all kinds of global occurrences.

While the Indian Broadcasting Company first began by transmitting news bulletins in Hindi and Bengali, the Indian State Broadcasting Service began increasing the frequency and number of news bulletins in the late 1930s, relaying them in other regional languages as well. Bijon Basu was perhaps the trendsetting newsreader to have influenced others like Debdulal Bandopadhay (who played a decisive role in Bangladesh's *Muktijuddha* (liberation war)), Upen Tarafdar (who developed *Sambad Bichitra* in the 1960s), Bibhuti Das and Nilima Sanyal, while English newsreaders included Melville De Mellow, Surajit Sen and others.[11]

The setting up of the Regional News Unit (in the 1960s and 1970s), coupled with the presentation of international news, *Gramin Sambad, Bichitro Sambad, Yuvavanir Sambad* and special news bulletins (during election or Emergency) popularized news items manifold. By 1954, the Bengali news programme came to be relayed from Delhi, while the transmission of regional Bengali news was to be made from the Calcutta station. Moreover, advertisements before and after news broadcasts came to be relayed from 1 April 1982, followed by primary channels from January 1985. War-time broadcasts in different Indian languages also came to be relayed from Delhi through the local radio stations. That AIR was to play a decisive role in the realm of war-time broadcasts became particularly evident during the Indo-Pak, Indo-Chinese and, most importantly, during the War of Liberation in Bangladesh wars (when news-broadcasters tried their best to uplift the morale of the *Muktijoddhas* or freedom fighters across the border).

Sports News

The popularity of AIR depended greatly on the transmission of news on sports. While the first sports news was relayed in English in 1930, its Bengali counterpart was broadcast in 1934 (with B.K. Bhadra and Rai Chand Boral's experimental relay of a soccer match between Calcutta and Mohan Bagan club teams). Live relays from the Calcutta station, however, began during 1947-8, following the India-Australia and India-West Indies cricket matches. Soon enough, Bengali commentaries were provided by towering sports-news-relayists like Ajoy Basu and Kamal Bhattacharya, who covered the India-Australia cricket matches in 1959 from Eden Gardens. The duo, along with Pushpen Sarkar, Berry Sarbadhikari and Pearson Surita lent their inimitable voices while relaying cricket and football events in English and Bengali on a regular basis, particularly following the 1967 Mohan Bagan *versus* Rajasthan League match.[12] Furthermore, the popular frenzy surrounding the Mohan Bagan-East Bengal matches (embodying the proverbial *Ghoti-Bangal* rivalry) proved to be so contagious that it drew even NRI Bengalis as well as Bengali women towards listening to commentaries, talks, interviews and discussions on soccer.

A special Sports Section of the Calcutta Station was formed in

1973 which sponsored the programme *Khelar Jagat* (later renamed
Krirangan). Moreover, radio stations in the major metropolitan cities
all used to broadcast a daily fare of 95 minutes of news on sports and
games.

AIR'S TARGET GROUPS

In its bid to facilitate India's transition into a welfare state, AIR
directed its programmes with the intention of serving special audience
groups such as farmers, tribals, women, children, youth, and the
armed services. The pluralist nature of Indian society also induced
AIR to arrange special programmes like the Urdu Service and Sindhi
programmes for linguistic and ethnic minorities.

Farmers

Post-Independence India was faced with a plethora of problems,
the foremost being sustaining agricultural productivity. In order to
ensure rural regeneration, AIR formed *Palli Betar Goshthis* (Rural
Broadcasting Groups) in the countryside. The tremendous popularity
of the *Pallimangal Ashor,* presented in a lively and interactive manner
between a fictitious *Morol* (village headman) and his associates
(Gobindo, Kashinath and others) kept the Bengali rural populace
completely enthralled. This programme proved extremely beneficial,
if not indispensable, to the peasantry as their awareness concerning
market prices (particularly of jute), weather reports, general farming
knowledge and other vital agrarian information became considerably enhanced. Experts having considerable farm-knowledge were
also brought in during questionnaire sessions with the peasants.[13]
Satyacharan Ghosh popularized *Mazdoor Mandalir Ashor* while
Pallimangal Ashor came to be replaced by *Krishi Jigyasha, Krishi
Kathar Ashor, Uno Jamir Duno Phashal* and the like. Among the
other rural programmes to be broadcast were *Panchali, Torja Gaan*
and *Ramayanpath* which sought to foster rural enlightenment by
addressing such socially-relevant issues as communal harmony, social
justice, national integration, rural health, literacy, and so on.

AIR had for quite some time been serving as a governmental
mouthpiece in promoting general health service for all. Through
its vast array of health-related programmes like *Apnar Swasthya,
Swasthya Jigyasa, Krishak O Tar Parivar,* and *Angan* from the 1970s
onwards it began to spread considerable awareness in matters relating
to family planning, rural polio vaccine drives, administration of oral

rehydration solution (ORS), etc., particularly among the rural communities. Following the recommendations of the Chanda Committee in 1966, governmental as well as commercial advertisements were introduced for the first time covering topics such as nutrition, family planning and sanitation.

The increasing popularity of the *Pallimangal Ashor* encouraged local science clubs to use folk songs in propagating scientific knowledge to the laity. Following the scientific spirit of the earlier radio programmes like *Bigyan Jigyasha* and *Bigyan Kathika*, later-day ones such as *Jana-Ajana*, *Bigyaner Niyomkanun*, *Mahaprithibi*, *Bibartaner Pathey Manush*, and *Chikitsha Bigyaner Itihas* focused primarily on astronomy and popular science.[14] Furthermore, by ushering in the Green Revolution through the Radio Rural Forums and the Farm and Home Units in 1956 and 1966 respectively, the indispensability of the wireless medium was proved without doubt.

Tribals

The Calcutta Radio Station tried to cater to the specific requirements of the socio-economically backward tribal communities through the *Santhali Anushthan*. It was conducted at first by Jadunath Tudu in the 1960s, with the help of Santhals who came to Calcutta for work. They focussed mainly on *Santhali* songs, poems, stories and talks (on agriculture, trade and craft, health, literacy and different festivities). Meanwhile, the presentation of news and plays (mostly adapted from the works of eminent Bengali literateurs) in Santhali enriched the Santhali language and literature, besides keeping the Santhali audience of Bengal and elsewhere enthralled.

Women

Of all the initial programmes targeted towards special audience groups, *Mahila Majlis* under Birendra Krishna Bhadra (*alias* Bishnusharma) was particularly significant. It was after the departure of Premankur Atarthi that Bhadra began conducting it with great finesse. In this particular programme, Bhadra spoke on wide-ranging and diverse subjects such as India's national history, Hinduism, Rabindranath's prose works, post-Miltonian poets, mythological tales, Egyptian travelogue, *Sri Ramkrishna Kathamrita*, humorous stories or *Ramya Rachana* and medicinal science. Moreover, in order to entertain women listeners (for whom this programme was meant), he read out their essays and letters, played the piano, recited poems and hymns, played gramophone records and even arranged a weekly *Panchali* (a class of Bengali poems celebrating the glory of a deity and often set to music) and *Kathakata Path* (professional practice of narrating scriptural and mythological story). In order to garner popular support for this programme, the conductors of *Mahila Majlis* began making earnest requests to middle-class Bengali women to overcome their hesitancy, and speak before the microphone on subjects of their choice! Not only were the senders' essays, letters, poems and house-keeping tips regularly read, they also got a chance to get those writings published in *Betar Jagat* (a Bengali radio magazine) editions from 3 January 1930 onwards. This provided an outlet for the literary aspirations of innumerable Bengali women, honing their creativity as never before.

The immense popularity of Kolkata radio station perhaps rested on two of its best-loved programmes—*Chotoder Ashor* and *Mahila Majlis*. By exploding the myth that sewing and cooking were the chief determinants in a woman's life, Bhadra (and others) sought to address the specific psychological and intellectual needs of the hitherto *purdahnashin* (veiled) women, fostering a common emotional bond amongst them.[15] Despite its soaring popularity, however, severe criticism from the wireless officialdom resulted in the imposition of considerable restraints on Bhadra, and the AIR's programme schedule too came to be strictly regulated. In October 1934 Bela Halder was brought in to step into Bhadra's shoes. She too followed the earlier trend and spoke on variegated topics such as Greek mythologies, Chinese folklore, and Vedic literature, while at the same time dwelling on the art of sewing, knitting and cooking.

Surprisingly enough, the authorities began displaying a lack of interest in the continuity of *Mahila Majlis*. Thus, Bhadra and Haldar were merely asked to fill up the slots by giving routine speeches; the term *Mahilader Janya* got scrapped, and the duration of the speeches too got restricted from 1936, finally culminating in Bhadra being replaced by subject-oriented speakers and gramophone records. The latter, on their part, delivered one-dimensional lectures on specific topics related mostly to their professions, which were devoid of the liveliness and interactiveness that had marked this programme earlier.

B.K. Bhadra combined in his personae the dual roles of programme executive as well as that of a radio artist. While presenting programmes he created a distinct style of his own, leaving behind an indelible mark of his profound erudition and extensive scholarship. Over and above the presentation of factual data, he was more interested in evoking the natural interest of his listeners, generating public appreciation for radio programmes in the process. Interestingly enough, *Mahila Majlis* (which came to be renamed as *Mahila Mahal* in 1936-7) came to be reinstated again from 1938 onwards under the aegis of Madhuri Dutta who tried to gauge listeners' response, answered their queries and published prize-winning poems. The second phase of the programme began with *Adarsha Grihini* (a play written and produced by Bhadra), followed by *Grihasthalir Katha—Griher Bandobasto* and *Garhastha Bigyan—Chelemeyeder Sikhadan*, with Bhadra being the speaker on both the occasions. For all practical purposes, therefore, by renewing his ties with the new set up, Bhadra was indeed chalking out the future course of action of the wireless medium.

Thus, under Bhadra's masterful tutelage and foresight, *Mahila Majlis* became one of the most successful and popular programmes ever to have been made by Akashvani Kolkata. Firstly, by identifying its target audience (women in this case, as they were the most loyal among radio listeners) and then by catering to their specific infotainment requirements, the pioneers at the radio station strove tirelessly to enhance the standard of their presentations. This women-centric cultural journey ushered in a kind of democratization, if not female emancipation, in Bengali society. Thus despite the initial authoritarian restraints, this programme soon started taking rapid strides in subsequent stages, under competent supervision and able guidance from the likes of Bela Dey and others, who successfully turned *Mahila Mahal* into an enchanting afternoon programme.

Youth

It was on 16 August 1970 that a separate channel for the youth called *Yuvavani* was launched, catering to youngsters between 15 and 30 years of age. Through this innovative venture, young people of both sexes were allowed to freely express, organize and present programmes of their own choice, through talks, interviews, discussions, drama, music, features and news. The objective behind this daily six-hour long service was to provide the youth with a forum for self-expression, inculcating in them a sense of purpose, involving them in the task of nation-building, fostering a scientific spirit in them and making them take pride in their nationality. Moreover, by providing them educational programmes, vocational guidance, honing their inherent creativity, promoting national integration and by supporting the less-privileged from among them, *Yuvavani* soon became a trendsetter thanks to its novel and humane approach.[16] Some of Delhi *Yuvavani's* regular features included *Firing Line, Down Memory Lane, Sports and Sportsmen* and *Echoes of a Generation*, while the Calcutta *Yuvavani* promoted programmes like *Jwabab Chai*. The 1981 circular also facilitated the participation of the non-youth in programmes such as these. Emphasis was primarily laid on introducing them to the history and culture of India, while opening a window on the world. Among Calcutta *Yuvavani's* popular programmes were *Path Chalte, Yuvavanir Mancha Theke, Pratibandhider Janya* and the year-end *Phire Dekha* which relayed interviews with eminent personalities, carried sports commentaries as well as poetical experimentations. Furthermore, since *Yuvavani's* audition procedures were simpler than in the general service, a number of aspiring, talented youngsters could be discovered through it, who have carved out their future careers with AIR. The only drawback was that these programmes were mostly restricted to the affluent, urban precincts of the metropolizes, thereby depriving the economically-challenged rural youth from getting adequate representation and due importance.[17]

AIR also sought to present educational programmes in an attractive curricular format. What began as *Bidyarthider Janya* in 1937 came to include many other educational programmes like *Pathdaan*. By inviting experienced academicians to the studio floors to render invaluable advice and suggestions to aspiring examinees, AIR tried in its own way to reach out to the economically deprived students in particular. Audio education of this nature was soon to become a supplementary teaching aid, encouraging students to participate actively in interactive discussions and academic quizzes, thereby reducing the number of school dropouts.

Children

The Calcutta radio station promoted the broadcast of the popular children's programme *Chotoder Baithak* from 1929 to 1942. This half-hour bi-weekly evening programme was brilliantly conducted by Jogesh Chandra Basu, who had joined AIR in 1927, dabbling in a few story-telling sessions for the young before he went on to conduct a programme specifically for children. Thus was born *Chotoder Baithak*, conducted endearingly by the childrens' favourite Golpodada (the title Basu adopted for this programme), who would start with his welcome address 'Calcutta Calling! Good evening children! Golpodada speaking. . . '. This clarion call would invariably attract young and old alike, so magnetic was his personality and so lively was his presentation!

That Golpodada's unique storytelling powers captivated children of all age groups and of different countries is borne out by the huge number of congratulatory fan mails that he received from his young Western audience! He single-handedly steered the children's programme of Akashvani Kolkata to new heights. His novelty lay in encouraging mutual correspondence amongst his young listeners (in India and the West), introducing the concept of the Radio Circle as well as arranging different competitions and prizes for participation in cultural activities, thereby making *Chotoder Baithak* one of its kind in the annals of AIR. However, the fun-filled story telling sessions received a rude shock with Basu's untimely death in 1933. His eldest son Kamal Kumar Basu, alias Dadubhai, Sourindramohan Mukhopadhaya, Bela Halder, Nripendra Krishna Chattopadhaya (fondly regarded as Dadumoni) and others tried to fill the void.

It was in the year 1941 that *Chotoder Baithak* received the new avatar of *Galpadadur Ashor* (GDA), ably conducted as it were by Nripendra Krishna Chattopadhaya. *Chotoder Baithak* of yore as well as GDA entwined in their personae the twofold objectives of providing entertainment and education to its student listeners, with the result that GDA prepared compilations of syllabi-centred questionnaires in consultation with eminent educationists with the purpose of preparing aspiring matriculation examinees. Although avowedly for children, GDA featured the young and the old alike. In its programmes, Nalinikanta Sarkar would regale the audience with his *Hashir Gaan*, B.K. Bhadra would narrate mythological tales while Saratchandra Pandit alias Dada Thakur would present puzzles and riddles.

Another milestone in children's programme was reached once Indira Devi (fondly referred to as Indiradi) joined the AIR as the first female Bengali announcer in 1943, whereupon she decided to start a programme primarily for kids and toddlers. Thus began the historic journey of *Sishumahal* from 1945, making its conductress a legend in her own lifetime. Indiradi's amiable disposition, her sweet and melodious voice, coupled with the songs, skits, stories, and recitations that she presented, regaled audiences, both young and old alike. Her Sunday morning programmes which would invariably begin with her endearing call *Chotto sona bandhura bhai, ador aar bhalobasha nao . . . Ki bhalo acho to shob?* (My dear little friends, take my love and affection . . . Hope all of you are well) made her an all-time favourite household name.[18] Realizing that GDA catered primarily to teenagers (*kishor*), she decided to conduct *Sishumahal* exclusively for 6-10 year olds, which she continued to do for almost four decades with great élan. A multi-faceted personality, an immensely creative and lively individual, a versatile genius with a profound insight into child psychology, she came to be universally loved, respected and trusted by her innumerable fans. Ivy Raha, Jayanta Chaudhuri, Promod Gangopadhyaya, Mihir Bandopadhyaya, Partho Ghosh, and Nirmalbhai, who followed her to host the programme, strove to maintain the same lofty standards subsequently.

A holiday special programme for school-goers came in the wake of *Chutir Ghanta* in 1990, when 'live' broadcasts were again brought back, in contrast to the now defunct *Chotoder Ashor* which had been an evening musical programme addressed primarily to rural teenagers.

Along with the Bengali programmes, the erstwhile English programme for children entitled *Calling All Children* (superbly conducted by Bulbul Sarkar and others) popularized Western music amongst young listeners.

Between 1957 and 1962, AIR Calcutta came to celebrate *Betar Saptaha* or Radio Week annually from the month of February, wherein the inauguration ceremonies were almost always accompanied by the popular children's programme *Ranjana* (conducted jointly by Indira Devi and Jayanta Chaudhuri). For this programme, some of the children's plays that were enacted comprised Prashanta Chowdhury's *Kumbhokarner Nidrabhongo*, Sukumar Ray's *Lakshmaner Shaktishel* and Leela Mazumdar's *Bok-bodh Pala*, which were carried out with the help of child-actors, after extensive rehearsals using real props and costumes!

The well-known Bengali litterateur Leela Mazumdar had a brief stint of seven years with the AIR (1956 to 1963), directing women's and children's programmes, wherein she came to receive considerable support from the likes of Bela Dey, Usha Bhattacharya, Sukumar Ray and above all from Jayanta Chaudhuri.[19] Despite her workload and temporary constraints, the vibrant cultural ambience of AIR inspired Mazumdar to concentrate on her literary pursuits. She began writing humorous stories such as 'Eastakutum', 'Taka Gachh', 'Tong Ling' and 'Holde Pakhhir Palak' jointly with Jayanta Chaudhuri—who read them aloud in the weekly episodes of *Galpadadur Ashor* (the popularity of which became synonymous with his name) in his unmistakably mellifluous voice, which kept the audience completely mesmerized and flooded the AIR studios with burgeoning fan-mails as well!

FREQUENCY MODULATION (F.M.)

AIR today has undergone a revolutionary transformation thanks to the innumerable F.M. channels in its booty. The F.M. channel started on an experimental basis from the Calcutta station around April 1980. Initially beginning with short durations (from both Calcutta A and B channels), it was extended as a 24-hour channel in 1995. Through its immensely popular and interactive Bengali talk shows like *Bhorai, Aaj Rate, Alapon,* and *Moner Kachhakachhi,* issues related to health, education, family planning, medical ailments and psychological disorders were extensively discussed.[20] Its inherent vibrancy thanks to its stereophonic sound system and novel phone-in systems have made the F.M. channels a universal favourite. Moreover, at a time when the higher echelons of our society have switched their allegiance to the 'idiot box', internet and other forms of portable entertainment (through ipods and so on), the timely introduction of F.M. channels has infused new vigour and fresh dynamism into the waning glory of the Indian wireless system. Furthermore, for the majority of unread listeners residing in the countryside, where the television still remains a distant dream thanks to the paucity of electricity, the F.M. channel is indeed a boon which ameliorates their physical exhaustion, provides them scope for recreation and transports them into a world of make-belief.

CONCLUSION

Mass communication in India began in a much larger way with the radio than with any other medium.[21] Indian broadcasting, which took off initially under amateur entrepreneurship, was followed in an organized way under imperial supervision. Yet gross political machinations on the part of the British Raj led initially to its lopsided growth. The apparently bleak scenario of AIR was however more than made up for by the pioneers of the various radio stations, who sought to envisage programmes with inherent egalitarian objectives in mind. Working under serious fiscal constraints and staff shortages (coupled with poor job prospects and meagre salaries), the visionaries manning the Calcutta Radio Station at the time of its inception[22] performed the apparently insurmountable task of striving towards cultural excellence. Through their Herculean endeavours, they provided the audience (belonging to different stratas of society) their feel of wholesome 'infotainment'. While doing so, they transformed AIR into a cultural mouthpiece of Bengali society, eventually leading to its considerable enrichment and rejuvenation in the post-Independence era as well. The present generation of AIR staff is faced with the challenge of living up to the legacy bequeathed by these pioneers, and of ensuring that the medium evolves in keeping with social, cultural and technological mores, so that it remains relevant in the lives of the people that it serves. Time will tell whether they are successful in meeting these challenges or not.

NOTES

1. U.L. Baruah, *This is All India Radio*, New Delhi: Publications Division, Ministry of Information and Broadcasting, Government of India, 1983.
2. Ajit Basu, 'Akashbani: Unmesh theke nana bikasher angane', *Korak Sahitya Patrika*, May-August 2002.
3. Partha Sarathi Gupta, *The Radio and the Raj (1921-1947)*, Kolkata: K.P. Bagchi, 1995.
4. A.L. Basham, *A Cultural History of India*, Delhi: Oxford University Press, 1975.
5. Pankaj Kumar Mallik, *Amar jug amar gaan*, Kolkata: Firma KLM, 1980.
6. Susanta Kumar Bhowmik, 'Swadhinata-uttar pashchim bange betar jagater itibritta', in Rahul Roy (ed.), *Paschim Banga: Phire Dekha*, Chinsurah: Pratiti, 2003.
7. N.K. Bhattacharya (ed.), *Satabarshe Banikumar: Smarane o barane*, Kolkata: Dasgupta, 2008.
8. H.R. Luthra, *Indian Broadcasting*, New Delhi: Publications Division, Ministry of Information and Broadcasting, Government of India, 1986.
9. Surya Sarkar, 'Kolkata betar: Natak', *Korak Sahitya Patrika*, May-August 2002.
10. Prabhat Kumar Das, 'Betar jatrapala: Atit o bartaman', *Korak Sahitya Patrika*, May-August 2002.
11. Basu, 'Akashbani'.
12. Bhowmik, 'Swadhinata-uttar pashchim bange betar jagater itibritta'.
13. Basu, 'Akashbani'.
14. Swapnamoy Chakrabarty, 'Bigyan samprachar o akashbani', *Korak Sahitya Patrika*, May-August 2002.
15. Bhowmik, 'Swadhinata-uttar pashchim bange betar jagater itibritta'.
16. Indira Biswas, 'Mahila majlish o Birendra Krishna Bhadra', *Tant Ghar Ekush Shatak*, 5, no. IX (2005).
17. Baruah, *This is All India Radio*.
18. Ratna Mitra, 'Betaare chhotoder janya samprachaar', *Korak Sahitya Patrika*, May-August 2002.
19. Leela Mazumdar, *Pakdandi*, Kolkata: Ananda Publishers, 1986.
20. Bhowmik, 'Swadhinata-uttar pashchim bange betar jagater itibritta'.
21. J.V. Vilanilam, *Growth and Development of Mass Communication in India*, New Delhi: National Book Trust, 2003.
22. Ratanchandra Das, *Kolkata betarer itibritta*, Kolkata: Antarik Prakashani, 2001.

6

Negotiating 24-Hour News: Satellite Television, Democratic Politics and Globalization in Contemporary India

NALIN MEHTA

INTRODUCTION

After four decades of state monopoly Indian viewers got their first taste of private television in the early 1990s. By 1998, the first of India's private 24-hour news channels was on the airwaves and by 2007 more than 300 satellite channels were broadcasting into Indian homes. Of these, 106 broadcast news in 14 languages and as many as 54 of these were 24-hour news channels in 11 languages.[1] These are conservative figures that do not include many foreign and local cable networks that also broadcast news.[2] Even so, the numbers are a stark illustration of how the Indian state lost control over television broadcasting despite its best efforts to the contrary. No other country in the world has such a concentration of private news channels as India. The creation of a television public has significant implications for democracy and this essay focuses on what 24-hour news means for India. It argues that the emergence of television news networks has greatly enhanced and strengthened deliberative Indian democracy. Commercial mass media stands at the junction of politics and the economy, enabling the entry of citizens onto the stage of politics, while simultaneously seeking to appropriate that energy for its own commercial benefit.[3] This is a claim that needs to be differentiated from the usual journalistic self-image of the fourth estate acting as vigilant defenders of democratic ideals. That notion should not be romanticized too much because news production itself is a cultural process that cannot be separated from its social environment. News producers always function under certain institutional constraints that are endemic to the news gathering process. Leftist and liberal scholars of the media differ in their emphasis but all agree that news production is always circumscribed by institutional filters.[4] News is 'more a pawn of shared suppositions than the purveyor of self-conscious messages'.[5] Yet the media are important, and while it is difficult to draw direct causal linkages, there is no doubt that they initiate and create a new sphere of political action.

Let me also clarify what I am not claiming. There is no evidence to show that satellite television has benefited Indian democracy if we understand it in the narrow procedural terms defined by the voting process alone.[6] A cursory glance at Indian voter-turnout figures shows that voter turnouts have not increased since the advent of satellite television (Table 1). My claim refers to a broader understanding of democracy as a deliberative process involving larger collaborative processes of decision making, identity and interest formation with the media acting as a crucial hinge. Democracy is intimately connected with mechanisms of public discussion and interactive reasoning. Indeed, the new disciplines of social choice theory and public choice theory are connected to ideas of individual values and their impact on decision-making.[7] In this context, Amartya Sen has famously shown that no substantial famine has never occurred in a country with a

TABLE 1: TURNOUT IN LOK SABHA ELECTIONS—1952-2004

General Election	Year	Male	Female	Total
1st	1952	–	–	61.2
2nd	1957	–	–	62.2
3rd	1962	63.31	46.63	55.42
4th	1967	66.73	55.48	61.33
5th	1971	60.90	49.11	55.29
6th	1977	65.63	54.91	60.49
7th	1980	62.16	51.22	56.92
8th	1984	68.18	58.60	63.56
9th	1989	66.13	57.32	61.95
10th	1991	61.58	51.35	56.93
11th	1996	62.06	53.41	57.94
12th	1998	65.72	57.88	61.97
13th	1999	63.97	55.64	59.99
14th	2004	61.66	53.30	57.65

Source: Election Commission of India, URL (consulted 23 October 2006): http://www.eci.gov.in/miscellaneous_statistics/votingprecentage_loksabha.asp

democratic form of government and a relatively free press.[8] When the audience for news expands, the shape of politics changes.

The publicness of mass media and television vastly differs from Jürgen Habermas' idealized conception of a 'rational' public sphere of citizens reading newspapers and then being spurred to logically debate matters of public importance in the salons and public spaces of eighteenth-century Europe. For Habermas, such a public sphere was central to the project of liberal democracy in the Western world,[9] but it has rightly been pointed out for a variety of reasons that such an idyllic public sphere never existed.[10] The public sphere is an important normative category and is crucial for democracy but in a way that substantially differs from that sketched by Habermas, and those that base their work on his ideas.[11] Politics now passes through a mediated arena and the media create a new kind of publicness that is de-spatialized, non-dialogical and received in settings spatially and temporally remote from the original context of production.[12] Reception is often at odds with the intentions of its creators—the recipient's own assumptions and expectations regulate how they are interpreted and appropriated. The meaning of the message is not static and takes different forms for different people.[13] The crucial point is that politics, unlike before, has to unfold in an open arena and in the glare of a new visibility that has a life of its own and is often difficult to control.

Of course, one must be careful not to exaggerate the influence of television. It is easy to fall prey to the 'myth' of media power and see 'Superman when it is really Clark Kent'.[14] The media's importance lies not in whether anybody is watching or is getting influenced, but in the assumption of it by political leaders and decision-makers:

The greatest media effects may not be measurable influences on attitudes or beliefs produced by media slant but the range of information the media make available to individual human minds, the range of connections they bring to light, the particular social practices and collective rituals by which they organise our days and ways. . . . The media organise not just information but audiences. They legitimise not just events and the sources that report them but readers and views. Their capacity *to publicly include* is perhaps their most important feature. . . . Moreover, visibility—public visibility—is of enormous importance even if few people bother to read or watch the news. So long as information is publicly available, political actors have to behave as if someone in the public is paying attention . . . even if the public is absent, the assumption of the public presence makes all the difference.[15]

It is in this context that television assumes an important role and—regardless of its actual impact on the voting public—becomes central to the political process.

This essay is divided into two parts. The first sketches the links between democratic culture and television by teasing out the social sources of news television. It moves beyond the political economy equation to argue that the rise of Indian news television can only be understood in the context of a society with a strong argumentative tradition of public reasoning. News channels tap into strong oral traditions and heterodox structures of social communication that Amartya Sen has labelled 'the argumentative tradition of India'.[16] For Sen, these traditions are an important support structure for the sustenance of Indian democracy.[17] I develop the 'argumentative Indian' argument further to show that it translates into 'argumentative television'. Indian television thrives on programming genres that marry older argumentative traditions with new technology and notions of liberal democracy to create new hybrid forms that strengthen democratic culture.

The second part of this essay provides a genealogy of Indian politics on satellite television that focuses on the specific ways in which the new medium has affected the daily spectacle of Indian politics. Satellite television has emerged as a new factor in the Indian political matrix since the mid-1990s and this section shows how political leaders and parties adapted their daily practices of politics to the 24-hour publicity it provides.

THE SOURCES OF ARGUMENTATIVE TELEVISION:
DEMOCRACY AND PROGRAMMING

The Argumentative Indian

Television has been called the private life of the nation-state; the medium cannot be understood in isolation from its social context. Different people's television is different. In Spain, the tradition of siestas and the propensity to go out late at night means that television schedules are different from, say, in Germany, which is a more 'privatized' society.[18] It has been argued that the tradition of cabaret and music hall makes variety programmes so popular in France. Similarly, the popularity of *telenovelas* in Latin America has its roots in literary traditions and radio serials. Cultures, of course, constantly change and cannot be reduced to simple equations. To the extent that we can pinpoint certain aspects of cultures, however, they cannot be separated from popular cultural forms like television.

It is the argument of this essay that a key factor in the rise and sustenance of Indian news television is that it forms a link with India's long dialogic and 'argumentative tradition' of heterogeneous debate. News television is successful because it feeds off and into precisely these traditions. Amartya Sen has argued that there is an intimate connection between these historical traditions and the sustenance of Indian democracy. He does not claim that the argumentative tradition has been a perennial, unchanging aspect of Indian culture or even to elevate it in relation to other sociological influences. The claim rather is that this tradition of public reasoning makes the roots of democracy stronger and easier to preserve.[19] To extend that argument further, news television plugs into this social practise and gives a new publicness to older traditions of debate and dissent. It combines these traditions with the existence of strong oral cultures and mediates them to a larger audience, negating space and time. It adds newer influences and technologies—SMS messages, audience polls, live public debates—and mutates the form to suit its own demands but in the process strengthens these traditions. India's argumentative traditions mutate into argumentative television.

First, what is this argumentative tradition? Traditions of public discussion have existed elsewhere in the world and India is not unique in this respect, but, as Sen argues, this is often an undernoted aspect of the Indian cultural milieu. He has shown that the idea of public dissent and reasoning has been an important component of Indian public life and religious life from the earliest writings. Drawing a genealogy of this tradition starting from religious epics like Valmiki's *Ramayana* to the dialogue between Krishna and Arjuna in the *Mahabharata*, he notes that the 'intricate arguments against Rama's and Krishna's orthodox views are elaborately accommodated in the texts themselves'. For instance, a pandit called Javali describes the actions of Rama, the hero of the epic, as 'foolish' in a long indictment, and though 'orthodoxy is shown to win at the end, the vanquished scepticism lives on', conserved in the dialogic accounts.[20] The crucial point is that while deep inequalities persist on lines of gender, class, caste and community, some of the most celebrated dialogues in ancient Indian writings came from women, like the 'arguing combat' between the woman scholar Gargi and Yajnvalkya in the *Brihadaranyaka Upanishad*. Similarly, the arguments presented by women speakers in the epics do not always conform to stereotypical cultural roles, as attested by Draupadi's scathing indictment of her husband King Yudhisthira in the *Mahabharata*, preserved in the sixth-century *Kiratarjuniya*.[21] Sen draws a long line from that tradition of dissent to the evolution of religious heterodoxy embodied by the rise of Buddhism, Jainism, the Lokayata philosophy of scepticism, the Carvaka philosophy of atheism and materialism, the Bhakti movement and the Muslim sufis in the middle ages who rejected social barriers, right up to eclectic debates on the question of religion in the court of the sixteenth-century Mughal Emperor Akbar. In Sen's view, Akbar's *rahe-aql*, the path of reason, which was symbolized by the royal championing of public discussions to resolve difference between religions[22] was the intellectual descendant of the Buddhist councils sponsored by the Emperor Ashoka in the third century BC. These were some of the oldest public meetings in the world to find public means of resolving conflict through dialogue and reasoning.[23]

Sen is not the only scholar who has explored these links. C.A. Bayly's study of social communication in early British India concluded that a strong 'information order' persisted and aided the rapid spread of nationalist ideas and new communication technologies like the printing press:

It was density and flexibility of indigenous routines of social communication which explains why north Indians were able to make such striking use of the printing press, the newspaper and the public meeting once those innovations finally began to spread rapidly amongst them in the 1830s and 1840s . . . [It] help[s] to explain why political leaders in a poor country with a relatively low rate of general literacy should have been able to create a widely diffused and popular nationalist movement so early.[24]

What colonial officials referred to as the lightening speed of 'bazaar rumour' was a 'picture of a lively social and political debate'. The techniques of this ecumene of communication varied from sophisticated notions of debate to poetic satire, puppetry, handbills, speeches and ironic visual displays during popular festivals.[25] The placarding of mosques and Sufi shrines was a common means of communicating with the wider community in Indo-Muslim cities and this was widely used, for instance, in the public protests against the marriage of James Kirkpatrick, the British resident at the court of Hyderabad (1798-1803), to a Muslim noblewoman Khair-un nissa.[26] Such patterns of political representation and debate extended along the Hindu-Muslim divide. A standard example is the 1810 political movement in Banaras against the new British system of house taxation which involved the vigorous and effective use of public communication strategies across the boundaries of caste and religion.[27] Christian missionaries were often surprised by how local officers, not just religious leaders, engaged them in complex debates which were a subset of larger questions that for centuries pitted Vaishnavite scholars against Buddhists and Jains, Siddhantists against the Puranas and devotional gurus against the orthodox.[28]

This ecology of communication was not restricted to elites and literate classes. Ranajit Guha's work on peasant insurgencies documents the centrality of strong oral cultures in the spread of peasant revolts in colonial India. The biggest factor was rumour, which was the trigger and mobilizer at the same time. During the anti-British uprisings of 1857, colonial officials often noted how news travelled 'with a rapidity almost electric'.[29] The speed with which it travelled from Persia to Banaras was immense, despite no substantial mechanisms of mass communication.

There is no doubt that these dense networks of social communication have persisted in modern India. After two decades of reporting on India for the BBC, Mark Tully observed that nobody could cover the country without taking into account its lively oral cultures, the fact that India is still very much a country where information passes by word of mouth:

Anyone who has joined a group of villagers huddled over a transistor set in the dim light of a lantern listening to news from a foreign radio station knows that the spread of information is not limited to the number of sets in a village. Go to that village in the morning, and you will learn that the information heard on that radio has reached far beyond the listenership too.[30]

Tully contends that oral cultures and the power of rumour were always strong rivals to government broadcasting through the years of government monopoly, particularly in a context where the print medium was free. After Indira Gandhi lifted the internal emergency and lost the general election of 1977, she attributed it to the power of political rumour. When asked by a visiting BBC director general why she lost despite controlling all channels of broadcast communication, she said that voters were 'misled by rumours'.[31] This was a sub-set of the deep-rooted nature of oral traditions. In Bengal, the cultural practice of animated conversation and discussion between friends has been given the nomenclature of *adda* and raised to such mythical status that it is now a central marker of Bengali identity itself.[32] These traditions should not be underestimated, as C.A. Bayly wrote of his time in India in the 1980s:

In this poor society, some forms of political and social knowledge were remarkably diffused: apparently uneducated people would come up to one in the bazaar to discourse on the demerits of Baroness Thatcher or Mr. Gorbachev, while educated people in east and south-east Asia, let alone Britain, seemed to struggle to understand anything of the external world.[33]

The point of the above discussion is to draw the long lineage and persistence of a vibrant and organic tradition of public reasoning, dissent, debate and oral tradition that cuts across classes, castes, religions and communities. The development of news channels as a prominent genre of satellite television can only be understood in this context. This is especially so because these traditions were kept out of the airwaves for five decades due to the state's monopoly. When the barriers were lifted it had a special liberatory resonance. News television, for the first time, provided the airwaves as a mass platform to extend the Indian propensity for argumentation and political debate. In such a society, news channels fit existing social nodes of communication and extend these linkages to mass audiences. If the genre of news channels had not existed, it would have had to be invented.

ARGUMENTATIVE TV: TALK-SHOWS, DEBATES AND MOBILES

If Indians can be characterized as argumentative, then Indian television can be characterized as argumentative television. Television feeds off existing traditions and remakes them. It is no accident that when Zee TV started the first private Hindi broadcasts, its first foray into current affairs, *Aap Ki Adalat* [Your Court], was not a regular news bulletin but based on questioning and argumentation. The format of that programme simultaneously symbolized the harnessing of television to the democratic tradition of transparency and the transformative nature of it as a spectacle. Styled as a people's court, each week the programme would bring a prominent political leader to the studio for a mock trial in a mock courtroom. The 'accused' had to face a litany of charges laid out by a 'public prosecutor' who led an inquisition in the presence of a live audience and in a kitsch Bollywood-style courtroom set that viewers were familiar with. The programme even had a court-reader who would announce each charge with the lines, 'Today in the people's court . . .' and a 'people's judge', normally a prominent journalist, who at the end of each hour-long programme would pronounce judgement on the politician's behaviour and a 'sentence'. The format allowed politicians an hour-long platform, interspersed with tough questioning and more than a touch of drama. This partly explains why they chose to submit themselves to such interrogations. It was the glamour of the new medium and the extended audience that it offered. It was the first time that mass audiences were getting an extended look at their leaders, and Zee began receiving sackfuls of letters from Hindi-speaking viewers in the remotest parts of the country. All of them wanted to be part of the studio audience. Some thanked Zee TV for starting programmes which would instil accountability in politicians while others wrote about how they cancelled all appointments on Sunday mornings to watch *Aap ki Adalat*.[34] By January 1994, Zee claimed that it was receiving more than 20,000 letters a day.[35] This popular response underwrote the economic market for such political programming in a culture that is underpinned by dialogic and heterodox lineage.

News channels created argumentative television by plugging into the social propensity for animated argumentation and dialogue and combining it with the language of liberal democracy and the spectacle of television. When the Bengali news channel STAR Ananda started operations in June 2005 it announced its launch by instituting daily live public debates between candidates contesting the Kolkata municipal election. These debates marked an important signpost in the political campaigning culture of the city. They were conducted in the city's open public spaces and took the form of public meetings where sometimes as many as some of 10,000 people turned up as live audiences in addition to regular television viewers.[36] The tapes of that programming make for riveting viewing. They show large public rallies of the kind that are familiar to observers of Indian politics but differ in one crucial aspect: these were joint political events, organized by a television channel and moderated by a STAR Ananda newsman as rival candidates debated their political views while their followers raised lusty slogans.

This was happening in a city which had been ruled by the same political organization, the Left Front, since 1977. The debates unleashed political passions and for the first two weeks, mini-riots broke out during virtually everyone of the daily events. Rival political groups attacked each other with swords and sticks. In one instance, petrol bombs were also used. The news anchors were roughed up for daring to ask tough questions and all this happened on live television. The debates created such a problem that the police commissioner of Kolkata called up the channel and asked it to stop, citing the fear of public rioting. As Suman Chattopadhyay, the founding editor of STAR Ananda, who also anchored these debates, explains:

It created such a furore and became such an instant hit ... I didn't even know ... that these two warring groups would come with daggers and bombs, and there was one shoot-out incident. . . . The police commissioner personally requested me 25 times. . . . He said to please withdraw this programme. . . . This is creating hell of a lot of *jhamela* [problem].[37]

STAR Ananda responded to the commissioner's suggestion with a public campaign for the strengthening of democratic traditions and debate. The editor went on air with news that the police commissioner wanted the public debates to stop and argued that this was a dangerous precedent for Bengali democracy. The important point here is that this tradition of public television debates was not a Bengali innovation. Hindi news channels like Zee TV and STAR News had run numerous such events in various constituencies during national and state elections across north India in the preceding five years. This is what STAR Ananda emphasized, along with the long Bengali tradition of public culture, *adda* and political activism that goes back to the Bengal renaissance of the nineteenth century.

On air, I said if debates are possible in Bihar . . . and in UP, Haryana, why shouldn't they be possible in Calcutta. It is your [police's] job . . . the law and order. Police commissioner said this is not our job. Our job is to maintain law and order. I said if something creates law and order problems, you should deploy sufficient number of policemen. He said I have other things to do. . . .

They forgot that Calcutta is a city where if you can host a good debate even on the most esoteric subject of the world . . . you will see 10,000 people in the crowd.[38]

The public appeal to democratic principles and Bengali-ness worked and the political violence ceased within two weeks. Many localities in Kolkata began to invite the channel to hold similar debates between contesting candidates and that single event turned STAR Ananda into a market leader in the Bengali news sphere. Following this success, a year later two more Bengali news channels started from Kolkata in 2006 in the run-up to the West Bengal assembly election. These two, Zee's 24 Ghanta and Kolkata TV, both followed similar programming formats of public debate that Ananda had started and developed these even further.[39]

Bengali television shows how news television feeds off, and into, liberal democratic values, which themselves are rooted in a long heritage of argumentation and debate. Argumentative television fits into broader cultural patterns, to the extent that they can be identified, but the very nature of the medium is such that they mutate into newer forms when mediated by television. In separate analyses of the uses of video technology for religious purposes in India, John T. Little and Philip Lutgendorf suggest that new electronic presentations are not overwhelming traditional religious performance genres.[40] Instead, a new layer of interpretation is being added to what is likely to remain a vibrant and multi-vocal cultural tradition. The impact on the traditions themselves is open to question but new formats are being used to enhance traditional formats. It is my argument that precisely the same thing is happening in the arena of politics with news television's focus on politics and civic life.

The most striking feature of Indian news television is its animated and highly argumentative tradition of programming. Critics often compare the style of news coverage unfavourably with Western channels like BBC and CNN:

If you compare Indian TV news channels to BBC you will appreciate the world of difference between those who invented the English language and those of us who have subsequently learnt to speak it. They are minimalist to the point that their lips find separation difficult. Our anchors and reporters whirr like fans on a hot day—fast and furious. The result is plenty of high speed mish-mash. As if they are reciting 'superkalifragilisticexpeallydocious' (Mary Poppins?) [sic] backwards.[41]

Such criticism, however, misses the point. Individual agency and institutional values are no doubt important but Indian reportage and presentation is a product of its cultural environment and can only be understood in that respect.

Notions of public debate and viewer agency constitute the lifeblood of Indian news channels. Here a distinction needs to be drawn between the daily reporting of current affairs and other genres of news television that also constitute significant drivers of democratic culture. Daily news production in the conventional sense is a culture subject to the structural and personal limitations of its gatekeepers[42]—news reporters, producers and editors. News production on television has been the subject of numerous critical studies ever since Lang and Lang established in 1953 that the nature of television coverage of General Douglas MacArthur's visit to Chicago in 1951 was significantly at odds with actual experience of participants on the spot. They concluded that:

... assumed reportorial accuracy is far from automatic. Every camera selects, and thereby leaves the unseen part of the subject open to suggestion and inference. The gaps are usually filled in by a commentator. In addition the process directs action and attention to itself.[43]

The medium mediates the message, as Marshall McLuhan emphasized. Yet there are vast numbers of journalists who do their jobs honestly and consider themselves as objective news gatherers. The problem of what constitutes legitimate news is a vexed one and summing up the arguments put forward by a range of ethnographers, sociologists and political scientists, Michael Schudson points to the fact that the quest for objectivity itself can be a source of distortion. As he sums up, five kinds of distortions are usually cited: news is said to be event-centred, action-centred and person-oriented; negative, detached; technical and official.[44]

All these filters operate in various forms on Indian news television as well. In the 2004 general election, for instance, a study of six 24-hour news channels over a two-month period spanning the election campaign found that more than 50 per cent of reportage in news bulletins was about the political campaign. However, five categories dominated 85 per cent of this coverage: party campaigning, electoral procedures, party politics, legal issues around the election and personalities. According to this detailed study, electoral issues like development, crime and economic reforms received scant attention.[45] Though news reportage does make a whole range of information publicly available, one may well question the relevance of news programming for purposes of democratic debate and public reasoning.

In this context, it is important to consider that news channels also cover current affairs through other programming genres as well, that typically do not feature in most analyses. These are the genres of public debates; regular talk shows focussing on political issues; political satire through puppetry and cartoons; daily opinion polls through SMS messages; and finally the concept of 'citizen journalists' who send in video clips through mobile phones and other means. The intensity and frequency of these genres varies from channel to channel but they are all significant components of Indian news programming. None of these formats is unique to India but they all feed on existing nodes of communication and indigenous forms of communication.

Let us first consider talk shows. They are one of the oldest genres of American television. They are studio-based, easy to produce and most importantly relatively cheap in terms of cost. They are one of the few television formats where the public gains 'full recognition' in the 'role of protagonist'. They differ from news debate shows because they present issues for public debate in the discursive format of conversation rather than formal debate or commentary. They are primarily oral, live-like and conversation is the mainstay. Phil Donahue is usually seen as the inventor of the talk-show concept where studio audiences became major players: 'The public is not in the dark of an orchestra pit. In a sort of orchestra of lighting, everybody is brought on stage and given a share of illumination.'[46] This is a format where hosts lose their spatial authority and the 'public is literally on centre stage'. The studio audience 'writes' the show as much as the presenter. Talk shows have been criticized for converting politics and conversation into spectacle but it has been pointed out that spectacle and politics have never been separated. The talk show can be seen as a terrain of struggles of discursive practices. Audience participants have agency on talk shows. Of course, the presenter directs the flow of conversation but there is no denying the fact that the audience is as much the driver as the presenter.[47] Through its discursive format and by making the news more comprehensible and interesting, talk shows increase the potential of 'rational-critical' debate.[48]

In the Indian context, talk shows and public debates in various forms have been embraced by news channels and harnessed explicitly in the political arena. Sociologist Ashis Nandy wrote that 'cricket is an Indian game, accidentally invented by the English'.[49] He based his argument on the psychological affinity between the complexity of cricket and a long tradition of abstractness in Indian thought. One could say the same for news channels and talk television. Indians are talkative and therefore Indian channels are talkative. The two NDTV general news channels, for instance, have always emphasized studio-based shows—all of which were anchored by its senior-most editors. Producers saw talk and debate as important for two reasons: They were a means of unique branding but such formats were also cheap to produce:[50]

The easiest television is talk television. It's the cheapest, easiest. . . . You call two guests, you talk to them and you kill half an hour. Half an hour, if you have to make a documentary is very expensive. Even if you have to use some moving images, it is expensive and takes a lot of time and effort. That is what has spawned this.[51]

Talk shows on news channels are highly political and serve as important agencies for political debate. Most of these talk shows have politicians sharing the same platform with a live audience and according to one presenter, audience members are increasingly turning more aggressive. The publicness of the platform gives audiences agency. The protection afforded by the publicness of live television often allows audience members to aggressively question politicians:

The average audience member now knows that he is not getting redressal as such, in terms of whatever his problems are. But he knows that he can put the participants on the mat and can also air his grievances to connect with others . . . those who have similar grievances. They [live audiences] have become more and more vocal. Earlier they were more reluctant to confront authority. Now they not just question authority, sometimes they become very ugly in accusing the authority. The attitude is you can't do anything to me right now, I am on air.[52]

During the 2004 general election, NDTV 24 × 7 had as many as nine programmes a week where the audience played a big part. These ranged from straight talk shows to public debates to vox populi based programmes where reporters travelled to constituencies and simply chatted to residents about their problems.[53]

The second important genre is that of political satire. It was started by Zee TV during the late 1990s when it produced a series of programmes using political parodies and the soundtrack of popular Bollywood songs. These were satirical clips that cleverly edited video footage of politicians over double-meaning Bollywood songs to make political comments. Zee also introduced political poetry in the form of *shayri*—Urdu couplets composed specifically in this case with the intent of political comment. These programmes formed an important part of Zee's coverage of the 1998 and 1999 general elections. It must be stressed that such programming only supplemented regular reportage of that event—it wasn't the mainstay of Zee's coverage— but it was an important intervention. It was yet another link in the long tradition of political satire and activity in India through the idiom of popular culture.

Historians have long documented how nationalist resistance to British rule manifested itself through subtle but meaningful variations in religious celebrations, bardic songs and theatrical productions. For instance, in Maharashtra, theatrical productions of *Kichaka Vadha* [The Killing of Kichaka]—the famous *Mahabharata* episode where the good Bhima kills the evil Kichaka—were used by nationalist writers in a way that represented Kichaka as the embodiment of British rule. The alteration was well appreciated by the audience and the play was banned by British officials in 1910 but such representations continued through other channels of popular culture, like lithographs. Such productions were subversive but difficult to control because they hid their political message in overtly religious overtones.[54] Puppetry and traditional theatrical performances constituted an important culture of communication through which political messages passed from town to town, as evidenced by the Vellore mutiny of 1806 and to a much greater extent in the great upheavals of 1857.[55]

It is important to clarify here what is not being claimed. The India of the twenty-first century is very different from the India of the nineteenth century. It is a democracy and modern means of communication have negated the need to resort to subterfuge in passing subversive messages through cultural performers. It is undeniable though that older cultural forms have reinvented themselves on television, mutating into new genres. This is the basis of argumentative television.

A good example is the January 2006 STAR News programme, *Deewar*, which focused on the split between the Gandhi and the Bachchan families. Former prime minister Rajiv Gandhi and Bollywood superstar Amitabh Bachchan grew up together and Bachchan became a Congress MP in 1984 before the two families split over the Bofors controversy in the late 1980s. Bachchan emerged in the 1990s as a star campaigner for the Samajwadi Party in Uttar Pradesh and this programme focussed on a public war of words between Rajiv's son, Rahul, and Amitabh Bachchan that was making headlines in the Indian media during that period. The show blurred reality and fiction, reconstructing the politics of the two families by inter-slicing real life footage and sound-bites of the protagonists with a reconstruction of inner-room politics through hired actors. The very name of the programme, *Deewar*, was symbolic because it was a play on the iconic Bollywood film of the 1970s which was the story of two brothers, one who became a policeman and the other a smuggler. The entire treatment was satirical. This was not a documentary-style reconstruction. *Deewar* fused the rumour of the political grapevine with the reality of public politics. For every real-life statement made by the protagonists, *Deewar* had a dramatized representation of what might have happened in backroom politics that led to it. None of this was substantiated through the standards of regular journalistic practice and the programme emphasized the fictional nature of the reconstruction but at the same time commented on contemporary politics and made public one popular version of what constitutes it.

Such satirical programming is *Kichaka Vadha* re-invented. These shows allow channels to make comments on issues, cutting across legal boundaries that define the limits of 'legitimate' news. STAR's weekly satirical show, *Poll Khol,* is based on precisely this premise. *Poll Khol* literally means 'open election', but it is also a play on a popular Hindi metaphor that means 'revealing the hidden story'. Anchored by popular comedian Shekhar Suman and an animated monkey, it's a political programme that uses humour, popular Bollywood soundtracks and real news footage to make political comments. According to the STAR editor who initiated it:

If you as an anchor went and said all those things on your programme you would be hauled over coals and you would dragged to court, but we can. . . . Its like writing an editorial. What *Poll Khol* does is to write an editorial, an Op-Ed page comment. It is only now that people in the political class are beginning to come to terms with a *Poll Khol*. It is biting satire and humour, its very black humour and it has got a very serious element to it as well. . . . Initially everybody thought, oh my, it was invasive, it was bad journalism, it was trivialising.[56]

Satire is a form used by all news channels. During the 2004 general election, Zee had a similar programme called *Chunavi Bhatti* [The Election Firing Pit] and Aaj Tak had *Chunavi Qawwali* [Election *Qawwali*], which fused comments on the political situation with *qawwali*, the form of musical melodies connected with Sufi Islam. Similarly, NDTV 24 × 7's *Double Take* and NDTV India's *Gustakhi Maaf* [Pardon Me] are daily puppetry shows based on political leaders.[57]

Such shows are important drivers of political culture of debate and significant cogs in the wheel of argumentative television. Talk and satirical television has been criticized for converting news into entertainment. Politics turns into a spectacle and its superficial aspects dominate. This is a valid point and one that news producers are more than aware of. Speaking of NDTV's popular weekly debating show *The Big Fight*, its creator acknowledges the limitations of form imposed by the imperative of packaging information and debate in a way that is entertaining to a mass audience.

TV is now increasingly entertainment. News is entertainment. You have to create some element of entertainment . . . people shouting at each other . . . or some kind of conflict. It is not always about information. I am not saying in the *Big Fight* you don't try to inform but if the entertainment element was not there the programme would probably not have survived. You have to package it. . . . First Punch, Second Punch [programme sections]. Otherwise who will see? There has to be some heat.[58]

That packaging, though, does not take away from the inherent argumentativeness and transparency of a programme like *The Big Fight*. Politicians appear every week and heatedly debate the issue of the day while an audience asks questions. Television does turn politics into spectacle but politics has always been about spectacle. They have never been separated.[59] Television merely provides another layer to that relationship.

Another cog in the construction of argumentative television is interactivity and the use of SMS and mobile phone technology. The rise of private telephony and mobile phones has coincided with the rise of the Indian satellite television industry. Modern communication technologies can only be understood in conjunction with each other, not in isolation, and both sectors feed off each other. From having no mobile telephones in 1998, India had 57.4 million mobile subscribers by mid-2005.[60] The people who own mobile phones are often those who also watch satellite television and television channels use mobile technology as a means for building linkages with their subscribers. This is done through SMS technology as well as mobile videos and both of these are important from the perspective of democratic culture.

The first method is popular opinion polls through mobile SMS technology. This is mostly done through SMS polls of viewers that are economically beneficial to channels as well as to telecom companies. News channels conduct opinion polls almost on a daily basis. When a Delhi court acquitted nine men accused of murdering model Jessica Lal in a Delhi bar, NDTV launched a 'Save Jessica Lal' campaign to protest against what it saw as a botched police investigation against politically connected individuals. The network asked viewers to SMS support for a petition to the Indian president and ran special shows on this theme. Some 84,000 NDTV viewers messaged their support by the end of the second day,[61] and in total, NDTV received more than 200,000 SMS messages pertaining to this campaign.[62] Simultaneously, the Delhi High Court, without waiting for an appeal, directed the Delhi Police to submit a report on its handling of the case and why it collapsed in trial courts.[63] The court ultimately overturned the previous verdict after fast-tracking proceedings and holding daily hearings.[64] The Delhi High Court's actions cannot be attributed to this public campaign alone; but television acted as a lightening conductor of popular public opinion, as NDTV's Managing Editor Sreenivasan Jain contended:

That just goes to show you technology has changed the face of mobilization completely. Because if this were like ten years ago and you were going door to door collecting signatures, which would have been its equivalent, it would have taken you many more logistics, just an army of volunteers. You didn't need any of that. You needed one rallying point on television.[65]

SMS activism has emerged in other countries as well.[66] SMS messages played a big part in rallying opposition protests in Manila that led to the fall of Philippines president Joseph Estrada.[67] The social impact of this interactive technology is undeniable although its exact nature is debatable. On Indian news television, SMS polling is so prominent that one commentator has gone so far as to call this phenomenon India's new 'tele-democracy'.[68] This 'tele-democracy' is restricted to the middle-class audiences of television channels but cannot be dismissed for this reason alone. To the extent that the nation itself is a 'daily referendum' news television's SMS polls represent mini-referendums on daily news. Even if they represent a small section of India, the daily exercise of voting represents a strong engagement of that section with the political process and a desire to be active in it.

Mobile video technology has also been co-opted into the news gathering process. Video clips emailed by viewers from mobile phones have featured prominently in coverage of various events, starting from the coverage of the Mumbai floods in July 2005.[69] STAR News, during the Mumbai floods, telecast nearly 150 such clips sent by citizens trapped in the floodwaters.[70] They documented conditions in parts of the city that STAR's own reporters could not reach and they came in after a prominent on-air campaign asking viewers to be the network's eyes and ears. Since then most Indian news channels have run similar campaigns asking viewers to turn into vigilante reporters and to send in video clips if they saw anything wrong happening in their neighbourhoods. Indian television has embraced this to such an extent that CNN, which runs an annual award series for young Indian journalists, instituted a new category in 2006—'CNN Citizen Journalist of the Year Award'. The term, 'citizen journalist' itself has been coined by CNN-IBN to refer to viewers who sends in videos. This offers the exciting possibility of flattening the gap between news producers and news consumers. Viewers turn into reporters and channels provide a public platform to air their pictures. Traditional journalists often disparage such techniques, arguing that this is not journalism in the conventional sense.[71] It is journalism, however, to the extent that it makes information available and is checked for accuracy. The marriage of television and mobile phones opens up many new possibilities for the spread of information and a consequent strengthening of democratic cultures through transparent debate.

GENEALOGY OF INDIAN POLITICS ON TELEVISION

TV Politicians

The previous section establishes the broad patterns of television's focus on society and politics. Let us now invert the lens and examine how politicians responded to satellite television and appropriated it. Satellite television did not change politics itself. It emerged as a new avenue through which politics was conducted; it added another layer to the complex palimpsest that constitutes Indian politics. This section builds this argument by providing a genealogy of politics on television.

During the decades of state monopoly over broadcasting, radio and television had always been harnessed to the service of the ruling party. News constituted little more than an audio-visual gazette of ministerial activities. Despite having control of the state's broadcasting apparatus, the Congress inaugurated the first move towards professional advertising for political purposes. It hired a professional advertising agency to plan and design its campaign on national security for the 1984 general election. Part of this campaign was the distribution of specially designed audio and video cassettes in remote and tribal areas. These productions evoked the memory of the just-assassinated Indira Gandhi, interspersed with the narrative voice of Bollywood superstar Amitabh Bachchan.[72] From the late 1980s onwards, however, it was the Bharatiya Janata Party (BJP) that adapted the best to new audio-visual technologies. The dissemination of political messages on audio and video cassettes was a vital component of the Ram-janmabhoomi agitation and the BJP acquired a well-documented reputation for adroit media management.[73] This is where detailed studies of the interface of Indian politics and television stop—in the mid-1990s.

The advent of 24-hour news, however, necessitates a fresh look at what happened to the politics-television equation after the rise of news channels. Twenty-four-hour news introduces a new dynamic into the political process. It introduces the element of permanent publicity and forces politicians to adapt to new forms of electronic mediation. Firstly, 24-hour news makes politicians visible on a daily basis. The kind of high publicity that politicians desire during election campaigns is now thrust upon them on a daily basis. The daily television camera symbolizes the scrutiny of public opinion. Even if that public is a 'phantom' one, the politician has to behave as if it is always there. The demands of 24-hour news force politicians to be on the campaign trail all the time. Anyone who has followed television reporters on their daily rounds of party offices in Delhi knows that it is often the insatiable drive of news channels to 'take the story forward' that induces party spokespersons to 'react' to the latest political controversy. Twenty-four-hour news leads to 24-hour politics.

The first manifestation of the induction of the 24-hour dynamic into politics was the rise of a new breed of politicians who understood how the medium worked and adapted to it. Political parties needed to mediate their message better but the demands of television also converged with this need. A good example of this new kind of politician is BJP General Secretary Arun Jaitely. Jaitely's politics can by no means be reduced simply to his television skills, but television undeniably played a big role in his rise within the BJP. He was still a relatively lightweight leader when during the 1998 general elections he was booked by NDTV to represent the BJP for seven straight hours of live broadcasting while the votes were being counted. The reason why NDTV picked him bears scrutiny. As Jaitely explains, he suited their requirements for producing short, crisp sound-bites.

I asked Prannoy [NDTV President] as to why he insisted on having just the two of us [Jaitey and Jairam Ramesh of the Congress] for 7-8 hours. He said, 'Let's say if Surjeet [Former CPI-M general secretary] had been here, or if let's say another old politician Sunder Singh Bhandari [senior BJP leader] had been here and I asked them for a reaction on these areas of Madhya Pradesh . . . I want a three sentence reply. I don't want an 18 sentence reply.'[74]

NDTV wanted Jaitely, and not Sunder Singh Bhandari, who was far more senior in the BJP hierarchy, because he could answer questions in the sound-bite idiom that fit its own demands.

It is television's need to find politicians who could adapt to it that fed into the rise of new television politicians in most parties. Such leaders were not necessarily official spokespersons for their parties, but television thrust that role upon them and they appropriated it. Television's need for giving a face to every story led to the representation of some leaders as credible representatives of their parties or governments, irrespective of their actual place within the hierarchy. This is apparent across the range of the political spectrum and particularly in the coverage of issues related to the government. A senior television manager sums up:

We have the emergence of these people like Sri Prakash Jaiswal in this government and I.D. Swamy in the last government who are available on any and every subject. On any story you need one bite from the government to give the government point of view and whether that person is an expert on that subject or not, you just go to him. He gives you the bite and you are happy. I don't think they are told . . . they are self-appointed. For them also it is an opportunity to get mileage. Ten-twelve years ago, these were all faceless people. Today they get a face. They are on TV.[75]

The publicity of television often helps political careers. It helps to be seen by cadres and to be seen by senior party leaders. From the point of view of television owners, this equation works in their favour. For NDTV's managers, this is an important reason why Delhi's politicians appear on its programmes: their peers and seniors often watch them. According to Prannoy Roy:

One politician told me, a senior minister in this government, he said there is an unwritten rule now, amongst all politicians . . . and maybe he was just telling me because I was sitting in front of him . . . that if you are in politics, you have to appear on NDTV once a month. You can appear on Doordarshan any number of times. But NDTV once a month. That's the standard rule apparently. So it does have an impact, partly on their own peers, on their leaders, and obviously it has an impact on the wider audience. Because they wouldn't waste their time otherwise.

We have a puppet show. One of the politicians was really upset that he wasn't made into a puppet. So he said why haven't you made me into a puppet? I will come and do my own voice-over also. They have obviously realised that television does further their careers, either with their own party people or with the electorate . . . that is not clear.[76]

Just appearing on news channels though is not enough. It is expertise in dealing with it that that distinguishes the new television politician. When private television channels first started, most politicians were largely ignorant about television politics. Some learnt quickly though. The BJP's Jaitely calls this the 'art of electronic media'. Enumerating the rules of this 'art', he reveals a telling description of how he nuances his behaviour and speech on camera to suit the demands of the medium:

The art of electronic media . . . political television . . . there are a few ground rules you must remember. The first is to give short, crisp, one line-two line answers. Two, be courteous. Three, don't be aggressive. Contrary to what people think, if you are aggressive and agitated, you don't give a correct impression. Four, you must know what your own target audience through television is. ... And therefore, a lot depends on how you dress up to how you speak, the language which you speak and so on. All that matters.[77]

Jaitely's response reveals a nuanced understanding of the special demands of television communication. But politics on television is about more than just appearing on the screen and giving good sound-bites. It is also about knowing when to give the sound-bites and where. The television age politician knows which channels to target and when appearances are most fruitful. Jaitely specifically talks about targeting what he calls 'high-viewership days':

I think over-exposure on TV is counter-productive. People will get bored of your face. Don't allow that situation to come. Therefore your appearances on television should be during the high viewership day. If you are there 365 days a year, believe it, people are going to get bored of your face. Therefore, if there is an election, you must go more frequently. If there is an important political event, you must go. For important debate you must go, not otherwise.[78]

This sophisticated understanding of media flows and the mechanics of television programming distinguish the television politicians.

The new television politicians are best understood by juxtaposing them with those who couldn't adapt to the new medium. None is more prominent than Sitaram Kesri, Congress president between 1996 and 1998. There is a widespread consensus among politicians and journalists who covered him on a daily basis that his fall as Congress president was intrinsically linked to his misreading of television politics. Arun Jaitely, for instance, is unequivocal that 'Sitaram Kesri was destroyed by television.'[79] That assertion, by itself, may not hold up to a close analysis of his career. Kesri's fall as party president, which paved the way for Sonia Gandhi's entry into politics, can be linked to a variety of complex political reasons that extend beyond the terrain of television, like his lack of a popular political base. For our purposes, the fact that such an assertion could be made is significant, irrespective of its truth. Television arguably played an important role in the perceptions of Kesri and its treatment of Kesri merits a closer analysis.

Kesri's tenure as party president also coincided with the rise of private television news and he was one of the few Congress leaders who embraced it wholeheartedly. According to one veteran Congress reporter, 'he was the only Congress president in the past two decades who reporters could meet anytime . . . he would give bites to us on a daily basis'.[80] Television reporters were welcome in Kesri's house every evening and often his day-to-day politics unfolded in their presence, as in the case of his public battle with former prime minister Narasimha Rao:

A very famous incident happened when the Congress manifesto was being released and there was a very big press conference organised at 24, Akbar Road. He was asked a question, what will you do with Narsimha Rao? He suddenly said that I have cut his ticket. The problem was that some cameras were taking cutaways and did not record that statement, he said it so suddenly. Some of us journalists said, *chacha* please repeat it. He asked us why and we told him his comment didn't come on the camera.

So he said that for you people I will say it again: 'I have cut Narsimha Rao's ticket.' He set a deadline for 4 p.m. for Rao to resign from the CPP. And he kept announcing in front of the camera that see, the resignation has still not come. After some time, he asked for Rao's resignation by fax.[81]

From the television reporters' point of view, Kesri was a dream politician. Here was a Congress president who was cutting off his predecessor, and a former prime minister, from the party's apparatus and was engaging in backroom manoeuvres in front of the cameras. He was always accessible and did not mind doing all his politics in the glare of the camera. Yet, it was precisely this element of transparency that worked to Kesri's detriment. Unlike Arun Jaitely's nuanced understanding of the 'art of television' Kesri in person was Kesri on camera. He was being transparent but it did not translate well on television. A typical example is a speech he once gave on getting Sonia Gandhi back into Congress politics: '*Agar Sonia Gandhi aayengi to ham topi utaar denge aur kapra-vapra sab chor denge* [If Sonia Gandhi comes back I will take off my cap and will take off all my clothes].'[82]

It was idiom that would have worked well in a Bihar village. On television, it made Kesri look uncouth. It is statements like these that made television channels and the Congress treat Kesri like a 'buffoon'. According to a senior editor, it was because of 'the way he looked and the way he spoke'. Kesri's visual imagery became more dominant than his politics, at least in the perceptions of television editors:

The image becomes more dominant than the individual. In Kesri, the image was not of someone who for 40 years had been a Congressman. The image was of someone who was a buffoon within the Congress . . . who spoke in a sharp Bihari accent. His image got the better of his actual deeds. That perhaps let them down. You can create a positive image and you can create negative images. In the case of Kesri, television created very negative images of them.[83]

The negative visual imagery may have had no bearing on his party's political fortunes at the elections. The decline of the Congress in the 1990s is part of wider political and sociological changes since the 1980s, but it did become an important factor in the perception of him within Congress decision-making apparatus and within the media. His image as a bad communicator alienated influential sections within the party. So much so that when he resigned as party president, even his nameplate was removed from outside his office within five minutes of the decision.[84]

It is not that Kesri was a rustic leader who wasn't polished enough by television standards, like the urbane English-speaking and city-based Arun Jaitely. Television's negative imagery was less to do with Kesri's speech and more to do with his failure to understand the force of television's mediated publicness. This can be illustrated better when we compare Kesri to another Bihari politician, Laloo Prasad Yadav. Unlike Kesri, Laloo is a mass leader who rose to power in Bihar on the back of caste-based social mobilization. Laloo's mass communication skills played an important role in his rise as a backward caste leader, but his refusal to speak the English-idiom of the upper middle classes often led to him being caricatured in national media representations as a simple 'country-bumpkin' during his early years.[85] This was precisely the image that Laloo used to his advantage on satellite television. His particular kind of country humour became a hit with television audiences and Laloo became a favourite of producers because his presence on a programme could demonstrably lift ratings. For instance, as union railway minister, when Laloo presented the 2004 railway budget in Parliament, viewer ratings for that event recorded a 72 per cent hike.[86]

Like Kesri, Laloo is accessible to television reporters. When a parliamentary delegation visited Pakistan in 2003, Laloo received widespread coverage and a television reporter recalls his panic when his Delhi bosses suddenly asked him to make a half an hour special programme on Laloo's popularity in Pakistan on the eve of the delegation's scheduled return. He just did not have enough pictures to make such a programme, and Laloo was leaving early next morning. He frantically knocked on Laloo's hotel room at midnight and Laloo immediately obliged with a late-night walk across Lahore's streets. The reporter got his programme and the channel got its pictures of Laloo charming local Pakistanis in the dead of the night. Unlike Kesri though, Laloo makes a clear distinction between his day-to-day politics and what he choses to show on television. On camera, he plays the rustic wit and woos audiences, but he is extremely careful about what he says and how he appears. Unlike Kesri, his daily politics is conducted off the camera. It is not uncommon for him to make strong political statements on camera and then tell reporters as soon as it is switched off that these were only for public consumption, that the actual position was something else.[87]

Trade Dressings: National Political Parties and Television

In the lead up to the 1999 general election, India's two principal parties—Congress and the BJP—formally took note of the rise of satellite television and took the first physical steps to adapt to it. Both parties redesigned their media rooms in Delhi to look like television studios, complete with trans-lit backgrounds. These were 'trade-dressings',[88] specially tailored to make their spokespersons look good on air and to use the medium to impress the party colours on viewers.

By the 2004 general election, the BJP declared that it was fighting the general election as much from the sky (from the satellite channels) as from the ground (Mitra, 29 March 2004: online). This was India's first national election which featured political advertising on television, and its cornerstone was an expensive BJP media campaign—India Shining—which cost Rs 650,000,000 (roughly $14.2 million at September 2004 exchange rates). The BJP's campaign manager, the late Pramod Mahajan, proudly proclaimed before the election:

This is the first election of the 21st century. . . . Slowly, in 20–25 years—maybe not in the next five–10 years—roadshows, *yatras*, public meetings and other traditional forms of campaigning will all be done on the electronic media. How you present yourself on television, how you look, how you dress, how you talk will be the main thing.[89]

In the end, though, the BJP's television-centric focus failed spectacularly—and it lost the national election. The reasons for the BJP's

defeat in that election were varied and if anything, demonstrated the
pitfalls of over-reliance on television. Television is another conduit
for politics, it cannot substitute politics itself. The failure of the India
Shining campaign, notwithstanding its costly implementation, is
testament to the importance India's political parties gave to television
at the start of the twenty-first century.

A little noted fact about the 2004 election is that much like the
BJP, the Congress too focussed a great deal on television. Its tactics
differed from the ruling party but there is no doubt that the party
saw television as a primary campaign vehicle as well. This was a
key recommendation of a confidential party blueprint for the 2004
general election that was submitted to the Congress president by a
specially appointed five-member committee. Under the chairmanship
of minister Pranab Mukherjee, this committee, among other measures,
recommended 'electronic warfare':

With the electronic media having taken campaigning into an altogether new
dimension . . . the Congress must, as in developed democracies, resort to highly
professional and politically fine-tuned electronic election warfare. This must
be separately conceived at the national/state/constituency level, with particular
attention paid to city cable channels at the constituency level. . . . The national
campaign on well-known satellite channels should include spots featuring the
Party's major national leaders. . . .
      Much more effectively than traditional public rallies, street corner meetings
and door to door campaigning, it is the electronic media which in 21st century
India, as in all developed democracies, has to emerge as the premier campaign
media.[90]

The committee recommended specialized training for Congress leaders in the art of television and the setting up of a professional media
department.

Accordingly, the Congress evolved a multi-faceted television strategy. Key Congress leaders in Delhi went through special orientation
sessions with specially brought in television professionals. They were
trained in media techniques to make them look good on screen. A
senior Congress leader explains:

To a certain extent we did train people also. How to face media. . . . How to
impress the people, with a colourful shirt. . . . It was media people also who helped
us. . . . The important thing is how do you look. Otherwise, people comment . . .
us ka muh dekh kar din kharab ho gaya [did you see how bad his face looked]. . . .
You have to do the decoration. Decoration is the part of the event.[91]

The 'decoration', including wearing the right colours on screen, was
an important part of the Congress campaign. The Congress and the
BJP differed on campaign issues but their focus on television as a
premier campaign medium was no different.

CONCLUSION

In the Hollywood film *The Truman Show* the central character, played by Jim Carrey, grows up, without knowing it, on a monster television set designed to simulate the real world. The television programme is created for the benefit of a voyeuristic live television audience and every action of Carrey's character is closely documented round-the-clock by hidden cameras. He grows up to adulthood oblivious, and in the glare, of this publicity until he realizes that his entire life has been nothing but a giant simulation of reality. Indian politics today is somewhat like the real-life equivalent of a mutated version of *The Truman Show*. The camera is always focussed on the protagonists but the difference is that India's Trumans, the politicians, know that it is there. Also, the 'set' that the camera focuses on is not a giant make-believe but is constituted by slices of the everyday reality of the Indian condition. Television's structural make-up ensures that channels focus on certain aspects of the reality, but there is no denying the fact that it is impossible to imagine Indian politics today without the ubiquitous television camera and the chatter on news channels. News channels are a new factor in India's political equations and have altered the political matrix. Different politicians adopt different tactics to deal with 24-hour news but the publicity engendered by 24-hour news has ensured that Indian politics will never be the same again. Television feeds into existing nodes of social communication. Older traditions of argumentation and debate mix with the technology of television to mutate into argumentative television. The argumentative nature of news television is a positive addition to Indian democracy because it adds to a culture of debate and public reasoning.

The publicity of television though is not value-bound. It is amoral and bound to be interpreted, used and subverted in various ways. A good example is the case of the 2002 Gujarat riots where the complexity in the interface between television and politics was on full display. A detailed analysis is outside the scope of this essay but Gujarat's Hindu-Muslim riots were the first in the age of 24-hour television, and as I have argued elsewhere, the politics of public violence unfolded on and around television.[92] Television became a lightning conductor for existing social conditions and 24-hour live news fundamentally altered the dynamics of the violence. Television coverage was a far cry from the days when only the official version of such events would be transmitted over the airwaves through the state-owned broadcasting apparatus. Indeed, in contrast to the private networks, Doordarshan's coverage in the first days of the violence repeatedly emphasized that matters were under control:[93]

In 2002, exhaustive live coverage of the violence directly pitted the national networks against the ruling party and turned the violence into a national issue in a way that was simply not possible before. Television brought the riots into the living rooms of viewers across the country and ensured that every act in the violence was 'seen' and debated on a daily basis. As such, the networks emerged as a vital new cog in the deliberative structures of Indian democracy.[94]

Conversely, it is also true that even though the detail in the coverage by the private networks was largely unflattering to the BJP, the pictures of the violence were interpreted differently by different audiences, and within Gujarat, the BJP managed to mediate their meaning to its political advantage.[95]

While India's private television industry has grown at a furious pace in the past decade the task of unearthing its social impact has barely begun. It is clear, however, that 24-hour news networks are now a permanent and influential factor in the Indian polity and it is no longer possible to imagine India without them.

NOTES

1. These numbers are based on data from Union Ministry of Information and Broadcasting and its master list of 303 channels: 216 are licensed Indian private channels, 60 are foreign-owned and 27 are run by Doordarshan. Data is updated until 30 June 2007. Ministry of Information and Broadcasting (5 November 2005; 11 November 2006); URL (accessed on 30 June 2007): http://mib.nic.in/informationb/CODES/frames.htm and Ministry of Information and Broadcasting, *Answer to Lok Sabha Unstarred Question No. 2056* (9 March 2006), URL (consulted 29 May 2006): http://164.100.24.208/lsq14/quest.asp?qref = 26637.

2. For example, Chhattisgarh's 24-hour news channel Akash News, set up in 2003, was never registered with the Ministry of Information and Broadcasting. Across the country, numerous cable operators also broadcast local news in their localities, without permission from the ministry as such. A good example is Delhi's Vaishali TV, a digital television service for residents of the suburb of Vaishali. Its news items range from the availability of parking space in the local shopping plaza to events in local politics. I am grateful to Ravish Kumar for information on Vaishali TV.

3. Arvind Rajagopal, 'Thinking Through Emerging Markets: Brand Logics and the Cultural Forms of Political Society in India', *Social Text*, 60 (Autumn 1999), p. 133.

4. The most celebrated leftist view is Chomsky and Herman's propaganda model. For a liberal view, see for instance Michael Schudson, *The Sociology of News*, New York: Norton, 2003, pp. 45-55.

5. Michael Schudson, *The Power of News*, Cambridge, Mass: Harvard University Press, 1995, p. 15.

6. Procedural models of democracy focus on the systems and institutions of democracy as symbolized predominantly by the act of voting. See, for instance, Graeme Gill, *The Dynamics of Democratisation: Elites, Civil Society and the Transition Process,* London: Palgrave Macmillan, 2000; Beata Rozumilowicz, 'Democratic Change: A Theoretical Perspective', in Monroe Price, Beata Rozumilowicz and Stefaan G. Verhulst (eds.), *Media Reform: Democratising the Media, Democratising the State,* London: Routledge, 2002, pp. 9-26.

7. Amartya Sen, *Rationality and Freedom,* Cambridge, Mass: Belknap Press, 2002.

8. Jean Dreze and Amartya Sen, *Hunger and Public Action,* Oxford: Clarendon Press, 1989.

9. Jürgen Habermas, 'The Public Sphere: An Encyclopedia Article', in Meenakshi Gigi Durham and Douglas M. Kellner (eds.), *Media and Cultural Studies Key Works,* Oxford: Blackwell, 2001, pp. 102-7.

10. Habermas' public sphere has been criticized for a variety of exclusions like gender, class and other non-liberal non-bourgeois spheres. See, for instance, Joan Landes, *Women and the Public Sphere in the Age of the French Revolution,* Ithaca, NY: Cornell University Press, 1988; Geoff Eley, 'Nations, Publics, and Political Cultures: Placing Habermas in the Nineteenth Century', in Craig Calhoun (ed.), *Habermas and the Public Sphere,* Cambridge, Mass: MIT Press, 1992; Mary P. Ryan, *Women in Public: Between Banners and Ballots 1825-1880,* Baltimore: John Hopkins University Press, 1990.

11. See for instance, Richard Sennett, *The Fall of Public Man,* Cambridge: Cambridge University Press, 1974.

12. John B. Thomson, 'Social Theory and the Media', in David Crowley and David Mitchell (eds.), *Communication Theory Today,* Cambridge: Polity, 1998, 1st pub. 1994, pp. 27-49.

13. John B. Thompson, *The Media and Modernity: A Social Theory of the Media,* Cambridge: Polity Press, 1995, pp. 34-41.

14. Schudson, *The Power of News,* p. 17.

15. Ibid., pp. 22-5.

16. Amartya Sen, *The Argumentative Indian,* London: Penguin, 2005, p. 14.

17. Ibid., p. 12.

18. Jan-Uwe Rogge and Klaus Jensen, 'Everyday Life and Television in West Germany: An Empathic-Interpretive Perspective on the Family as a System', in James Lull (ed.), *World Families Watch Television,* Newbury Park: Sage, 1989, pp. 80-115; Gabriele Kruetzner and Ellen Seiter, 'Not All Soaps are Created Equal: Towards a Crosscultural Criticism of Television Serials', *Screen* 32, no. 2 (1991): pp. 154-72.

19. Sen, *The Argumentative Indian,* p. 30.

20. Ibid., p. 47. Sen quotes Jāvali from Makhanlal Sen, *Ramayana: From the Original Valmiki,* Calcutta: Rupa, 1989.

21. Sen, *The Argumentative Indian,* pp. 7-9.

22. For Akbar's tradition of debates see S.A.A. Rizvi, *Religious and Intellectual History of the Muslims in Akbar's Reign with Special Reference to Abu'l Fazl, 1556-1605,* Delhi: Munshiram Manoharlal, 1975, pp. 108-40, 203-22.

23. Sen, *The Argumentative Indian,* pp. 3-33, 47.

24. C.A. Bayly, *Empire & Information: Intelligence Gathering and Social Communication in India, 1780-1870,* Cambridge: Cambridge University Press, 1996, p. 2.

25. Ibid., pp. 181-5. See also the contributions in S. Freitag (ed.), *Aspects of the Public in Colonial South Asia, Journal of South Asian Studies* (Special Issue) 14, no. I (June 1991).
26. Bayly, *Empire and Information*, p. 92. The story of the marriage is told in great detail in William Dalrymple, *White Mughals: Love and Betrayal in Eighteenth Century India*, New York: Viking, 2003.
27. Bayly, *Empire and Information*, p. 206. In this context, see also Gyanendra Pandey, *The Construction of Communalism in Colonial North India*, Delhi: Oxford University Press, 1990, pp. 24-50.
28. Bayly, *Empire and Information*, pp. 191-2.
29. Ranajit Guha, *Elementary Aspects of Peasant Insurgency in Colonial India*, Delhi: OUP, 1983, pp. 258, 226-76. The quote is from J. Kay and G.B. Malleson. Rumour was not a uniquely Indian experience—all pre-literate societies experienced this phenomenon in some form and Guha specifically documents how it worked in the French Revolution.
30. Mark Tully, 'Broadcasting in India: An Under-Exploited Resource', in Asharani Mathur (ed.), *The Indian Media: Illusion, Delusion and Reality Essays in Honour of Prem Bhatia*, Delhi: Rupa, 2006, pp. 285-6.
31. Ibid., p. 287.
32. Dipesh Chakrabarty, *Provincializing Europe: Postcolonial Thought and Historical Difference*, Princeton: Princeton University Press, 2000, pp. 181-8.
33. Bayly, *Empire and Information* 1996, p. ix.
34. Sevanti Ninan, *Through the Magic Window: Television and Change in India*, Delhi: Penguin, 1995, pp. 60-1.
35. S.C. Bhatt, *Satellite Invasion of India*, Delhi: Gyan Publishing, 1994, pp. 215-16.
36. The average daily live audience count was estimated to be 500-1,500. Interview with Uday Shankar (Shanghai: 22 August 2005), CEO and Editor, STAR News, 2003-7.
37. Interview with Suman Chattopadhyay (Kolkata: 22 December 2005), Founding Editor, STAR Ananda.
38. Ibid.
39. Ibid.
40. John T. Little, 'Video Vacana: Swadhyaya and Sacred Tapes', in Lawrence A. Babb and Susan S. Wadley (eds.), *Media and Transformation of Religion in South Asia*, Philadelphia: University of Pennsylvania Press, 1995, pp. 254-83 and Philip Lutgendorf, 'All in the (Raghu) Family: A Video Epic in Cultural Context', in *Media and the Transformation of Religion in South Asia*, Philadelphia: University of Pennsylvania Press, 1995, pp. 217-53.
41. Shailaja Bajpai, 'It's TV Not Radio, Silence Sometimes Helps', *The Indian Express*, 26 September 2006, URL: http://www.indianexpress.com/story/13395.html (consulted 27 September 2006).
42. David Manning White ('The "Gatekeeper"—A Case Study in the Selection of News', in D.M. White and L.A. Dexter (eds.), *People, Society, and Mass Communications*, New York: Free Press, 1964, pp. 160-72) first used the term to denote an editor, 'Mr. Gates', of a mid-Western newspaper that he studied in a ground-breaking study on the crucial role of individual preferences in news selection.
43. G. Land and K. Lang, 'The Unique Perspective of Television and its Effect: A Pilot Study', in J. Corner and J. Hawthorn (eds.), *Communication Studies: An*

Introductory Reader, London: Arnold, 1953 (4th reprint 1993), p. 195.

44. Schudson, *The Sociology of News*, p. 48.
45. Centre for Advocacy and Research, Viewers Forum (2004), *Election 2004: Monitoring of TV Coverage*. URL: http://www.exchange4media.com/e4m/media_matter/matter_260604.asp (consulted 15 July 2006).
46. Paolo Carpignano, Robin Andersen, Stanley Aronowitz, and William DiFazio, 'Chatter in the Age of Electronic Reproduction Talk Television and the Public Mind', in Bruce Robbins (ed.), *The Phantom Public Sphere*, Minneapolis: University of Minnesota Press, 1993, pp. 108-10.
47. Ibid., Stephen Harrington, '"The Democracy of Conversation": The Panel and the Public Sphere', *Media International Australia incorporating Culture & Policy*, 116, Digital Anthropology (August 2005), pp. 75-87.
48. Harrington, 'The Democracy of Conversation', p. 75.
49. Ashis Nandy, *The Tao of Cricket: On Games of Destiny and the Destiny of the Games*, New York: Viking, 1989, p. 1.
50. Interview with Rajdeep Sardesai (Delhi: 25 January 2005), Managing Editor, NDTV, 1997-2004.
51. Interview with Pankaj Pachaury (Delhi: 9 January 2005), Senior Editor, NDTV India.
52. Ibid.
53. The shows were: *The Big Fight; The X Factor; We, The People; The Big Story; Small Talk; Chai Stop; University Talk* and *Village Voice*.
54. Christopher Pinney, *Photos of the Gods: The Printed Image and Political Struggle in India*. London: Reaktion Books, 2004, pp. 68-71.
55. Bayly, *Empire and Information*, p. 208.
56. Interview with Uday Shankar (Mumbai: 12 January 2005), CEO and Editor, STAR News 2003-7.
57. The NDTV shows are based on the popular BBC show *Spitting Image* that ran in Britain in the 1980s. Conversation with Arun Thapar (New Delhi: 20 December 2004), producer and presenter, *Double Take* and *Gustakhi Maaf,* NDTV.
58. Interview with Rajdeep Sardesai.
59. Carpignano et al., 'Chatter in the Age of Electronic Reproduction Talk Television and the Public Mind', p. 94.
60. Telecom Regulatory Authority of India, *Consultation Paper on Mobile Number Portability*, no. 7/2005, Delhi (22 July 2005), p. 3.
61. N.a. (25 February 2006) 'NDTV 24 × 7 Launches "Fight for Jessica Lal" SMS Campaign', URL: http://www.indiantelevision.com/headlines/y2k6/feb/feb315.htm (consulted 26 February 2006).
62. NDTV (n.d.), URL: http://www.ndtv.com/fightforjessica/jessicamessages.asp (consulted 30 October 2006) (n.a., 'NDTV 24 × 7 Launches "Fight for Jessica Lal" SMS campaign').
63. 'Delhi High Court Takes Up Jessica Lal Murder Case', *The Hindu*, 25 February 2006, URL: http://www.hindu.com/2006/02/25/stories/2006022514320100.htm (consulted 26 February 2006).
64. Omkar Singh (18 December 2006), 'Jessica Lal Case: Manu Sharma Convicted', URL: http://www.rediff.com/news/2006/dec/18jessica.htm (consulted 19 December 2006).
65. n.a., 'NDTV 24 × 7 Launches "Fight for Jessica Lal" SMS campaign'.
66. Jacob Adelman, 'U for U', *TIME Asia*, 12 July 2004.

67. Howard Rheingold, *Smart Mobs: The Next Social Revolution*, Cambridge, Mass: Perseus Publishing, 2003.
68. Rajdeep Sardesai, 'Sonia's "Sacrifice"', 4 April 2006, URL: http://www.ibnlive. com/blogs/rajdeepsardesai/1/7751/sonias-sacrifice.html (consulted 5 April 2006)
69. Interview with Uday Shankar (22 August 2005).
70. Ibid.
71. This, for instance, was an argument made forcefully by BBC World's main presenter Nick Gowing in 'Tyranny of Real Time: Cruel and Arbitrary', Asialink Lecture, Melbourne University, 28 August 2006.
72. J.S. Yadava and Zahoorul Haq, *Election Campaign: A Study*, Delhi: Indian Institute of Mass Communication, n.d., pp. 9-11.
73. Arvind Rajagopal, *Politics After Television: Religious Nationalism and the Reshaping of the Indian Public*, Cambridge: Cambridge University Press, 2001.
74. Interview with Arun Jaitely (Delhi, 24 January 2005), General Secretary, BJP.
75. Interview with Rajdeep Sardesai.
76. Interview with Prannoy Roy (Delhi, 28 October 2005), President and Wholetime Director, NDTV.
77. Interview with Arun Jaitely.
78. Ibid.
79. Ibid.
80. Interview with Manoranjan Bharti (Delhi, 25 January 2005), National Bureau Chief, NDTV India.
81. Ibid.
82. Ibid.
83. Interview with Rajdeep Sardesai (25 January 2005).
84. Interview with Manoranjan Bharti.
85. Sankarshan Thakur, *The Making of Laloo Prasad Yadav: The Unmaking of Bihar*, Delhi: Harper Collins, 2000.
86. PricewaterhouseCoopers, *The Indian Entertainment Industry: An Unfolding Opportunity*, Delhi: Federation of Indian Chambers of Commerce and Industry, March 2005, p. 54.
87. Interview with Bhupendra Chaubey (Delhi, 19 December 2006), Chief Political Correspondent, CNN-IBN.
88. Interview with Arun Jaitely. As BJP general secretary, Jaitely initiated the conversion of the BJP media room in 1999.
89. Interview with Pramod Mahajan on *The Big Fight*, NDTV 24 × 7 (telecast April 2004).
90. Pranab Mukherjee, Mani Shankar Aiyar, Prithviraj Chauhan, and P.R. Das Munsi, *Assembly Elections 2003: Evaluation Lok Sabha Elections 2004: Recommendations, Report Submitted by the Mukherjee Committee*, Delhi, 25 December 2003, p. 24.
91. Interview with Oscar Fernandes (New Delhi: 21 December 2004), General Secretary and Chairman, Central Election Authority, Congress (I); Union Minister of State (Independent Charge), Labour and Employment.
92. Nalin Mehta, 'Modi and the Camera: The Politics of Television in the 2002 Gujarat Riots', *South Asia: Journal of South Asian Studies* XXIX (3 December 2006): pp. 395-414.
93. Doordarshan largely followed the government line on Gujarat. Similarly, at the

All India Radio, a staffer was transferred when the radio network broadcast a critical discussion on the government's role. See generally, Aakar Patel, Dileep Padgaonkar, and B.G. Verghese, *Rights and Wrongs: Ordeal by Fire in the Killing Fields of Gujarat, Editors Guild Fact Finding Mission Report* (3 May 2002), Delhi.
94. Mehta, 'Modi and the Camera', p. 414.
95. Ibid.

7

New Culture at the Periphery: The Story of 'Musical North-East'[1]

RAKHEE BHATTACHARYA

Ethno-cultural identity is north-east India's strength. Each of the eight states of the north-east has evolved a unique form of ethno-culture which can mesmerize people with its marvellous rhythm, tune and aesthetics. Along with its astounding natural beauty, this rich ethno-culture could be the most important component for the region's economy, provided it is properly commercialized. But the people of the region have always favoured more preservation than commercialization, whereas the balance between the two could bring wonders here. Emphasis on preservation has over the years; created a closed mindset; the region has never tried to establish a link with India's 'mainland' culture, and thus has been forced to remain at the 'periphery'. People from the rest of India hardly know anything about this rich cultural diversity of this region, neither have the people of the north-east ever shown their interest for the 'mainstream' culture. Rather a Western cultural ambience, especially music, has dominated the region since the colonial era. This cultural distance from the rest of India is glaring. But a recent countrywide popular cultural force, viz., the musical reality show, has suddenly brought a phenomenal change in the region. This has dramatically transformed the image of north-east India's isolationist cultural identity and has brought the region closer to the mainland. The growth of satellite television, sponsorship and communication network along with the euphoria of the people have made this wonder to happen. It is therefore interesting to explore as to how popular music has set the tune of cultural transformation in the north-east and what role does the concept of economic gains play behind it. The present essay, in trying to address these questions, also examines whether a similar change has occurred in the mindset of the 'mainlanders' to break the regional barriers in the context of this changing phase of cultural perspective of north-east India.

CULTURAL PARADIGM OF NORTH-EAST INDIA: QUESTION OF TRADITIONAL IDENTITY

North-east India is traditionally known for its rich ethno-cultural diversity, which has made it distinctly different from the rest of India. The typical melodies, rhythms, tunes, instruments and aesthetics across its astoundingly beautiful hills and valleys constitute north-east India's most visible identity. This cultural pluralism,[2] which is one of the striking features of the north-east, has also manifested itself in its colourful social fabric. Since India's Independence, the question of modernization of north-east India and its linkages with the rest of India have always been contradicted with the preservation of the rich ethno-cultural identity. Nehru, for example, always felt the necessity of respecting 'tribal' sentiment:

The problem of tribal areas is to make the people feel that they have perfect freedom to live their own lives and to develop according to their wishes and genius. India to them should signify not only a protecting force but a liberating one. Any conception that is ruling them and that they are the ruled, or that customs and habits with which they are unfamiliar are going to be imposed upon them, will alienate them.[3]

Yet, after so many decades of Nehru's fantasy and policy about the north-east, it is clear to see that the dynamics of socio-cultural practices within the region have not always remained harmonious as intra-ethnic rivalries have surfaced over and over again. On the other hand, the idea of preservation and protection of their ethno-culture has become an imperative for the people of the region to realize the importance of cultural interaction and then convergence with the rest of India. The region has remained so confined within its indigenous cultural boundary[4] that even intra-regional cultural exchanges have never gained any momentum.

To the outsiders, north-east India has always been known for its bamboo culture. The region's culture is identified with the bamboo dance of Mizoram, Bihu dance of Assam, Naga dance of Nagaland, and Manipuri dance of Manipur. They are performed mainly during the Independence Day or Republic Day celebrations in New Delhi or on the national channel, Doordarshan. This apart, their songs, music, lyrics and dance have received attention by social anthropologists for academic research. But these unique cultural forms have never really got a chance to reach the mass of the Indian audience, except perhaps the Manipuri dance. Similarly, the 'mainstream' culture has also never been able to penetrate the region due to lack of response and interest. Even the closest neighbours of the north-east—West Bengal, known as the 'cultural capital of India' and Orissa, with its world famous tradition of dance—have hardly found any cultural space to interact with north-east India. This lack of exchange, interaction and knowledge about the world of *each other* has divided 'north-east India' from 'Other India' in terms of a cultural boundary. This boundary has eventually led to a cultural gap along with other socio-political and economic differences, and the region has got conveniently projected as an 'exclusive' territory of India. It has always mystified outsiders with its exclusivity and ethnicity, which is grossly different from that of others. This enormous cultural gap has created a typical *north-east* mindset, which has never showed any zest to establish any link with India's 'mainland' culture. This isolationist tendency, to a large extent, has kept the region on India's 'periphery'. People from 'Other India' hardly know anything about the rich cultural identity of this region, neither have the people of 'north-east India' ever displayed any interest for the 'mainland' culture, thereby both making themselves culturally distant from each other. The mindsets of the mainlanders and north-easterners have never converged.

The gap in traditional culture discussed above has gone hand in hand with a similar gulf in the pursuance of popular culture. For example, popular Indian songs and Bollywood music, which unite the 'Other India', surpasses even geographical boundaries to unite Indian diasporic community across the world, and has tremendous impact on all our Asian neighbours including Pakistan, could hardly make any impact on the people of north-east India. The main reason for this cultural gap is language; the mainstream Indian language Hindi is not the popularly spoken language in north-east India. Rather English is much widely spoken and is the accepted language due to the influence of Western missionary education since the colonial era. The people of the region, being more Westernized in language and manners, became fond of Western movies and music from the very beginning. Therefore, popular music in north-east India was primarily dominated by English songs and music, and most of the local people sing Western songs and play the Spanish guitar. The north-easterners' passion for music therefore implied love not for Indian but for Western music. Thus the ethnic identity and Western affinity in north-east India's music always kept the region in a different cultural space from the 'Other India', and there never existed any awareness to explore each other. Each lived with its own cultural specificity and within its own cultural domain. As Ashok Kumar Jha has argued:

The north-eastern region of India is as diverse as it is breathtakingly beautiful. Yet, most Indians have never tried to explore the region for various reasons, safety and security among them. The most striking reason, however, is the very low awareness about the region. Obsessed with Pakistan and the Kashmir valley, our national media only wakes to the concerns of the north-eastern region when there is a major terrorist strike or a natural catastrophe.[5]

To trace the reason, one needs to look at the history of the north-east, which can briefly be seen in three stages—pre-colonial, colonial and post-colonial. As Lal Dena has pointed out, during the *pre-colonial era*, except for the Meiteis of the Imphal valley and the Assamese in the Brahmaputra valley, the hill people remained essentially outside the orbit of India's Hinduism and its culture. Thus north-east India was not really included in the process of Indianization; rather it had much better connections with its East and South-East Asian neighbours.[6] Sanjiv Baruah has found strong ethnic and cultural affinities between the north-east and countries like Tibet, Bhutan, Burma and the Indo-China region, but not with mainland India.[7] This ethno-cultural bondage and connectivity got destroyed during the *colonial era*. For their economic and strategic interests, the colonial rulers ruthlessly isolated north-east India by drawing boundaries with its close South-East Asian allies, and introduced policies of distinction for the people of north-east from the rest of India. The British emphasized the concept of preserving 'tribal'[8] identity of the north-east. Since the region had never had any cultural link and geographical accessibility with other parts of India, its truncation from its close neighbours on the other side truly 'isloated' it. In the words of B.B. Kumar:

Their (colonials) policy of gradual segregation of the tribals and non-tribals, hills and the plains; segregation of the tribal population by introduction of the 'Inner Line Regulation', creation of 'non-regulated', 'backward' and 'excluded' areas/tracts was able to break centuries of historical, cultural, social and religious continuum and connectedness. The colonial theories/myths—the myth of race, core-fringe conflict, isolation—colonial misinterpretation of history and culture further deepened the impact.[9]

Such ruthless 'restructuring of north-east India' by the colonial rulers forced the region to remain at the periphery. Even in the *post-colonial era*, this peripheral status was rarely broken. Rather the north-east became further distanced from the mainstream due to its persistent political-economic swings along with Nehru's policy of protection. This set in motion a gradual resentment in the region that manifested in ways of separatism, secessionism, insurgency, and above all, hatred and denial of the 'mainland'. So over the years, any attempt at cultural convergence with the mainstream has been termed as 'cultural imperialism' by the new generations of north-east India. On the other hand, such gap in connection and understanding has also created misnomers in 'Other India' about 'north-east India'. As aptly argued by Mrinal Miri, there can be broadly two views of north-east India: the view from inside and the view from outside.[10] The outsiders' view imagines north-east as a unitary entity, inhabited by vaguely differentiated 'tribal' people who seem 'racially distinct' from Indians elsewhere. And the insiders' diverse view caters to tribes, communities, languages, ethnicity, culture, tradition, and so on. Miri has termed the insider's view as 'egocentric predicament'. Such egocentricity amongst insiders and misnomers amongst the outsiders have pathetically widened the problem of integration both within 'north-east India' as well as with 'Other India'.

To break such age-old cultural barrier of two Indias, affinities, understanding and contacts could have been the best modes, but unfortunately this has never really happened. The people of 'Other India' treated them as 'aliens' and the people of 'north-east India' treated the mainlanders as 'foreigners' in their soil. In the words of Kumar,[11] in north-east, 'colonial education and left ideology—as in Manipur—weakened nationalist feeling'. Instead of mainstream education, culture and nationalism, the north-east people started accepting and preferring missionary education and Western culture. Thus political discourse reshaped the cultural destiny of north-east India in all spheres, even in popular culture, which became vastly different from 'Other India'. Western singers like Bob Dylan instead of Indian singers like Kishore Kumar or Mukesh became icons in north-east India's popular music world. As mentioned rightly by Dasgupta,[12] when Dylan was awarded the Pulitzer Prize for his music, little did he know that for some people in eastern India, it was one of the proudest moments of their lives. Dylan made an incredible impact on north-east India's popular music. Lou Majaw, a singer from Shillong, the 'cultural capital of north-east', began the city's musical tradition of celebrating Bob Dylan's birthday in 1972 and ever since Shillong pulsates with Dylan music. To understand the euphoria of Dylan's music, Dasgupta[13] further mentioned that 'on 26 October 2007, Shillong hosted an ensemble of 1,730 guitarists, trying to break the Guinness record held by 1,721 musicians from Kansas City, Missouri, who had gathered in that Midwest American city to play Deep Purple's 'Smoke on the Water' the year before. Last fall, the Indian mountain air resonated with 'Knockin' on Heaven's Door', beating of the rhythm of every Meghalayan heart filled with love for Dylan.' To understand further the euphoria for Western music in north-east India, Jha[14] has reported that

Recently world famous musician Eric Martin reluctantly staged a show in Shillong and was surprised by the incredible response. More than 20,000 people thronged the venue and cheered the artist, who was amazed by their knowledge and fondness for Western music. Almost every youth in the region loves to play some instrument or the other, but guitar takes pride of place among them.

These incidents can reflect the degree of affinity and closeness of north-easterners towards Western popular music.

Interestingly enough, this Western cultural affinity is predominant only amongst the 'tribals' of the region but not necessarily amongst the 'non-tribals'. A large percentage of Bengali and other communities, who have settled here for generations, are not a part of north-east's popular Western culture. Thus, even within the region, the cultural divide is prominent amongst different communities. The widely acclaimed Tagore songs in India and overseas have hardly had any impact amongst the people of north-east, despite the fact that Bengalis are the second largest community in the region. This perception gap in the cultural domain has flared the distinctions between communities and resulted in animosity. Lack of 'Indianness' in the mindset and cultural paradigm of north-easterners, and lack of 'belongingness' in the mindset of 'outsiders' in the region has become a critical cause of conflict and division here. Communal violence due to other economic and political issues across the region over and again has further accentuated distrust and hatred amongst the communities. The two worlds of 'tribal' and 'non-tribal' have existed for years within the same geographical boundary, but in different identifiable cultural spaces.

SUDDEN CHANGE AT THE PERIPHERY:
INDIA'S POPULAR MUSIC AND REDEFINITION OF IDENTITY

The conflict, bloodshed and violence of north-east India has never found a peaceful solution since Independence, despite innumerable attempts and measures by the Indian government. Development initiatives along with additional benefits to the Scheduled Tribe population in the region have never broken the barrier with main-stream India. Hatred, grievances and resentment against the non-north-easterners have always remained. For example, in Meghalaya, the non-tribals are termed as *Dkhars* (outsiders) by the local tribals. But a silver line has recently shone in the region which has remained perpetually disturbed due to such conflicts. The region has transformed suddenly and now manifests itself as a cosmopolitan and harmonious land showing a spirit of tolerance and acceptance. This miracle has happened, at least in some of the states in north-east India like Meghalaya, and the messiah there is none but Amit Paul, the *Indian Idol* hero. Amit Paul from Shillong, set a new era in the north-east in the year 2007 when he made it to the final of the *Indian Idol* musical contest of Sony TV and became the first runner-up on the basis of public votes. Since then a magical transformation has occurred in the society of the region, and with this transformation, north-east India has entered into a new historical era—an era of *Indian Idol*. This era for the first time is marked by a spirit of *harmony* in the region.

As Jaideep Mazumdar has argued, the history of Meghalaya, granted statehood in 1972, can be divided into two distinct phases, before and after the *Indian Idol* contest.[15] The earlier phase of Meghalaya is identified with killings, riots, and violence against non-tribals; and the latter phase is seen as a return of harmony with cosmopolitan ethos. The agent of this transformation has been Amit Paul, a Meghalayan Bengali, whose family was driven out from a tribal locality during a gruesome communally violent incident in Shillong. It is ironical that the boy from an ostracized family could bring hope of unity and friendship between tribes and non-tribes, and bridge the gap of hatred with love and trust. The kind of mass mobilization that Amit has made possible amongst the people of Meghalaya, cutting across the barrier of tribal and non-tribal, has led to a cultural revolution in the state. The gathering for Amit Paul in the Khasi tribal locality, Mawlai, where non-tribals are simply non-existent, has surpassed the gathering of 20,000 for Eric Martin, the Western singer! An unprecedented number of Amit fans gathered and waited for hours for their idol. Once he reached the venue there was frenzy with teenagers and adults who started dancing and singing songs. The venue was packed with a 30,000 capacity crowd.[16] Thus a 24-year-old could finally break the age-old cultural boundary, reach the hearts of north-east India and make, for the first time, Indian popular music more *popular* than Western music in north-east India. The chief minister of Meghalaya was rightly enthusiastic, since no political equation had ever solved this conflict; he declared Amit as the 'brand ambassador for peace and harmony'. One must not forget here that before Amit, another north-easterner, Debojit Saha from Silchar, created similar cultural euphoria amongst Bengali and Assamese communities in Assam by winning the *Sa Re Ga Ma* title in 2005. He too helped to break the barrier between these two communities in Assam. In the words of Debojit, 'Amit Paul and I are both from north-east, a region hardly known to the outside world. We know the hurdles we have crossed to reach our desired destination.'[17]

Who played the key role behind such magnanimous success? It was none but India's private satellite television network, which deserves a big applause at this hour. Satellite television network has actually acted as the catalyst to penetrate into the heart of 'Isolated north-east India' and made it possible to shatter the 'Berlin wall' of tribal and non-tribal. It has also made possible a change in the xenophobic mindset of the north-easterners, at the same time reversing the attitude of 'Other India' towards this region. Amit's achievement made the people of north-east India feel proud of themselves when their region came into the limelight. The achievement came in a talent search drive which gave the talented singers of north-east India an opportunity to perform before the Indian audience. And most of them, enchanted and captured the hearts of 'Other India'. This is possibly the first time in history that the people of the region to expressed their joy and pride as a 'north-easterner' and the region spontaneously rejoiced as a singular identity, forgetting at least for that time being the other heterogeneous identities and conflicts. As Nalin Mehta has rightly argued, 'satellite television was the catalyst for this political mobilization and engendered new cultural processes in the context of identity formation in the north east.'[18] Mehta further asserts:

Amit Paul became a vital link for this process of reconciliation because his success in a national television competition, by bringing the north-eastern state, often relegated to the periphery in the mainstream consciousness, into the limelight, enabled a new mobilization based on the boundaries of the political map of the state, rather than one based on ethnicity.[19]

This TV show not only transformed the typical *north-east* mindset, but also transformed the *Other India* mindset about this region, and united the north-east diaspora across the globe. 'Tribalism',[20] considered to be one of the crucial ills of the region, affecting national unity for so long, got submerged in such remarkable achievement. North-east India is no longer identified and perceived as the 'periphery' of India, at least in the paradigm of India's popular music!

MONEY, MEDIA AND A *NUEVO CULTURE*

This cultural *renaissance* in north-east India, as already noted, became possible due to the boom of India's satellite television, which is a part of India's incredible progress in information and communication technology. The phenomenal achievement in technology and communication network has practically reshaped India's image in the world and has earned respect and repute. The pathbreaking success in IT and electronic media, which has reached to the remotest corner of the country today, along with the extensive use of other digital devices, have made an unbelievable impact on the everyday life of the nation. It has improved the regional connectivity, initiated people-to-people contacts, and established linkages amongst various non-state actors. This has undoubtedly created a *nuevo* sociocultural dynamics amongst the pan-Indians. The key player behind such transformation is India's recent economic success and its experiment with Liberalization-Privatization-Globalization (LPG). It is a fact that the story of India's economic growth due to its policy of LPG has not left any aspect of its society and culture untouched, not even its entertainment sector. Television, for example, can be regarded as one of the most successful arenas of India's LPG policy. The electronic media could never achieve optimum returns during the time of state ownership and monopoly. Ever since the sector was privatized, the scenario has magically changed due to the entry of competitive players with innovative ideas. Further, the induction of satellite television has enabled TV to reach every nook and corner of the country and to bring the Indians from all corners on one platform—that of popular culture. People in the remotest corner of Arunachal Pradesh of north-east India can now watch TV shows through satellite connection. The perspective of this audio-visual media has got transformed with the coverage of hundreds and thousands of audiences, and as a consequence the normal demand and supply equation has set in. The demand for more shows at the popular level began to increase, leading to competitive players with qualitative performance to capture the market.

Indian Idol is one such successful show in the current decade, which has created mass hysteria amongst the Indians, cutting across caste, class, region and religion. This show is an adaptation of *American Idol*, which was started by Simon Fuller in 2002 in America. Sony Entertainment Television bought the India rights from the makers of *American Idol* and created history. Every corner of India became a part of the contest, because it provided an opportunity to young musical talents to compete in this show. This has boosted the spirit of oneness and the euphoria of *Indianness*, especially amongst the youth. One can already sense the pride and confidence that Indians have gathered recently due to these commendable economic success. This *Indianness* is succinctly expressed in Stern's words:

The languages used in most mass media communications and in education at all levels are provincial, but most of the ostensible messages are Indians: in popular culture, current affairs, geography, history, the social science, sport, fun. The underlying message is: This is India and you are its citizens. [21]

Thus India's policy of privatization has undoubtedly given a 'fillip' to its 'entertainment sector' with unprecedented financial inflow. This adds another success story to India's ever-developing service sector, where creativity is being commercialized through the small screen and has opened the opportunities for talented Indian youths, even from small towns and the periphery. These opportunities in the long run are now looked upon as viable career options, as one can see a positive correlation between the expansion of economy with its incredible service sector and the earning opportunities for skilled persons. Artists of popular arts get fresh exposure and new scope and competition, which was a distant dream before, as the field was monopolized by a select few with their authoritative power nexus. TV channels, including Sony Entertainment, have brought in change by providing fair competition for singers from all parts of the country, along with wide economic incentives. Big business houses and corporates today do not hesitate to invest in such popular musical shows in the TV industry. The involvement of big money drives the entire team of these shows, from producers, sound recordists or set makers, singers, and judges, to perform well. Such commercialization of creativity, which is solely performance-oriented, provides space to young Indians to work hard.

A similar success story can be seen in cricket, now India's most popular sport, which has been on upward track by dint of a successful shift to the commercial paradigm, known as the Indian Premier League. Players are auctioned in the open market on the basis of their performance. Investments in such entertainment sectors through sponsorships or ownerships have become one of the most lucrative options for big companies and businesses today, since the returns are assured, given the game's huge popularity and the lucrative sponsorship opportunities through satellite television.

The other significant business space, as relevant to the present discussion, has been created through India's mobile phone network. This new communication mode is fast making the world flatter, where a new generation has emerged with global and modern identity which cuts the barrier of regionalism and ethnicity. The role of mobile phones has become indispensable in these popular TV shows, as the voice of audiences has become more important than the verdict of judges for the singers. Making public opinion polls and giving the voting rights to the audience to choose their favourite singer through SMS or calls from mobile phones has boosted financial flows tremendously. Crores of rupees are being generated through such programmes, and network companies like BSNL, Airtel, Hutch and Reliance could see their fortunes touching the sky! Thus the prospect of huge economic gains actually fuels such popular programmes. It is estimated that 70 million votes were received on SMS or over phone lines for the winner of the *Indian Idol* in 2007—Prasant Tamang of Darjeeling. Crores of rupees were spent by the business persons to set up phone booths to enable the people to vote for their favourite contestant.

Information and communication network has undeniably set in a new era of human civilization and modernity, in which mass mobilization is possible through the electronic media. Even two decades ago, India could never dream of such a scenario. Digital devices are now the prime actors to expand the modern service sector, which embraces even various aspects of popular culture like music, movies, sports, and other shows, thereby helping enormously to create an urban professional middle class. India's tremendous success in IT and ITES has already given country a sense of pride. Its emerging 'knowledge economy' has given birth to a strong empowered middle class. This class can now think beyond the bare necessities of life, and can spend on creativity and entertainment; thus their aspirations and dreams have also soared high. This 'knowledge economy' has given a strong back-up to our 'entertainment economy' through its skills, technologies and network, and now the two compliment each other.

The roles, functions and aspirations of the emerging middle class can very well be reflected in their expenditure pattern. As Leela Fernandes has argued:

While emerging opportunities for the consumption of newly available commodities represent the public face of the benefits of economic liberalization, the central figure in such representation of consumption is the urban middle class. The urban middle class, in effect, represents a hegemonic socio-cultural embodiment of India's transition to a committed liberalizing nation.[22]

For example, conscious, aware and capable urban middle class parents are keen to spend more money on their children's competence and all-round development. The propensity to spend therefore has multiplied in urban India, ranging from better and higher education to sports, modelling and other popular activities, which were never in the priority of spending before. Shows like *Indian Idol* or *Miss India* are the eye openers, which provided the space to fulfil the aspirations of urban Indian parents of the twenty-first century!

CONCLUSION: TOWARDS AN *INCREDIBLE INDIA*

It is time therefore revisit and re-examine the components and patterns of expenditure in the emerging middle class of urban India. Apart from traditional food and durable items, Indians are now spending more on quality education, better health, increasing entertainment and expanding creativity, which in the long run will give a boost to the capability index. This will widen the freedom of choice for the next generation of India. More importantly, it breaks the barrier of India's traditional gender perspective. Thus, the estimation of expenditure on traditional education for average Indian urban household should be replaced by the estimation of expenditure on modern skills for such households. 'Skills' can include education and other creative endowments which are popularly accepted by average urban Indians today but were considered to be social taboos before. This expenditure on individual skill building in urban India in all possibility will find a much higher figure today than it was two decades before. This reflects that *India is Changing* along with an improved level of living and an open mindset. So, for an average urban Indian, the propensity to spend is no longer limited to traditional food and non-food durable items like cars. In fact, it has extended to even non-traditional heads like creativity, popular culture, travelling and other entertainments. The economic stability of this emerging class is the engine behind the success story of modern India, which is dismantling all the regional barriers, ethnicities and conflicts, replacing these with a modern identity and based on a new culture which has the force to unite the people in one forum that is *India*, and may well give another chance to the rest of world to say *Incredible India*!

NOTES

1. The phrase 'Musical North-east' was first used by Ashok Kumar Jha in his article entitled 'India's Musical North-east', *Ohmy News*, 2007, available at http://english.ohmynews.com/articleview/article_view.asp?at_code = 432504 &no = 380894&rel_no = 1
2. Niru Hazarika, 'Ethnic Autonomy: A Challenge to Indian Democracy', in B.B. Kumar (ed.), *Problems of Ethnicity in the North-East India*, Delhi: Concept Publishing Company, 2007, p. 110.
3. Nehru wrote the foreword to Verrier Elwin's *Philosophy of NEFA*, Shillong: NEFA Administration, 1957, cited by H.N. Das, 'Ethnic Aspirations and Insurgency in the North-Eastern Region of India', in Kumar, *Problems of Ethnicity in the North-East India*, p. 84.
4. The term 'Cultural Boundary' is used by S.M. Patnaik in his article 'Tribe and Problem of Cultural Boundary', in S.K. Chaudhury and S.M. Patnaik (eds.),

Indian Tribes and the Mainstream, New Delhi: Rawat Publications, 2008, p. 53.

5. Jha, 'India's Musical North-east'.

6. Lal Dena, *In Search of Identity: Hmars of North-East India*, Delhi: Akanksha Publishing House, 2008.

7. S. Baruah, 'Between South and Southeast Asia North-east India and Look East Policy', Ceniseas Paper 4, Guwahati, p. 198.

8. For more layers on this, see S.K. Choudhury and S.M. Patnaik, 'Introduction', in Choudhury and Patnaik, *Indian Tribes and the Mainstream*, p. 2.

9. B.B. Kumar 'Ethnicity and Insurgency in India's North-East', in B.B. Kumar (ed.), *Problems of Ethnicity in the North-East India*, Concept Publishing Company, Delhi, 2007, p. 17.

10. Mrinal Miri 'Two Views of the North-East', in B.B. Kumar (ed.), *Problems of Ethnicity in the North-East India*, Delhi: Concept Publishing Company, 2007, p. 3.

11. B.B. Kumar, 'Ethnicity and Insurgency in India's North-East', in Kumar, *Problems of Ethnicity in the North-East India*, p. 17.

12. Ruma Dasgupta, 'Love of Dylan', *Span*, XLIX, no. 3, May-June 2008.

13. Ibid.

14. Jha, 'India's Musical North-east'.

15. Jaideep Mazumdar, 'The Hills are Alive: A Local Lad on National TV Unites a State', *Outlook*, 1 October 2007.

16. *Shillong Times* (a local daily), 29 September 2007.

17. Quoted by Anand Soonda, 'Meghalaya, Darjeeling in India an Idol Frenzy', 13 September 2007, available at www.singlung.com/print/897.html

18. Nalin Mehta, 'Introduction: Satellite Television, Identity and Globalization in Contemporary India', in *Television in India: Satellites, Politics and Cultural Change*, London: Routledge, 2008, pp. 1-12.

19. Ibid.

20. Dena, *In Serach of Identity*, p. 176.

21. Robert W. Stern, *Changing India: Bourgeois Revolution on the Subcontinent*, 2nd edn., Cambridge: Cambridge University Press, 2003, p. 31.

22. Leela Fernandes, *India's New Middle Class: Democratic Politics in an Era of Economic Reform*, London: University of Minnesota Press, 2006, p. 137.

8

Nationalism and Entertainment: A Study of Colonial Bengali and Gujarati Theatres

SUNETRA MITRA

INTRODUCTION

The emergence of the modern play and public theatre in colonial Bengal and Gujarat was an urban phenomenon and should be seen in the background of a much wider process involving the rediscovery of classical literature and the modernization of regional societies and politics. The public theatre evolved from the assimilation of local theatrical forms and practices which had been in vogue for long and novel organizational and theatrical features borrowed from the English play houses. New features that were incorporated into the public stage were the management of theatre companies as business enterprises, the practice of ticket sales and the introduction of new visual stage settings and props borrowed from the nineteenth-century Victorian stage. The essentially patriotic character (as revealed from the content of the plays) of the public stage demonstrates it was deliberately and necessarily selective about what it took from the West. The plays that were staged questioned the veracity of colonialist knowledge, disputed its arguments, pointed out contradictions, and rejected its moral claims. Even when it adopted the modes of thought characteristic of rational knowledge in the post-Enlightenment age, it could not adopt them in their entirety, for then it could not constitute itself as a nationalist discourse.[1] The public stage with its offerings based on well-known stories from myths and legends, combining heroic characters, themes of romantic love with an endless scope for commercial gains, fulfilled the urgent need for entertainment that amalgamated aspirations to high taste, entertainment and popular sentiment. The reach of the new literacy was hardly enough to sustain a radically novel prose drama. Not surprisingly therefore the turning to tradition and history was a vital element of theatrical and artistic innovation in the last decades of the nineteenth century. This essay, in an attempt to explore the interconnectedness between colonial theatre, nationalism and entertainment in colonial Bengal and Gujarat, examines the way nationalism as an ideology was suited to the formation of theatre and later appropriated to further the pecuniary gains from theatre.

THE NATION STAGED

The need for native theatres—whether Bengali, Parsi or Gujarati— was felt in the first quarter of the nineteenth century. Initially there was a strong emphasis on producing English plays which eventually gave way to vernacular plays. The trend towards indigenous themes and adoption of vernacular as the medium of exchange was encouraged by the process of cultural rediscovery which was on full swing then. The natives were searching for a self-identity that could take them beyond the humiliation of being ruled. Taking the cue from the scholarship of British Orientalists and the work of institutions like the Asiatic Society of Bengal and the Gujarati Vernacular Society, several members of Bengali and Gujarati literature became serious and proud scholars of Indian antiquity.

When the tenets and principles of Western drama started influencing Bengali and Gujarati theatre (both Parsi as well Gujarati) there was a strong inclination for indigenous texts and subjects, which continued to thrive and find various avenues of expressing itself even in the midst of Western style of theatre that had been adopted by the Indians. Sudipto Chatterjee, writing in the context of development of Bengali theatre, observes that the literati were confronted with two compelling factors in their desire to refashion a compensatory national identity. While on one side stood the great tradition of Sanskrit theatre, its plays and their need to be translated and/or emulated, on the other side there was the example of colonial English theatres of Calcutta, their plays and mostly their proscenium stage whose mode of production, as the natives thought, was a good idea to follow.

Gujarati theatre too appropriated many techniques of Victorian stagecraft and fed off the imperial image of the Raj. It responded to the challenges of modernity by using drama for the revival of vernacular traditions. Efforts at appropriation and imitation, a quest for identity and search for roots could be noted in Gujarati theatre as well. Towards the second half of the nineteenth century, the beginning of Gujarati theatre (Parsi-Gujarati theatres initially and then the emergence of Gujarati theatre) had marked a new epoch in the urban life of Bombay and its public culture. Initially, it was Bombay's merchants (a considerable section of whom consisted of Parsis and Gujaratis who had migrated to Bombay following Gujarat's merger with Bombay Presidency in 1818),[2] who pressed for theatre as an enhancement of civil society, a source of 'good humour' and 'desirable tone of feeling'.[3] Between 1842 and 1878, following the English theatre pattern and Parsi groups' adaptations, the Gujaratis independently started their theatrical activities. They too began with translated English plays but gradually, playwrights felt encouraged to compose plays based on mythological and historical themes, a trend that continued henceforth. According to Hasmukh Baradi, the noted Gujarati thespian and theatre historian, the process should be viewed as an endeavour made by various theatre companies to probe and evaluate the extraordinary profession of drama not only as an instrument for earning money but also for cultivating taste, and for testing it as an instrument to gratify the popular inner urge for fun, adventure and entertainment.[4]

THEATRE IN BENGAL

The Dramatic Performances Control Act effectively marked the end of direct political activism, what little had been demonstrated in the Bengali public theatre, although some plays continued to be proscribed at the slightest hint of any seditious intent. Thereafter, most plays produced by the commercial companies looked mainly at making money. Garrulous advertisements to attract bigger audiences became commonplace. Making plays commercially viable became the biggest concern for even director-producers like Girish Chandra Ghosh. Ghosh was one of the leading dramatists and director-actor-trainers of the Bengali public theatre in its first phase. His forced transformation into a playwright was a stroke of good fortune for Bengali theatre since it was his huge dramatic corpus that finally gave to Bengali theatre what Dutta had earlier called 'a body of sound classical dramas to regulate the national taste'.[5] Chatterjee points out that the question of 'national taste' dominated Girish Ghosh's thinking. Defending the role and position of the actor in a conservative society, he wrote:

{I}f we in the theatre can explain to (the society) . . . that the discipline of the actor is, like all other disciplines, expressive of the nation's civilization—only then will the actor win the respect he deserves, the prize of his life long striving, the fruits of his single minded dedication from a civilized society.[6]

To make the theatre 'expressive of the nation's civilization' was a daunting task and cannot be achieved through simple historical dramas, blindly religious mythological plays, socio-satiric farces and social tragedies. Girish Ghosh had thought of a theatre that would be far above the ordinary. Stage for him was more a reality of the mind, a commentary on the social realities. He constantly used metaphors that examined the socio-historical moment he was living in. Aesthetically, comments Sudipto Chatterjee, Ghosh's feet were on two rocking boats at the same time, Western dramaturgy and Indian aesthetics.

Ghosh's plays were packed with socio-political significance. For example, in *Sribatsa-Cinta*, Ghosh expressed the need for violent political upheaval. Utpal Dutt, Bengal's much revered thespian, noted that it is the French Revolution that Ghosh was talking about in *Sribatsa-Cinta*, where the macrocosm of the gods is integrated with the human world.[7] In the 1890s, when Ghosh wrote and directed *Chanda*, it dealt once again with the theme of revolution and political intrigue. In this play, Ghosh displayed his ability to analyse dictatorial regimes, a lesson he must have drawn from observing the situation then in India. *Chanda* narrowly escaped proscription on account of being a historical play but *Siraj-ud Daula* (1905), *Mir Qasim* (1906) and *Chattrapati Shivaji* (1907) being more explicit in their content were all banned by the Dramatic Performances Control Act. While *Chanda* and *Chatrapati Shivaji* were plays set in pre-British India, *Siraj-ud Daula* and *Mir Qasim* were directly about how the British came to rule Bengal.[8] Thus the latter were banned with good reason on the part of the government. In the last two plays Ghosh did not use metaphor, the subject itself was metaphoric. Siraj was the last independent ruler of Bengal who lost the Battle of Plassey more due to treachery than chivalry of his enemies. The story of *Mir Qasim* on the other hand was that of a titular head who saw his kingdom being destroyed as his power to save it. Both plays presented history with great accuracy and patriotic fervour that it became difficult for the British administration to ignore them. The plays were considered politically provocative and consequently proscribed.[9]

Bengali theatre in the age of Girish Ghosh went far beyond the prescribed parameters of the 'babu theatre' (theatre patronized by Bengali babus or gentlemen). It embraced a wider audience and preferences as its ingredients. And having attained its own autonomous status as valid artistic/performative articulation, this theatre of the last quarter of the nineteenth century was necessarily responding to the socio-political situation. The development of this theatre coincided with the growth of 'culture industry' as a business sector. As theatre business became more lucrative, it came to justify itself in business terms defined by popular hits. In many instances, therefore, the power of market economics reduced the theatre and its projected themes as ideological strategy rather than the realization of a national imperative. This nexus between theatre and commercialism becomes evident in the context of the plays that were written and staged for production by Girish Ghosh and Amarendranath Dutta between 1903 and 1910, the heydays of nationalism in Bengal. This was the period when social and religious movements, so prominent down to the 1870s, were being swamped by a rising tide of revivalism, which was again intimately bound up with the emergence of more extreme varieties of nationalism.[10] A new controversy over cultural ideals, between modernistic and Hindu-revivalist trends emerged. The Swadeshi mood in general was closely associated with attempts to combine politics with religious revivalism, which was repeatedly used as a morale booster for activists and a principal instrument of mass contact. Increasingly, Hinduism was sought to be used as the principal bridge to the masses, appealing both to the imagination as well as to fear.[11] This trend was reflected in the theatres of Girish Ghosh, who despite his ideological position used the same for furthering the economic gains of the theatre where he worked as an employee.[12] Time and again Girish Ghosh bemoaned the fact that theatre had become subject to the commercial aspirations of the theatre owners. Theatre management appreciated the popularity of such themes and emphasized staging plays with similar contents to earn more revenues. The leading theatres of the city—the Star, Emerald, Classic—fully utilized the favourable situation created by the popularity of these plays. Correspondingly, there was a surge of such plays and very soon the mythological plays were replaced by more tangible, historical accounts that dealt with characters from history. While these plays definitely strengthened the financial base of the theatre companies, the authenticity and quality of the plays deteriorated correspondingly. Sensationalism and gimmicks became the hallmark of the historical plays. These plays and many of the lesser directors and theatre managements capitalized on the sentiments that had swept across the length and breadth of the country, thus exploiting the appeal of nationalism and using it as a saleable commodity, comments Apareshchandra Mukhopadhyay. Apareshchandra explains how these so-called historical plays were envisaged and put on stage. He says that while depicting a particular historical character a few 'platform speakers' were created. These characters were mere protagonists and hardly different from others. Almost invariably one would find two opposing camps—the oppressor and the oppressed. One group sacrificing their lives for their motherland while the other group opposing such moves. Thus the historical plays came to represent stereotypes that only counted on the instant excitement they could generate among the public. The audience was carried away by such depictions but the plays could not have a lasting impression on their minds. Girishchandra lamented, 'These days I no longer pen down plays, rather scribble down a few scenes filled with excitement. The management keeps the ones that suits their taste and need and scraps the rest.'[13]

Drawing upon historical subjects was readily adopted by the theatre companies as the easy path to quick success and popularity. Apareshchandra notes that so popular and easy had this trend in historical depiction become that even a young boy studying in Standard Three could come up with a full-fledged play that was staged and had considerable viewership! Neither the audience nor the critics raised their voice against such a tendency. Before this, playwrights hesitated about the quality of their plays, but the surge of nationalism broke all dams of restraint as in the bid to save the motherland there emerged new playwrights almost overnight. It is, however, undeniable that these budding playwrights did revive and receive an opportunity to alter their economic well-being. And it can be safely inferred that unless these theatres had great pecuniary potentials a number of theatres would have been compelled to pull down their shutters.[14] Apareshchandra Mukhopadhyay further notes that the year 1905 heralded the 'historic age' in Bengali theatre. He particularly mentions the contributions of Bankimchandra Chattopadhyay in literature and Girish Ghosh in theatre in translating the spirit of nationalism to these very powerful conduits of public opinion. Apareshchandra notes that the success of the play *Siraj-ud Daula* reversed the sagging fortunes of the Minerva Theatre. Prior to the staging of *Siraj-ud Daula* Minerva had a sale of tickets worth Rs 150 or 200. But *Siraj-ud Daula* saw the proceeds soaring to Rs 1,500.[15] Apareshchandra records the sale of tickets thus:

the play *Siraj-ud Daula* opened on 24 Bhadra 1312 (September 1905).

Sale of tickets for Siraj-ud Daula

1st night	Rs 821
2nd night	Rs 798
3rd night	Rs 773

It ran for a total of twenty-five nights. On an average the play had a sale of Rs 700 per night on all the twenty-five days of its performance. The last time the play was staged has been dated 19 Falgun 1312 (February 1903) and the sale of tickets recorded was Rs 361. On the first night of the play a Muslim audience composed two lines in praise of Girish Chandra which said, 'O Girishchandra, please accept the blessings of the entire Muslim community' (p. 125).

He regretted that Mir Qasim had to flee from the battlefield after suffering defeats and on each occasion the same dialogue was repeated, 'Unless I made an exit, who would protect Bengal?' Every time the dialogue was repeated the audience burst into thunderous applause. The play *Mir Qasim* opened on June 16, 1906.

Sale of tickets for Mir Qasim

1st night	Rs 1,080
2nd night	Rs 1,016
3rd night	Rs 1,015
4th night	Rs 1,028
Last show	Rs 570

Like *Siraj-ud Daula*, *Mir Qasim* ran continuously for more than twenty-five nights. The average sale of the tickets per night was nine hundred rupees. Compared to *Siraj-ud Daula* the sale was more by two hundred rupees.

Rival theatre companies of the time notably Star tried to compete with Minerva. The Star came up with *Palashir Prayaschitta* written by Kshirodprasad Vidyabinod. It opened on the sixth night of *Mir Qasim* at Minerva. The plays though had Mir Qasim as the central character, the stories were substantially different and hence no comparison can be made so far as the plot was concerned. Both the plays had been banned by the British government and hence had aroused much interest among the audience. But *Palashir Prayaschitta* failed to generate much enthusiasm and from the financial standpoint it not very successful. The other historical play *Nurjahan,* written by Dwijendralal Ray, opened in March 1905 with much fanfare. The proceeds from the sale of tickets were remarkable the first few nights after which the sale plummeted considerably and by the eighth night it came down to Rs 136. On the ninth show together with *Alibaba* it managed to make a mere Rs 349. Minerva landed in a crisis. However, when *Nurjahan* was tagged with *Toofani* the sale once again rose and, on the tenth night of its performance, the sale went up to Rs 630. The sale gradually increased to Rs 1,000. Dwijendralal Ray's later plays like *Mebar Patan* (Fall of Mewar) introduced in the stage the notion of universal brotherhood against the background of Mughal-Rajput conflict. The other play *Rana Pratap Singha* too touched upon this notion. The plays proved successful commercially. Of course, a lot of compromises were affected keeping in mind the audience taste and preferences.

However, the competition that ensued over the depiction of historical plays remains incomplete without referring to the play *Protapaditya* of Kshirodprasad Vidyabinod, the play first put up by the Star Theatre on Saturday 15 August 1903. Amarendranath put up the play by the same name rendered suitable for stage production by Haranchandra Chakravarty on 29 August 1903 at the Classic Theatre. *Protapaditya* had been instrumental in restoring the reputation of Star, which was passing through an extremely bad patch. However when pitted against Classic it was no match. The sale of tickets at Classic soon surpassed the sale at Star. During the time when advance sale of tickets had not yet become a regular practice, people queued up at the Classic from 2 p.m. onwards. On the second day of opening of the play, overwhelmed by the rush for tickets, the ticket seller at the counter went to Amarendranath for solution. On Amarendranath's instruction, counters were to be opened from 2 p.m. since then. The sheer volume of tickets sold spurred Amarendranath to bring out the following advertisement:

We did not sing ourselves our own victory. The fact of our tickets even upto Four-Rupee ones being entirely disposed of long before 8 p.m. on both the first and the second nights—indicates our position. All the leading actors and actresses are Classic's own; hence the success! The others they simply beat the air—because, lame cannot jump, a blind cannot paint, a dumb cannot sing, never if he tries his best.[16]

Protapaditya at Star was equally successful and it went houseful on successive shows. But while 'full house' Star recorded a total sale of Rs 600 to 800, Classic would record a sale of Rs 1,800 to 2,200. The Star could never imagine the extent of sale to such level. In fact, when Amarendranath, after taking over Star Theatre, increased the sale of tickets to Rs 2,000, one of the proprietors of the Star Theatre, Hariprasad Basu told Amarendranath: 'When we used hear from people that people are lampooning at the Classic and the sale goes up to Rs 1,800 to 2,200 and so on successive days, we ruled it out as unreal. Now we see that such huge sale is not poetic imagination rather quite a possible feat.'[17] However, that happened later and there ensued cut-throat competition between the two companies. The newspaper reviews that came out invariably compared the rendition of the plays by the two rival groups. The *Indian Mirror* of 16 September 1903 wrote,

... Taken as a whole, *Protapaditya* is one of the most successful historical plays ever produced on the boards of Classic Theatre. Faults it has no doubt, but in view of the educational effects of the theme on the present-day Bengalees, and the masterful manner in which that theme has been worked upon, one might unhesitatingly exclaim, as Cowper did with regard to England,—'With all my faults I love thee still'.[18]

The *Bangabasi* of 26 Bhadra 1310 (September 1903) thus commented about the play at Classic: 'We are pleased to watch the performance of Pratap at Classic. Amarendranath himself is Pratap. . . .'[19]

Rangalay discussed the merits and demerits of plays performed at the Star and Classic from a comparative angle,

Now we will discuss the two Pratap's. Pratap at Star recites well but often it hears like sermon. Pratap at Classic well matched the role, good at dialogue delivery and acts well too. But he suffered from slippages in intonation and accentuation. Many a times the dialogues did not synchronize well. Classic's Pratap is not a dedicated actor. He is an artist true, but he avoids hard work. He lacks an eye towards detail and once he manages to overcome these limitations, Classic's Pratap would become incomparable. Despite these shortcomings Classic's Pratap invokes interest—one wants to see and hear him perform. Personal magnetism, which is like an asset for the actor, Classic's Pratap seems to have it in abundance. Pratap at Star lacks vitality and is morbid. Classic's Pratap is animated, there is no trace of morbidity anywhere. Classic's Pratap better served the purpose for which the plays have been put up at Star and Classic . . . Star basks in age-old charm, in Classic one sees youth and vigour. Star is restrained, Classic is brimming with exuberance. People will judge the plays according to their tastes and preferences. We preferred the acting at Classic.[20]

The other play of this genre that aroused intense public interest as well as reflects the spirit of competition among theatre groups comes out very neatly from the staging of the play *Chattrapati*. *Chattrapati* directed and written by Girish Ghosh opened at Kohinoor Theatre on 15 September 1907, *Chattrapati* being enacted by Danibabu. Amarendranath too was staging the play at Minerva, himself playing the title role. The depiction of the same character by two eminent actors created a sensation among the viewers. On this occasion as well Amarendranath stole the show. Minerva Theatre once again scored a resounding victory. The handbill that came out shortly after this proudly proclaimed:

Glorious Victory! Grand success in competition! The hour of trial is over! We are proud to acknowledge with thanks the unanimous verdict of public opinion, which declared itself unmistakably in favour of the success of our performance and it is with no small satisfaction that we find that chorus of acclamation and unbounded admiration with which our reference was hailed by an admiring press was but the precursor of the still more glorious success, which we have achieved in the open field of competition and that our thrilling performance which has already excited the enthusiasm of our friends and the envy of our enemies is now declared even by the most fastidious critic to be decidedly the Best.[21]

Even the *Statesman*, published and edited by an English, wrote on 17 November 1907:

The popularity of *Chattrapati* is manifest from the large audience which are attracted to the Minerva Theatre on every occasion that this thrilling play is billed. Though it has been running for about ten weeks now, the large auditorium was crammed in every part and early in the evening the sale of tickets had to be stopped, the large overflow helping to fill the adjacent play-houses. Babu Amarendro Nath Dutt was in excellent form and the entire company played up to his high standard.[22]

The way nationalism was used as an effective way of pulling audience becomes evident from the way a victory over the colonizers by a native football team was used for advertising the successful running of a play, thereby heightening its appeal. The play was *Baji Rao*, the Maratha Peshwa at the Great National Theatre which was then working under the tutelage of Amarendranath Dutt. On its opening night, Mohun Bagan, one of the oldest football clubs of Calcutta and India, scored a victory over East Yorkshire and won the Indian Football Association Shield—no mean achievement by a native football team. The victory of Mohun Bagan had been a moment of victory for the natives for it shattered the myth of the invincibility of the dominant master race. Even an hour before the play started, very few seats had been filled up but in the next one hour an unprecedented rush of audience created history. The audience, carried away at the victory of Mohun Bagan, were equally swept by the phenomenal acting and rendition of the play. The following Saturday Amarendranath Dutt, the director and hero of the play, brought out an advertisement which read: 'Mohun Bagan has won the Shield, *Baji Rao* has gained the victory.'

With the opening of *Baji Rao* at the Great National Theatre, Minerva staged *Chandragupta* of Dwijendralal Ray. But in its competition with *Baji Rao*, Minerva landed into severe financial difficulties. Despite being such a well written play *Chandragupta* failed at the box office. Later on, however, the play was saved through brilliant portrayal of the role of Chanakya by Danibabu. Despite suffering huge losses on the opening six-seven nights, it managed to revive after a week.

What one can infer from the above narrative is the immense popularity of nationalist plays, which quite successfully made use

of the current political situation and the resultant emotional out-
burst that it created. Thus, play after play with similar content was
produced and staged. Not all the plays were equally successful and
one notices that the really good ones came from the masters of the
game. Girish Ghosh and Amarendranath, ably assisted by such great
playwrights as Dwijendralal Ray and Kshirodprasad Vidyabinod,
staged plays which inspired generations of viewers and served twin
purposes of not just generating nationalist feelings but also create
opportunities for big earnings for individual theatre companies. Thus,
nationalism as a subject was ably exploited for the cause of theatre—a
cause that not only fortified the economic foundations of theatre but
also popularized it at a time when other kinds of subjects were not
much available for stage adaptation. Commercial theatre made the
principle/ideology of nationalism accessible to an indefinitely large
and undifferentiated audience. Thus, nationalism as an ideology was
detached from the high culture of the elite politics of the Congress,
associations and aristocratic ritual and became open and available to
citizens prepared to pay for admission. The public that was addressed
was treated as equal, emptied of specific characteristics of status,
family and individual personal identity.[23]

THE STAGE IN GUJARAT

Turning to Gujarati theatre, one finds that even there the themes
were largely similar. Nationalism was a potent theme and, following
the emergence of Mahatma Gandhi in national politics, Satyagraha
became a dominant theme of Gujarati theatre. Given the markedly
commercial character of Gujarati theatre, the popularity of nationalist
plays reinforces the hypothesis that the ideology well fitted the
pecuniary aspirations of the theatrewallahs. Interestingly, in Gujarat
such dominance of patriotic themes showcased the cause of national
as opposed to community interest. The existence of profitable professional theatre, regardless of origin and content, satisfied ones
who saw the arts and more specifically theatre here as a marker of
national maturity.[24] As the titles of the plays suggest, there was strong
emphasis on legends and mythological contents such as Narmad's
Ram-Janaki Darshan (1876), *Draupadi Darshan* (1878), and *Raja
Bharathari* (The Legend of King Bharathari). This tendency can
be explained by the Gujarati elite's sudden interest in its language,
literature and history. The search for 'classical poets' and ancient
glory must have reinforced this tendency. Though in the initial phase
of its development a number of indigenous popular practices had

been intentionally kept out of the stage in 1893, Vaghji Asharam Oza reincorporated elements from Ras and Garba (folk dance) in the play *Trivikra*, at Gaity Theatre in Mumbai. Ras and Garba after this became a regular feature of the Gujarati drama. Another play that belonged to this category was *Nrusinh Avatar* by Manilal Nabhu-bhai Dwivedi. Staged in 1896, the popularity of the play rested on the depiction of the characters, native diction by Chandals, colloquy of the jester, sarcasm arising from belligerent stage-directors and the introduction of parallel minor farce. Mulji Asharam Oza's *Mahasati Ansuya* is another play worthy of mention. In 1908 the play became a 'hit' in Mumbai. It celebrated the ideal married life of sage Atri and his virtuous wife Ansuya. A 'play within the play' had, in contrast dwelt on the bitterness a marriage could generate. The surge of popularity earned by the play compelled the owner to publish it in 1911. A very notable theatre production in the post-Narmad period was *Kanta* by Manilal Nabhu-bhai Dwivedi. The play introduced elements of fiction in the plots involving historical characters. The essential elements of Sanskrit and English theatre traditions, for example incidents parallel to those in *Uttara-Rama-Charita* and *Vikramorvashiya* as well as characters adapted from the impressions of Hamlet and Macbeth were inducted in *Kanta* employing the Western playwriting techniques. Dayashankar Visanji edited and modified the play to make it suitable for stage, renamed it *Kulin Kanta* and staged it in Mumbai in 1889. Soliloquy, dramatic flourish and lyrics were considered to be *Kanta's* strong points. The portrayal of the villain was an attractive aspect of the play.

The list of such plays produced and directed during the entire phase of theatrical activities in Gujarat is inexhaustible. What made such subjects popular was their easy availability as also the audience's familiarity with the characters and themes. Thus in Gujarat where commercial viability was a major consideration the fact that a play could always be put together from readily available mythological and historical characters accounted for the popularity of such plays. Moreover in Gujarat where a clear hiatus existed between the literary world and the world of theatre and where the owners or proprietors finally decided the content of the plays there was a definite crisis of good plays with diverse, contemporary themes and thus myths and history were used as easy substitutes for alternative themes.

Incorporation of contemporary events into plays had been a constant plea of many of the Gujarati thespians who duly recognized the poor literary standards of the commercial Gujarati plays. The relationship between art and literature and their interdependence was tried to be extolled and a few protracted instances of making Gujarati theatre come of age was made by Bapulal Nayek and later a whole crusade was launched by Chandravadan Mehta, who single-handedly changed the face of Gujarati theatre. There was a very significant aspect of nationalism around that time which again had became prominent in Gujarati theatre—it was the candid depiction of Gandhian Satyagraha and other contemporary political events of importance, despite the fears of censorship and proscription. In fact, many of the plays could not see the light of the day but the endeavour continued. In *Amar Asha*, a play written by Manilal, one of the scenes alluded to a call to revolt against the British rule. A scene showed sprightly British soldiers swarming the salt pans in order to guard against Gandhiji's 'illegal' entry but running away on seeing him approaching the site. The British Agent in Vadodara took exception to the scene and consequently the Mumbai police department issued a notice and stopped its performances for three months. Such a play adequately brings out the general anti-imperialist mood prevalent in the larger society.

Between 1915 and 1919 Bapulal Nayak's plays were agog with patriotic fervour. He used many of the plays written by Nrusinh Vibhakar dealing with contemporary social issues. For example, Bapulal Nayak dramatized Vibhakar's *Sudha-Chandra*, a play voicing the popular aspiration for freedom. In 1917, Vibhakar wrote *Madhu-Bansari*, a play dealing with the campaign launched by the Home Rule League. The play earned laurels for excellence in direction, choreography and a vigorous plot and ran uninterrupted for two years in Mumbai. In the play *Kund-bala*, Mulshankar Mulani depicted the relationship between the princedoms and the British officers on deputation. The British government was alarmed by the play and introduced the practice of granting censorship certificates without which the plays could not be staged. In 1920 when Gandhi launched his Satyagraha campaign, Mulshankar wrote *Dharma-Vir*, based on the event. It echoed the spirit of Swadeshi or home-made goods. The administration however did not allow it to be staged. In 1928, the rebel poet Prafulla Desai wrote *Balato Dav*, which depicted several anecdotes relating to Satyagraha. Spectators thronged Bharat Bhuvan to see the performance and the play could be performed only under police protection. Its writer Prafulla Desai thus earned the revered title of 'rebel playwright'. Gaurishankar Vairati's play *Swamibhakta Samant* was so filled with patriotism that the city magistrate of Karachi issued a warrant for Vairati's arrest. Vairati disguised himself in a Sindhi costume and journeyed to Vadodara overnight. The legal

tangle was later resolved in Karachi with the intervention of Manu-
bhai Mehta, the then state administrator of Vadodara, and assistant
of Maulana Abul Kalam Azad. Vairati later settled in Vadodara.

CONCLUSION

The professional commercial theatres of the late nineteenth- and
early twentieth-century Gujarat and Bengal thus enacted the crisis
of colonialism and by extension the power of nationalism. They
contained elements that could cause disruption by using the aesthetic
revolution of new technologies in professional formations. The
theatre through depiction of nation and nationalist themes enacted
a historical narrative of racial supremacy. Thus these theatres—
whether in Bengal or in Gujarat—institutionalized the enactment of
metahistorical nationalist fantasies. The eponym of nation and theatre
thus rested on assumptions that sat together uneasily. On the one
hand, the theatre was reflective of the national character, identifying
national models in dramatic literature. In this scheme, the theatre
as the actualizing mechanism of drama reflected national types as
figured in the plays and at the same time exhibited national character
in the way the plays were produced. The theatre in that sense was
a system of organization that reinforced national behaviour. On the
other, the theatre as popular form of art deployed 'tradition' as a motif
to legitimize contemporary attempts to reconstruct political, social
or cultural identity. History thus became the dearest ally as well as
potentially the greatest threat to those seeking to refashion popular
and community perceptions to political or economic ends.[25]

NOTES

1. Partha Chatterjee, *Nationalist Thought and the Colonial World: A Derivative
   Discourse?*, Delhi: Oxford University Press, 1986, p. 41.
2. Sonal Shukla, 'Gujarati Cultural Revivalism', in Sujata Patel and Alice Thorner
   (eds.), *Bombay, Mosaic of Modern Culture*, Delhi: Oxford University Press, 2003,
   p. 88: Also see Francoise Mallison, 'Bombay as the Intellectual Capital of the
   Gujaratis in the Nineteenth Century' in the same volume.
3. Kathryn Hansen, 'Parsi Theatre and the City, Locations, Patrons and Audiences',
   in *Cities of Everyday Life*, Sarai Reader, 2002, p. 40, available at http://www.
   sarai.net/publications/readers/02-the-cities-of-everyday-life/02parsi_theatre.
   pdf
4. Hasmukh Baradi, *History of Gujarati Theatre*, tr. Vinod Meghani, Delhi: National
   Book Trust, 2001 (originally in Gujarati, 1997).
5. Michael Madhusudan Dutta, *Madhusudan Rachanabali*, ed. Ksetra Gupta,
   Kolkata:, Sahitya Sansad, 1982, cited in Sudipto Chatterjee, 'The Theatre of the

Bengal Renaissance', in J. Ellen Gainor (ed.), *Imperialism and Theatre: Essays on World Theatre, Drama, and Performance*, London: Routledge, 1995, p. 30.

6. Girish Chandra Ghosh, *Girish Rachanabali*, ed. Debipada Bhattacharya, vol. 3, Kolkata: Sahitya Sansad, 1972, pp. 840-1, cited in Chatterjee, 'Theatres of Bengal Renaissance', p. 31.

7. Utpal Dutt, *Girish Chandra Ghosh*, Delhi: Sahitya Akademi, 1992.

8. For the details about the plays and their content, see books by Pulin Das, Darshan Chowdhury, Ajit Kumar Ghosh and Kiranmoy Raha. The works by these authors provide exhaustive discussion about the plays and playwrights of the Bengali stage.

9. Dutt, *Girish Chandra Ghosh*, pp. 33-4.

10. Sumit Sarkar, *Modern India, 1885-1947*, Chennai: Macmillan, 1983, p. 70.

11. Ibid., p. 120.

12. In an article entitled 'Pauranic Natak (Mythical Plays)', Girish Ghosh explained why he repeatedly fell back on mythological themes. A careful reading of the article reveals that the plays that Girish Ghosh churned out actually reflected his personal understanding about audience preferences as well as what really mattered for a play to be successful. Girish Ghosh wrote, 'A play or a poetic composition to be beneficial for the race needs to focus on nationalist feelings. India's nationalist self is her religiosity. Notions of national welfare cannot erode that spirit of India. India is religious. . . . For a play to be generally accepted therefore, religion has to be taken recourse to . . . for a play to be truly Indian one cannot do without religion.' And this is where Girish Ghosh's limitation becomes apparent—he equated Hinduism as presented in the legends and the religiosity of the mass of Indians. One comes across two very extreme kinds of reactions to such an attempt by Girish Ghosh. The *Sadharani* of 12 February 1882 wrote, 'The foundation of the National theatre can finally be justified. A true mythological play has been mounted, the Hindus could once again get a book to read, plays found their language, the language found a force of its own, Krittibas and Kalidas once again rejuvenated, Girishchandra could recognize his own native land, took his place and we have duly got rid of the malignancies arising out of Madhusudan's attempt to belittle the brave exploits of Rama and Lakshmana and we whole-heartedly thank Girish Ghosh for his brilliant writing and thus rid ourselves of our great limitations.' Another significant but negative review came out in the pages of *Aryadarshan*. It attacked Girish Ghosh for excessive gimmickry and use of spectacle. It accused Girish Ghosh of using clowns instead of actors in his plays. 'Such attempts help in earning easy applause and popularity', it wrote ('Abhimanyubadh o Rangabhumi', *Aryadarshan*, Agrahayan 1288).

13. Cited in Apareshchandra Mukhopadhyay, *Rangalayey Trish Batsar*, Kolkata: Papyrus, 1991, p. 126.

14. Ibid.

15. Ibid., p. 108.

16. Ramapati Dutta, *Rangalayey Amarendranath*, ed. Debjit Bandopadhyay, Kolkata: Dey's Publishing House, 2004, pp. 238-40.

17. Ibid., p. 239.

18. Ibid.

19. Ibid., p. 240.

20. Ibid.

21. Ibid., p. 292.

22. Ibid.
23. Jurgen Habermas, *The Structural Transformation of the Public Sphere*, tr. Thomas Burger and Frederick Lawrence, Cambridge and Massachusetts: MIT Press, 1962.
24. Alan Filewood, 'Imperialism, Empires and Canadian Theatre', in J. Ellen Gainor (ed.), *Imperialism And Theatre: Essays on World Theatre, Drama and Performance*, London & New York: Routledge, 1995, pp. 56-70.
25. Crispin Bates, *Beyond Representation*, Delhi: Oxford University Press, 2006, p. 16.

9

Changing Contexts, New Texts: Analysing the Transforming Text of Post-1980 Bengali Cinema

SHARMISHTHA GOOPTU

INTRODUCTION

This essay analyses a profound transformation of Bengali regional language cinema since the early 1980s, a transformation that fundamentally changed the industry and one that can arguably be attributed at least partly to the creation of a Bengali television watching public in the same period. It focuses on a trend that emerged in mainstream Bengali cinema during the 1980s and was sustained thereafter, and brought into prominence a new configuration of elements, earlier marginal to Bengali films. This transformation was to do a lot with mainstream Bengali cinema's increasing adaptation of what are commonly known as the 'masala' or 'formula' elements of Bombay cinema,[1] such as racy dialogues, stereotypical villainous characters, stylized fights and song-and-dance sequences. This new genre, which has commonly been discredited as the Bengali film industry's totally unimaginative imitation of the popular Hindi language cinema of Bombay, completely altered what had been the dominant aesthetic of Bengali cinema till about the mid-1970s. Till this point, Bengali cinema was marked by its close relationship with Bengali literature, a Bengali middle class world-view, greater realism than Bombay cinema or other mainstream regional cinemas, and naturalistic acting styles. But since the early 1980s it was radically transformed by a growing adoption of the 'formula' elements commonly identified with popular Hindi cinema. Industry sources, however, indicate that this new trend was successful in boosting the Bengali film industry, which had been swamped by a severe economic crisis since the 1970s. The industry's crisis was caused by a host of factors: the most important of these was the Bengali middle- class audience's shift to television as a result of an increasingly un- satisfactory film-going experience in this period. The creation of a Bengali television public in the early 1980s shifted audiences from the cinema theatres, thereby significantly reducing film revenues in Kolkata,[2] till then the prime market for Bengali films.[3]

On the face of it, the new 'masala' trend of Bengali films of the 1980s was symbolic of the Bengali industry's capitulation to the dominant paradigm of Indian popular cinema as epitomized by the Bombay film industry. I would, however, argue that the complexities of Bengali cinema of the period after 1980 cannot be fully comprehended if the reference is restricted to the master-template of Bombay cinema. For, while there was definitely a growing affinity with the dominant paradigm of Bombay cinema, there was also a very structured move towards evolving a distinctive product that could appeal to very specific sensibilities among the regional film-going public. In other words, what was emerging was a new strategy for niche marketing, and to that extent, the transformation of Bengali cinema during the 1980s was part of a larger case of 'product differentiation' that had made it possible for the regional film industry to hold its own against the larger presence of Bombay cinema. The distinctive aesthetic of Bengali cinema till the latter half of the 1970s, evidenced in its literariness, realism and naturalistic acting styles, might in part be understood in terms of the Bengali industry's need to differentiate its product: to offer that which was relatively lacking in the dominant Bombay/Hindi cinema, and which the 'better' class of Bengali film- goers, the middle-classes, might easily identify with. Such product differentiation was closely tied to the idea of a 'serious' Bengali cinema as opposed to a 'commercial' Hindi cinema, and was ruptured by the 1980s' transformation of the text of the mainstream Bengali film, strongly criticized for being a crass imitation of Bombay. However, as this essay argues, the 1980s trend that transformed Bengali cinema, rather than being an aberration of sorts, may be understood in terms of a mutation of the regional film industry's existing paradigm of product differentiation, and its need of securing a niche market against more dominant visual cultures. In the 1980s, such a niche market needed to be secured both against the presence of the dominant Bombay cinema and the new television culture in middle-class homes.

A TRANSFORMED TEXT: TELEVISION, HINDI CINEMA AND
A REVERSAL OF THE MIDDLE-CLASS'S CINEMA HABIT

I would like to start my discussion of the 1980s' Bengali film by drawing upon some responses that capture the dominant view on the transforming aesthetic of Bengali cinema in this period. In its issue of 7 March 1987, the Bengali film magazine *Anandalok* published a letter from a reader in south Calcutta, who was very dissatisfied with the current trend of Bengali films, and noted, 'If Bengali directors continue making copies of Hindi films it will be difficult to get audiences to the theatres.'[4] Like him, other observers, both among film-goers and industry persons, agreed that Bengali films were simply becoming second-rate copies of the commercially more viable Bombay cinema. Between January and May 1995, *Anandalok* carried a series of interview-based features titled 'Bengali Films: Why the Crisis?', which presented the views of industry persons on the then state of Bengali cinema and the Bengali film industry. Several among these indicated that the crisis of Bengali cinema was to be blamed on the 1980s' transition to a mindless reproduction of the Hindi film formula, which militated against the sensibilities of the Bengali audience and their expectations of a Bengali film. In his interview to *Anandalok*, Bengali art-house director Gautam Ghosh noted:

Audiences no longer get the kind of clean entertainment that Bengali films offered in the '50s, '60s and even in the '70s. Everything is a copy of cheap films from the South or Hindi films. Audiences are not appreciating such films. Women have comprised the principal audience base of Bengali films; there was a saying that if women like a film it would be a hit. This segment of the audience is rejecting Bengali films based on a Hindi film formula. . . .[5]

Among others, senior actor Soumitra Chattopadhyay observed, 'Hindi films are pushing Bengali cinema against the wall and the industry is responding with its second-rate copies of Hindi films.'[6] Another very indignant senior actor, Subhendu Chatterjee, coined the phrase 'Hingla film' (hybrid of Bangla and Hindi) to describe this new brand of Bengali cinema. As he put it, 'Only the language of these films is Bengali. The rest is an uninspired copy of Hindi films.'[7]

The question then arises: who were the targeted consumers of this much-discredited new genre? A comment by Anjan Chowdhury, the initiator and one of the leading directors of this genre, points to the answer. In an interview on 11 February 1995 in *Anandalok*, he noted, 'Today, the audience for Bengali films are those people who do not have TVs and VCRs in their houses. The people who pull rickshaws, sell fish, are vegetable vendors, are the ones who now spend money to come and watch films in the theatres.'[8] This comment condenses into a few words a crucial transformation in the history of the Bengali film industry, namely, a change in its principal audience base, which may be crucially linked to the new trend in mainstream cinema.

The transformation of the principal audience base of Bengali cinema can be traced back at least to the end of the 1970s as the outcome of a reversal of the Bengali middle-class's cinema-going habit. A television centre was set up in Calcutta in 1975 as part of the expansion of the national network Doordarshan. While it was rather ramshackle, its Bengali language programming proved rather successful.[9] As the television network's popularity grew, Bengali film industry lost out on a sizeable chunk of its audiences with the proliferation of television sets in middle-class homes. By the first half of the 1980s, TV culture had become common in Calcutta homes, with middle-class women, the mainstream industry's most stable audience segment[10] showing a preference for the homely experience of television viewing as opposed to the more formalized practice of film-going. Until the rise of television, for women, particularly housewives who did not work outside the home—and whose hours of work and leisure were not clearly structured, film-going had been a structured diversion from the daily routines of work and leisure. In Calcutta, the 3 p.m. 'matinee' show mainly catered to ladies who could most easily make it to cinema shows in the afternoons, when husbands were away at work and children were at school or taking their afternoon nap. Yet, even these few hours of a 'get-away' often involved the making of alternate arrangements for children left at home, older relatives who needed to be cared for, and the like. Interviews with women who were in the age group 30-45 years in the mid-1980s[11] revealed that the coming of TV meant that they could now watch two films every week, one Bengali and another Hindi, aired on Doordarshan, in the comfort of their homes, and without the additional expenditure or adjustment in their daily schedules involved in film-going.

The 1980s also saw the proliferation of video culture which meant that viewing choices were no longer restricted to the fare offered by the neighbouring movie theatres, or even the films shown on Doordarshan. Most of the women I spoke to specifically appreciated the new TV-video culture of the period because it gave them the opportunity for repeat viewing of their favourite films from the 1950s, 1960s and 1970s, that were not in circulation in the theatres. During the 1980s, the first Hindi mega-serials *Buniyad*, *Ramayan* (78-episode series, 1987-9) and *Mahabharata* (96-episode series, 1989-

90), also fundamentally altered the viewing priorites of those who had access to television. The two epic serials, in particular, enjoyed unprecedented popularity.[12] They were projected as a counter to the 'sex and violence' of mainstream Hindi cinema in particular, and were greatly instrumental in entrenching a TV culture in middle-class homes.

Home viewing also became the order in middle-class homes as the chain of theatres showing Bengali films became more and more déclassé during this period. In the above-cited interview to *Anandalok,* director Gautam Ghosh also pointed to the decline of movie theatres as a principal reason for the turning away of Bengali audiences from films to television: 'Theatres are in a very bad state. There is no air-conditioning, seats are broken. Even sound-boxes are in bad shape. Consequently, the quality of projection is inferior . . . it is easier to watch films on TV or video, and that's what people have been doing.'[13] Likewise, actress Madhabi Chakrabarty noted, 'Most theatres still don't have air-conditioners. Fans are barely operating. The theatres are unbearable. . . .'[14] It needs to be mentioned here that among the more prominent regional film industries, Bengali cinema was the hardest hit by the TV culture of the 1980s because unlike Bombay or the southern film industries which had a 'popular' orientation, the Bengal industry was oriented to cater to middle-class audiences, or a niche market. This segment being the most likely to have access to the comforts of home viewing were very easily drawn away from the deteriorating cinema experience.

According to articles in the film magazines *Anandalok, Cinema Jagat* and *Ultarath,* Bengali audiences were also showing a marked preference for Bombay films, made in colour and with superior technical qualities as compared to Bengali films being made on very tight budgets that could not accommodate colour film or the latest technology. In the 1960s, Bombay cinema largely made the transition from black-and-white to technicolour, showcasing foreign locations, as in Raj Kapoor's *Sangam* (1964), and embodying overall a consumerism that was attractive for its dream-like quality for the mass of Indian filmgoers. The Shammi Kapoor or Rajendra Kumar starrers of those years flaunted plush homes, fancy telephone sets, cigars, carpeted hotels, night clubs, cabaret dancers and elaborate hairdos, a flagrant diversion from the anti-consumerist state ideology and the rhetoric of Nehruvian socialism. The Bachchan films of the 1970s had a similar consumerist subtext, played out as the backdrop to the angry subaltern's rise as a power player. The consumerist subtext of Hindi cinema also produced a degree of sexual openness and license, epitomized by the Helen cult, the cabarets and the Westernized gangster's moll in the Bachchan films. In sharp contrast, Bengali films of the same period largely projected an alternate aesthetic. They were closer to the socialist paradigm of 1950s' Hindi cinema, set in middle-class milieus and generally projecting a sexually restrained femininity even when constructing the good woman-bad woman binary. While this schema was tied to middle-class conceptions of 'cultured Bengaliness' and a more serious brand of 'Bengali' cinema as opposed to a 'commercial' Hindi cinema, by the end of the 1970s Bengali film audiences were showing a preference for the overall package of attractions offered by Hindi films, primarily in view of the degenerating technical qualities of the black-and-white Bengali cinema.

Another factor adding up to the alienation of middle-class audiences from Bengali cinema was the death of matinee idol Uttam Kumar in 1980. Uttam Kumar had attained an iconic status in Bengali cinema by the end of the 1960s, through his on-screen pairing with actress Suchitra Sen. He was the industry's winning face, with whom a whole generation of middle-class Bengalis had closely identified. Though his last films had not done too well, Uttam Kumar's name was able to draw audiences, and till the time of his death the formula for success in the industry had been a combination of star power and a good script, preferably drawn from Bengali literature. However, with Uttam Kumar gone, and with the growing popularity of Bombay films and television seriously affecting the industry, there was a period of floundering for new viable formulas, and a drift away from the industry's established paradigm of a middle-class world-view and audience base.

THE SHIFTING PARADIGM OF THE 1980s:
SATELLITES AND MIDDLE-CLASS AUDIENCES

In response to the challenge posed by Hindi cinema and television, a section of the industry came up with a more uninhibited brand of the middle-class paradigm of Bengali cinema in the latter half of the 1970s. This was somewhat in keeping with the emergence of more overt sexuality in contemporary Bengali literature, for instance, by drawing upon the cabaret culture that was a rage in Calcutta in the 1970s. A series of films emerged with cabaret settings and appearances by leading cabaret artists. As in Calcutta's professional theatre at this point, this referencing of the city's much-talked-about nightlife was evidently calculated to draw Calcutta's middle-class audience, which had been the industry's mainstay. Others conceived double versions, in Bengali and Hindi, incorporating the so-called 'masala' elements of the Bombay formula to try breaking into a larger market. Simultaneously, there were efforts to bring in actors from Bombay to add star value to Bengali productions. However, cabarets and double-versions mostly fell flat, or at the most were one-time successes. For instance, both Bengali and Hindi versions of the Uttam Kumar–Sharmila Tagore starrer *Amanush* (1975) made by Bombay-based Bengali producer-director Shakti Samanta were hits, but the same director's other double version *Ananda Ashram* (1977), with the same star cast, failed at the box-office. On the other hand, the mostly B-grade Bombay actors who were brought into Bengali films from the end of the 1970s could not make much difference in the overall scheme of things. The industry was at an all-time ebb, when a new director Anjan Chowdhury released his first film *Shatru* (1984), which though apparently derived from a 'Bombay formula' was significant for being able to make room for a new orientation of the text of mainstream Bengali cinema.

Shatru is the story of an honest police inspector who is transferred to a corruption-ridden village and his subsequent struggles to fight the oppressive agents and bring justice to the underprivileged. By this time, this was a clichéd plot in Bombay cinema: the figure of the police inspector, particularly, had been played with since the early 1970s and had reached iconic proportions through the screen persona of Amitabh Bachhan. *Shatru*, and the later films of Anjan Chowdhury were also liberally spiced with the formula elements of Hindi cinema, the song-and-dance, fights and rousing dialogues. What is significant, however, is that in *Shatru* Anjan Chowdhury for the first time brought to Bengali cinema a configuration that overturned the pre-existing middle-class orientation of the industry, and pandered to more subaltern groups. I will briefly discuss two crucial elements of this new brand of popular cinema that stood out against the established paradigms of the mainstream Bengali cinema.

A key figure in the films of Anjan Chowdhury is the figure of the police inspector. As in *Shatru*, the police inspector, in most films of this genre, is the righteous face of law who fights to bring justice to the underprivileged. Interestingly, while this figure had been a staple in Hindi films since the 1970s, there was, till the first half of the 1980s, no such figure as the conventional hero of Bengali films. In his entire career, which spawned more than two decades (1948-80), superstar Uttam Kumar played an inspector in just one film (*Thana*

Theke Aschi, 1965), and this was something of an experimental film, within the bounds of mainstream cinema. Moreover, Uttam's psycho-analyst-like detective's character in this film had nothing in common with the figure that literally fights to bring justice to the subaltern in *Shatru*. In fact, one of the main selling points of Anjan Chowdhury's films has been the figure of the inspector-hero as the savior, generally played by the same actor, Ranjit Mallick, who has become an icon of post-Uttam Kumar Bengali cinema by virtue of this larger-than-life star persona. It is instructive to note that it was from the 1980s that Bengali cinema started having action heroes.

Aside from the inspector action-hero, a key figure of the Anjan Chowdhury brand of films was the domestic help who suddenly assumed a heightened significance in the plot. While the figure of the domestic help has been prominent in a few earlier Bengali films [*Bhranti Bilash* (1963), *Subarnagolak* (1981)], these were primarily part of the more marginal genre of comedy. In most of these films, the domestic help is the comical figure, whose idiocy is played upon to create absurd situations for generating laughter. In other films, the prominent role assumed by this figure is part of a fantasy that is eventually broken at the end of the film. For, as argued by Henry Jenkins and Kristine Brunovska Karnick (1998) in the case of classical Hollywood, comedy is a genre that creates situations for inversions of the established norms of society, but also ensures a reversal to the 'normal' order at the end of the film.[15] However, in the Bengali films of the 1980s and thereafter, the domestic help is neither the comical figure who gets pushed around, nor is his prominence in the plot constrained by the bounds of fantasy. Rather, he is projected as a more crucial component of the daily lives of middle-class families, and someone who deserves respect on his own terms. Two significant themes in Anjan Chowdhury's films are the domestic help's romance and eventual marriage to his employer's daughter, and of the aged domestic help as the father-figure who protects his employer's family from various mishaps. In the case of the former, there is no subplot of a mistaken identity, where the young domestic help would typically turn out to be his employer's long lost friend's only son, and hence the legitimate claimant for his daughter's hand. Here, unlike in Hindi films with a similar plot, there is no attempt to eventually naturalize the subaltern figure's coupling with a woman above his class. On the other hand, various episodes in these films are centered round the question of giving the aged domestic help the respect he deserves. Whether to touch his feet as a mark of respect, or not, becomes an issue between the conceited and selfish members of the household and the ones who are portrayed as being more fair-minded, though in real-life this would never be an issue or a practice in middle-class households. A typical sequence, involving the aged domestic help, is available in *Bourani* (1991) produced and directed by Bhabesh Kundu, with script and dialogues by Anjan Chowdhury.

Such themes in the films of Anjan Chowdhury and others assume relevance with reference to the crisis of viewership in Bengali cinema discussed earlier. With middle class audiences turning away from the theatres to television by the end of the 1980s, the industry was looking beyond the metropolis for its primary viewership. So, while Bengali films had premiered in Calcutta theatres till the end of the 1970s, advertisements in newspapers such as *Ananda Bazar Patrika* indicate that by the latter half of the 1980s, openings were generally in theatres in the districts. With middle-class city-based audiences preferring television to film theatres, producers had no option but to reach out to the less lucrative sectors of the Bengali film market, and aggressively target the rural hinterland. In addition to the factor of the alienation of the 'better' class of Calcutta audiences, there was also the case of local distributors being unable to compete with Bombay distributors in the exhibition circuit in Calcutta, where the best theatres were. Through the 1980s, most film magazines carried articles which complained that a large percentage of Bengali films made each year were rotting in cans for local distributors simply did not have access to the kind of money that was being offered to local exhibitors by Bombay distributors. The outcome was that fewer and fewer Bengali films were being able to show in Calcutta during these years. In such a situation, if the regional industry was to have a market at all, it would be in those relatively lower priority sectors where the competition of Bombay cinema was relatively less. This was in the districts where the second and third order theatres were. However, in order to find a niche market in these sectors, mainstream Bengali films would have to offer a product that targeted certain dominant sensibilities of filmgoers in these sectors, and hence the changing orientation of Bengali cinema of the 1980s, with its greater emphasis on issues of social justice.

The trend indicated by the changing text of Bengali films was confirmed through interviews with industry persons. Sri Panchanan, a leading publicity agent since the 1960s, indicated that the main consumers of mainstream cinema from the end of the 1980s were the 'simple people of the villages' (*gramer sadharan manush*).[16] It bears out Anjan Chowdhury's statement, in the interview cited earlier in this essay, that by the 1990s, the principal audience for mainstream Bengali cinema was a class of people different from its erstwhile middle-class patrons. True to Chowdhury's observations, these audiences may be typified by the figures of the rickshaw puller, fish-seller and vegetable vendor, in other words, mufassil and rural Bengal.

The new orientation of Bengali cinema was doubly confirmed in the trend of a total departure from social realism into the realm of folk and fantasy. In 1994, the industry had its biggest hit of the time, *Beder Meye Jochhna* (Jyosna, the Snake Charmer's Daughter), which was an Indo-Bangladesh joint venture, and the remake of a 1991 super-hit Bangladesh film of the same name based on a folktale of the love-story of a princess brought up among snake charmers. The film drew heavily on the cult of snake worship in rural Bengal and the related folk culture and was literally a filmed version of the *jatra* or indigenous theatrical performance popular in both rural West Bengal and Bangladesh. For most industry persons, it was a non-film, and generally considered the lowest ebb of Bengali cinema for its loud melodrama and heavy theatricality. Yet, by the end of its first year, it was declared the industry's greatest success story. Chiranjeet Chatterjee, the actor who played the male lead in the film, said in an interview, 'millions of people over the years have thronged cinema halls to see this film over and over again. I have met hundreds of people who told me that they had seen it more than 25 times.'[17] *Beder Meye* spawned a whole genre of folk in Bengali films, which was a complete departure in the industry's established ethos of social realism.

Interestingly, however, after the coming of satellite television, *Beder Meye* or the Anjan Chowdhury films were shown on privately owned satellite channels and became accessible to a segment of the urban middle-class audience who would never have seen these films in a movie theatre. This points to the complex relation of television and Bengali cinema of this period. Significantly, the individual who was principally active in initiating the launch of Bengali satellite television was actor Prosenjit Chatterjee, who has been the superstar of Bengali cinema since the late 1980s. His career was shaped by the genre of post-1980 Bengali cinema discussed in this essay, his audience base concentrated in rural and small town Bengal, where he is a contemporary equivalent of what Uttam Kumar was to the Bengali middle-class youth in the 1950s and 1960s. It was mainly through his efforts that Subhash Chandra Goel of Zee TV agreed to launch the first Bengali television channel Zee Bangla. According to a recently published article, 'Prosenjit understood the potential of satellite television in the mid-nineties. . . . In 1994-5, he concentrated on building the new generation television industry and also acted in some television serials himself.'[18]

Through satellite TV telecasts, Prosenjit's films, which had limited runs in city theatres, acquired an audience within middle-class homes in Calcutta. Satellite television was a boost to the Bengali film industry since the mid-1990s, after Zee Bangla was launched, and many film stars began a parallel career in television serials. By 2007, at least eight privately owned Bengali language satellite television channels were broadcasting into Bengali homes, and among these several included film-based content. Therefore, where on the one hand TV snatched the industry's Calcutta market, on the other, it was largely through satellite TV that mainstream Bengali cinema made it back into middle-class homes, and it was television that provided the film industry its principal buffer during one of its most crisis-ridden phases.

ALTERNATE MEDIA SYSTEMS, OVERLAPPING VISUAL CULTURES

Though the transforming text of post-1980 Bengali cinema was, in many respects, indistinguishable from Bombay cinema, it would not be fair to look upon this trend solely in terms of a crisis-ridden regional cinema's unimaginative imitation of Bombay. Rather, it was a very structured move on the part of industry persons to work out a new principle for niche marketing, in a situation where Calcutta was no longer the principal revenue zone for the industry. Incidentally, the end of the 1980s marked the return of the love-story in Bombay cinema, which was saturated by overdoses of violence in the previous decade and a half. However, there was, as such, no parallel resurgence of the love-story as a formula in Bengali cinema,[19] indicating that what was happening was not something quite as simple as the lifting of formulas from Bombay. Accordingly, while there has been a tendency to look upon the 1980s Bengali cinema as an unimaginative, unintelligent and overall blatant imitation of Bombay and the southern mainstream cinemas, I would argue that this phase needs to be understood in terms of the Bengali film industry's growing need for a 'product differentiation'. The changing text of Bengali cinema in the 1980s was in the direction of offering something that neither Hindi cinema nor TV could offer: a unique local brand, most closely identified by an audience segment which had never been directly catered to. Rather than superimposing Bengali cinema on a Bombay template, I would argue that the Bengali film industry during this phase was in a very dynamic relation with both Bombay cinema as well as the new TV and video culture of the period. Whatever the production values or the so-called 'crassness' of the post-1980 Bengali films, it is significant that they were able to tap a segment of the film market that was substantial, and which eventually made way for the industry's recovery.

The effort to get beyond the constraints created by the growing penetration of Bombay films into the regional market as well as the loss of audiences to television led to the creation of a very distinctive aesthetic in Bengali films, which is best understood when we look into the parallel cultures of Hindi cinema and television. This essay has, therefore, tried to point to the dynamics between alternate media systems and the greater need to look at each in relation to the others if we are to understand the complex and overlapping nature of contemporary visual cultures and their audiences. To place it in perspective, one might, for instance, refer to the burgeoning body of research on contemporary Indian cinema, which, while rich in itself, is generally found wanting in its referencing of parallel media systems, most importantly satellite television, or the more recent FM radio boom in India.

NOTES

1. Bombay's name was changed to Mumbai in 1995. I refer to it here as Bombay because this was its name for the period referred to here.
2. Calcutta was officially renamed as Kolkata in 2001. I use the previous name Calcutta since it was called so in the period referred to here.
3. Till the end of the 1970s, Bengali films were normally released in one of the three theatre chains for Bengali films in Kolkata, and had their first run in the city's movie theatres.
4. *Anandalok*, 7 March 1987.
5. *Anandalok*, 28 January 1995, p. 41.
6. Soumitra Chattopadhyay, *Anandalok*, 25 March 1995, p. 28.
7. Subhendu Chatterjee, *Anandalok*, 8 April 1995, p. 23.
8. Anjan Chowdhury, *Anandalok*, 11 February 1995, p. 36.
9. Bhasker Ghose, *Doordarshan Days*, Delhi: Penguin/Viking, 2005, pp. 25-6.
10. Gautam Ghosh, *Anandalok*, 28 January 1995.
11. Interviews conducted in Kolkata in November-December 2005, in 12 households in the Bhowanipore, Kalighat and Cornwallis Street areas.
12. Arvind Rajagopal, *Politics After Television: Religious Nationalism and the Reshaping of the Indian Public*, Cambridge: Cambridge University Press, 2001.
13. Gautam Ghosh, *Anandalok*, 28 January 1995, p. 41.
14. Madhabi Chakrabarty, *Anandalok*, 28 January 1995, p. 40.
15. Henry Jenkins and Kristine Karnick Brunovska (eds.), *Classical Hollywood Comedy*, New York: Routledge, 1998.

16. Interviews with Sri Panchanan, 23 July 2004; 13 August 2004; 14 December 2004.
17. Tapas Ganguly, 'Hero No. 1', *The Week*, 16 November 1997.
18. Kakoli Poddar, 'Bengal's One-Man Industry', *Society*, November 2006, p. 140.
19. The only Bengali hit of the 1980s and early 1990s that was an out and out love-story, *Amar Sangi* (1987), with Prosenjit and Bombay actress Vijeta Pandit, as against a series of super-hit Hindi love-story films made in Bombay during the same period. [*Qayamat Se Qayamat Tak* (1988), *Maine Pyar Kiya* (1989), *Aashiqui* (1990), *Dil* (1990), *Saajan* (1991), *Dil Hai Ke Manta Nahin* (1991).]

10

Partition Memory and Refugee Experience: A Study of Literature and Cinema in Post-Colonial Bengal

MONIKA MANDAL

INTRODUCTION

The Partition of India is a much-debated issue in the history of South Asia. In August 1947, after over a year of tortuous negotiations in the midst of communal (religious) riots and killings throughout India, leaders of the Indian national movement—predominantly from the Indian National Congress and the Muslim League—and representatives of the departing British colonial government agreed to the decision to divide India into the Indian Union, with a Hindu majority, and Pakistan, with a Muslim majority. Furthermore, Pakistan was composed of two geographically separate (more than 1,250 miles apart) and culturally and linguistically different parts: West Pakistan (now known simply as Pakistan) and East Pakistan (now known as Bangladesh). An estimated 10 million people, primarily Hindus, Muslims and Sikhs, were forced over the next few months to abandon their homes where they had lived for generations and migrate to either India or Pakistan. Muslims fled to West and East Pakistan, while Hindus and Sikhs fled to India. Families were divided, friends and neighbours were left behind, and mass confusion developed as where to go and what to expect when they reached there. All of these factors created tremendous tension, which led to religious hatred, riots and murders. Corollary to the Partition of India, Bengal was also geographically and culturally divided into two parts: East Bengal became Pakistani East Bengal or East Pakistan while the rest of Bengal became West Bengal in India. The Hindu Bengali refugees who came in droves from East Pakistan to West Bengal following the Partition had to make a new life in the difficult circumstances, particularly in the overcrowded city of Calcutta.

The influx of migrants from East Pakistan brought in many literary talents to West Bengal, who expressed their social and professional insecurity in their writings from the very beginning. But the surprise of the story lies in the prominent voicelessness of the writers of the earlier generation on the theme of Partition and its immediate aftermath. Commenting on this inexplicable silence of the earlier generation of writers, this essay points to a polyphonic increase of words and narratives by the writers of the later period. It also intends to bring to light a mid-zone, translucent and hence lesser known writers who steered their way through these two extremes of voicelessness and polyphonousness and thereby made a world for themselves, a unique world of digression—a digression that gives in as it were, to a counter-revolt, a revolt that is as quiet as the self-denying and becomes the metaphor of their poetic being. Even though the Partition of the Indian subcontinent registered an awesome tragedy in an apparently callous and unpromising time, unlike other such historical events that spontaneously produce memorable artistic creations in literature or cinema, artistic works produced as a result of the Partition have not been adequate to the occasion. The Partition never figures directly in Ritwik Ghatak's film; rather it is an interesting memory image of a destructive event that had far-reaching consequences. While littérateurs like Tarapada Roy, Sunil Ganguli and Manindra Gupta gave vivid representations of the Partition and its aftermath in their works, the essay forcefully argues that Ritwik Ghatak was perhaps the only contemporary film-maker who focused on detailed visual and aural commentaries of Bengal in the socially and politically tumultuous period from the late 1940s to the early 1970s. The essay specifically focuses on Ghatak's treatment of the Partition and its associated perils that posed fundamental questions to human existence in society.

PARTITION AND/IN BENGALI LITERATURE

Bengali literature was in a healthy state when Partition took place. Tara Shankar Bandopadhyaya, Bibhuti Bhusan Bandopadhyaya and Manik Bandopadhyaya were in their literary prime. Poets like Jibananda Das, Samar Sen, Subhas Mukherjee and Birendra Chattopadhyay were also in full flow while Buddhadeb Bose, Sudhindranath Dutta and Bishnu Dey promised a great future for Bengali poetry. The Pragati Sahitya Andolan inspired by social commitment promoted the idea of 'modern' literature of the late 1930s that drew largely from the Marxist perspective. The purpose of the Pragati Sahitya Andolan, in short, was to make out of literature miraculous means of protest and propaganda, which would be realistic in its spirit and mass-friendly in its soul. Modernity that was stealthily imposed by the colonial rule on the native literature found its operative idiom in the wedlock with the discourse of Pragati Sahitya Andolan. Literature was however enjoying the quintessence of realism. The famine of 1943, for example, had served before the writers a delectable palate to try their intellect and to endure commitment. The year 1936 witnessed the birth of Nikhil Bharat Pragati Lekhak Sangha in Lucknow. Two years later, the second congress of that association was held in Calcutta. The poet Rabindranath Tagore sent his congratulatory messages to the congress. The amended constitution of the association adopted in the congress stated that the goal of the association would be to inculcate the spirit of radical ideas into the fold of Indian literature and strengthen progress through scientific rationality.

A number of novels written during the first two decades following Partition deal with the tragedy, directly or indirectly. These included *Pranganga* (1949) by Abinash Saha, *Durobhashini* (1951) by Narendranath Mitra, *Pancha Parba* (1954) by Banaphool, the works of Ramesh Chandra Sen, *God Shrikhanda* (1957) by Amiya Bhushan Majumder, *Bolmik* (1958) by Narayan Sanyal, *Tabu Bihanga* (1960) by Shaktipada Rajguru, *Neel Aagun* (1963) by Saroj Kumar Roy Choudhury and *Panka Palbal* (1964) by Bibhutibhushan Mukhopadhyaya. In fact, in these novels, what one would identify as effects directly linked to the Partition actually appear as autonomous processes, to be dealt with in isolation from the event that shaped them. Thus the refugee problem is treated repeatedly as a problem of the 'present', without trying to unravel the process of its genesis. Indeed, refugee colonies and refugee existence become the backdrop for narrating other stories—stories of women's struggle, of the poor, of family life, of interpersonal relations, and many other aspects of social life. In other words, the aspects of Partition enter more as description than as a unified aesthetic comprehension.

The unpleasant situation of the displaced and their helplessness became the theme, which was sincerely studied and more genuinely described than before. Such realism could be found in *Akaal*, an anthology of poems edited by Sukanta Bhattacharya, *Nabanna*, a powerful play by Bijan Bhattacharya or in Bibhutibhusan's famous novel, *Asani Sanket*. Thus the writings of this period were self-consciously realistic and remarkably sensitive to their contemporary world. Sympathies with the rural poor and rationalism of the Left were very much a part of the changing political climate of Bengal though the class orientation of the authors bound them to the familiar nationalist bourgeois/liberal ideological framework.[1] The famine of 1943 fostered similar literality and excitement out of Subhas Mukherjee, Samar Sen and the likes.

Interestingly enough, none of the writers of the earlier generation cared to (or 'dared to') devote attention to the most singularly discussed event of the period—the Partition of 1947. They were too pre-occupied with the communal riots that followed the long awaited independence or the independence itself as a final point of their dreams. The poems written during this period represented two distinct streams: the conscience of the poet, paralysed by an unwarranted retributive justice called the 'riot', and a euphoria out of an image of a braver, newer world. Subhas Mukherjee published *Agnikon* in 1948, in which poems like 'Agnikoner Tallat Jude' and 'Ekti Kabitar Janya' celebrated bowing and scraping for the promised land, i.e. the independent motherland in vision. It is noteworthy that the Communist Party of India (CPI) passively accepted the transfer of power and was not vocal with its later popular slogan 'Yeh Azadi Jhuta Hai' (this is pseudo independence), thus justifying the mute standpoint of the poet Subhas who was then a member of the party. Subhas could not afford to look beyond the euphoria of the celebration. Nirendranath Chakrabarty published his first book of poems *Neel Nirjan* in 1954, comprising a selection of his best poems. The impact of the riot is prominent in one of the poems 'Taimur', but the overall mood of the book is romantic. Birendra Chattopadhyay's *Natun Maas* (1951) or *23rd January* (1953) bears anti-slavery overtones, albeit with a predominance of the enchanted smile of euphoria. Even Jibananda Das's *1946-47* sailed in the same boat.

It was only with the subsequent breed of poets of the 1950s that the Partition came up as an evocative subject of poetry. It was a subject to be militant about, a subject to feel anger and distress, a subject to romanticize, a subject to cry for, and a subject to make a statement. This group included the poets of the *krittibas* set, especially Sunil Ganguli and Tarapada Roy. Sunil's poetic sensibility could not deny the aftermath of the historic truth, while it became for Tarapada a galaxy to wander about. The days of nightmare became alive once again in Sunil's *Charabali Podabali, Maandhaata* and *Bangaldesher Hriday Hote*. In his second book of poems, *Eka Ebang Kayekjan*, Sunil recreated the bleak memory of the post-Independence tales of the disillusioned metropolitan life, challenged by poverty, hunger, lost love, political turmoil and spiritual void. Even as late as 1972, when Sunil published *Aamaar Swapna*, the wound was still as live in his memory. *Jodi Nirbasan Dao* or *Dhatree* tastes as bitter. In his journey from his first mega novel *Eka Ebang Kayekjan* to *Purba Paschim*, Sunil has always been articulate about sufferings borne primarily out of this singular political fiasco. Some kind of displacement is visible from the temperament of *krittibas* in totality and therefrom an ejaculation of anger and violence negotiated in sensuality. To pursue beyond the mutilated body of a nation, the general poetic sensibility thus took a swing towards a rare kind of physicalism, hitherto unappropriated.

Tarapada Roy, from his very first book of poems *Tomar Pratima* (1960), focused on Partition and the enforced emigration. In the second edition of his book in 1972, he made it more relevant with reference to the Bangladesh war of liberation of 1971, speaking for the deprived and the deceased. The series of poems named *Bangladesh* ends in absolutely astounding images of eternal return. The branches have been torn apart from the roots and these have been for him the injury of his life, 'ironically the fountainhead of his counter production'. Even in his later writings, there has always been this typical melancholic strain—the memory of an integrated family life, teardrops for a land, never to be returned to. The literary practice of the *krittibas* group structured this displacement into a metaphor to combat the social and spiritual calamities and it is only too blatant a truth that in the post-*krittibas* era mainstream modern Bengali poetry has obediently followed this as the principal discourse.

Manoranjan Hazra's *Managare Dabanal* (1946) is one of the two novels with communal riot as its theme. The Muslim League's call for Direct Action is seen as the immediate cause of the riot. Calcutta's experience of the preceding years of quickly organizing demonstrations, barricades or guerrilla battle is used in the novel for raising overnight an armed nucleus of communal organizations in different localities. The novel goes on to narrate that the newspapers did not report the unity of the factory workers, and their defence of a girl's hostel during the period of unrest. Probir, a communist, joins hands with his friend Osman, a former Muslim Leaguer, to resist the rioters and to organize relief for the riot-stricken. In the second novel dealing with the riots, while describing the events of 16 August 1946, Saroj Kumar Raychaudhuri in *Mahakal* (1946) says:

The situation rapidly went out of control. Looting and plunder, burning, murder, mob violence—nothing was left to the imagination. One felt, that the traditional values and culture that have developed over hundreds of years had been shorn-off in a matter of moments, and the people of Bengal had returned to those pre-historic barbaric days of the past.[2]

The riots, which fed on a growing lumpenization of the unemployed poor, become the theme in 'Ijjat' (1950), a short story by Baren Basu. A young unemployed boy from a lower middle class family represents this lumpenization in the story. According to the boy, the riot led to erosion of human values, morality and conversed social stability. He vividly described the human carnage caused by murder, arson and looting of property.[3]

However, during the 1950s, with the sense of euphoria steadily diminishing, the band began their voyage from the opposite harbour. Increasing joblessness, turmoil in regional politics, adulterated daily necessities, and above all the unsettling refugee crisis could hardly be regarded as harbingers of a socialist revolution. The youth thought it better to caricature Nehruvian policies than sing ballads for an improbable world. In terms of Bengali poetry, this gave birth to a very de-familiarized language, expressionistic, candid, often uncouth, thereby enabling Sunil and his colleagues to grab their share of popularity. Refugee distinction, the memory of an undivided Bengal and the generation of fury and helplessness became the principal and relevant discourse in Bengali poetry. But the story of shifting colours goes on. In his *Swarganagarir Chabi* (1980), and specifically in 'Bharatbarsher Manchitrer Opar Danriye' and 'Ekti Oitihasik Ukti', we find the enraged Sunil of *Ekq Ebang Kayekjan* (1965) settling down as a conformist, adopting the lines in favour of communal harmony and the national meta-narrative. Sunil received Bankim Puruskar (Bankim Prize) in 1983, and the Academy in 1985. Success comes to those who can read the pulse of the state and refurnish their language with the statistic discourse. Thus the metaphor of displacement is itself displaced enough.

Is it only to decree one's stately dome, that the verses written on the Partition were scribbled? The answer might be a yes or nothing at all. This is only too obvious when literature becomes an echo of the voice of the state. Processions of refugees, homeless and landless people gathering at the Sealdah station, hungry Bengal screaming in distress—are all there in Sunil's writings. But by the 1980s he is a pro-establishment Sunil, trying to cater to newer generation of readers, titillating them with the feigning of commitment.

The characteristic feature of modernity in literature is its pre-occupation with dislocation. *Krittibas* and the later poets have all embraced this discourse. However, it was only in the poems of Tarapada Roy that we find more layers to the exploitation of displacement than what Dipesh Chakraborty defines as the 'three-dimensional discourse of refugee memory'. Between the two editions of *Tomar Pratima*, Tarapada has not merely been sentimental about the lost past or painted an ideal rural habitat or made stories of Hindu piety; rather he portrays the human misery caused by displacement, likened to feelings of isolation, anguish, and longings to become 'unborn' or return to the mother's womb.

In this context, it is relevant to mention one enviably productive poet of a later generation, namely Manindra Gupta, who has been writing since the 1990s and whose individual life itself is a recital in displacement. In his childhood, he had to shift from his homeland Barisal to the valley in Assam after the Partition. His prose works reflect the prerogatives of this outrage of perpetual exile. Gupta named his autobiography *Akshay Mulberry* where he reminisces a childhood sport with friends, hand in hand they would spin around an old mulberry trunk babbling 'here we go round the mulberry bush, the mulberry bush, the mulberry bush, in a cold and frosty morning'. But with the growing pace he would lose his friends and remain a solitary star. The dislocation of beings brings this man closer to the people sharing identical experiences. His prose finds motifs in the displacements of the Eskimos, the Red Indian clans, the Nagas and the Chakmas.

Is not poetry born out of such catastrophes? When the East Pakistanis were butchered by the military of their western counterpart, the literary scene in Bengal was inundated with remarkably reflective poems. Every little magazine published special issues on 21 February to lend its support to the Bengali language movement in Bangladesh. However, the same magazines seem to be mostly unconcerned about the Chakmas, who are abused, looted and robbed of their honour, only to be finally kicked out of their homeland, previously East Pakistan, to seek shelter in north-east India. Manindra Gupta's writings are thus unique to read and feel, particularly if the reader suddenly liberates himself from his media-trained eyes, statistic aesthetics, and cultural heterogeneity. Gupta's poetry represents a *jihad* (religious war) against progressivism and colonial modernity and carries us far back into one primordial origin where there is no more conflict between men, no more deconstruction and no more displacement.

In an important compilation of essays, *Chhere Asha Gram*, the author Dakshinaranjan Basu recount memories of their native villages of East Bengal belonging to some 18 districts. These essays capture the sense of tragedy that the division of the country created. The essays capture the everyday struggle of the Hindu Bengali refugees who were to begin a new life in the difficult circumstances of the overcrowded city of Calcutta.[4] To become an *udvastu* (refugee) was considered by them to be an extreme curse. If and once this curse befalls on someone through no fault of his own, he naturally draws sympathy and compassion from others. This could indeed be the language of one's self-pity as well. But when a refugee speaks in this language of self-pity, he speaks, obstinately, for the nation.

By the time it was 1947, the poets of the 1940s had already acquired some amount of fame in Bengal. A Buddhadeb Bose or a Sudhindranath Dutta mastered recognition and authority. Poets like Subhas and Birendra Chattopadhyay—ideological in their poems that placed the idea of the emancipated world in contrast to the general poverty around—had to perpetuate the jargons of progress. They might have been allured by the successful poetic career of their predecessors. Thus the colonial discourse of progress engineered a sense of governmentality in the works of these poets. One would suspect that they must have nurtured a dream of establishment in a new nation, speaking in terms of a new state's language while strangely and ironically remaining silent on the Partition issue.

Jibanananda Das, the renowned Bengali poet, wrote *Jalpaihati* in 1948 just on the eve of the Partition. The novel deals with the lives of the Hindus of Jalpaihati and the potential refugees. Yet, in Hindu homes, Muslim men who had hitherto been underlings, were entering bedrooms, asking for *bidis* and even wanting to marry Hindu women. It was an attack on the prevalent class distinctions in cultural practices with the reversal of rituals of deference, which become the 'moment' of realization of the inevitability of migration for many genteel families. Jibanananda's struggle with this cultural problem is best seen in his inherent identification with the plight of the *bhadra mahila* and his simultaneous attempt to 'resolve' the issue through the marriage of Wajed Ali to a Hindu girl, Sulekha.[5] Sabitri Roy's novel *Swaralipi* (1952), set in the period between 1946 and 1951, on the other hand, was an attempt to describe how the Partition had changed the economic and social institutions and traditional ties in 'both the Bengals'. It described the plight of the refugees in India and the problems faced by the erstwhile Hindu zamindars of East Pakistan.[6]

The literary discourse reflected in the production of poetry and novel in post-Partition West Bengal brings to light an important difference between the specific historical developments of these two literary forms. Historically, the novel in twentieth-century Bengal developed by changing a specific 'philosopher' literary language, moving towards increasing simplicity of narration of growing complex social processes. The development of 'counter experiential' vision and ideal linguistic styles, best found in the poetry of Jibanananda Das and Bishnu Dey, severally, settled the issue of distance between the logical conditions of the production of a poem and a text's formal structure.

PARTITION, REFUGEES AND BENGALI CINEMA: THE ROLE OF RITWIK GHATAK

Ritwik Ghatak remains the most celebrated Bengali filmmaker who focused on detailed visual and aural commentaries of Bengal in the socially and politically tumultuous period from the late 1940s to the early 1970s. In 1948, Ghatak and other ambitious Bengali directors like Mrinal Sen began to regularly meet and discuss about films and moviemaking at a teashop in Calcutta called Paradise Cafe.[7] Ghatak also organized a trade union for the underpaid studio workers and technicians in Calcutta.[8] One of Ghatak's first intensive engagements with cinema was in 1950 as an actor in Nemai Ghosh's Bengali film, *Chinnamul* (The Uprooted), with which Bengali's cinema's tryst with Partition and the refugees began. The film depicts the story of a group of farmers from East Bengal who are forced to migrate to Calcutta under the stress of Partition. *Chinnamul* used Calcutta's Sealdah railway station as a location and real refugees as characters and extras. That station had political importance as a site where thousands of refugees entered the city during and after Partition.

During Ghatak's lifetime, Bengal was twice physically set apart —in 1947 by the Partition engendered by the departing British colonizers and in 1971 by the Bangladeshi war of independence.[9] In his work, Ghatak critically addressed the question of identity in post-independence Bengal.[10] The formation of East Pakistan in 1947 and Bangladesh in 1971 motivated Ghatak to seek through his films the cultural identity of Bengal in the midst of new political divisions and physical boundaries. More importantly, Ghatak was an important actor in and observer on Bengali culture. His films represent an undoubtedly unique viewpoint of post-independence Bengal. It has been unique in his films because, he has pointedly explored the fallout of the 1947 Partition of India in Bengali society, and has been influential because he has set a standard in his films for newly emerging 'alternative' or 'parallel' cinema directors. The majority of Ghatak's films are narratives that focus on the post-Independence Bengali family and community, with a sustained critique of the emerging petite bourgeoisie, specifically in the urban environment of Calcutta. In this context, Ghatak utilizes a melodramatic style and introduces a mode novel to Indian cinema. His melodrama combines popular and classical idioms of performance from Bengal and India that are merged with Stanislavskian acting and Brechtian theatrical techniques.

In his films, Ghatak consistently displayed these three components to convey both utopian and dystopic visions of 'homeland'. He employed Bengali folk music and framed Bengali landscapes to inform his audience, both aurally and visually. His representations of Bengali women as symbolic images of joy, scrrow and nostalgia that he associated with the birth of the Indian state can be analysed with reference to the scenes of two of Ghatak's most illustrious films, *Meghe Dhaka Tara* (A Cloud-Covered Star, 1960), and *Subarnarekha* (The Golden Line, 1962; also the name of a river in Bangladesh). These films illustrate the critical relationship between women and landscape, and sound and music, which became so fundamental to his representation of a 'resistant' narrative of the new Indian nation.

Ghatak viewed the division of his native Bengal as mishandled and ill conceived. Government officials, he believed, gave barely a thought to the devastating impact that such a division would have on millions of people. He spent his entire artistic life wrestling with the consequences of Partition: particularly the insecurity and anxiety engendered by the homelessness of the refugees of Bengal.[11] In his films, he tries to convey how Partition struck at the roots of Bengali culture. He seeks to express the nostalgia and yearning that many Bengalis had for their pre-Partition ways of life.[12] In fact, at times Ghatak becomes quite outspoken about India's Independence and Partition. In response to an interviewer's question regarding what personal truth had inspired his films, stories and plays, Ghatak replied: 'Being a Bengali from East Bengal, I have seen the untold miseries inflicted on my people in the name of independence—which is a fake and a sham. I have reacted violently towards this and I have tried to portray different aspects of this in my films.'[13]

Ghatak discussed the common thread in most of his films, particularly in *Meghe Dhaka Tara* (1960), *Komal Gandhar* (The Gandhar Sublime, 1961; in the Indian classical musical system, an E-flat), and *Subarnarekha* (1962). As he stated:

Against my intention the films *Meghe Dhaka Tara*, *Komal Gandhar*, and *Subarnarekha* formed my trilogy. When I started *Meghe Dhaka Tara*, I never spoke of political unification. Even now I don't think of it because history will not alter. The cultural segregation caused by politics and economics is a thing to which I cannot reconcile myself, as I always thought in terms of cultural integration. This very theme of cultural integration forms the theme in all three films.[14]

In his films, he often exhibited his preoccupation with the union of East Pakistan and West Bengal within the heart of society and family in Bengal. Through the post-Independence Bengali 'family', Ghatak expressed the transformations that had occurred within Bengali culture. As his films exhibited, 'families' are often not the traditional Bengali family, but 'alternative', 'surrogate' families, like the theatrical troupe in *Komal Gandhar* or the wandering group of misfits in *Jukti Takko Ar Gappo* (Arguments and a Story, 1974), who were displaced urban lower middle-class refugees searching for a home. Ghatak visually and aurally articulated a new Bengali homeland by utilizing a melodramatic style comprising Bengali, Indian, European and Russian elements, and a historical narrative that would lead to the event, explaining why it had happened at that time.

Meghe Dhaka Tara

Meghe Dhaka Tara is set in the late 1950s in Calcutta. The story revolves around a Bengali lower-middle-class refugee family who are victims of Partition and who are now struggling for survival in a *bustee* (slum) on the outskirts of the city. The eldest daughter Nita (Knowledge), has given up her college studies in order to work. She is the breadwinner of the family. Her elder brother Shankar, who would normally be the head of the household, is eccentric and irresponsible. He spends his days singing, practising scales and classical Indian *khayals*,[15] with the dream of becoming a great singer. Nita's old father teaches in a small school nearby and her mother maintains the house. Nita's selfish younger siblings, Gita and Montu, are still in school. In her bleak life, Nita has only one thing to look forward to: the return of Sanat, a young scientist to whom she hopes one day to marry.

Through many twists and turns of the plot, Nita's family becomes increasingly dependent on her earnings. Nita's father and Montu both undergo debilitating accidents and Shankar leaves home for Bombay to become a singing star. Sanat does return, but falls in love with and marries Nita's sister, Gita. The stresses and strains of Nita's life take their toll. She develops tuberculosis and, although she is desperately ill, continues to work to support her family. Shankar returns from Bombay, now an accomplished classical singer, to find Nita wasting away with a terminal illness. Shankar takes her to a sanatorium in the hills where she remains, uncertain whether she will live or die, and forgotten by her family.

Subarnarekha

Subarnarekha begins in a setting similar to that of *Meghe Dhaka Tara*. A lower middle-class family lives in a *bustee* on the outskirts of Calcutta immediately following the Partition. This *bustee* is a camp, called 'New Life Colony', for refugees from East Bengal. The narrative of *Subarnarekha* focuses on Sita, whose mother and father were killed during Partition, and who is being raised by her elder brother, Ishwar. Ishwar has also taken in a poor, low-caste boy named Abhiram. They move to the Bengali countryside for a fresh start when Ishwar gets a job as an assistant manager in an iron foundry. Sita spends her life caring for her unmarried brother, until she grows into a young woman and falls in love with Abhiram. Ishwar is determined to find a high-caste Hindu husband for Sita and demands that she should never see Abhiram again. Ishwar proceeds to arrange Sita's marriage, yet Sita, resolved to marry Abhiram, escapes with him to Calcutta on her wedding night.

Once again living in a *bustee*, the newly married couple have a child, Binu, and Abhiram finds work as a bus driver. One day, he accidentally runs over a child and an angry mob kills him. Sita is forced to earn money for her and Binu. She begins to sing for paying customers, and thus unwittingly becomes a prostitute. One night, Ishwar, on a business trip to Calcutta, visits Sita in a drunken stupor to avail himself of her services, not realizing that this prostitute is his sister. In shock at seeing her brother in these circumstances, Sita kills herself. At the conclusion of the film, Binu is placed under the care of Ishwar, who although devastated, attempts to move on for the sake of his nephew.

Nagarik

By the time Ghatak directed *Nagarik* (Citizen) in 1952, in artistic terms, he was a gifted writer. The opening shot of the film with the camera travelling over the girders of Howrah bridge in Calcutta and the as-yet anonymous narrator's voice saying, *Aami take dekhe chhilaam. Aami take chine chhilaam* (I saw him. I recognized him) has already perceived the flow of time. History has become memory and memory has become history. Within minutes we are plunged into the lives of an impoverished refugee family from East Bengal living mostly with a hope in Calcutta, waiting in vain for life to turn for the better. On the crowded streets of a big city, millions of people come and go everyday. Just one of them, a very ordinary citizen, is our Ramu. He spends his days on the streets in search of a job. His eyes are full of dreams; he cherishes to build a small house. Ramu's family depends on his father's meagre pension.

The film ends both on a note of despair as well as hope, as the impecunious family has to move to poorer lodgings as their potential breadwinner—the young protagonist—fails to get a job. But long after the film is over, the image of Probha Debi stays in the memory as the all-sustaining mother. Her strength, compassion and vulnerability give credence to the opening images of the film and the narrator's observations. It also gives dignity to humanity, impoverished and up-rooted by history, and enhances its stature.

Bari Theke Paliye

Ghatak's next film *Bare Theke Paliye* was for young children. In this film, a village schoolmaster's son, Kanchan, runs away from home and arrives in metropolitan Calcutta. During his adventures in the city, he meets Haridas, a *channa chur wala* (person who sells snacks), who sports a false beard and turns out to be an unemployed schoolmaster, apart from being a refugee from East Bengal and a victim of the Partition. When Haridas learns that Kanchan has left home without informing his mother, he becomes very concerned. The little boy asks him in turn about his mother and Haridas tells him that she is no more and that she died in great suffering. Here the word 'mother' acquires dual significance as the giver of life to an individual and then as a symbol for the motherland that was unified Bengal. This is more so because of the opening words of the ditty that he sings to sell his wares: *amaar naam Haridas pathe ghuree baaro mash* (My name is Haridas and I walk along the pathways all the year around). He is not just an unemployed teacher turned into a gram seller, but also an eternal wanderer in search of the beacon of truth and compassion, due to the refugee status conferred on him by the politics of nationalism.

Komal Gandhar

Komal Gandhar is a serio-comic movie with lilting folk music of East Bengal and songs of revolution. With wit and razor-sharp perception, it chronicles the divisive forces already at work within the cultural movement of the Communist Party of India. There is a teasing of dual movement within the structure of the film. On the one hand, there is a forward movement of the young troupe of actors entertaining ordinary people in the small towns and the countryside, with the hope of sharing their own idealism with them; and on the other there is also the powerful, nostalgic pull of the past, which is still alive. The leading performer in the film talks of his mother, living on the other side of the river Padma, as he stands on its banks at Lalgola in West Bengal. He looks at the land on the other bank and wants his beloved to see it. This is the eastern province, which then formed part of a new country called Pakistan. He tells confidently that his mother practically died of starvation, which implied two things at the same time: physiological and spiritual lack of nourishment. The body and spirit or soul are wounded, on occasion, simultaneously and fail almost at the same time, when faced with unspeakable violence, which is, in turn, interpreted as an historical inevitability by chroniclers!

There are other unconcealed references in the film to the Partition. The camera moves forward rapidly on the railway track at Lalgola to simulate a subjective angle from the point of view of the engine that comes to a halt abruptly to create a collision-like effect; and the screech of the brakes of the engine is again a cry of lament for the immediate past and the destruction of a more congenial way of life before politics and the blessings of modern civilization vitiated it. Since cinema deals largely in time and associative memory, one may suggest that in its conception, this cinematic idea contains within it Fazlul Haq's dream of a federation of East and West Bengal as independent of both India and Pakistan. In retrospect, it dose not seem such a far-fetched notion, as both East and West Bengal lost heavily on the economic as well as the cultural front through the Partition of the subcontinent. The East became a humble dependent state of Pakistan and remained so until it broke away in 1971 to form Bangladesh. The only link between East and West Pakistan was religion. In terms of culture, language and temperament they were poles apart. Finally, the folk song in *Komal Gandhar: Ey paar padda! O paar padda moddikhane char tahaar moddhe boshe aachen shibbo shaudagaur* (The Padma [river] on this side! The Padma river on the other side . . . in the middle is the sand bank, on which is sitting Sib Saudagar) speaks of the vital composite culture that existed before the division of the province placing the two halves, east and west, in different countries.

Titas Ekti Nadir Naam

Titas Ekti Nadir Naam is Ghatak's intermediate film made in Bangladesh in 1972. It does not deal directly with the Partition, but it tackles the moral, ethical and political problems connected with displacement. It is an impressive film about the dissolution of a fishing community in the early 1920s. The river changes course and begins to shrink, the fishermen panic and disperse and their land is taken over by a community of traders. The final tragedy and the irony of this change is witnessed by a dying woman and a child, running through the paddy fields, playing with a leaf whistle.

In Ritwik Ghatak's *Meghe Dhaka Tara* and *Subarnarekha*, the activities of 'women' and 'homeland' are inextricably intertwined in setting, sound, and song. Adding and forming habits with introductions filled with socio-historical observations and critiques, Ghatak creates a cinema that offers a complex vision of post-independence Bengal, where both dystopian and utopian futures are seen for his Bengali homeland. It is the most certain method of retaining the *status quo* of endorsing the work of opportunistic mediocrity. In an atmosphere where our cultural attitudes and artefacts have been identified with the objectification of effete feudal Brahminism and European humanism inflicted on us by the colonials, Ritwik's work is the violent assertion of our identity. It is the cry of the dying girl in *Meghe Dhaka Tara*, which echoes through the hills, our right to live.

The division of Bengal, which was responsible for her tragedy, was only the immediate symptom of a broader division. The impetus, not only to the obvious narrative content of his films, but to their very language, was the system and its values, while maintaining a façade of a hoary culture. The contradictions of a society that could have modernized itself after attaining formal independence are the prime cause of a deeper division. The middle class is seen at the unsteady apex of the inverted triangle, brought about by the three-way division central to the structure of *Meghe Dhaka Tara*. The feminine principle, borrowed from our earlier lower level of materialist culture, also suffers the cruel mother; the multiple allusions to Durga on the rich sound track reinforce the pattern.

Thus, when Ritwik Ghatak uses what were earlier merely religious symbols, he secularizes them through juxtaposition. For example, the Bahurupi in *Subarnarekha* and even the deserted airport are both 'archetypes'. In a society which is only now trying to break away from feudal relations, it is inevitable that secularization remains one of the foremost functions of the artiste. As a refugee, Ghatak is compelled in his work to transmit and continually revise Bengal's cultural memory, identity, and history.

CONCLUSION

Bengali literature and cinema focusing on the theme of Partition present the underside of history. They bring out the continuities of human consciousness. And Partition cannot just be historicized as an event of the past. In actuality, that 'past' has been perpetually digging into the present. The creative writer in the subcontinent has been working and reworking the Partition in fiction, if only to come to grip with the dynamic thrust of human consciousness struck by both the collective as well as the individual tragedy. To understand the relation between the actual social conditions and the reality of the individual's experience, writers are constantly evolving new strategies, to confront the actuality of the historical and cultural event of Partition. In their vast panoply of images and symbols, irony and narrative point of view, the picture of Partition and refugee situation is viewed from different perspectives and angles. This is a difficult phenomenon for literature and films to grapple with. These mediums, as pointed out at the beginning of this essay, focus on individuals, private sorrows and particular situations, which, nevertheless, acquire a representative value and indicate the general trend of the time.

NOTES

1. Tarashankar Bandopadhyay, *Tarashankar Rachanabali*, vol. V, 1st edn., Calcutta, 1973, p. 418.
2. Saroj K. Raychaudhuri, *Mahakal*, Calcutta, 1946, p. 202.
3. Baren Basu, 'Ijjat', *Parichaya*, October-November 1950.
4. Dakshinaranjan Basu (ed. and comp.), *Chhree Asha Gram*, Calcutta, 1975.
5. Jibanananda Das, 'Jalpaihati', in *Jibanananda Rachana Samagra*, Calcutta: Pratikshan, 1985, pp. 295, 321.
6. Sabitri Roy, *Swaralipi*, Calcutta, 1952, pp. 293-303.
7. Mrinal Sen, 'Paradise Café', in Mrinal Sen, *Montage: Life, Politics, Cinema*, Calcutta: Seagull Books, 2002, pp. 105-9.
8. See Sen, *Montage*, and Ritwik Ghatak, *Cinema and I*, Calcutta: Ritwik Memorial Trust, 1987, p. 110, for details of Ghatak's union activities.
9. For an elaborate and insightful discussion on the 1947 Bengal partition, see Joya Chatterji, *Bengal Divided: Hindu Communalism and Partition, 1932-1947*, Cambridge: Cambridge University Press, 2002. For the Bangladesh War of Independence and the birth of Bangladesh, see Richard Sission and Leo E. Rose, *War and Secession: Pakistan, India, and the Creation of Bangladesh*, Berkeley: University of California Press, 1990.
10. Ghatak, *Cinema and I*.

11. Dipesh Chakrabarty, 'Remembered Villages: Representation of Hindu Bengali Memories in the Aftermath of Partition', *Economic and Political Weekly*, 10 August 1996, pp. 2143-51.
12. Ranabir Samaddar (ed.), *Reflections on Partition in the East*, Delhi: Vikas, 1997.
13. Ghatak, *Rows and Rows of Fences*, p. 92.
14. Ashis Rajadhyaksha and Amrit Gangar (eds.), *Ghatak: Arguments and Stories*, Bombay: Screen Unit, 1987, p. 92.
15. For details on this musical tradition, see Sumati Mutatkar, *Aspects of Indian Music*, Delhi: Sangeet Natak Akademi, 1987, pp. 84-9.

11

Retelling the Holocaust in Film and Literature

PRIYA SINGH

INTRODUCTION

As an area of study, the Holocaust has experienced virtually unrivalled controversy and excitement. In fact, in the recent past, works on the Holocaust reveal a richness of thought and sophistication of interpretation. Holocaust is the most widely used English term to designate the 1933-45 war against the Jews, a war that began with book burnings and culminated in the burning of human beings in the crematoria and lime pits of Nazi occupied Europe. Although the word Holocaust suggests an apocalyptic destruction, it is felt by many contemporary historians that it also has an unfortunate sacrificial connotation related to the biblical burnt offering congruous with a Christian interpretation of Jewish history, thereby rendering it in their opinion morally repugnant. Nevertheless, it is the most widely accepted term in popular and scholarly discourse. The Hebrew word *Shoah*[1] is the preferred alternative and is used liberally in all forms and variants of writing. The Biblical word meaning ruin, calamity, desolation, was reintroduced in modern Hebrew to suggest the cataclysmic destruction of European Jewry that transformed conceptions of God, society and humanity; yet *Shoah* is considered to be free of the affirmative theological overtones of the Greek-derived Holocaust and said to be more accurately signifying the rupture in the Jewish collective consciousness engendered by the destruction of one-third of the world's Jewish population.

Irrespective of the term used, the Holocaust or *Shoah* continues to be the single most significant factor in the life of the Jews to the extent that life is viewed through the veil of this apocalyptic event as is evident in the ethos of persecution that governs their mental make up. Consequently, the Holocaust has assumed the character of a national trauma, which finds a myriad of voices in the form of varied reflections and multiple analysis in newspaper articles, contemporary writings, both fictional and non-fictional, moreover, theatrical and cinematic depictions of the ghastly event continue to dominate the Jewish cultural arena. This essay is in the nature of an attempt to provide a concise insight into the obsession with the *Shoah* by way of an analysis of the same in terms of its depiction in cinema and literature.

In the words of Frank Stern,

the Holocaust has no analogy in other historical events or past ruptures that were reflected in the arts. Holocaust themes, decades after the event, belong to our understanding of Western art and aesthetic commemoration, be it in literary or visual form, in the performing arts or in architectural monuments of remembrance. The arts, the aesthetic representations, particularly in film have become a visual and often virtual *place of memory*.[2]

The further we move away from the era of the Holocaust, the more we are able to see that many forms of documentation and personal recollections are substituted by aesthetic forms that depict these experiences and memories. Literary and visual styles deal with cultural legacies, stories, narratives, and myths, and are defined by the common denominator to 'tell it' to new generations who, in turn, have cultural perceptions and expectations that are different from those generations who have witnessed the Holocaust.[3]

MULTI-DIMENSIONAL REPRESENTATION [4]

In representing the Holocaust, there are at least three dimensions that need to be reflected in all aesthetic, intellectual, and educational deliberations. First, the events, the recollections, the individual cases that are told or depicted in the work of art are rooted in history, in the period of the Holocaust, the 1930s and the 1940s, in Germany, and in those countries that were occupied by Nazi Germany. In other words, the Holocaust is definitely not a timeless event, a fate outside history, a mythical catastrophe. It is an event, an immense cultural rupture that was enacted by human beings, and that occurred in historical time and geographical space. The Holocaust has a chronology and geography and the development of the State of Israel always was related to the Holocaust. Anti-Semitic waves and historical revisionism that denied the singularity of the Holocaust influenced the perception of the *Shoah*. There was a new self-understanding of European Jewry and a new role of the *Shoah* in the evolving European Jewish identities. Literature and cinema became assets of this development, a young generation of writers and film directors, actors and artists of Jewish origin belonged to this creative change. Eventually, the cultural and intellectual confrontation with the *Shoah* could develop in parallel and also different ways in the three centres of world Jewry: North America, Europe, and Israel. Moreover, the historical confrontation with the *Shoah* has its chronology and its geography as well.

Second, innumerable aesthetic representations of the Holocaust were produced during the years of the Holocaust (for example, in the form of music, paintings, diaries, and drafts for stories, memoirs or the songs of the Jewish partisans). Much of these works today are represented in local, regional, or national exhibitions in Europe, North America, Australia, and Latin America, and many of these works are integrated into contemporary culture. Today, these operas, musical pieces, poems, and plays are performed, can be heard on audio, and can be seen on video recordings. Actors, directors, and writers who survived, contributed with their experience in the camps, in the underground, with their manifold ways of overcoming despair, persecution, and betrayal to post-war works of art.

The third representation is different from those works of art that were created after the event, in the immediate post-war period or the decades since then. Representations of Holocaust experiences and themes since 1945 reflect as much the Holocaust as the spirit of the time in which writers, poets, painters, actors, dancers, or filmmakers were turning to the past. The cultural context is twofold. It contains the recollections of the Holocaust, and it contains a conscious or unconscious reflection of the artistic, social, and intellectual climate at the time of production of the work. As they belong to different periods in the cultural confrontation with the Holocaust, they reflect different attitudes of artists, audience, and aesthetic climate. The culture of confronting both the memory of the Holocaust and its ongoing aesthetic representation is not static but a historical process in itself. The observation of difference holds true as well for the American, European, and Israeli perspectives on the Holocaust. These differences can be seen in film-language, aesthetics, acting, and, even more important, narration and contextual messages of the films that refer to the cultural developments in each country.

Hence, three general aspects should be considered when discussing or analysing, cinematic, literary, or other aesthetic representations of the Holocaust: first, the historical context of the narratives in works of art; second, the presence of the voices both of the perished and the survivors; and third, the differences in style, time, and space of the representations.

LITERARY AND CINEMATIC DEPICTIONS:
TEXTS AND IMAGES

The Holocaust was not an aberration of history, it was the ultimate and inevitable consequence—the final solution, in other words—of a long historical discourse.[5]

As Raymond Federman remarked,

It is necessary to speak, to write, and keep on writing (lest we forget) about the Jewish Holocaust during the Nazi period even if words cannot express this monstrous event . . . it is impossible to speak about the Holocaust because words cannot express this monstrous event.[6]

This statement very aptly describes the dilemma faced by Holocaust writers in every corner of the world.

There have been innumerable efforts at the level of fictional depiction of the Holocaust, whether in the form of a novel as in the case of Martin Amis' *Time's Arrow* (1991), Anne Michael's *Fugitive Pieces* (1996), Cynthia Ozick's *The Shawl* (1980), documentary fiction in the form of D.M. Thomas' *The White Hotel* (1981), autobiographical fiction as in the depiction by Jerzy Kosinski in *The Painted Bird* (1965), or the controversial factional representation by Thomas Keneally in *Schindler's List* (1982), still more in the melodramatic format as in the case of William Styron's *Sophie's Choice* (1979) and even in the nature of a historical polemic as represented by Helen Darville's *The Hand that Signed the Paper* (1994).[7]

The German Jewish writer Anna Seghers' *The Seventh Cross* (*Das siebte Kreuz*) is one of the more well-known examples of German literature during the period of the Second World War. According to Dorothy Rosenberg, who wrote the afterword for the 1987 Monthly Review Press edition of the work, statistics indicate that 319,000 copies of *The Seventh Cross* were sold in the first twelve days alone, and the novel was printed in German, Russian, Portuguese, Yiddish and Spanish by 1943. A film version starring Spencer Tracy and produced by MGM premiered in 1944. The book was well-received in Germany, particularly in the East as the author was supposedly a Communist, and some of the 'heroic' or sympathetic characters in *The Seventh Cross* are also members of the Communist Party. In fact, the libretto of German composer Hans Werner Henze's *Ninth Symphony* is based on *The Seventh Cross*. The story of this novel is rather simple: there are seven men who have been imprisoned in the Westhofen camp, who have decided to make a collaborative escape attempt. The main character is a Communist, George Heisler; the narrative follows his path across the countryside, taking refuge with those few who are willing to risk a visit from the Gestapo, while the rest of the escapees are gradually overtaken by their hunters. The title of the book comes from a conceit of the prison camp. The current officer-in-charge has ordered the creation of these seven crosses from the trees nearby, to be used when the prisoners are returned—not for crucifixion, but a subtler torture: the escapees are made to stand all day in front of their crosses, and will be punished if they falter.

Seghers, who had fled Nazism and lived in Mexico until her return to post-war Germany, wrote at the end of her novel *The Seventh Cross* about those who were persecuted, and tried to resist: 'All of us felt how ruthlessly and fearfully outward powers could strike to the very core of man, but at the same time we felt that at the very core there was something that was unassailable and inviolable.'[8] The worst nightmares of Western culture had come true. A historical rupture had swept Europe that had never been experienced by mankind. Years later it was called Holocaust. In 1945, there were no categories, no theories, and no philosophical or psychological deliberations but there were tens of thousands of images—Photographs in black-and-white, and in colour, filmed footage in black-and-white, and in colour. The liberators could never forget the images they had seen when liberating the camps in the East and in the West. They wanted the world to see what they had seen, as did those survivors who wanted to tell, to speak out.

Another celebrated figure in Holocaust literature is writer Primo Levi, a Jewish-Italian chemist, Holocaust survivor and author of memoirs, short stories, poems, essays and novels. He is best known for his work on the Holocaust, and in particular his account of the year he spent as a prisoner in Auschwitz, the death camp in Nazi-occupied Poland. *If This is a Man* (published in the United States as *Survival in Auschwitz*) has been described as one of the most important works of the twentieth century.[9] His only novel, *If Not Now, When?*[10] (in Italian, *Se non ora, quando*) was published in 1984. It traces the fortunes of a group of Jewish partisans behind German lines during World War II as they seek to continue their fight against the occupier and survive. With the idea of reaching Palestine to take part in the construction of the Jewish national home clearly their ultimate objective, the partisan band reaches Poland and then German territory before the surviving members are officially received in territory held by the Western allies as displaced persons. Finally, they succeed in reaching Italy, on their way to Palestine. The book had its origin in Levi's train journey home, narrated in *The Truce*. At one point in the journey a band of Zionists hitch their own wagon to the refugee train. Levi was impressed by their strength, resolve, organization and sense of purpose. Primo Levi became a major literary figure in Italy and *The Truce* became a set text in Italian schools.

On being liberated, Levi had to experience an odyssey through Eastern Europe and Germany before he could reach his homeland of Italy. In later years, he recalled his feelings when the southbound train stopped in Munich, and he was walking through the streets of this German city, now in ruins. He could not understand why neither the Germans nor the world could perceive and realize what the surviving Jews and all those who had been alive at the time of liberation had experienced. The world had to face the images that were shown in newsreel shows in the movie theatres or in special screenings and documentaries all over the Western world. Survivors had kept diaries, and began to write memoirs, essays, poems, plays, novels, or newspaper articles. The world had been silent, and had turned its eyes away. Now, so it seemed to many survivors, the world should see, hear, and learn. This period is characterized by documentaries and documentary style in fiction films. Novels and biographical fictions depict the concentration camp universe, and the plight of the survivors.

The immediate responses to the Holocaust in literature, and in the performing arts, particularly film, were defined by this two-fold experience of liberator and the liberated. However, the shadow over Europe that the death mills had cast remained, although later voices claimed that the immediate response was silence and a visual blackout. This perception ignores the cultural and political realities of the early post-war period in Europe when the remnants of European Jewry, the survivors, the returnees, the images of hundreds of former concentration camps and camps of annihilation, and the public process of de-Nazification and bringing Nazi criminals against humanity to trial created a visible and hearable environment. The victims of the Holocaust, and of World War II, were at the very centre of public attention and rejection. In fact, the screens of the film theatres, which reopened in the spring and in the early summer of 1945, were full of documentary images, the newspapers and journals full of stories. By 1946 and 1947, the first feature films dealt with the Holocaust (Poland: *The Last Station*; Germany: *The Murderers Are among Us*, *Marriage in the Shadows*, *The Path Is Long* and *Morituri*).[11]

Given the disconsolate state of the German mind in the immediate post-war period, it is amazing to apprehend that since 1946, no other film culture has produced as many films dealing with the Holocaust, Jewish issues, Nazism, and anti-Semitism as has Germany. Most astonishingly, this happened earlier than in France, the United States, and Israel.[12]

There can be no doubt that the Holocaust poses one of the most fascinating challenges to creators of visual culture. How can the actor or director represent images of the Holocaust without offending survivors? Which images are necessary to convey the horror, the suffering, and the daily struggle to survive? Which cinematic elements are able to create a visual legacy that will convincingly tell generations to come about this immense rupture in European, German and Jewish history and culture? [13]

Victor Klemperer was a German Jewish scholar, a businessman, journalist and eventually a Professor of Literature, specializing in the French Enlightenment at the Technische Universität, Dresden. Notwithstanding his conversion to Protestantism in 1912, and his strong identification with German culture, which he regarded as his own culture, Klemperer's life started to worsen considerably after the Nazi rise to power in 1933. He kept a diary, which from 1933 through the end of the war provides a unique day-to-day account of life under tyranny and the struggle for survival among Jews in the Third Reich. This diary also insightfully details the Nazis' perversion of the German language for propaganda purposes, which Klemperer would use as the basis for his later book *LTI—Lingua Tertii Imperii*.[14]

Chiefly, Klemperer's diary chronicles the daily life of restricted Jews during the Nazi terror, including the onset of a succession of prohibitions concerning many aspects of everyday existence (e.g. finances, transportation, medical care, the maintenance and use of household help, food and diet, and the possession of appliances, newspapers, and other items). Particularly harrowing are accounts of 'suicides', household searches, and evacuations of friends, mostly to *Theresienstadt* (Concentration Camp).[15] In addition, the diary hints at the profound paucity of information Klemperer and his fellow victims had available to them concerning the nature of atrocities being conducted in places such as *Theresienstadt* following transports and evacuations.

Klemperer, who survived inside Germany, also describes in his diary in 1945 that from a Jewish community numbering over five thousand in Dresden in 1933, just one hundred German Jews could be counted—and these people immediately became active in public functions.[16] The same happened in Berlin, Hamburg, Frankfurt, Munich, and other cities. Among those who had lived through the Third Reich were many public figures who had emigrated from Germany whenever one wave or another of anti-Semitism made it unbearable to live there. Among those who returned were many artists, actors, directors, writers, journalists, or German Jews who had been active in politics or anti-Nazi organizations. Others, who had survived the Nazi period but were not allowed to work in their professions because of the Nazi racial laws, now tried to return to their work. In the late 1940s and early 1950s, a series of films emerged from the newly founded Deutsche Film Aktiengesellschaft Studios in Babelsberg, which dealt in one way or another with questions of guilt, sin, ethics, and the German Jewish context. Emphasizing historical narrative as a means to explain the crimes of the recent German past, such films included Kurt Maetzig's *Marriage in the Shadows* (1947) and *Council of the Gods* (1950), Erich Engels's *The Blum Affair* (1948), Wolfgang Staudte's *Rotation* (1949), and *The Kaiser's Lackey* (1951) based on a novel by Heinrich Mann.[17]

The common theme of these works was how non-Jewish Germans had failed to preserve their humanism, morality, and decency, and how German Jews had deceived themselves in dreaming of German decency and revealed in an almost semi-documentary manner the deterioration of the status of the Jews in Berlin. These films contained many details of daily life that were not emphasized or explained. The filmmakers could rightfully assume that everyone in the audience would understand because everybody had been witness to similar scenes in everyday life. Until this day, these remain as the few outstanding works of collective German remembrance.

Immediately after the war, the writer Alfred Dölin returned in a French army uniform, and the writers Stefan Heym and Hans Habe returned with the U.S. Army. The writer Friedrich Wolf and his son Konrad, who later became one of the most outstanding German film directors, returned from Moscow; Anna Seghers from Mexico; Arnold Zweig and the painter Lea Grundig from Palestine; and Stephan Hermlin from Switzerland. The writer Wolfgang Hildesheimer became an interpreter at the Nuremberg Trials. Actresses and actors such as Ida Ehre, Elisabeth Bergner, Lilli Palmer, Peter Lorre, Curt Bois, Ernst Deutsch; the director Fritz Kortner; and, for a period, even the famous director Fritz Lang tried to re-enter professional life in post-war Germany.[18] They and other returned exiles had an immense impact on the re-presentation and representation of Jewish topics within the emerging post-war culture. Hence, many of the early films are not just about Jews and the Holocaust but are produced with the participation of actors, directors, composers, or producers of Jewish origin.

A film, which was also shown in North America and Israel, Israel

Becker's *Long Is the Path* (1948), depicted the fate of a Polish Jewish family from 1939 onwards, and focused on the post-war experience of the survivors, as Jewish displaced persons in Germany. In this respect, the film was exceptional because in most of the later films the gendered situations deal with Jewish-non-Jewish German relationships. Around the same time, another Jewish survivor of Nazi persecution, the young Arthur Brauner, started his career as a film producer in Berlin. His desire was to produce a movie about the Holocaust that would reach out to millions and convey a democratic, antiracist, humanistic, and spiritual message. The result was a film titled *Morituri* (Those Who Are Bound to Die; 1948, Germany; dir. Eugen York, based on an idea by Arthur Brauner), which is almost forgotten today, begins with a concentration camp scene. The film is based in occupied Poland and deals with the story of a doctor, who deems as not fit for work those men whom he believes are strong enough to escape the very same night to freedom.[19]

It is said that images on the screen and connotations in the minds of the audience can have a very complicated relationship. Since the early post-war documentaries about the camps of annihilation, any image that refers to the Holocaust is drawing on a cultural blueprint that exists in the minds of millions. The images of discrimination, of isolation, of social death, and the ensuing deportation and murder are not cinematic imaginations but reflections of collective experiences—and thus collective memories—that invaded all strata of cultural creativity and social life.[20] Moreover, it is important to remember that films that face the past have to be seen within their cultural and political contexts. Mainstream politics and ideologies also influenced film production. The Cold War shaped the cinematic imagination not only in the East Bloc, but also in the West. In the late 1950s, works such as *The Diary of Anne Frank* (1952, United States), Elie Wiesel's *The Night* (1958, France), and André Schwarz-Bart's *The Last of the Just* (1958, France) were read by millions in Europe, Israel, and America. Beyond all other national recollections such as resistance and collaboration, being a soldier or a Nazi, victim or perpetrator, surviving hero or perished victim, a central narrative evolved that dealt not just with the heroes of World War II but with the specific, unique, and singular annihilation of European Jewry. The cinematic shift to the *Shoah* outside Germany began in France with Alain Resnais's documentary *Night and Fog* (1955, France). Since the 1960s, aesthetic styles were probed that would help find a new film language to combine at once the unique and the universal of the *Shoah*. The Czech film *Demanty noci* (Diamonds at Night, 1963;

dir. Jan Nemec, based on a novel by Arnost Lustig) is a convincing example of this development. In 1960, the Italian film *Kapo* (dir. Gillo Pontecorvo) showed the ethical problems of Jewish concentration camp inmates, a topic that fascinated more and more Italian, French, and American filmmakers.[21]

The film, *Nackt unter Wölfen* (Naked among Wolves, 1963, Germany; dir. Frank Beyer, based on the novel by Bruno Apitz, which in 2004 is still a bestseller), shows how inmates of the Buchenwald concentration camp hide a child in the last few weeks before liberation. The father is deported, but the child lives, which is a basic feature in recent films such as *Life Is Beautiful* (1998, Italy; dir. Roberto Benigni).[22] The focus on children in hiding, their suffering, and their survival fascinated French filmmakers and can be seen in Claude Berri's *The Old Man and the Boy* (1967); Louis Malle's *Lacombe Lucien* (1973) and *Goodbye Children* (1987); and Andrzej Wajda's *Korczak* (1991, France, Germany, Poland).[23]

Another important film of the early 1960s contributed immensely to a new film language in the representation of the Holocaust. Camera work and historical research, sound and image, text and acting were admirably combined in Konrad Wolfs film *Sterne* (Stars; 1961, Germany). The film shows an episode in the deportation of Jews from Saloniki that implies the awakening of the moral consciousness of an ordinary German soldier. The opening sequence of the film creates images of deportation trains that can be traced forward and found, for instance, in *Schindler's List*. Films such as *Professor Mamlock* (1959, Germany; dir. Konrad Wolf) and *Sterne*, with their many images of Jews and persecution, established central Holocaust-related icons of collective memory. These films structured the perception of German Jewish relations. Thus, for many viewers, these representations of history sometimes became synonymous with the history itself. Nevertheless, there remained a strong element of ambivalence.[24] The first Israeli fiction films, mostly with funding, directors, and production firms from abroad, that referred to the Holocaust such as *Hill 24 Does Not Answer* (1955), *Jonathan and Tali* (1953; dir. Henry Schneider), *The Pillar of Fire* (1959; dir. Larry Frisch), and *The Basement* (1963; dir. Nathan Gross) combine the stories of Holocaust survivors with Zionist resurrection. It is not always clear whether remembrance of the *Shoah* is more important than building the new Jewish state, or whether the Zionist rebirth is just another historical asset of collective Jewish recollections.[25] These films are imbued with the danger of marginalizing the *Shoah*, which is a general characteristic of this period. But even in marginalized forms, such films succeeded in keeping the visual memory alive. A younger generation of authors and filmmakers had to develop new perspectives.

The transition from the immediate post-war period to the 1960s influenced filmmaking and past related public discourse. Now that many stories had been told, deeper layers of individual and collective problems, of ethical and emotional attitudes, of ambiguities and doubt, of guilt and antagonistic memories demanded their adequate aesthetic representation.

REPRESENTING THE TRUTH

After the anti-Semitic wave that swept Europe in 1959-60, academic and political debates about the social, intellectual, and political causes for the success, the terror, and the outcome of the politics of National Socialism led to a wave of remembering. This was enforced by the huge impact the Eichmann trial in Jerusalem had on the political cultures in Israel, the United States, and Europe. The trial became an international visual event, and Hannah Arendt's critical essay *The Banality of Evil* continues to be a controversial topic until this day.[26] In the decades since the 1960s, public debates were often initiated by works of literature, plays, and, most important, films representing various facets of a world divided into victims, victimizers, and their respective bystanders. The play and film *The Diary of Anne Frank* has to be mentioned here, and theatre plays of the early 1960s such as Rolf Hochhuth's *The Deputy* that dealt with the role of the pope in the time of the Third Reich, Max Frisch's *Andorra* that illustrated the fatal impact of anti-Jewish prejudice, and Peter Weiss's docudrama *The Investigation* that dwelled on the crimes and psychologies of Nazi criminals. Such aesthetic works of the early 1960s provoked highly emotionalized public controversies, and contributed to a growing awareness of the singularity of the Holocaust, but such debates were usually followed by periods that focused on other aspects of public life and reflections of the past. In the 1960s in West Germany, a history book reform introduced relevant material on the Holocaust in the German school system. In the 1970s, the debate about a controversial play by Rainer Werner Fassbinder, *The Rich Jew,* aroused public consciousness as did the historians' debate about the singularity of the Holocaust in the late 1980s, the debate about the crimes of the German Wehrmacht and the Holocaust Memorial in Berlin in the 1990s, and the resurfacing anti-Semitic sentiments in the early 2000s that have much to do with reactions to the Israeli-Palestinian conflict.[27] These debates are reflected in European, American, and Israeli films as was the Holocaust indirectly in the classic French film *Hiroshima Mon Amour* (1959; dir. Alain Resnais).[28] Such debates kept, and keep; issues related to the Holocaust on the agenda and were echoed in France and the United States as well as other countries.

In a nutshell, while examining the evolution of Holocaust films from the immediate post-war period until the 1980s, it can be contended that classics like *The Search, The Diary of Anne Frank* and *The Shop on Main Street* prefigure the double-narrative structure that characterizes many subsequent Holocaust films.[29] These films introduce the Jewish genocide into their narratives and imagery more candidly than contemporary scholars have acknowledged. Their optimism and universalism reflect the politics of the period when they were released. The NBC mini-series *Holocaust* marked and influenced the shift toward the production of historical docudramas, graphic representations of the atrocities committed against the Jews, and the portrayal of Jews as complete characters rather than faceless victims of Nazi mass murder.

Since the 1980s there have been thematic changes in the most popular genre of Holocaust films, the biopic. Biographical pictures convey the limits and possibilities of the individual to affect the outcome of an event of this magnitude. Over the decades, different types of individuals assume more prominence than others in Holocaust biopics.[30] Although movies about Hitler (*The Empty Mirror*) and Nazi fellow travellers (*Hamsun*) continue to be made, Gentile rescuers and resisters and Jewish victims and survivors have replaced perpetrators and their accomplices as the favoured subjects of such films. This shift has been an international phenomena rather than the consequence of the 'Americanization' of the Holocaust, as Alvin H. Rosenfeld has asserted. *Bonhoeffer: Agent of Grace* is one of the spate of movies about religiously motivated Christian resistance to Nazism. Wajda dramatizes Janusz Korczak's gentle courage as a means to promote contemporary Jewish-Polish reconciliation. While *Europa, Europa* dwells primarily on Solomon Perel's masquerade as a Hitler Youth, it also presents the Soviet alternative to Hitler's rule in a critical light. *Triumph of the Spirit* deals with the amoral choices made by those who survived Auschwitz, but it clearly blames the German perpetrators for constructing an environment that necessitated a Darwinian struggle for survival among its inmates.

The growing publishing industry created an almost universal canon of novels, biographies, autobiographies, memoirs, and scholarly works on the *Shoah*. The cultural transfer between Europe and North America was intensified and more literary and visual works were created by younger generations. Students in Los Angeles, Tel Aviv, and Berlin were reading the works of Primo Levi and the poems of Paul Celan, although much of German-language literature was confined to Europe. Very often, novels and films based on these works rekindled reading interests and discussions.[31]

Beginning with the first post-war films produced in Germany, Austria, and Poland, filmmakers of a new generation faced the legacy of the past and created works that are still seen and discussed. East European directors, such as Andrzej Wajda, included visual connotations of the Holocaust or Polish Jewish life in their films. The cinematic depictions in most European countries and North America increasingly began to cover all areas of Holocaust remembrance and representation. Cultural remembrance, scholarly debate, public discourse, and cinematic creativity became interwoven, although only film and novels reached out to a broader public and tried to combine the contradictions of serious commemoration and entertainment.

The 1960s brought with it a growing awareness of ethnic diversity and related problems.[32] Sidney Lumet directed what is now regarded as an outstanding film, *The Pawnbroker* which surpassed everything that the universalistic and simplistic 1959 George Stevens version of *The Diary of Anne Frank* could accomplish. The references to the Holocaust became at once universalized and Americanized. Woody Allen with his comedies, Paul Mazursky with *Enemies, a Love Story,* and Mel Brooks with his humour running over the top were all striving for new territory. Increasingly, the ethnic reference to Jewish American life was becoming inseparable from representations that included the Holocaust and Israel.

In Israel, particularly after the Israeli-Arab war of 1967, some films allowed for parallels between Nazi Germany and the Arab States while others, in the 1970s and 1980s, discussed the role and problems of immigrants with reference to the European past.[33] This was different from Europe where the historical dimension was at the very centre of any reference to the Holocaust. Anti-Semitism, discrimination, deportation, collaboration, and the relationship of victim and perpetrator and survival were and still are historical dimensions of such films with different foci defined by national history, the state of historical consciousness, and remembrance.

Holocaust films are replete with visual quotes, back—and fore-shadowing of images that haunt our imaginations. Before we, the audience, analyse and discuss such films, these 'cinematic memories' are already freely crossing borders in a virtual cinematic world between Europe, Israel, and North America. As images, they subtly construct our visual memory. In the future, the memory of the Holocaust will be defined less by the recollections of the survivors than by the representations of the filmmakers, scriptwriters, novelists, and playwrights. This is even happening to some extent today. With distance, in time, the virtual becomes increasingly the real. Most filmmakers have employed traditional genres and assumed audience familiarity with Holocaust cinema, images, and symbols. What has changed over time is which genres and themes are most commonly used by filmmakers to make the Holocaust relevant to audiences who are removed in time and often place, from the genocide perpetrated against European Jewry during World War II. In choosing film as a measure of popular perceptions of the Holocaust, one does not imply that the written word is no longer an important tool for raising public awareness but a recognition that the visual media plays an increasingly larger role in that process.[34]

UNDERSTANDING CAUSALITIES

Beyond issues of deportation and concentration camp horrors, beyond the relation between perpetrators and victims, many German and Austrian films also deal with the period before 1939. Some general differences can be mentioned. It has been observed that while the American filmmakers usually are more interested in the camp realities, the French filmmakers deal with the French involvement under Nazi occupation, with collaboration and resistance, and include *Shoah*-related issues. Italian filmmakers focus on the context of Fascism and everyday life. Polish, Czech, and Hungarian filmmakers still have to grapple with the two periods of totalitarian rule and brutality, and other film cultures only began in recent years to turn to their history under Nazi occupation. It is increasingly being felt that in the coming decade, such differences will become less important as European film cultures develop more and more forms of cooperation and co-productions. The *Shoah*-related visual discourse will become more European while the literary discourse may still focus on the specific national experience. Works by a younger generation that freely commutes between Europe, Israel, the United States, and other countries indicate that the *Shoah* increasingly is not only perceived as a universal theme but that the creators of such works, be it literature or film, are much more mundane and cosmopolitan than the artists of the immediate post-war period. Indeed, the internationalization of the Holocaust as a symbol of evil and the production of movies by countries with minimal connections to the event call for explications that go beyond analysing feature films as expressions of national collective memory.

It was characteristic of German historical consciousness in the first three post-war decades after 1945 that the cultural discourse, including the cinematic discourse,[35] centred on the pre-war years, either the demise of Weimar democracy or the events surrounding the November pogrom of 1938, the so-called Crystal Night (*Reichskristallnacht*). A recurring topic, which sometimes unfolded from the perspective of children or youth, was the depiction of the help—or failure to help—of non-Jewish Germans, and of the horror that Jewish bourgeois life faced. These films portrayed growing up in Germany, desperation, loss, and emigration. With the increasing importance of television, many productions were initiated by German television stations, particularly in the 1970s and 1980s. Television became a central medium for imagining the so-called German Jewish symbiosis, for representing Jewish history in Germany, and particularly for depicting the fate of the Jews in Nazi Germany. Many of these fiction and non-fiction films incorporated images of exile and of Israel. Usually, this was a cinema of reconciliation, void of the terror of extermination, void of the individual faces of perpetrators. Films about Jewish suffering were almost a welcome salve for the living-room audience, as they often conveyed to the spectator the message that he or she could switch over and identify with the victim. In short, these films had a strong redemptive connotation, e.g. *Europa, Europa* (1991, Germany; dir. Agnieszka Holland, based on the autobiography of Salomon Perel) about the Jewish Hitler Youth Salomon which was not really successful in Germany.[36] This film indicated that the depiction of concentration camp realities, of heroism, as for instance in the remarkable *Uprising in Sobibor* (1987, United States; dir. Jack Gold, based on the memories of survivors from the Sobibor camp) or problems of survivors that were characteristic for a number of American films such as *The Pawnbroker* (1960; dir. Sidney Lumet) or *Enemies, a Love Story* (1989; dir. Paul Mazursky, based on the novel by Israel Bashevis Singer), and the controversial Italian film *The Nightporter* (1973; dir. Liliana Caviani) switched to more detailed and individualized depictions. Gendered narratives became a focus, and taboos that had been characteristic for Holocaust representations were questioned to reach a more sophisticated and less idealizing level of cinematic representation.

Facing the perpetrators, though, became central for smaller productions, often documentaries or docudramas, for instance, by Erwin

Leiser. Two outstanding docudramas that have to be mentioned are Theodor Kotulla's 1977 film about the SS commander of Auschwitz, *Aus einem deutschen Leben* (From a German Life) and *The Wannsee Protocols* (1987, Germany; dir. Heinz Schirk).[37] The first depicts scenes outside the gas chambers and the visit to Auschwitz by Heinrich Himmler. The second film is the story of the infamous meeting of high-ranking Nazi officials in a Wannsee villa who discuss and decide on the Final Solution. In 1943, Fritz Lang, in Hollywood, directed *Hangmen also Die!* that depicted the Czech resistance and the killing of Heydrich. This is an important film with references to the Holocaust that contributes to the discussion of problems related to anti-Nazi resistance. In general, films concentrating on the perpetrators are rare as it is often easier to depict the suffering of the victims than to individualize, to give name and identity to, the perpetrators. *Music Box* (1989, United States; dir. Constantin Costa-Gavras) is an exception since the film depicts convincingly how a Nazi perpetrator becomes an honourable member and beloved father in American post-war society until the truth about his criminal past is revealed. Since the 1980s, Israeli films react to the political shifts to the Right in Israeli politics. Zionist myths and problems of historical consciousness that refer to the ambivalence of instrumentalizing Holocaust remembrance are subtexts in such Israeli films as *Link Gun* (1979; dir. Ilan Moshensohn), *Hide and Seek* (1986; dir. Dani Wollman), *The Summer of Aviya* (1988; dirs. Eli Cohen and Gila Almagor), *Because of That War* (1989; Orna Ben-Dor), which portrays the popular singer Yehuda Poliker as a child of Holocaust survivors.[38] German films, of this period, particularly television mini-series, focus on German everyday life under National Socialism or 'bring to life' novels and memoirs. The serious fiction films of the decades after 1945 display a higher narrative and aesthetic quality.

MOVING SITES OF MEMORY

Since the 1950s, the aesthetics of visually remembering on the screen were sometimes a hidden and sometimes an open discourse that transformed the Iron Curtain in Germany into a filter of cultural confrontation between the politics of memory in the East, and those in the West. One could observe two major tendencies: either the search for new cinematic ways to vary Holocaust narratives, or the imaginative use of elements of the Holocaust to come to terms with more recent social or political problems in post-war society.[39] In one way or the other this also holds true for French, Israeli, and other film cultures. Some films tried to use Jewish characters to restore the image of the decent soldier or to stress images of the heroic anti-Fascist fighter. Others combined concepts of anti-Fascism and philo-Semitism with subplots that involved Jews, or mixed social critique with things Jewish. This was very often the case with directors of the so-called New German Film of the 1970s. There is almost no film by the directors Rainer Werner Fassbinder or Wim Wenders or Volker Schlöndorff without such hidden and open references, usually leading to contextual problems.[40] Certain elements, keywords, or images became stock representations of the past in Germany, and very often the term *memory* became almost automatically loaded with meanings related either to the Holocaust or to the war.

In the mid-1970s, the 'high noon' of the post-war era, one of the more outstanding German films about the Holocaust was produced in East Germany. It captured many awards, including an Oscar nomination for Best Foreign Film. Even today, *Jakob the Liar* [41] (1974; dir. Frank Beyer) has not lost its power. The film was based on a bestseller written by Jurek Becker, who as a child together with his father had survived the Lodz ghetto and then grew up in Berlin to become one of the most important German Jewish authors and scriptwriters of German post-war literature, film, and television. *Jakob the Liar* is considered to be a watershed, and since then, films about the Holocaust have to be measured against this cinematic backdrop. Though full of humour and irony, the film does not indulge in false happy endings, it does not yield easy answers, but it does insist on humanity and hope. In the closing scene of the film, all of the protagonists are deported, and from inside the train, we see them remembering the distant past and imagining the unfulfilled future. Spielberg's *Schindler's List* already indicated with its final colourful scene in Israel that history, and Jewish history as well, goes on beyond the shadows of the Holocaust. Istvan Szabo's *Sunshine* (1999; Canada, Germany, Hungary) begins in nineteenth-century Hungary and ends in post-Communist Budapest. It deals with the life story of a bourgeois Jewish family which shows that despite anti-Semitic persecution and racist murder, some survived and guaranteed the continuity of European Jewish life. The same holds true for Roman Polanski's masterpiece *The Pianist* (2002; Canada, France, Germany, Poland) that begins with the German attack on Poland and ends with the first post-war concert of the Polish-Jewish soloist. The last two films are European co-productions and reflect this new tendency in European filmmaking. Israeli filmmakers and theatre directors investigate the meaning of the past for the crisis of Zionism at the beginning of the twenty-first century. The film *Don't Touch My Holocaust* (1994; dir. Asher Tlalim) connects Holocaust remembrance with the experiences of Israelis of Oriental and Arab origin. These productions, thus, achieve universal and provocative meaning, and overcome another limit, an exclusive Jewish perspective that could be found in Israeli culture.[42]

Widely received films such as *Marriage in the Shadows, Night and Fog, Jakob the Liar, Shoah, Schindler's List, Life is Beautiful, Sunshine,* and *The Pianist* establish lasting cinematic images of memories and remembrance that are quoted again and again. A few of the lesser-known films are worth mentioning. These deal with the public German discourse on remembering and representing the Holocaust and 'things Jewish' in contemporary Germany. The first is the film by Thomas Brasch, co-written by Jurek Becker, *The Passenger—Welcome to Germany*. This, in fact, is an extraordinary cinematic work on film as a medium of memory, and, at the same time, a fundamental critique of Nazi cinema. The audience does not really know whether this is a memory or the realistic depiction of past events, because the whole film is about making a movie about perishing in the Holocaust, and about survival, and about the eventual memory of these past events. Through these obscuring layers, the film, in fact, questions our whole concept of memory—and memory on a public level. Jurek Becker published another novel, *Bronstein's Children* that was transformed into a movie for German television in 1990 (dir. Jerzy Kawalerowicz). The film tells the story of Jewish families in East Berlin in the 1970s. The narration is unpretentious, the story familiar to every Jew who has lived or has grown up in post-war Germany. The film is set in 1970s East Berlin. The imagined, abstract Jew has become a real Jew, who lives in Germany before and after unification. The film indicates the new self-consciousness of a younger generation of German Jews—and quashes any residual stereotyping that might occur on the public level. The Austrian film *Gebürtig* (2002; dir. and author of the script, based on his novel, Robert Schindel) takes up the ambiguities of growing up Jewish in Vienna after 1945 and can be compared to the Berlin film.[43] Both films deal with the culture of antagonistic memories and with the relevance of the *Shoah* for the contemporary Jewish-non-Jewish dialogue.

Together with a relevant number of other cinematic representations, most films that have been mentioned thus far inform an on-going cultural debate about two crucial problems: the generational dimension of memory, and the pitfalls of constantly surpassing the limits of representing the Holocaust and Jewish themes on the screen.

The 1980s culturally set the stage for what has become the renewed German Jewish or Austrian Jewish experience since the early 1990s. Since then, we have increasingly to deal with cinematic and literary images of German Jewish and Austrian Jewish self-understanding in a German civil society. Authors such as Robert Schindel, Robert Menasse, Doron Rabinovici, and Elfried Jelinek in Vienna, and later, Thomas Brasch, Jurek Becker, Stefan Heym, and Esther Dischereit in Berlin opened new dimensions in their aesthetic references to the *Shoah*.[44] The Jewish perspective is not just focused on Germany from the outside, either from America or Israel, but it is increasingly a perspective from inside Germany. As they face the past in their own cultural productions, Austrian or German Jews do not need deputies anymore, a fact that could already be seen in France or Hungary. The debates of the 1980s and 1990s about the limits of the representation of the *Shoah* seem to be over.

Although scholars have debated for many years whether there can or should be limits to the representation of the Holocaust, we come to understand that these limits are only defined by the limits of the cultural consensus of a given period. Often, the term *limits* seems to be another word for *taboo* or the feeling of uneasiness when specific touchy topics of the Holocaust are the subject of aesthetic representation. Films that are preoccupied with problematic or marginal aspects of the *Shoah* will doubtlessly follow in the coming years. Beyond all questionable and purely market-oriented film productions, this development indicates a shift in cinematic culture. The *Shoah* as a historical event and all its repercussions have been established on the screen. The focus is not *that* the story has to be told but *how* it has to be told to achieve the cultural ambition—to 'tell it'.[45]

Filmmakers in many countries have overcome imagined boundaries and self-imposed limitations that contradict their cinematic project. The images of the *Shoah* produced today are by no means authentic reproductions but they are authentic insofar as they represent the artistic challenges to tell it to new generations. The outstanding films produced between 1946 and 1948, and this cannot be stressed enough, could also be revived through serious and thoughtful remakes. In twenty-first-century Western culture there are no limits to the aesthetic representation of the *Shoah*, though, this does not mean that financial or thematic aspects of film production cannot interfere with content. The general problem, though, that is characteristic for popular culture remains on the agenda: the balance between historical narrative and contemporary need for good entertainment is not always easy to master. Results of historical research and public debates on problems relating to the culture of remembrance and the *Shoah* interfere with aesthetic representations in film, literature, or architecture as the international debates on *Schindler's List* and the architecture of the Jewish Museum in Berlin indicate. The necessary balance, though, can also be disregarded when pure entertainment becomes more relevant than historical accuracy. Joseph Vilsmaier's 1998 film of the famous a capella band, Comedian Harmonists is an example of a convenient representation of the past. The immense conflicts between the Jewish and non-Jewish members of this group at the time of the Nazi's rise to power are smoothed down and polished for the sake of an idealized German Jewish past. Films of this ilk, as entertaining as they may be, always flirt with the danger that the aesthetically brilliant and pleasing representation of a by-gone world may turn out to be a one-way road out of history, where remembering becomes a means to forget. Among widely read novels, this phenomenon occurs as well. Bernhard Schlink's novel *The Reader* and a further illustration of this wave of entertaining by obmission is the widely debated film *Aimé and Jaguar* (1998, Germany; dir. Max Färberbök, based on the biographical fiction by Erika Fischer), which won two prizes at the 1999 Berlin Film Festival for the leading female actresses.[46]

Such debates are not limited to German films. In the past, there have been many debates on Mel Brooks's sharp satirical comedy *The Producers/Springtime for Hitler* (1969; United States) that refer back to discussions on Charles Chaplin's *The Great Dictator* (1940; United States) and on Ernst Lubitsch's *To Be or Not To Be* (1942; United States), and resound in the critique of Roberto Benigni's *Life is Beautiful* (1998; Italy) or in the discussions about the French-Rumanian co-production *Train of Life* (1998).[47] All of these films try, more or less successfully, to tell their stories with humour, music, and a satirical edge. The fact that all of them are well represented in the video market, and that some of them have become classics or even cult movies, illustrates their impact on the visual consciousness of generations.

Well-known Holocaust comedies like *Life is Beautiful* and *Jakob the Liar* and lesser known ones like *Train of Life, Genghis Cohn* and *Mendel* have either managed to succeed or fail at blending humour and pathos. In *Genghis Cohn*, the murdered Jew gets the last laugh as a ghost who haunts the German who killed him. The downtrodden Jews of *Jakob the Liar* elevate Jakob into a hero because he has overheard a radio broadcast about the impending liberation of his ghetto. Seeing how this raises their morale, he fabricates more stories, even though he owns no receiver to confirm them. The father in *Life is Beautiful*, to prevent his son from succumbing to despair, pretends the deadly purpose of a concentration camp is really an elaborate game. *Train of Life* invokes the stock characters and harebrained scheme found in much Yiddish literature about the *shtetl* to enable a village of doomed Jews to evade their oppressors. The young lead character of *Mendel* naïvely imagines what secrets his survivor parents have been concealing from him and eventually summons up the courage to fight against injustice as the resistance fighters of his adopted homeland of Norway did.[48] Although not all of these films were equally effective as comedies, they employ humour in ways that respect the victims and censure the perpetrators without trivializing the suffering of the former or exonerating the latter.

Moreover, many Holocaust historians have stridently criticized what has been termed as the Hollywood version of the Holocaust. Indsdorf, for example doubted whether Hollywood directors could portray the event in sufficiently complex terms and resist relying on epic effects, melodrama, and stars whose previous roles often undermine their credibility as characters trapped in the maelstrom of Nazi genocide.[49] Similarly, Avisar also maintained that 'unlike the personal drives of west and east European filmmakers, who deal with the Holocaust in order to explore and express their national traumas, the American interest in the subject is motivated by other considerations which are not necessarily rooted in a genuine concern with the disturbing truth of the historical tragedy.'[50]

Most historians believe that American public awareness of the Holocaust developed as a response to Israel's trial of Adolf Eichmann at the beginning of the 1960s. Yet the American film industry accounted for 40 per cent of the movies about the Holocaust produced between 1945 and the 1960s.[51] The blanket criticism of American films about the Holocaust also fails to take into account significant changes over the last twenty years in how movies get produced and distributed. First, there is the resurgence of independent filmmaking. Second, venues for the screening of films have proliferated with the advent of cineplexes, film festivals, network television movies, premium movie cable stations, and VCR and DVD players. Finally, the size of the audience reached by the films has grown with the use of new communications technologies like the Internet. Globalization not only extends the influence of the Hollywood image of the Holocaust abroad but also enriches Hollywood productions with the perspectives of foreign actors, crews, and directors recruited to work on American films. A case in point is Steven Spielberg, who hired many cast and crew members who were Croatian, English, German, Israeli and Polish and viewed classic foreign films about the Holocaust to imbue *Schindler's List* with a European look.[52]

Many of these entertainment films doubtlessly trivialize the Jewish experience, but we should never forget that there are many other movies on the subject that do not trivialize, and that do not reach the American or Israeli movie theatres. German films about the Holocaust are part of a cinematic and broader cultural discourse. Many are referential and self-critical. There can be no doubt that most films are, in a broad sense, cinematic contributions to the serious debate on Holocaust remembrance and on film as one of the aesthetic sites of the *Shoah* in Western culture—as ambiguous as some of them may be.

Such ambiguities highlight the very existence of ongoing pro-ductive endeavours to remember the pain and the feeling of loss. Remembering always implies a process of forgetting, and we have to be conscious of the fact that we do not know all the time what to remember and what to forget. To raise didactic fingers whenever works of art provoke an audience is a general problem of culture. In the case of aesthetic representations of the *Shoah* it figures as a byproduct of public discourse.

Concerning Europe, though, we should never forget that images of Jewish women, men, and children on the screens fill a real void that exists in European society as different from North America. Such films revitalize images of the past for popular imagination. They create a whole world of imagined Jews that may perhaps not always live up to historical research or to our knowledge of Jewish social life and culture. Younger European generations, however, may find here sources for learning about their own families and emotional resources for the development of their identities. We know that neither the grandparents of the generation of younger non-Jews nor elementary or higher education can provide what all of these films, regardless of their educational or entertainment value, try to establish—images of something that today's Europe can never be part of, namely, the European Jewish experience of the past. These films fill a cultural and social void. They are the visual representation of a cultural longing, and of remembrance. It might seem base that films facing the past actually serve this sort of purpose. But, in fact, that is the essence of art, cinematic aesthetics, and movies about the Holocaust.

There can be no doubt that in the years to come more stories will be told about the Holocaust. At the same time, we will witness a newer and younger generation of authors and filmmakers. Kurt Maetzig's *Marriage in the Shadows*, Steven Spielberg's *Schindler's List*, Istvan Szabo's *Sunshine*, and Roman Polanski's *The Pianist* are films that can be seen as four outstanding contributions to the visual confrontation with the *Shoah* and related issues since 1947. They highlight the transition from the mid-twentieth century to the first decade of the twenty-first century. They focus on specific personal narratives and pose questions of guilt and responsibility while avoiding the cliché of good and evil and stressing the ambivalences imbued in the experience of the *Shoah*. The 2003 production by Arthur Brauner, *Babij Jar* (2003, Germany; dir. Jeff Kanew) about the mass killing of 33,000 Jews in 1941 by Nazi soldiers, is a very emotional and personal narrative that does not shy away from images of brutal mass shootings or from the complicated relationship of Jews and Ukrainians.[53]

In fact, the 1990s produced not only the maximum number of Holocaust movies but these films as a group achieved more critical and popular acclaim than their predecessors. A cursory survey of some of the best-known films from the 1990s reveals the calibre of this body of work.[54] *The Nasty Girl* (1990), directed by Michael Verhoeven, unmasks the antagonism and obstructionism of a German city toward a teenager conducting research into local complicity in executing Nazi policies during the Nazi era. *Korczak* (1990) directed by Andrzej Wajda, portrays the ultimately futile efforts of the famed Jewish-Polish educator to shield the orphans under his care from the deprivations of the Warsaw ghetto and prevent their deportation to Treblinka. *Europa, Europa* (1991), directed by Agnieszka Holland, traces the incredible survival of a Jewish boy whose Gentile appearance and knowledge of foreign languages gained him entry into the Soviet Young Communists League and German Hitler Youth. *Schindler's List* (1993), directed by Steven Spielberg, portrays the transformation of a war profiteer into a rescuer of Jews amid the backdrop of the decimation of the Jewish community of Krakow. *Under the Donim Tree* (1994), directed by Eli Cohen, delves into the mindset of Israeli children whose parents perished in the Holocaust. *Les Miserables* (1995), directed by Claude Lelouche, imagines how a modern Jean Valjean would have reacted to the plight of the Jews in Vichy, France. *Shine* directed by Scott Hicks, records how the son of a survivor escapes his abusive father and becomes a celebrated pianist. *The Harmonists* (1997), directed by Joseph Vilsmaier, recalls the formation and dissolution of a German singing group comprising Jewish and Gentile musicians. *Life is Beautiful* (1998), directed by

Roberto Benigni, uses humour to show the touching devotion of an Italian Jew to his wife and son in a concentration camp. *Sunshine* (1991), directed by Istvan Szabo, spans the twentieth century to follow the attenuation and recovery of Jewish identity of several generations of Hungarians during the Hapsburg Empire, interwar period, German occupation, Soviet occupation and post-communist era.

The number of documentaries made about the Holocaust in the last decade surpasses the number of feature films released in this period but the extent to which documentaries influence collective memory about the Holocaust is often questioned by Holocaust historians. The reason attributed to this is that their distribution tends to be limited to Jewish and Independent Film festivals, art theatres, the Public Broadcasting System, and cable stations like the Arts and Entertainment Network and the History Channel. Only a few documentaries that win Oscars or receive rave reviews from nationally syndicated film columnists ever land on the shelves of major video-store chains. Nevertheless, Holocaust scholars tend to prefer the authenticity of documentaries over feature films because the former rely on movies taken by the Nazis themselves, newsreel footage, photographs shot by journalists and soldiers when the camps were liberated, photos preserved by the survivors and perpetrators, and interviews with the eyewitnesses to the event. However, the usage of these 'actualities' should not mask the intensive editing of material to substantiate the stance directors assume when they interpret what they have compiled. For instance, Claude Lanzmann's *Shoah*[55] merits the accolades it has received for revealing the bureaucratic nature of the Final Solution, the widespread hostility of Poles towards Jews, and the psychological wounds that burden the minds of the Jewish survivors. Yet in order to shorten *Shoah* to its final 9 hour-length, Lanzmann cut out over 340 hours of the film and he staged situations simulating experiences survivors had endured during the Holocaust to force them to 'relive' the moment. In questioning the appropriateness of Lanzmann's methods, one is not denying the searing impression *Shoah* leaves on its viewers but merely pointing out that making documentaries involves directorial abridgement and emplotment.

Another popular genre which has evolved recently along with the incorporation of the Holocaust into the public school curriculum and the concomitant demand for age appropriate movies on this topic is that of Holocaust films made for children.[56] They have the challenging task of replicating the horrors of the Holocaust without traumatizing their target audience. These films are often based on best-selling children's books. *Alan and Naomi* based on a novel by Myron Levoy, uses buddy genre to depict the experiential gulf between an American boy and a girl who witnessed the Nazis' murder of their father. *Swing Kids* directed by Thomas Carter, provides an object lesson in how political and peer pressure dissolve friendships among a group of adolescent jazz enthusiasts. *The Island on Bird Street* based on Uri Orlev's book and *The Devil's Arithmetic* based on Jane Yolen's novel ransplant the plots of children's classics into the Holocaust and thereby transform an event that is remote into something familiar. Lois Lawry's book *Number the Stars* demonstrated that the rescue of the Jews in Denmark appealed to young readers since it resolved a dangerous situation with a happy ending. Disney's *Miracle at Midnight*, a TV movie based on the rescue of the Danish Jews in Denmark during the Holocaust, follows the same formula.

Movies about neo-Nazis and skinheads comprise the most numerous group of films from the 1990s that refer to the Holocaust.[57] These exposes of contemporary right-wing extremism usually fall outside the purview of Holocaust cinema. Yet they consciously forge a link between the third Third Reich and today's racist movements. Political neo-Nazis and skinheads make more than a fashion statement when they decorate their bodies with swastika tattoos, hang Nazi banners and pictures of Hitler on the walls of their rooms and espouse white supremacist doctrines. They seriously believe that the Final Solution should serve as a model for a future race war conducted against the minorities they stigmatize as aliens or inferiors. That the neo-Nazis and skinheads portrayed in movies produced in different parts of the world vary so little in the clothes they wear and the viewpoints they articulate is a symptom of the Globalization of neo-Nazism. Thus *Rosenzweig's Freedom* underscores the similarities between Hitler's goals and tactics and neo-Nazi violence against asylum seekers and immigrants in reunified Germany.

Since the end of World War II, the rescue of Jews has afforded filmmakers with inspiring plotlines about righteous heroes saving innocent Jews from arrest and deportation. In the 1950s, Bruno Bettelheim attributed the popular appeal of *The Diary of Anne Frank* as a play and movie to its implicit confirmation of Anne's faith in human goodness by failing to depict Anne's suffering at Auschwitz and death in Bergen-Belsen.[58] As *Schindler's List* amply attests, contemporary movies about rescuers of Jews neither idealize their protagonists nor spare their viewers from seeing the terrible fate that awaited the majority of Jews who never found someone like Schindler to protect them.[59]

In the first decades after World War II, movies like *The Juggler*, *The Pawnbroker* and *Sophie's Choice* fixated on the mental instability of survivors forever scarred by their experiences of deprivation, dehumanization, and loss. The television broadcasts of *Holocaust* in 1978 and *Skokie* in 1981, as well as the increasing prominence of Elie Wiesel, which culminated in his receiving the Nobel Peace Prize in 1986, recast the image of the survivor in a more positive light.[60] The survivor has become 'emblematic of Jewish suffering, Jewish memory, and Jewish endurance'.[61] The recent films about survivors encompass a greater range of characterizations of those who lived through the Third Reich's attempt to eradicate them.[62] Their brush with death can intensify their faith in Judaism or their atheism as is evident in the fierce debate between the two protagonists of *The Quarrel*.

The flurry of movies about the children of perpetrators and victims mirrors the maturation of the post-war generation. The offspring of parents who were either implicated in Germany's commission of genocide or managed to survive are now authoring books, memoirs, and screenplays or are directing movies about how these events have left an imprint on their lives, too. The denial of the past or hypocrisy about it can drive an inquisitive adolescent literally up a tree if she rattles the skeletons in her town's past, as *The Nasty Girl* vividly illustrates. *Left Luggage* illustrates that covering or digging up the past can be a source of alienation or intimacy between survivors and their offspring. Movies about second-generation children are the fictionalized counterparts of the documentaries Alan Berger discusses in his book *Children of Job*. Both kinds of films confront 'issues such as the survivors "conspiracy of silence", parents who wanted either to micromanage their children's lives or who, conversely, were emotionally, unavailable, and feelings of being unworthy'.[63]

Several notable Holocaust films have been released since 2000 and the biopic is still the most popular genre.[64] *Max* speculates about how Hitler ultimately chose to pursue a career in politics rather than in art. *Hitler: The Rise of Evil* re-enacts how he emerged from the obscurity as an embittered war veteran to become chancellor of Germany. On the one hand, while the plots and settings of the *Pianist* and *Nowhere in Africa* received critical acclaim and commercial success, *The Grey Zone*'s visceral realism, on the other, repelled audiences. The percolation of the Holocaust into the mainstream of pop culture is evidenced in *X-Men*. Therein the audience witnesses how the villain's loss of his parents in the Holocaust fuels his fears that humanity will persecute mutants like himself.

And that is where we are more than a half century after everything, maybe only on the screen, in the movies, but maybe in real life as well. Cinema is always the mind's eye, seeing beyond the mirrors of reality. It might force an encounter with a painful past; it might serve a redemptive function; it might trivialize; it might deconstruct stereotypes. But through cinema, no matter what its purpose, we start to swim again. We face the past.[65] The shadow of the Holocaust extends far into the future, far beyond the screen.

CONCLUSION

The question inexorably asserts itself: Does there exist another way, another language, to say what is unsayable? The image perhaps? Can it be more accessible, more malleable, more expressive than the word? Can I admit it? I am as wary of one as of the other. Even more of the image. Of the filmed image, of course. One does not imagine the unimaginable. And in particular, one does not show it on screen.

ELIE WIESEL[66]

Film changes the rule of the historical game, insisting on its own sort of truths, truths which arise from a visual and aural realm that is difficult to capture adequately in words. This new historical past on film is potentially much more complex than any written text, for on the screen, several things can occur simultaneously—image, sound, language, even text—elements that support and work against each other to render a meaning as different from written history as written was from oral history.

ROBERT ROSENSTONE[67]

Many Holocaust scholars have tended to share Elie Wiesel's skepticism about the ability of popular feature films to depict the Holocaust without rendering it photogenic, resorting to generic formulas of epic struggles between good heroes and evil villains, or imposing edifying endings on an unmitigated tragedy. Ilan Avisar's criticism of *Schindler's List* typifies this line of reasoning when he says that the message implied in Spielberg's project is one that focuses on exhilarating qualities of courage and moral strength at the expense of an excruciating recognition of the genocidal evil that prevailed over a period of years and at the cost of millions of lives.[68] Similarly, Omer Bartov maintains that Schindler's story fosters a distorted perspective of history because within the context of the Holocaust, it was so unique as to be untrue in the sense of not reflecting (or even negating) the fate of the vast majority of victims who were in turn swallowed up in a unique and unprecedented and therefore (at least as far as Hollywood conventions are concerned) unrepresentable murder machine.[69] Claude Lanzmann, spoke in the same vein categorizing fiction as a transgression and pledging that he deeply believed there are some things that cannot and should not be represented.[70]

Roberto Benigni's *Life is Beautiful* elicited even more severe condemnations than *Schindler's List*. Richard Schickel of *Time Magazine* loathed Benigni's manipulation of emotions because 'sentimentality is a kind of fascism too, robbing us of judgment and moral acuity'.[71] David Denby of the *New Yorker* decried the picture's happy ending as tantamount to Holocaust denial.[72]

The criticisms levelled at *Schindler' List* and *Life is Beautiful* are premised on two assumptions. The first asserts that since the Holocaust is 'unique' and 'exists outside of human meaning', it can never be accurately represented in cinema or literature. Lanzmann extends this opinion to its most radical conclusion. The second assumption concedes that even though it might be possible to approximate what the Holocaust was like in feature films and novels, such portrayals must mirror the reality that most of the Jews died, most of the Germans collaborated with the perpetrators or remained passive bystanders, and most of the victims sent to the showers were gassed.[73]

Holocaust educators and historians are bothered by both of these caveats. In their opinion, human beings planned, implemented, condoned, perished in, resisted and survived the Final Solution. Consequently, it should not be regarded as a supernatural phenomenon beyond human comprehension and representation.

Scholars like Robert Rosenstone value both the accomplishment of feature films in popularizing the Holocaust and the unique capacity of the medium to make history come alive. In his opinion, 'Film lets us see landscapes; hear sounds; witness strong emotions as they are expressed with body and face, or physical conflict between individuals and groups.' For a mass audience, he continues, 'film can most directly render the look and feel of all sorts of historical particulars and situations'.[74] Similarly, Alison Landsberg argues that motion pictures can serve as 'prosthetic memories' that can 'bridge the temporal chasms that separate individuals from the meaningful and potentially interpellative events of the past'.[75]

NOTES

1. See Omer Bartov, *The Holocaust: Origins, Implementation, Aftermath*, London: Routledge, 2000.
2. Frank Stern, 'The Holocaust: Representing Lasting Images in Film and Literature', in Konrad Kwiet (ed.), *Contemporary Responses to the Holocaust*, Westport: Praeger, 2004, p. 193.

3. Ibid., pp. 194-7. Also see Sue Barker, *Holocaust Fiction*, London: Routledge, 2000.
4. See Stern, 'The Holocaust' for greater details on the dimensions of the Holocaust.
5. See Claude Lanzmann, *Shoah: An Oral History of the Holocaust; The Complete Text of the Film*, New York: Random House, 1985.
6. Quoted from an Internet Article by Raymond Federman, 'The Necessity and Impossibility of Being a Jewish Writer', p. 1, available at: http://www.federman.com/
7. See Sue Vice, *The Holocaust Fiction*, London: Routledge, 2000.
8. Anna Seghers, *The Seventh Cross*, tr. James Austin Galston, Montana: Kessinger Publishing House, 2005, p. 338.
9. See Primo Levi, *If This is a Man*, tr. Stuart Woolf, London: Everyman's Library, 2000.
10. See Primo Levi, *If Not Now, When?* London: Penguin Books, 1987.
11. See Anne Insdorf, *Indelible Shadows: Film and Holocaust*, Cambridge: Continuum, 1983 and Andrea Reiter, *Narrating the Holocaust*, Cambridge: Continuum, 2000.
12. See Insdorf, *Indelible Shadows*.
13. See Stern, 'The Holocaust'.
14. See Victor Klemperer, *The Lesser Evil: The Diaries of Victor Klemperer 1945-59*, tr. Martin Chalmers, London: Orion Publishing, 2004.
15. Ibid.
16. Ibid.
17. See Stern, 'The Holocaust'.
18. Ibid.
19. Ibid.
20. See Marlon Kaplan, *Between Dignity and Despair*, Oxford: Oxford University Press, 1997.
21. See Lawrence Baron, *Projecting the Holocaust into the Present*, Lanham: Rowman and Littlefield, 2005.
22. Ibid.
23. See Andre Pierre Colombat, *The Holocaust in French Films*, Lanham: Rowman and Littlefield, 1993.
24. See Stern, 'The Holocaust'.
25. See Idith Zertal, *Israel's Holocaust and the Politics of Nationhood*, Cambridge: Cambridge University Press, 2005.
26. See Lawrence L. Langer, *Admitting the Holocaust: Collected Essays*, New York: Oxford University Press, 1995.
27. See Insdorf, *Indelible Shadows*.
28. See Colombat, *The Holocaust in French Films*.
29. See Baron, *Projecting the Holocaust into the Present*.
30. Ibid.
31. Berel Lang, *Writing and the Holocaust*, NY, London: Holmes and Meier, 1988.
32. See Stern, 'The Holocaust'.
33. Ibid.
34. See Baron, *Projecting the Holocaust into the Present*.
35. See Insdorf, *Indelible Shadows*.
36. See the memoir of Salomon Perel, *Europa, Europa: A Memoir of World War II*, New York: Wiley, 1997.

37. See Insdorf, *Indelible Shadows.*
38. See Stern, 'The Holocaust'.
39. Ibid.
40. Insdorf, *Indelible Shadows.*
41. See Jurek Becker, *Jakob the Liar: A Novel*, New York: Arcade Publishing House, 1975.
42. See Toby Haggith et al., *Holocaust and the Moving Image: Representations in Film and Television Since 1933*, London: Wallflower Press, 2005.
43. Ibid.
44. Lang, *Writing and the Holocaust.*
45. See Stern, 'The Holocaust'.
46. See Haggith et al., *Holocaust and the Moving Image.*
47. Ibid.
48. See Baron, *Projecting the Holocaust into the Present.*
49. See Insdorf, *Indelible Shadows.*
50. See Ilan Avisar, *Screening the Holocaust*, Bloomington: Indiana University Press, 1988.
51. See Baron, *Projecting the Holocaust into the Present.*
52. Ibid.
53. See Stern, 'The Holocaust'.
54. See Baron, *Projecting the Holocaust into the Present.*
55. Ibid.
56. Ibid.
57. See Haggith et al., *Holocaust and the Moving Image.*
58. Ibid.
59. Ibid.
60. Ibid.
61. Ibid.
62. Ibid.
63. Ibid.
64. Ibid.
65. See Stern, 'The Holocaust'.
66. Quoted from Baron, *Projecting the Holocaust into the Present*, Lanham: Rowman and Littlefield, 2005, p. 1.
67. Ibid.
68. See Avisar, *Screening the Holocaust.*
69. See Bartov, *The Holocaust.*
70. See Lanzmann, *Shoah.*
71. See Baron, *Projecting the Holocaust into the Present*, p. 3.
72. Ibid.
73. Ibid.
74. Ibid. p. 6.
75. Ibid.

12

Representation of the Armenian Genocide in Popular Culture

SUSMITA BHATTACHARYA

INTRODUCTION

Medz Yeghern (Great Calamity), *Medz Vochir* (Great Crime), *Aghet/ Aghed* (Catastrophe), or *Haykakan Tseghaspanuthyun* (Armenian Genocide)—all these expressions have become inseparable elements of Armenian collective consciousness and national identity construction. These terms refer to the atrocities and mass annihilation through forced deportation and other gruesome means, committed against the Armenian population of the Ottoman Empire along with the Assyrians, Greeks and others by the political party Committee of Union and Progress (CUP) (*Ittihad ve Terakki Jemiyeti*), popularly known as the Young Turks during and after the World War I. The Armenian Genocide began in 1915 and culminated in the flight or expulsion in 1921-2 of the survivors who after the war had returned to the region of Cilicia.[1] The Armenians mark the date 24 April 1915 as the beginning of what they regard as the genocide, the night when the Ottoman government arrested about 250 Armenian intellectuals and com-munity leaders in Constantinople, and later executed them.[2] It is estimated that altogether one and a half million Armenians perished during this period, and the rest were forcibly driven out from their millennia-old ancestral homeland, and most of the tangible evidence of their three thousand years of material and spiritual culture were wiped out.

The Armenian Genocide, the second most-studied case of genocide,[3] has divided the world community on the question of recognition of the perpetrations by the Ottoman government against the Armenians during World War I as 'Genocide'. Whether or not the deaths of hundreds of thousands of Armenians during First

World War amounted to genocide is a matter for heated debate and remains a highly sensitive issue. Though a large number of historians and scholars[4] categorized it as genocide, there are some scholars who question this. Many countries like Canada, France, Italy, Russia, forty-two states of the USA, and several international organizations like European Parliament, UN Sub-Commission on Prevention of Discrimination and Protection of Minorities have officially recognized the genocide. But still there are many others who have resisted calling it as genocide. On the one hand the Armenians, particularly the diasporan communities all over the world, are actively engaged in gaining formal recognition of the crime as 'genocide' both by the Turkish authority and the international community. On the other hand, the Turkish government refuses to accept the term genocide as an accurate description of the events.[5]

ARMENIAN GENOCIDE AS A THEME OF POPULAR CULTURE

Popular culture both as an academic discipline and as a subject of multidisciplinary studies has undergone a long process of evolution and is still in a formative stage. The meaning of 'popular' and the meaning of 'culture' essentially remain contested concepts, and we are yet to receive a universally accepted definition of popular culture. Discourses concerning the connotation, scope, dimension, content and other related issues of popular culture are still going on. But if 'popular culture' is considered to be the widespread cultural element in any given society, and if we accept the 'collectivity', 'mass impact' and 'mass involvement' as some of its basic characteristics, the 'Armenian Genocide' undoubtedly fits into this category and obviously can be regarded as a theme of Armenian popular culture. Here I would like to share the view expressed more than once by many of my friends from this ethnic community, like Vachegan Tadevosyan, Narine Sahakyan, Naira Mkrtchyan, Anush Matevosyan and many others, that it is rare to find a family either in Armenia or especially in the diaspora, which has not been devastated by the blow of this crime against humanity. The Armenian Genocide thus inexorably has become an integral part of the Armenian collective consciousness. Razmik Panossian writes in his book entitled *The Armenians: From Kings and Priests to Merchants and Commissars*: 'It is impossible to understand 20th century Armenian consciousness—particularly until 1988—without situating the Genocide at its very centre. The elimination of the Armenians from their historic lands in the Ottoman Empire was the ultimate "Catastrophe".'[6]

April 24 has turned into a significantly solemn date for the entire Armenian community around the world, which commemorates it as part of their culture. On the night of 23-4 April 1915, hundreds of Armenian political, religious, educational, and intellectual leaders in Constantinople were arrested, deported to Anatolia and ultimately eliminated. Though the dispersed community started commemorating the day since 1919, it was confined to requiem services and programmes in which they read sympathetic messages from government officials, foreign dignitaries and religious leaders. It gained a new dimension and momentum in the year 1965 when the fragmented Armenian diaspora from all corners of the globe succeeded in coming together in large numbers for a united commemoration of the fiftieth anniversary of the 'Armenian Genocide' along with their counterpart in Soviet Armenia, where the occasion was observed for the first time since the 1920s. And Tsitsenakaberd in Yerevan became a pilgrimage for the members of the community.

It was during this period that a new wave of nationalism revived which engendered the 'Campaign for Recognition of the Armenian Genocide'. The Armenian world burst into frenzied activities aiming at reaching this goal. They started insisting on the use of the word 'Genocide' by the world community instead of the less forceful term massacres, which does not necessarily imply intent to eliminate a people. The politics centring genocide recognition also took its root at this time and began to affect the Armenian political identity in the diaspora, especially after the 1970s. To be precise, in 1973 the assassination of two Turkish consular officers in California by an elderly survivor of the genocide and obvious reference and description of the forgotten genocide in the press coverage revived the issue after long years of silence.

The campaign that started in the mid-1960s turned into a popular movement, especially in the years following the outbreak of anti-Armenian violence in the Azerbaijani industrial city of Sumgait in 1988 and the Karabakh crisis and subsequent developments in the Caucasus. Suddenly along with other issues, genocide became current, and immediate spontaneous associations with 1915 were made everywhere. It no longer remained a haunting, terrible memory but turned into a living reality.

The main objective of this international movement, as suggested by the campaigners, is to create greater awareness about this tragedy and fight for its official recognition worldwide; to promote the necessity of prevention of occurrence of such crime anywhere in the world; to educate and make the world community as well as the new Armenian generation understand the Armenian Genocide and realize its ramifications across the world.

The Armenian Genocide was not an issue anymore after the Lausanne Treaty of 1923. In the initial years the diaspora communities tended to internalize their frustrations, hostility, suffering, and even creative and constructive talents. Survivors and their immediate descendents had to bear the traumatic past with them, discreetly commemorating the Great Crime *Metch Vochir* in a community framework. Step by step though, with various contributions from eminent personalities like Franz Werfel and Raphael Lemkin, and the adoption of the Convention on the Prevention and Punishment of the Crime of Genocide by the UN General Assembly on 9 December 1948, a new awareness was created among the Armenians that crystallized in massive public celebrations held in 1965 and henceforth a new political assertiveness was formed towards official recognition among the Armenian diaspora.

It took two decades for the survivors of Armenian Genocide and the succeeding generations to cope with the psychological and emotional trauma caused by the calamity, world communities' indifference to the plight of the exiled Armenians, and particularly the apathy of the great powers, and the Turkish attempts to deny or rationalize the crime. During the period between the two World Wars, the dispersed community concentrated their collective energies on refugee and relief resettlement, creation of a new diaspora infrastructure of cultural, educational, and religious institutions and above all on adjustment to the host countries. Then once they were successful in making a niche in the host societies after absorbing the shock they made their voice heard.

The genocide had a profound impact on the Armenian national identity. The millennia-long evolution of collective identity formation on historic territories came to an abrupt end. Though the genocide is not the only defining characteristic of 'Armenianness', it has come to be a dominant feature, particularly among the diaspora. It transformed the identity of the survivors into a community of genocide victims. It was no longer a diaspora of merchants, labourers, fortune seekers, intellectuals and political exiles. Rather, it was of refugees, starving survivors and a deeply scarred people. Moreover, the diaspora and the homeland no longer co-existed as two parts of the same nation, with their strong reinforcing links. Since the homeland was completely decimated—physically lost—the diaspora no longer had the option to return and was condemned to live in dispersion. Decades after 1915, the genocide remained—and for many still remains—the core attribute of modern Armenian identity, woven with diasporan identity. Close to a century after the event, its legacy is distinctly reflected through the literary lens.

At present the issue of genocide along with the movement has permeated among all sections and layers of the Armenian diasporan society everywhere, from the USA to Iran, from France and the United Kingdom to Lebanon, from Argentina to Australia. The present generation of diaspora Armenians afflicted by the trans-generational trauma has engaged in concentrated effort in pursuance of their goal. While there are eminent scholars like Richard Hovannisian, Vahakn Dadrian, Gerard Libaridian, Lorne Shirinian and many others engaged in academic research, analysis and publications to legitimize the claim, the personalities in different fields of popular culture have been busy in presenting the issue in their respective ways.

The Armenians lost their ancestral land and their millennia-old heritage. What remained were collective memories. The new generation of diaspora Armenians are concerned with memory—how to preserve the memory of the remaining survivors. With this end in view, the campaigners and supporters of this highly sensitive, complex and debatable issue exploited various forms of popular culture like literature, films, documentaries and music.

Since this paper cannot include all these forms of popular culture exploited by the campaigners, it therefore attempts to project 'Armenian Genocide' only as a highly sensitive and complex issue which has been portrayed in some of the well-known novels and films, as representatives of popular culture.

COLLECTIVE MEMORY THROUGH LITERARY LENS

Literature has always been one of the forces that forge the morality and sensitivity of a civilization so that the question may be seen as a way of testing the fundamental attitudes and convictions of that civilization. The memory of the genocide, as the most important event in the recent history of the Armenian people, the unresolved injustice, the indomitable pain and mourning over the colossal loss, persisted in the diaspora and served as the common thread stringing together the diasporan literature. The memory of the genocide reverberated in literature as a source of identity, a leitmotiv or a hidden theme. Successive generations of diasporan writers tried to confront the catastrophe (*aghet*), comprehend it, and deal with it. Diasporan Armenian literature in one way or another relates to the genocide.[7] They are representations of collective memory.

Khente (The Fool) (1993) by Raffi, whose real name was Akop Melik Akopian, is not a novel of the Armenian Genocide of 1915-23 *per se*, since it was originally published in 1881 and deals with the Russo-Turkish War of 1877-8. But this masterpiece should be mentioned for its importance in understanding the historical context of the Armenians in the Ottoman Empire in the late nineteenth century. It can be argued that if Raffi's messages of Armenian self-sufficiency had been more widely heeded, the tragedies of the 1890s and 1915 might have turned out differently. Long before the large-scale massacres began, Raffi called for action, unity, and self-reliance. Many of his criticisms of the Armenian community of the time are equally as applicable today as they were nearly 125 years ago. He foresaw what was in store for the Armenians if they did not actively seek to change their fate.

Adam Bagdasarian's *Forgotten Fire* (2002) is a brutally vivid, utterly compelling and elegantly written narrative fiction based on the tape recording of the verbal recounting of the author's great-uncle's experiences during the Armenian Genocide. His novel covers the years 1915-18 when a boy, Vahan, the youngest member of the wealthy, influential and well-respected family of an Armenian lawyer from Bitlis, Turkey, is stripped of everything simply because he is an Armenian.

Forced to watch his father and uncle being escorted out of their lives by the Turkish police, his brothers shot dead in his backyard, his grandmother being murdered by a rock-wielding guard, and his sister take poison rather than being raped by soldiers, twelve-year-old Vahan Kendarian abruptly begins to learn what his father meant when he used to say 'steel is made stronger by fire . . . '. His secure world in the lap of luxury is shattered as the 'genocide' begins. After a forced march, he loses all other members of his family one by one. He faces hunger, destitution, beatings and sexual abuse and is forced to live a life he would never have dreamt of. He tries to run, that results in his three years struggle to survive alone in a country torn by war and hatred of his race. He lives on begging, pretending to be deaf and mute, dressing as a girl, hiding out in the basements and outhouses, and even living for a time with the 'Horse-shoer of Baskale', a Turkish governor known for nailing horse-shoes to the feet of his Armenian victims. Time and again, the terrified and desperate boy grows close to someone, only to lose him or her in an appalling and violent death. However, somehow Vahan's incredible strength and spirit help him to endure even knowing that each day could be his last. Through his experiences he develops, matures, and strengthens his resolve. Vahan is forced to grow into a man reaching freedom, as he escapes to the safe haven of Constantinople in 1918. *Forgotten Fire* is thus the story of one boy's search for the survivor inside himself. It is the story of a lost nation and a powerful celebration of the resilience of the human spirit during the darkest of times. It is inspiring to see a person like Vahan moving ahead in life under such horrible conditions.

This fragment of the narration tells us how close was the place to their heart, which the Armenians had to leave forcibly.

As far as an Armenian from Bitlis was concerned, Bitlis was the centre of the world: her mountains were the highest, her soil the most fertile, her women the loveliest, her men the bravest, her leaders the wisest. (*Forgotten Fire* by Adam Bagdasarian)

Nancy Kricorian's first novel *Zabelle* (1997) is an exuberant and magical tale of an Armenian woman's life, spanning from her childhood in Ottoman Turkey to grandmotherhood in modern America. In vivid poetic prose, Zabelle recounts the story of a lively heroine whose ordinary life is infused with ghost and memories of her extraordinary past. A child at the outbreak of World War I, Zabelle Chahasbanian was forced to join the death march with her mother, grandparents, and two brothers for hundreds of miles out of Turkey to Ras Al-Ain in the Syrian desert. Her father was taken from their home at the outbreak of the violence in April 1915 and was never heard from again. The starvation, deprivation, and Turkish attacks during the trek prove too much for her mother, grandparents, and baby brother, and with her elder brother, she is left an orphan with only her best friend Arsinee to console her.

Her marriage is arranged with an older man in America, and she emigrates to the Armenian enclave in Watertown, Massachusetts, where she begins a quiet but emotionally restive life. Although she is now a world away from the remote village where she was born, she remains captive to its old-world traditions—caring for her family, cleaning her house, tending to her garden, and generally suspicious of anyone who is not Armenian.

The novel notes that the assimilation, which brought richness to succeeding generations of Armenians, did not work for Zabelle. Zabelle, despite being educated, confined her world to her family, home, and church once she came to America. Zabelle dealt with the terror that had overwhelmed her in the world that she had fled–in silence. There was no coming to terms with the anger and sadness that she—and the other survivors, both male and female—felt toward the Turks for their murderous acts as well as toward the international community for failing to redress the loss. The only time Zabelle revisits her past is in her sleep, when the nightmares set in.

Like Zabelle Chahasbanian, most of these women have died. Their heroic experiences, however, both in the old and new worlds are vital to understand how the Armenian diaspora, like other groups of immigrants, have maintained their ethnic identity and have been nourished by it.

Peter Balakian's memoir is about growing up as an American in a family that was haunted by a past too fraught with terror to be spoken of openly. *Black Dog of Fate* (1997) is set in the affluent New Jersey suburbs where Balakian, the firstborn son of his generation, grew up in a close, extended family, at the centre of what was a quintessential American baby boom childhood. Yet despite this calm exterior, at the centre of his family's memories lay the dark spectre of a trauma his forebears had experienced during the genocide of 1915. The unforgettable figure of the story is Balakian's grandmother, a survivor and widow of the genocide who speaks in fragments of metaphor and myth when she cooks Armenian delicacies. Balakian moves from childhood memory to history to his ancestors' lives, and lastly to the story of a poet's coming of age in the unfolding recovery of his sense of identity.

In all of this germ madness there seemed to be some deeper, more pervasive anxiety being expressed. Some pathological fear that I sensed in my grandmother when she hovered over me, incessantly brushing her hand over my hair and asking me, How are you, what can I do for you, are you OK? Eench, eench, eench. [What, what, what] For my grandparents' and parents' generation, perhaps the world was a place conspiring to kill you. After the Genocide, the fear of death was different from the fear of mortality. In this atmosphere of deep anxiety, our family was far from the optimistic mood of suburbia. As my grandmother said to me as I lay on my bed recovering from the measles, 'Sleep with one eye open; know the evil eye.' (*Black Dog of Fate: A Memoir: An American Son Uncovers his Armenian Past* by Peter Balakian)

A trend in the recent past has been to translate literary works originally written in the Armenian language into English, the universal *lingua-franca*, to reach out to the broader masses and to let the victim's side of the story be marketed to the world. For example, *Bloody News from My Friend* (1996) is a collection of twelve poems translated by Peter Balakian and Nevart Yaghlian from the original works of Siamanto (1878-1915).

Siamanto, whose real name was Atom Yarjanian, was one of the most eminent poets of the twentieth century, and was among the

Armenian intellectuals executed by the Turkish government at the beginning of the genocide.

Don't be afraid. I must tell you what I saw, so people will understand /the crimes men do to men. For two days, by the road to the graveyard. . . . (*Bloody News from My Friend* [tr. Peter Balakian and Nevart Yaghlian])

The collection depicts the atrocities committed by the Ottoman Turkish government against its Armenian population with special reference to the 1909 massacres in Adana. The collection of twelve poems bears the imprint of the genocide in a language that is raw and blunt; often eschewing metaphor and symbol for more stark representation. Siamanto confronts pain, destruction, sadism, and torture as few modern poets have. The pieces are accompanied by a critical introduction by Peter Balakian, which places Siamanto's poems in a proper literary and historical context.

'What do you remember, Ma?'
'I remember many things but I can't remember my mother's face.'
'Tell me what you remember.'
(*Daughters of Memory*, a story by Peter Najarian)

With *Daughters of Memory* (1986), Peter Najarian becomes one of the first, if not the first, author-artists born in the Diaspora to engage in self-reflexivity and tackle the issue of past—memories that keep escaping descendants of Armenian survivors. Through self-reflexivity, Najarian positions himself within the narrative of his survivor mother and creates a whole new landscape for mapping the identity construction of a specific segment of diasporic Armenians: the generation of non-Armenian-speaking Armenian-Americans.

I always keep raisins in the house. They keep me alive. Ever since the desert I keep raisins in the house. In the desert all we had to eat was a handful of raisins a day. Without those raisins I wouldn't be alive now. (*Daughters of Memory* by Peter Najarian)

This is an unusual novel about women as a source of inspiration in society, interwoven with the commentary of three elderly Armenian women who survived the genocide. The three women's conversation centres on the facts about life in America and the days gone by. The author also embarks on a personal search to understand more about the hardships experienced by his grandmother, a young peasant who was killed in the Syrian desert. The plot of *Daughters of Memory* is simple. Zeke, 'a big-nosed, bald', Armenian artist, is reviewing his life's work. He ends up confronting the spirits of history, and of his maternal grandmother, who perished in the desert wastelands of

Mesopotamia. The story of the author and that of his protagonist are almost synonymous. It is his life story and the stories of his mother that he transposes to his character. As the narrator embarks on this journey of self-excavation and redemption, trying to give shape to the image of his grandmother, the reader encounters the many layers and crosscurrents of history through which his identity is formed and transformed. *Daughters of Memory* is a series of interwoven vignettes detailing Zeke's, and by extension Peter's attempt to grasp his unwritten and ruptured history. The narration is punctuated with a female chorus of survivors from his mother's generation.

Passage to Ararat (1996) by Michael Arlen (original name Dikran Kouyoundjian) is a remarkable account of one man's journey to learn more about what his father tried to block from his memory— the tragedy of the Armenian Genocide. It is a true story with the resonance of a novel. The author travels to Armenia and Turkey to learn first-hand about the history and culture of his forebears. In this fascinating voyage, there is humour and sadness. Arlen tells a story as large as a whole people, yet as personal and focused as the uneasy bond between a father and son. In his search to learn about Armenia and Armenians, he has written about anyone who has ever tried to come to terms, not just with a father, but with a father's fears.

I was born in 1915 on the Anatolian plateau, beneath a ubiquitous sky whose iridescent blue was like a fine lace veil covering my eyes. I saw the world through the openings and around the edges of the scalloped filet. I remember seeing the reaching branches and green leaves of the oak tree like hands in prayer, the grooves in the brown-gray tree bark like empty rivers, and the drifting of woolly cloud shapes like prehistoric beasts. I didn't know what to call these blue-edged pictures before my eyes, but I saw them clearly in the hours before my death. (*Three Apples Fell from Heaven* by Micheline Aharonian Marcom)

Three Apples Fell from Heaven by Micheline Aharonian Marcom (2002) is a novel set in 1915-17, reveals the Armenian Genocide in poetic language that conjures images of desperation and absolute agony yet allows love and strength of spirit to filter into this overwhelming narrative. Marcom's passion for her Armenian heritage spills into the novel as she brilliantly weaves religion, landscape, and the daily rituals of Anatolian Armenians into her chapters about a people doomed to the atrocities of the Turks. Possibly one of the best pieces of fiction written about the Armenian Genocide, Marcom brings the experience into vivid focus with the precision of a talented writer and studied historian. Drawing on the experiences of her grandmother, a survivor, Marcom recorded the many voices of the Armenian massacre and diaspora. Anaguil, a young Armenian girl taken in by her neighbour, a Turkish Muslim family after her parents' deaths, trying to hold on to her culture; Sargis, a student hiding from the Turkish police in his mother's attic, writing poetry as he loses his mind; Lucine, a servant at the American embassy, and the consul's mistress, Rachel, who has known all of them and who speaks after her death from the bottom of a well; Maritsa, a Muslim woman who wishes she were a boy—all these characters and others voice their stories in interconnected chapters of this book.

We never talked about the massacres. It was as if we had forgotten about our past troubles, but often they would surface in different ways. (*The Road from Home: The Story of an Armenian Girl* by David Kherdian)

The Road from Home: The Story of an Armenian Girl (1988) by David Kherdian, a poet and anthologist, is the biography of his mother, Veron Dumehjian and her unique and gripping story of courage, survival, and hope. Veron was born to a prosperous family that lived in the Armenian quarter of the city of Aziziya, Turkey. Her early childhood was idyllic, until 1915 when the Turkish government, after years of persecuting its Christian minorities, decided to rid Turkey of its Armenian population. Veron was deported with her family and survived incredible hardship and suffering until at the age of 16, she left for America as a 'mail-order' bride.

In *Mayrig* (1991) with all the poignancy of a man at his mother's deathbed, holding fast to her hand and reflecting on the story that will no longer be theirs but his alone, Henri Verneuil begins the journey back to a childhood lovingly remembered. It is an odyssey that takes us not only through time but through the complex landscape of relationships and emotional milestones in which the young Achod Malakian grew into manhood. The steamer to France, the search for a place to live, a poor man's summer vacation, looking for work, the nightmare of school, these are only some of the places this story takes us. It tells a universal tale of all men and women who, one way or another, are exiled and reborn, heartbroken and hopeful, defeated and triumphant.

Antonia Arslan's debut novel *Skylark Farm* (2004) chronicles the life of a family struggling for survival during the Armenian Genocide in Turkey in 1915. At the centre is Yervant, who, at thirteen, left his home in the Anatolian hills of Turkey to study at an Armenian boarding school in Venice. After forty years, in May 1915, he is planning a long-awaited reunion with his family at their homestead, Skylark Farm. Unfortunately at this time, Italy enters the Great War and closes its borders. Simultaneously in Turkey, Yervant's family begins a brutal odyssey of forced marches and prison camps, hunger and humiliation at the hands of the Young Turks. In this novel the author draws on the memories of her own family to tell the story of the Armenians, and a nostalgic longing for a lost homeland and lost happiness. It was made into a movie by the Italian directors the Taviani brothers and screened at the 57th Berlin Film Festival, 2007.

The Promise at the Sea (2004) by Vitali Ianko is the story of Nargiz and her family that intermingles tragedy and romance. It is a story filled with love, betrayal, suspense, and miraculous escapes. Readers of this fictionalized memoir will come away with a much clearer sense of what happened during the Armenian Genocide. The story is narrated by Nargiz, the last survivor and a medium, who is devoted and obliged to remembering her lost loved ones. Nargiz wavers between the frightened young girl who barely survives the years of the Armenian Genocide, and the sharp older woman she becomes. Sad, funny, strange, and based on a true story, this book is a long caravan of thoughts and reminiscences carrying a weighty notion: tell to remember, and remember to keep the dead alive.

Florence Soghoian in *Portrait of a Survivor* (1997) writes a moving story telling the personal journey of a mother and daughter as they miraculously live through the violence. The author asks what her mother Shnorhig and grandmother Vartouhi had in them that allowed them to endure the atrocities, the only two of a family of eighteen to survive. Their deep religious convictions and strength of character gave them the faith and hope not to give up. So beyond revealing a very well-documented period of history, there is an underlying message in this sensitively-written portrait: no matter how terrible life may seem, do not give up. This is a fascinating story of transformation of a sixteen-year-old girl Shnorhig, from a tortured survivor of cruelty, violence and brutal hardships during the marching and living in refugee camps, to a happy elder woman, from a deprived Armenian to abundant American. This is saga of intensive sojourn in the New World.

I look at my olive tree, and I know that my family members 80 years ago did not suffer and die in vain. They live on. In that olive tree. In my heart and soul. (*Portrait of a Survivor* by Florence Soghoian)

Time and space had lost meaning and measure. From dawn to sunset the caravan was prodded ahead. No hope was left among the exiles; any reserves of faith that they might escape the hell that hounded them had dried up. Darkness continued to drape their days. How was this going to end? And where? When? (*Death and Resurrection: A Novel of the Armenian Massacres* by Antranig Antreassian)

Death and Resurrection (1988) is by the well-known Armenian-American author Antranig Antreassian, himself a survivor of the tragedy. The story vividly and dramatically talks of life on the deportation trails, the resistance of some and the ultimate death for many in the deserts of Mesopotamia. The novel traces the difficulties encountered after the Armenians established an independent republic in 1918 and concludes with the subsequent establishment of the Soviet Republic of Armenia in 1920. The chapters 'The Death of an Armenian City', 'Toward the Desert of Death', 'Aleppo', 'Last Way Station Before the End and Der Zor', 'Dominion of the Dead' deserve special mention.

Affinity with Night Skies (2005) by Astrid Katcharyan is the biographical novel of Astra Sabondjian, born into culture and privilege in late nineteenth-century Armenia. From her earliest days, savage wars force a nomadic destiny on her, through five countries, for more than forty years. Set against a historical and political backdrop, the story analyses the psychological perspectives of a reluctant heroine. Refusing to be a victim, and driven by a mission to build a safe haven around the people she loves, she meets spine-chilling fate head on. Astra, idealistic, radical and passionate, marries her hero, a well-known newspaper editor and political activist. But living in an empire seething with brutality and ethnic intolerances, mortal dangers are never far away. Forced to abandon her personal dreams, she reaches deep into her creative talents, which take her to unexpected heights, but then in life she must learn to always expect the unexpected.

REMINISCENCE IN VISUAL IMAGES

Films, an integral part of popular culture, nowadays have also become a very important means for the campaigners of the genocide to voice their opinions and present their side of the happenings to the world. While discussing about the films depicting this sensitive issue in a lucid but heart wrenching manner, the below-mentioned films are well acclaimed.

Ararat (2002), written and directed by Armenian-Canadian director Atom Egoyan loosely based on the siege of Van during the Armenian Genocide, attempted to revisit the 1915 mass murder of the Armenians in Turkey by way of the life of painter Arshile Gorky. It also portrayed the present-day traumas of the Armenians in Toronto. In *Ararat*, Egoyan deals with the historical consciousness of diasporic Armenians as a communal group. He, as the director and screenwriter of the film, emerges as an author-historian, the collective memories of his subjects and communal group become his object of study and representation. A modern meditation on memory and intergenerational trauma *Ararat* tells the juxtaposed story of four families, all lost in their nightmarish personal and national histories and all trapped in some sort of denial. What unites these unrelated characters is a complex web of relationships surrounding the production of the film-within-the-film, intended by its fictional director Edward Saroyan (Charles Aznavour). This complex and powerful tale of the Armenian Genocide is based on the very clever use of the 'film within a film' technique. Both Egoyan's film and the film within the film are called *Ararat*. Mt. Ararat occupies a prominent place in the ethos of the Armenian nation and its mythology. Ani [Arsinee Khanjian], an art history professor who has just finished a book on the most famous genocide survivor, Gorky, lectures on the painter's life and work. In her lectures she expounds movingly on one of Gorky's greatest paintings, 'Portrait of the Artist and His Mother' (1928-36), which the film portrays as an essential touchstone to Armenian cultural identity. Celia attends these lectures to heckle Ani about her father's death. Her expertise is employed for the project. She spends considerable time on one of Gorky's masterpiece from his figurative years and argues that it alludes to the theme of genocide. The film is an artful re-creation of documented events, much of which has been taken from Clarence Ussher's 1917 memoir, 'An American Physician in Turkey'. Ussher, played by Bruce Greenwood, appears as a character in the film within the film.

Ararat has an especially deep personal resonance. One paradoxical question that *Ararat* confronts is whether it is possible to leave the past and its pain behind while retaining lessons that can be absorbed only by chewing on history's bitter residue. *Ararat* showed how an 87-year-old historical trauma still reverberates through the lives of contemporary Armenians living on another continent. Gorky's spirit is the most powerful of the many ghosts haunting *Ararat*. There are recurrent images of the painter (played by Simon Abkarian), who immigrated to the United States in 1920 (he committed suicide in 1948), contemplating the canvas and weeping as he applies the finishing touches. 'The only concern was to find a way to give voice to a true history, to retrieve it from oblivion and make the viewers ask themselves why they have never heard of it.'[8]

La masseria delle allodole (*The Lark Farm* Berlin Film Festival 2007) is considered to be an important and stirring contribution to the culture of reminiscence. Its screenplay is based on an eponymous novel (2004) by Antonia Arslan and directed by the Italian directors Paolo and Vittorio Taviani. The film deals with the human effects of persecution, political violence and with the desire to rebel against fate. It is a film filled with vivid images and meaningful gestures. In one scene, a Turkish soldier stands awkwardly next to an opulently set table. He carefully picks up the soup bowl, lifts it into the air, pauses for a moment, and then slowly pours the soup over the damask tablecloth. The horror begins with the insignificant, setting the stage for the unimaginable in the most polite of ways.

In another scene, Turkish servants suddenly refuse to unload the truck belonging to their Armenian masters, saying that it's too late in the day for work. A short time later, the masters, already earmarked for slaughter as enemies of the people, have been reduced to sobbing bundles of flesh as they beg for their lives. This is how genocide begins.

The novel traces the life of the Avakians, a respected middle-class Armenian family that lives in a provincial city, hoping that things will not take a turn for the worse. The film begins with scenes of beautiful women wearing long dresses, filmed in the light of a Vermeer painting. The family patriarch has died, and Colonel Arkan (André Dussollier) in spite of being a Turkish bows to pay his respects to the deceased. But then Arkan receives his orders from Istanbul, that he promptly obeys. In only a few scenes, the directors depict the mixture of obedience and cowardice, of expediency and vileness that has always made ethnic cleansing and pogroms possible. The men and boys are crucified, castrated and hacked to pieces, and the women are sent on a starvation march into the deserts of eastern Anatolia.

The role of Amine Avakian has been played by Arsinée Khanjian, an Armenian-Canadian who lost part of her own family. In one scene the severed head of her husband is thrown into her lap. 'She was adamant about acting in our film. She felt that it was a sort of obligation to her murdered great-grandparents. We promised her that we would only shoot this scene once, and without rehearsal', says Paolo Taviani. 'According to the script, she was supposed to scream. But all that came out was a muffled silence. We left it that way.'[9]

The film My Son Shall Be Armenian (2004-5) by the noted filmmaker Hagop Goudsouzian depicts the struggle of a people with over 300-year-old history, against oblivion and for official recognition of the first genocide of the twentieth century. A reflection on the Armenian identity, this movie follows the filmmaker and five other Montrealers of Armenian descent as they return to the land of their forebears in search of survivors of the 1915 genocide. Goudsouzian weaves a moving account of the centenarians and the touching reactions of the New World travellers to a poignant film about the need to make peace with the past in order to move into the future.

At the outset of their six-year adventure, the film retraces the deportees' route through Deir ez Zor in the heart of the Syrian desert on the bank of Euphrates where thousands of their forefathers were massacred. Just eight hours before their departure, however, their visas are denied by the Syrian authorities, and they are forced to change routes. As the little band combs the Armenian countryside to find survivors they meet with horrifying sights which bring them face to face with brutal pictures of the past—men lined up behind one another so that they are killed by a single bullet, two people tied together and one shot before being thrown into water so that the other one is dragged down to a watery death—acts driven by a will to systematically destroy a people. These compelling images of the film are accompanied by a stirring narration script by Michel Langlois, read by Goudsouzian.

The filmmaker says he wanted to 'go beyond the Armenian identification with sufferings' so that his son 'may grow up experiencing joy and pride in his origins'. Dedicating *My Son Shall Be Armenian* to his father and his son, Goudsouzian wishes to link the past to the future so that the future generations of Armenians will no longer have to bear the burden of silence. The film also asserts the determination to prevent such gruesome history from repeating itself.

Screamers (2006) is a documentary film-directed by Carla Garapedian featuring on the Multi-Platinum, Grammy-Award winning American rock band from Gledale, California System Of A Down. This critically acclaimed movie is an impassioned synthesis of concert, film and political expose about the rock group's intensely personal campaign to stop genocide. Chronicling the band's efforts to persuade both the British and US governments to recognize the Armenian Genocide, *Screamers* also traces the history of modern-day genocide—and genocide denial—from the first occurrence in the twentieth century in Turkey, to today in Darfur. Commentary and interviews with Pulitzer prize-winning author Samantha Power (*A Problem from Hell: America and the Age of Genocide*), survivors from Turkey, Rwanda and Darfur, FBI whistleblowers, and Hrant Dink, who was murdered in Turkey after appearing in this film, shed light on why genocides recur. Passive politicians and corporate interests have conspired to turn a blind eye to genocides as they are happening. We say 'never again' but we don't mean it.

Mayrig (Mother) is a 1991 semi-autobiographical movie about an Armenian family was forced to leave its homeland in order to escape certain death from the Turkish army. The movie is a masterpiece not only because it is based on real happenings—the story of one family that represents the story of survival of the entire nation—but also because it shows, in a very sensitive manner, the life of one man from his difficult but happy childhood until the very heights of his successful career. It demonstrates that care and unity within family are the cornerstones of happiness, even when you pass through the hardest times. It is about the sacrificial care and boundless love of every father and every mother for their child. And nothing is more important for a person in his life than to make his parents proud and happy.

The campaigners of the recognition of Armenian Genocide have also exploited documentaries, another visual medium with a strong mass appeal. *Armenia: The Betrayed*, is a powerful 45-minute documentary made by BBC News with significant material, logistical and other support from the Gomidas Institute and other organizations like the Armenian National Committee of America (ANCA), and the Armenian National Institute (ANI). This documentary followed by a presentation by Ara Sarafian on the Armenian Genocide in Van, was broadcast on 26 January 2003 on BBC *Correspondent Two* at 19:15 GMT. In a special *Correspondent* to coincide with the Holocaust memorial week, Fergal Keane investigated how a terrible slaughter, three quarters of a century ago, has returned to haunt the relationship between Turkey and its Western allies. The programme also discloses how President George W. Bush and his predecessor Bill Clinton both broke promises to the Armenian community that they would recognize genocide. Talking to Armenian survivors, Turkish officials and key political figures in the United States, the *Correspondent* investigated a story of terrible slaughter, political intrigue and a people betrayed.

The director and producer of the movie, James Miller, 34, was killed in the Gaza Strip when an Israeli armoured vehicle opened fire and wounded him in the neck. He had been making a documentary on house demolitions in Palestinian areas. According to his colleague Fergal Keane, they were due to receive medals of honour in Beirut for that film. Keane said 'I was fortunate to have worked with James in Turkey for *Correspondent*. He was truly moved by what he saw in Van and wanted to make more documentaries on the Armenian Genocide.'

Some of the other documentaries on this issue worth mentioning are: *Turkey: A Family Erased* (2008), a PBS documentary directed by George Kachadorian, *The Forgotten Genocide* (2007) by the ABC World News, *The Armenian Genocide* (2007) a 52-minute documentary by French Director Laurence Jourdan distributed by TIME Europe, *Germany and the Secret Genocide* (2006) by Armenian Film Foundation showcasing the role of Germany in the Armenian Genocide, *Twenty Voices* (2007) twenty stories by Armenian Genocide survivors, produced by Twenty Voices, *Turkey Facing up to Past* (2006) by ABC on Orhan Pamuk and the Armenian Genocide, *The Armenian Genocide*, (2006), a Two Cats Production, a critically acclaimed PBS documentary by Emmey Award winning director Andrew Goldberg, featuring interviews with the leading experts in the field like Pulitzer Prize winning author Samantha Power and *New York Times* best-selling author Peter Balakian, in addition to never-before-seen historical footage of the events and key players of one of the greatest untold stories of the 1900s. Goldberg gives a voice to a people and an occurrence that has been kept quiet for far too long. *The Armenian Genocide* is narrated by Julianna Margulies and includes historical narrations by Ed Harris, Natalie Portman, Laura Linney and Orlando Bloom, among others and *Armenia: Genocide Denied* (2002), a 31-minute 50-second documentary by Journeyman Pictures.

CONCLUSION

More and more scholars, historiographers, sociologists and historians from the US, Germany, Israel and even Turkey are now openly extending their support to the efforts of the Armenians for securing formal international affirmation and recognition of the 1915 genocide by Turkey and the world community and condemnation of such a heinous act in any other country. Notable among those who have joined the campaign are Orhan Pamuk, Taner Akçam, Halil Berktay, Israel Charny, Ragip and Aysenur Zarakolu, Glendale-Hilmar Kaiser, Dobkin, Marjorie Housepian, Donald Miller, Lorna Touryan Miller, Israel Charny and Fatima Müge Göçek. The Armenian Genocide Recognition campaigners have gained the support of the people at large to their cause as well. More than 20 countries including France, Italy, Russia, Canada, Switzerland, Lebanon, Sweden, Greece, the European Parliament and Argentina along with 42 states of the USA have officially confirmed that the massacres of 1915 perpetrated by the Young Turks against the Armenian population was 'Genocide'.

It may be noted that considerable success of the campaigners and supporters of the universal genocide recognition movement in drawing attention and gaining support from a larger section of the world community is proof enough of the expanding scope, growing effect and importance of various forms of popular culture. It further conveys that the various forms of popular culture are not only sources of pleasure and entertainment but play a significant role in strategically pursuing and achieving desired goals.

The Armenian Genocide has passed into the previous century and even previous millennium, but to the Armenian community the issue still remains current. The collective memory still stirs deep passions among the descendants of the victims. In some ways they are imprisoned in their past and feel their liberation depends on acknowledgement through acts of contrition and redemption. With the expanding horizon of popular culture, development of communication and distribution system, the media of popular culture like films and literature have become an effective way of conveying the totality and enormity of the Armenian Genocide to the world community. They have become strong and powerful instruments to contextualize the memory and achieve their mission—formal confirmation and recognition of the crime perpetrated during the first quarter of twentieth century and ending of the scourge of genocide from the surface of this earth.

NOTES

1. Richard Hovannisian, 'Etiology and Sequelae of the Armenian Genocide' in George J. Andreopoulos (ed.), *Genocide: Conceptual and Historical Dimensions,* Philadelphia: University of Pennsylvania Press, 1997.
2. Vahakn N. Dadrian, *The History of the Armenian Genocide: Ethnic Conflict from the Balkans to Anatolia to the Caucasus,* New York, Oxford: Berghahn Books, 2003; Peter Balakian, *The Burning Tigris: The Armenian Genocide and America's Response,* New York: Perennial, 2003; Richard Hovannisian, 'Etiology and Sequelae of the Armenian Genocide'.
3. R.J. Rummel, 'The Holocaust in Comparative and Historical Perspective', *Journal of Social Issues,* vol. 3, no. 2, 1 April 1998.
4. Richard Hovannisian, Gerard J. Libaridian, Vahakn N. Dadrian Donald Bloxham, Merrill D. Peterson, Samuel Totten, Eric Markusen, Alex Alvarez, Herbert Hirsh, Israel W. Charny, Steven L. Jacobs, Roger W. Smith, Donald E. Miller, Lorna Touryan Miller, Yair Auron, Altuğ Taner Akçam, Fatima Müge Göçek, Joe Verhoeven, George J. Andreopoulos, Robert Melson, Gerard Chaliand, J.M. Winter and others.
5. 'Q&A: Armenian "genocide" dispute', BBC News Europe, 10 July 2008, http://news.bbc.co.uk.
6. Razmik Panossian, *The Armenians: From Kings and Priests to Merchants and Commissars,* New York: Columbia University Press, 2006.
7. See Rubina Peroomian, *Literary Responses to Catastrophe: A Comparison of the*

Armenian and the Jewish Experience, Atlanta: Scholars Press, 1993; idem, 'New Directions in Literary Responses to the Armenian Genocide', in Richard G. Hovannisian (ed.), *Looking Backward, Moving Forward: Confronting the Armenian Genocide*, New Brunswick, NJ, and London: Transaction Publishers, 2003.

8. Arsinee Khanjian relaying the words of her husband, Atom Egoyan, at the annual Bay Area Armenian National Committee's 'Hai Tad' (Armenian Cause) Evening, 6 March, 2004. Internet http://www.ancsf.org

9. Internet http://www.spiegel.de

13

The Construction of Martial Race Culture in British India and Its Legacies in Post-Colonial South Asia

KAUSHIK ROY

INTRODUCTION

The making of 'martial races' was a technique of the European powers to utilize Afro-Asian demographic resources for military purposes. The colonial armies depended on local manpower. This was because indigenous population was cheaper and physically more inured for operating in the climate of the colonies compared to the European soldiery. The European overseas empires were all racial constructs where physical difference, usually pigmentation, marked out the colonizers from the colonized.[1] The concept of 'martial races' was used to ascribe martial status on some groups among the colonized who became military and political allies of the colonial state. The Hausas, one of Africa's most famous 'martial races' formed the nucleus of British-led West African Frontier Force, just like the Sikhs in the Sepoy Army during the late nineteenth century.[2]

The colonial employers ascribed the colonial soldiers with martial identity for several reasons. Identity creation aided battlefield cohesion. An exotic identity generated pride of craft on part of the warriors. Groups based on personal and clan affinities along with language and place of origin became more cohesive when they acquired an identity generated by the Empire's institution to which they owed allegiance. Moreover, crafting separate identities also prevented the genesis of any sense of homogeneity among the colonized. This ensured 'divide and rule' resulting in consolidation of the colonial regime.

The Sepoy Army constituted a crucial component of British colonialism in India. It consumed 35 per cent of the government's revenue and was one of the largest government employers in India.

Hence, the army constituted a crucial interface between the British colonizers and the colonized in the subcontinent. This essay attempts to analyse the creation of martial race culture by the colonial army and its legacies after decolonization. The post-colonial armies of India and Pakistan after 1947 absorbed the martial race cultural artefacts. In addition, certain communities within the subcontinent also mobilized themselves by using the martial race concept. In fact, what started as an elite culture introduced by a colonial institution became part of the popular culture among the inhabitants of modern South Asia.

THE 1857 MUTINY AND THE SEARCH FOR THE 'MARTIAL RACES'

After conquering India, the British initiated a twofold division for controlling the colonized. In the early nineteenth century, Indian society was divided into martial and unmartial castes. The *Purbiyas* (Brahmins and Rajputs from Awadh and Bihar), conceived as a martial caste, was heavily recruited in the Bengal Army.[3] After the 1857 Mutiny, the British turned from the high castes towards the non-Hindu groups like the Gurkhas, Sikhs and the trans-Indus Pathans. This turnaround was partly due to the fact that mostly the Brahmins and the Rajputs engineered the 1857 Mutiny. Hence, the British in the aftermath of the Mutiny distrusted them. This policy shift was legitimized on ideological grounds by the British belief that Hindu religion bred servility and passivity, thereby inviting subjugation. Hence, the conviction that high caste Hindus could rarely be martial.[4]

In the post-1857 Mutiny era, the British came to view Indian society as composed of martial and unmartial races. The theory advanced to justify this bipolar division is known as the Martial Race theory. This shift from caste to race as an analytical category to understand the colonial society was partly influenced by the emergence of race theorists among the Western intelligentsia during the late nineteenth century. They tried to analyse the rise of great powers and subsequent degeneration of nations with the help of quasi-biological race theories. And colonial scholar-officials like W.W. Hunter and Denzil Ibbetson, to name a few were influenced by the racial determinism of the nineteenth-century Western academicia.[5] In British conceptualization, there was much similarity between caste and race. Religious underpinning, occupational and hereditary manifestations determined the nature of a caste/race in British eyes.[6]

Important scholar-officials of the Raj like Hunter and Herbert Risley conceptualized castes as ethnologically based races.[7] Lieutenant Colonel J.M. Wikeley, an officer of the 17th Cavalry, who could be taken as a representative of the British officer corps, stated in 1915, 'there are many types of race, distinguished from one another by their moral and physical characteristics'.[8]

The Raj initiated the Handbook Project for knowing the 'other', that is, the indigenous society, in order to classify the potential 'martial races'. This project had the support of Risley. In the words of Risley, the Handbook Project was an amalgam of ethnography and ethnology. Ethnography means collection of descriptive details on physical characteristics, social usages and cultural customs of the various groups of people. The assumption of the British officers was that similar customs among the different groups point to blood kinship among them, which in turn played a crucial role in social evolution. Ethnology attempts to explain the behaviour of human aggregates such as tribe and clan, by comparing and analysing the facts collected by ethnography.[9] The production of this sort of literature on the 'martial races' could be categorized as a kind of Orientalist discourse because the British officers engaged with creating an authoritative and superior body of knowledge about the 'others'—the colonized communities—and essentializing their inherent traits.[10]

This sort of classification was linked with the strengthening of colonial authority. The British officers wrote the Handbooks in an attempt to understand, and then command the 'martial races'.[11] As Edward Said has pointed out, Orientalism as a mode of discourse was characterized by supporting institutions like colonial bureaucracies.[12] In the case of the Handbook Project, the Sepoy Army supported this project of understanding the 'other'.[13] In order to ascribe identities to the groups who joined the army, it was essential that the officers knew about their habits and mentality. The British officers acquired knowledge about the Indian soldiers to dominate them but in this process also came to develop affection for them. Field-Marshal Birdwood, the Commander-in-Chief of India from 1925 to 1930 reflects in his memoirs 'long daily marches with one's men helped one to get to know them well, to enter into their lives and become truly fond of them'.[14] So, the British Orientalist project in India was not merely a game shaped by power equation, as Said would have us believe.[15]

In the production of this discourse, a symbiotic alliance emerged between the Handbook authors and the colonial state's intellectuals. The army officers writing Handbooks depended on the ethnographic accounts churned out by Raj's official and unofficial personnel. The army believed that 'martial' groups must possess a martial past. So, fabrication of glorious history of the 'martial communities' became essential. The British perceived the Scots as Highlander warriors. The Highlanders were the British Army's 'martial race'. For manufacturing the Highland tradition of the 'martial' Scots, the British state's intellectuals falsified facts and created a 'new history' of the Scots.[16] This process was also evident in colonial India. Vincent Smith, a Bengal Civil Service official-cum-historian of late nineteenth-century Raj aided Captain Eden Vansittart in fleshing out the historical details regarding the 'glorious past' of the Gurkhas.[17]

In the early nineteenth century, the British discovered the Gurkhas who were known in the indigenous society as *parbattias* (highlanders).[18] For the British, the Gurkhas were the Indian equivalent of the Scottish Highlanders. The British invented the term 'Gurkha'. Originally, there was no Gurkha community in Nepal. A district in the north-east portion of the Gandak basin occupying the region between Tirsuli-Ganga and Sweti-Gandak rivers was known as Gurkha. This region's principal town which was 55 miles to the west of Kathmandu was also known as Gurkha. The British conviction was that the ancestor of the race whom they termed as Gurkhas hailed from the Gurkha district. A dynasty named Gorkha under Prithvi Narayan Shah united central Nepal in the eighteenth century. The imperial myth went on to state that since the people from this district conquered Nepal before the British intervention, they were martial.[19]

The Raj's policy makers accepted the theory of Aryan invasion of India. It was believed that the Aryans after conquering the land of the Dravidians settled down. For occupational purposes, three groups emerged within the Aryans: Brahmins, Kshatriyas or Rajputs, and the Vaisyas. The second group who constituted the original martial races provided hereditary warriors to the subcontinent from time immemorial.[20] In the 1920s, Professor R.L. Turner argued that in the medieval age, when pressed by the Muslim invasion of India, many Rajputs migrated into Nepal from north India. These Rajputs intermarried with the Mongoloid tribes of Nepal and their offsprings, that is the Gurkhas, inherited the martial instincts of their Rajput forefathers.[21]

Thanks to the influence of Darwinism, in the nineteenth century, the race theorists believed that acquired characteristics could be inherited and thus a human hierarchy based on superior and inferior qualities emerged.[22] The imperial officers were obsessed with the idea of purity of blood. The Scottish Highlanders were obsessively proud because they believed in a common ancestry and an exclusive identity which put them above the others.[23] So, the Handbook authors were at pains to learn about intermarriages between the various clans. They feared that coupling among the various clans would result in mixing of impure blood and this in turn would destroy the genes carrying military prowess. The Magars and Gurung tribes from central Nepal were dubbed as Gurkhas and recruited in the army. Vansittart noted that the Magars never married Gurungs and vice versa.[24] Many Gurkha pensioners settled down in the Almora district. They intermarried with the local women. Due to intermixture of blood, the British did not consider their progeny as Gurkhas. Rather, the British categorized them as Kumaunis.[25]

In the late nineteenth century, Captain A.H. Bingley, the Sepoy Army's expert on the Rajputs noted:

Certain clans of Awadh and the North-West Provinces which are probably connected with aboriginal races are looked down on by the blue blooded Rajputs of Rajasthan, who regard them as spurious, and thus practically disown them.[26]

Since, the Eastern Rajputs (Rajputs of Awadh and Bihar) by marrying non-Aryan races had lost their purity, Bingley believed that they retained their status by the connivance and goodwill of the Brahmins. As a result, argued Bingley, the Brahmins exercised undue influence on them.[27] In the aftermath of the 1857 Mutiny, the British regarded Brahmin influence over the Rajputs of north India as unfavourable. So, the Raj turned towards the Rajputs of Rajasthan who were considered by both British officials and later by the citizens of post-colonial India as true Rajputs.

The Punjabi Muslims were another favoured 'martial' group of the late nineteenth century. They were recruited from the salt ranges of western Punjab. The men recruited were retainers of the war-like semi-autonomous chiefs who were reduced to submission by the Sikhs under Ranjit Singh.[28] Probably, the British recruited them in the belief that they could act as a check on the Sikhs. Due to the British experience in the metropole, the chiefs of the Punjabi Muslims were granted commissioned ranks in the army.

In the Highland society of Scotland, the chief of the clan was the father of the family. He exercised power over his tenants. So, when the British government ordered the clan chiefs to raise regiments, the clan members joined the units because they perceived that by joining the regiment they were paying rent in kind to their clan chiefs. The British realized this peculiar trait of the Highlanders, and hence allowed the companies to be captained by the gentry of the clans including Campbell, Murray and Grant.[29] The British in India considered the Punjabi Muslim chiefs as equivalent to the Scottish clan leaders. The *Chaudhuris* (headmen of the village), also known as *Thakurs*, were given commissioned ranks in the cavalry because the British belief was that being social superiors they could control their relatives and retainers who joined as *sawars*.[30]

CONSTRUCTION OF MARTIAL RACE CULTURE IN THE REGIMENTS

The next step was to create distinct martial identities for different groups of sepoys by accommodating the various martial communities within the diverse ethnic regiments. It was a sort of colonial insurance policy because in case of any probable mutiny, the different martial race regiments, such as the Sikhs and the Gurkhas, could be set against each other.[31] Major General S. Cotton, commander of the Peshawar Division, articulated this policy in a despatch to the Adjutant-General dated 1860:

To produce and bring into operation that feeling of antagonism naturally existing between the castes or races of which the Indian Army is composed, by the formation of corps of distinct races, so that one would become effective check on the other. I would recommend therefore the gradual conversion by voluntary transfers of the present mixed corps into homogeneous regiments wholly composed of . . . race and caste, and drawn from as far as possible from the same province. . . . Thus regiments of . . . Sikhs, Dogras, Mazbis, Afridis, Punjabi Muslims etc. would be established.[32]

The imperialists tried to strengthen the martial culture imposed among the recruits through the mechanism of long-term enlistment (up to twenty years) and intense identification with the regiments.[33]

In order to fuse regimental ethos with ethnic loyalty, the army headquarter started giving the name of the community which provided personnel to the unit. Most of the personnel of the 1st Burma Rifles were Gurkhas. In 1890, the name of this unit was changed to 1st Battalion of the 10th Gurkha Rifles.[34] For instilling community ethos, the British opened up separate recruiting depots for different 'martial races' who joined the army. Before 1886, there was no centralized system of recruiting for the Gurkhas. Every regiment sent out its own recruiting parties and the recruits were brought to the regimental headquarters. In 1886, the Gurkha recruiting depot was opened at Gorakhpur.[35]

Among the Scottish Highlanders, a particular type of dress (tartans and kilted skirts) worn by the personnel of the Scot regiments fostered ethnic identity.[36] For integrating the Indian communities within the Western military system, Western style uniforms of the sepoys and the *sawars* was modified to incorporate indigenous elements like turbans and sashes.[37] Such elements of indigenous dress code were utilized by the Raj for making group identities more acceptable to the communities joining the army. In the Sepoy Army also the British emphasized peculiarities of dress for constructing identities of the different ethnic groups. For ascribing distinct identity to the different 'martial' regiments, the details of uniform varied from unit to unit. While the 1st Sikh Irregular Cavalry had blue turban, drab kurta and red pyjamas, the Jat Horse had red turban, blue kurta and white pyjamas.[38] Footwear constituted a part of the cultural baggage which aided identity construction. The sepoys found socks uncomfortable and expensive. So, the Punjabi soldiers wore Peshawari *chappals* (indigenous slippers) which they found not only comfortable but also inexpensive. Though the *chappals* reduced military efficiency, still the British tolerated it in order to respect the soldiers' cultural sensibilities.[39]

One of the vital components constituting British sponsored martial identity was religion. The imperialists encouraged a sort of modified Hinduism among the Gurkhas. The aim was to establish a cleavage among the *pahari* Hinduism of the Gurkhas and the traditional Hinduism of the high castes of north India. Eric Hobsbawm states that traditions had to be invented for constructing identities.[40] The colonial military also constructed and selected a certain set of practices. Minor Hindu deities like Deorali, Chandi and Devi, which were not popular among the north Indian Hindus were worshipped in the Gurkha regiments. Further, the military authority constructed a shrine of Deorali in every Gurkha regiment and on the seventh day of the Dussehra festival the whole regiment visited this shrine in a parade ground procession.[41]

Religion also constituted a crucial component of the imperial sponsored identity for the Sikhs. The imperial aim was to manufacture a separate religion, that is, Sikhism, and a distinct social identity based on that set of religious practices.[42] Birdwood jots in his memoirs:

The Indian Army does much to foster and keep pure the Sikh religion, with its worship of one God. A Sikh priest known as a Granthi, is maintained in every regiment enlisting Sikhs, and it is his office to read the Granth Sahib regularly and to instruct recruits in Gurmukhi. The major festivals of Sikhism are observed as far as possible as regimental holidays, and it was always our custom to attend the Gurdwara (Sikh temple) on such occasions. . . . On the line of march in a Sikh regiment the Granth Sahib is carried by some of the men in the place of honour at the head of the column, wrapped in a fine silk cloth and attended by a Sikh escort.[43]

In order to create a separate identity of the Sikhs from the Singhs (non-Sikh Indians whose surnames were Singh), the British officers insisted upon the Sikh soldiers in the Sepoy Army to wear *pugris*. And even after Independence, the *pugri* remains a crucial component of Sikh culture.[44]

INDIGENOUS DYNAMICS IN THE CONSTRUCTION OF MARTIAL RACE CULTURE

Construction of martial identities not only depended on imperial policies but also on the indigenous epistemology and indigenous preference or lack of it for military service. Thus, in the construction of the 'martial races', the cultural preferences of these communities and the corpus of indigenous knowledge played an important role.

The British were eager to ascribe martial identity to the 'natural warriors' of India. The imperial belief was that the Vedas designated the Rajputs as the soldiering class.[45] Vansittart depended on the Limbu *Vamsavali* while writing about the Gurkhas. In the last decade of the nineteenth-century Havildar Purandhoj Limbu of the 2nd Battalion of the 4th Gurkha Rifles cooperated with Vansittart in classifying the tribes of eastern Nepal. Again Jemadar Assaram Burathoki of the 2nd Battalion of the 1st Gurkha Rifles assisted Vansittart in locating the vernacular papers regarding the Nepalis and translating them.[46] From early twentieth century, the Newars of Nepal were also amalgamated within the Gurkha fold and recruited in the army. For constructing a martial past of the Newars, the British made use of the Newar *Vamsavali* that chronicled the history of Nepal from AD 1056 to 1388.[47]

An important element of the Western notion of martiality was masculinity.[48] Bingley was strengthened in his belief regarding the superiority of the western Rajputs (Rajputs of Rajasthan) over the eastern Rajputs from some Indian proverbs. Bingley quotes a proverb *Purab ki beti aur paschim ke beta*. This indicated the custom of the eastern Rajputs marrying their daughters to the western Rajputs of clans ranking higher than themselves.[49] In other words, the 'Orientals' played a conspicuous part in the Occident's attempt to define the 'other'. So, Said's assertion that the Orient was never able to speak about itself nor able to represent its history, and the Occident only spoke for the Orient,[50] cannot be sustained.

To some extent, economy shaped the culture of the inhabitants. The Scots joined the British Army because life for them was bleak and hard, occasionally devastated by famines. The land was infertile and the herds of cattle were inadequate to sustain lives. So, sheer necessity forced them to raid the prosperous Lowlands. Pillage and plunder made skill at arms a sheer requirement and the consequent warrior tradition became the ultimate in masculine achievement. This was reflected in Gaelic verse throbbing with the love for weaponry.[51] Back in India, the Pathans were a favourite 'martial race' of the British. The Pathans joined the Sepoy Army because of rising population and the operation of deficit economy in the Indus region.[52]

After the 1857 Uprising, the British preferred the Rajputs from Rajputana than the Rajputs from Awadh and Bihar. So, the British were interested in recruiting the Rajputs from Bikaner. However, they were not willing to join the army because they found the return from agriculture much more lucrative. Canal water ensured bumper crops, hence a high return from land.[53] After the First World War, the Raj faced problems in recruiting adequate number of Sikhs because they became mechanics and made more money than was possible in military service.[54]

Indigenous military culture also aided imperial stereotyping of certain communities as martial. The Rajputs and Jats of western Punjab who accepted Islam in the medieval age were termed as Punjabi Muslims by the British and they were enlisted in the Sepoy Army. Before 1849, a large number of Muslim Rajputs from tribes like Ghakkars and Awans from Jhelum and Rawalpindi districts used to join the cavalry of Ranjit Singh's army. The Jats around river Ravi constituted the backbone of the Khalsa military.[55] The British preference for the Jat Sikhs encouraged many job-hungry Hindu Jats in Punjab to accept Sikhism.[56] And these Sikh Jats became the most favoured 'martial race' of the Raj from 1880 onwards.[57]

Certain communities, due to their particular type of interaction with their physical environment and past history, became readymade soldiers for the Raj. Before 1814, Purbiya deserters from the Company's Bengal Army drilled the Nepal Army's personnel. And most of the personnel of the Nepal Army were from Magar, Gurung and Limbu tribes who were most heavily recruited by the British in the aftermath of the Anglo-Nepal War of 1814-15. In British perception, the members of these tribes comprising the Gurkha community were born soldiers because of their military training and the terrain in which they grew up. Lieutenant Colonel R. Sale Hill, officer of the 1st Gurkha Light Infantry in 1874 commented: 'the

Gurkhas acquaintance with forest, makes him perhaps as a pioneer in the jungle, almost unrivalled with his *kukri* to suit himself with, he is quite at home'.[58] Hence, the British used the Gurkhas armed with *kukris* for close quarter combat in the jungle-clad mountains of the north-west frontier. And *kukri* as a component of the martial Gurkha culture is now accepted by the Gurkha community in India and Nepal.

The groups which were designated as martial did not depend totally on the choices and biases of the imperial elite. The assumptions inherent within the indigenous society also shaped the Martial Race construct. The Tarkhans and Lobanas among the Sikhs were not respected by the members of this community, because they were carpenters and water carriers. So the British decided not to recruit the Sikhs practising these two professions.[59]

LEGACIES OF THE MARTIAL RACE CULTURE

The Martial Race theory was also a technique to keep the politically conscious, university-educated middle class out of the army.[60] The illiterate communities were categorized as 'martial races'. This was because the imperialists assumed that education might breed disloy-alty. In 1883, Field-Marshal Roberts, Commander-in-Chief of India (1885-93), warned the Commander-in-Chief of the British Army, the Duke of Cambridge: 'There is a danger for us if . . . in future Indian soldiers might develop political feelings especially due to spreading of education by the government.'[61] The Punjabi Muslims were favoured because they were illiterate and did not like to attend the schools.[62]

Punjab comprised of 9.7 per cent of the total area of British-India,[63] and the Sikhs accounted for 6 per cent of the province's population in 1911.[64] Between 1914 and 1918, 877,068 combatants were recruited from India. Of these recruits, about 250,000 came from Punjab.[65] Between 3 September 1939 and 31 August 1945, the Indian armed forces absorbed 2,581,726 recruits. Of them, 103,114 were Pathans from the North-West Frontier Province, 120,280 were Gurkhas from Nepal, and Punjab provided the largest number, that is, 754,551.[66]

The post-colonial Indian and Pakistani militaries are also tainted by the legacy of the martial race culture. To illustrate the point: those Indian officers who had initially joined the Sepoy Army, after 1947 rose to occupy high positions in the Indian Army, and continued to display the convictions of the British officers. General J.N. Chaudhuri, the Sandhurst-trained officer who fought for the Raj during the Second World War and became the Commander-in-Chief of the Indian Army

(1962-6) is one such example. Chaudhuri seemed to be following in Roberts' shoes when the former in his autobiography narrated:

The best type of infantryman has always come from solid, stolid, yeoman farmer stock. This breed produces a type who is strongly built, used to hard work and adverse living conditions, observant and wise in field craft. He has individuality but is not over-imaginative, too much imagination being a handicap when faced with the machines of destruction. He has the peasant's basic ruthlessness, an indifference to the vagaries of nature and a stubborn determination.[67]

Like Roberts, Chaudhuri also assumed that the spread of civilization and education resulted in the dying out of the breed of the 'hardy peasants',[68] the yeomen farmers, who constituted the martial warriors in British eyes. The irony is that though Chaudhuri was a Bengali, a group castigated by the British as an unmartial effeminate community, he believed in the British sponsored concept of 'martial races'.

Armies remain important in the post-colonial polities of Sou'h Asia. Between 1947-50, about 70 per cent of the national budget of Pakistan went to the Pakistan Army.[69] The Indian Army is the third largest land force in the world. Till this date, while the one million strong Indian Army remains over-dependent on the Sikhs and the Gurkhas, the 400,000 Pakistan Army continues to recruit 'Punjabi Muslims' from Rawalpindi, Attock, Campbelpur and Jhelum districts of Punjab, and Pathans from the Kohat and Marolan districts in the North-West Frontier Province. These five districts, known as Potowar regions, contain only 9 per cent of Pakistan's male population but are over-represented in the army.[70] According to the 1951 census, the Punjabi-Muslims constituted one-fourth of the Pakistani population but they occupied 80 per cent of the posts in the army.[71] The Akali Dal in 1973 demanded greater recruitment for the Sikhs in the Indian armed forces.[72] In 1981, though Punjab contained only 2.45 per cent of India's population, the Punjabis accounted for 15 per cent of the personnel of the Indian Army. In 1991, the Sikhs comprised of 20 per cent of the Indian Army's officer corps.[73] Stephen P. Cohen rightly says that independent India failed to raise new regiments from the lower castes.[74]

The martial race culture came to haunt independent India and Pakistan. The percentage of Sikhs in the population of Punjab rose from 60.75 in 1981 to 62.95 in 1991 while that of the Hindus decreased from 36.93 to 34.46 per cent in the same period. Competing economic interests of the Hindu and Sikh traders strengthened the Hindu-Sikh divide in Punjab. The terrorists in Punjab used Sikhism for mobilizing support against the Indian state. The Punjabi terrorists not only got financial support from the Sikhs living overseas but also used the Sikh gurdwaras.[75] In 1982, several thousand Sikh servicemen met at the Golden Temple Complex to discuss demands of the Akali Dal.[76] Many Sikh officers of the Indian Army also joined Sant Jarnail Singh Bhindranwale's terrorist group. The most famous among this lot was Shahbeg Singh who in 1971 had organized the Mukti Bahini in Bangladesh against the Pakistanis. Shahbeg Singh was also instrumental in fortifying the Golden Temple Complex before the Indian Army attacked it.[77] On June 1984, in the immediate aftermath of Blue Star Operation, 1,500 Sikh soldiers in the army barracks at Bihar, Maharashtra, Tripura and Rajasthan mutinied.[78] Despite massive unemployment in India, the Gurkhas constituted more than 10 per cent of the personnel of the Indian Army.[79] And the recent Gorkhaland demand is also aiming to rally the Gurkhas in the Indian Army around this issue.

In 1965, there were only 13,000 Bengalis of East Pakistan in the Pakistan Army and none of the Bengali Muslims occupied senior positions. This was one of the reasons behind the Bengali upsurge under Mujibur Rehman. This finally led to the secession of East Pakistan which in 1971 became Bangladesh. And the successive interventions in politics by the Pakistan Army have been to maintain the Punjabi predominance against the Sindhis and the Baluchis.[80]

CONCLUSION

Edward Said's characterization of the Orient, as a land of snake-charmers, magic, mysticism, romance, exotic beings, and remarkable experiences as almost a European invention, could partly be applied to the case of the British construction of the martial race culture. However, Said's formulation that Orientalism represents merely Europe's 'otherness'[81] needs to be qualified in the context of the British project of building the identities of the 'martial races'. Imperial experience in the metropole also shaped the identity construction scheme in the colony. This was most evident in the case of Scot Highlander-Gurkha syndrome. Nevertheless, the imperial construction of the martial warriors was not an epistemological project undertaken by the British alone. Both the British and the Indians (albeit from an inferior position) participated in this process and also contributed to it. In fact, the Martial Race ideology was a bag of competing and fractious ideas, and absorbed a lot of indigenous elements. Due to the vested interest of the 'martial races' and military traditions, which are in turn products of the martial race culture, both India and

Pakistan have failed to broaden their respective army's recruitment base. The strongest legacy of the Martial Race theory is increasing communal consciousness in the post-colonial South Asian society. In the post-1947 era while the Indian Army remained over-dependent on the 'martial races', several communities also organized their resistance against the central government by utilizing the martial race construct.

NOTES

1. David Killingray, 'Guardians of Empire', in David Killingray and David Omissi (eds.), *Guardians of Empire: The Armed Forces of the Colonial Powers c. 1700-1964*, Manchester: Manchester University Press, 1999, p. 2.
2. Bruce Vandervort, *Wars of Imperial Conquest in Africa: 1830-1914*, Bloomington/Indianapolis: Indiana University Press, 1998, p. 96.
3. Douglas M. Peers, ' "The Habitual Nobility of Being": British Officers and Social Construction of the Bengal Army in the Early Nineteenth Century', *Modern Asian Studies*, 25, no. 3 (1991), pp. 545-6.
4. Channa Wickremesekera, *'Best Black Troops in the World': British Perceptions and the Making of the Sepoy, 1746-1805*, Delhi: Manohar, 2002, p. 84.
5. Susan Bayly, 'Caste and "Race" in Colonial Ethnography', in Peter Robb (ed.), *The Concept of Race in South Asia*, Delhi: Oxford University Press, 1995, pp. 165-70.
6. Peers, 'Habitual Nobility', p. 548.
7. Chandar S. Sundaram ' "Reviving a Dead Letter": Military Indianization and the Ideology of Anglo-Indians, 1885-91', in P.S. Gupta and Anirudh Deshpande (eds.), *The British Raj and its Indian Armed Forces: 1857-1939*, Delhi: Oxford University Press, 2002, p. 51.
8. J.M. Wikeley, *Punjabi Musalmans*, 1915, rpt., Delhi: Manohar, 1991, p. 2.
9. Eden Vansittart, *Notes on Nepal*, 1896, rpt., Delhi: Asian Educational Services, 1992, pp. i-ii. iv.
10. Lionel Caplan, *Warrior Gentleman: 'Gurkhas' in Western Imagination*, Providence/Oxford: Berghahn Books, 1995, p. 1.
11. Caplan, *Warrior Gentleman*, pp. 1-2.
12. Edward W. Said, *Orientalism: Western Conceptions of the Orient*, 1978, rpt., Delhi: Penguin, 2001, p. 2.
13. Wikeley, *Punjabi Musalmans*, Preface.
14. Field-Marshal Birdwood, *Khaki and Gown: An Autobiography*, London/Melbourne: Ward, Lock & Co. Limited, 1941, p. 63.
15. Said, *Orientalism*, pp. 7-8.
16. Hugh Trevor-Roper, 'The Invention of Tradition: The Highland Tradition of Scotland', in Eric Hobsbawm and Terence Ranger (eds.), *The Invention of Tradition*, 1983, rpt., Cambridge: Canto, 1995, p. 17.
17. Vansittart, *Notes*, p. i.
18. Eden Vansittart, *Gurkhas*, 1906, rpt., Delhi: Asian Educational Services, 1991, p. 48.
19. Ibid., p. 48; R.L. Turner, 'The People and their Languages', in W. Brook Northey and C.J. Morris, *The Gurkhas*, 1927, rpt., Delhi: Cosmo Publications, 1987, p. 65.

20. Wikeley, *Punjabi Muslims*, p. 2.
21. Turner, 'People and their Languages', in *The Gurkhas* by Northey and Morris, pp. 64, 68-9.
22. Peter Robb, 'South Asia and the Concept of Race', in Robb (ed.), *Concept of Race*, pp. 3-4.
23. John Prebble, *Mutiny: Highland Regiments in Revolt, 1743-1804*, 1975, rpt., Harmondsworth, Midddlesex: Penguin, 1977, p. 21.
24. Vansittart, *Gurkhas*, p. 49.
25. C.J. Morris, *The Gurkhas: An Ethnology*, 1933, rpt., Delhi: Low Price Publications, 1993, p. 126.
26. Captain A.H. Bingley, *Handbook on Rajputs*, 1899, rpt., Delhi: Low Price Publications, 1999, p. 26.
27. Bingley, *Rajputs*, p. 27.
28. Tan Tai Yong, 'Sepoys and the Colonial State: Punjab and the Military Base of the Indian Army, 1849-1900', in Gupta and Deshpande (eds.), *Indian Armed Forces*, p. 30.
29. Prebble, *Mutiny*, pp. 21, 25.
30. *Memorandum by Colonel L.B. Jones commanding 3rd Cavalry*, Dera Ghazi Khan, 22 October 1874; *Ethnic Elements of Indian Army, Records of Chief Commands, Notes and Minutes by Napier of Magdala*, Mss.Eur.F.114, 5(4), India Office Records (hereafter IOR), British Library, London.
31. Richard G. Fox, *Lions of the Punjab: Culture in the Making*, Delhi: Low Price Publications, 1990, p. 145.
32. From Major General S. Cotton, to the Adjutant General of the Army, no. 723, 26 July 1860, *Correspondence and Memoranda on the Organization of the Indian Army, Notes and Minutes by Napier*, Mss.Eur.F.114, 5(3).
33. Vandervort, *Wars of Imperial Conquest*, p. 216; *Notes on the Indian Cavalry*, by Major General H. Tombs, commanding Awadh Division, *Ethnic Elements, Notes and Minutes by Napier*.
34. Morris, *Gurkhas*, p. 131; Confidential Circular Memorandum, Lieutenant Colonel E.B. Johnson, Offg. Adjutant General of the Army, 1862, *Correspondence and Memoranda on the Organization of the Indian Army, Records of Chief Commands, 1865-76, Notes and Minutes by Napier*, Mss.Eur.F.114, 5(2).
35. Morris, *Gurkhas*, p. 130.
36. Prebble, *Mutiny*, p. 21.
37. Bernard S. Cohn, 'Representing Authority in Victorian India', in Hobsbawm and Ranger (eds.), *The Invention of Tradition*, p. 183.
38. Boris Mollo, *The Indian Army*, Poole, Dorset: Blandford Press, 1981, p. 95.
39. Vivien Ashima Kaul, 'Sepoys' Links with Society: A Study of the Bengal Army, 1858-95', in Gupta and Deshpande (eds.), *Indian Armed Forces*, p. 144.
40. Eric Hobsbawm, 'Introduction: Inventing Traditions', in Hobsbawm and Ranger (eds.), *The Invention of Tradition*, p. 1.
41. Vansittart, *Gurkhas*, pp. 54-5.
42. Fox, *Lions of the Punjab*, p. 140.
43. Birdwood, *Khaki and Gown*, pp. 65-6.
44. Kaushik Roy, 'The Construction of Regiments in the Indian Army: 1859-1913', *War in History*, 8, no. 2 (2001), p. 139.
45. Bingley, *Rajputs*, p. 26.
46. Vansittart, *Notes*, pp. ii-iii.
47. Turner, 'People and Their Languages', p. 67.

48. Caplan, *Warrior Gentleman*, p. 101.
49. Bingley, *Rajputs*, p. 28.
50. Said, *Orientalism*, pp. 6-7.
51. Prebble, *Mutiny*, p. 22.
52. Birdwood, *Khaki and Gown*, p. 140.
53. Edmund Candler, *The Sepoy*, London: John Murray, 1919, pp. 122, 128.
54. Anirudh Deshpande, 'Military Reforms in the Aftermath of the Great War: Intentions and Compulsions of British Military Policy', in Deshpande and Gupta (eds.), *Indian Armed Forces*, p. 191.
55. Memorandum by Major R.E. Boyle commanding 11th Bengal Lancers, *Ethnic Elements, Notes and Minutes by Napier*.
56. Roy, 'The Construction of Regiments in the Indian Army', p. 138.
57. Papers on different classes from which the Punjab Frontier Force is recruited, *Ethnic Elements, Notes and Minutes by Napier*.
58. The Gurkhas, Note by Sale, March 1874, *Ethnic Elements, Notes and Minutes by Napier*.
59. Papers on the different classes from which the Punjab Frontier Force is recruited, *Notes and Minutes by Napier*.
60. Deshpande, 'Military Reform in the Aftermath of the Great War', p. 188.
61. General Frederick Roberts, *Correspondence with England while Commander-in-Chief in Madras: 1881-85*, Simla: Govt. Central Printing Office, 1890, pp. 64-5, L/MIL/17/5/1615, IOR.
62. Papers on the different classes from which the Punjab Frontier Force is recruited, *Notes and Minutes by Napier*.
63. Rajit Mazumder, 'Military Imperatives and the Expansion of Agriculture in Colonial Punjab', *International Journal of Punjab Studies*, 28 (2001), p. 173.
64. Apurba Kundu, *Militarism in India: The Army and Civil Society in Consensus*, Delhi: Viva, 1998, p. 170.
65. S.D. Pradhan, 'Indian Army and the First World War', in Dewitt Ellinwood and S.D. Pradhan (eds.), *India and World War I*, Delhi: Manohar, 1978, pp. 58, 60.
66. Nandan Prasad, *Expansion of the Armed Forces and Defence Organization: 1939-45*, Delhi: Combined Inter-Services Historical Section (India & Pakistan), 1956, Appendix 16.
67. General J.N. Chaudhuri, *An Autobiography*, as narrated to B.K. Narayan, Delhi: Vikas, 1978, p. 180.
68. Chaudhuri, *Autobiography*, p. 180.
69. Ian Talbot, 'Does the Army shape Pakistan's Foreign Policy?', in Christophe Jaffrelot (ed.), *Pakistan: Nationalism Without a Nation?*, Delhi: Manohar, 2002, p. 314.
70. Ian Talbot, 'The Punjabization of Pakistan: Myth or Reality?', in Jaffrelot (ed.), *Pakistan*, p. 59; Kaushik Roy, 'Good Governance versus Bad Governance in South Asia: Civil-Military Relations in India and Pakistan, 1947-2000', *Asian Studies*, 18 (2000), p. 92.
71. Christophe Jaffrelot, 'Nationalism Without a Nation: Pakistan Searching for its Identity', in Jaffrelot (ed.), *Pakistan*, p. 16.
72. Stephen P. Cohen, 'The Military and Indian Democracy', in Atul Kohli (ed.), *India's Democracy: An Analysis of Changing State-Society Relations*, 1988, rpt., Delhi: Orient Longman, 1991, p. 133.
73. Apurba Kundu, 'The Indian Armed Forces' Sikh and Non-Sikh Officers' Opinion of Operation Blue Star', *Pacific Affairs*, 67, no. 1 (1994), pp. 48-9.

74. Stephen P. Cohen, 'The Indian Military and Social Change', *Institute for Defence Studies and Analyses Journal*, 2 no. 1 (1969-70), p. 22.

75. Satya Pal Dang, '"Cross-Border" Terrorism in Punjab', in V.D. Chopra (ed.), *Rise of Terrorism and Secessionism in Eurasia*, Delhi: Gyan Publishing House, 2001, pp. 155, 157-61.

76. Kundu, 'The Indian Armed Forces' Sikh and Non-Sikh Officers', p. 60.

77. Kundu, *Militarism in India*, p. 177.

78. Cohen, 'Military and Indian Democracy', in Kohli (ed.), *India's Democracy*, p. 127.

79. Sandy Gordon, 'Indian Security Policy and the Rise of the Hindu Right', *South Asia*, 17, no. s1 (1994), p. 202.

80. Roy, 'Good Governance versus Bad Governance in South Asia', p. 92.

81. Said, *Orientalism*, p. 1.

14

Women and Sports in Colonial Bengal: A Process of Emotional and Cultural Integration?

SUPARNA GHOSH (BHATTACHARYA)

INTRODUCTION

Calcutta, as the administrative capital and industrial entrepôt of the British Empire in India, was a centre of imperial enterprise and endeavour. The Europeans here not only operated as imperial governors but also shaped cultures in acting as colonizers. Here, 'culture' is taken up not as a static concept but as a dynamic frame. According to Giroux,

Culture is not seen as monolithic or unchanging, but as a site of multiple and heterogeneous borders where different histories, languages, experiences and voices intermingle amidst diverse relations of power and privilege.[1]

Culture is thus a contested terrain which raises questions around the categories of race, class and gender. There is also a strong connection between culture and sport where the latter consists in the orderly activity of a group or two opposed groups.

In the late nineteenth century, the British recreated in India, a culture and lifestyle fashioned in upper middle-class Britain. Hence, alongside tea parties and cocktails on the lawn, they introduced various individual and team games for themselves. Consequently, many clubs sprang up in the city of Calcutta for the above-mentioned purpose. However, the anti-Indian prejudice among the British in India was powerfully exercised in the composition of their class. The Indians were largely excluded from the social world of the Europeans. Amidst such exclusion, was there any possibility of cultural integration in the field of sports so far as women were concerned? The present essay seeks to address this issue. How did the British transmit the need of sports to the middle-class Bengali *bhadramahila* in the British-run Anglo-Indian schools and colleges modelled on the British public schools of the nineteenth century? The paper will further investigate the unfulfilled desires and emotions of some women along with the factors that facilitated sporting activities among Bengali women in the twentieth century.

WOMEN AND SPORTS DURING THE COLONIAL PERIOD

When European schools were first founded they catered almost exclusively to Europeans or Anglo-Indians.[2] The first Official Code of Regulation for European Schools (1883-5) restricted admission mainly to 'Europeans', defined as persons of European descent, pure or mixed, who retain European habits and modes of life.[3] It excluded all natives of India whatever their religion may be. Burmese, Chinese, all other Asiatic, Armenian and Asiatic Jews were also excluded from this definition.[4] Some time later, Armenians, Jews and Parsees, who were British-Indian nationals, were included in the term 'European'.[5] However, there is clear evidence from the earliest records of some of the oldest schools that from the very beginning a sprinkling of children of other Indian communities were admitted.[6] For instance, in Loreto House in 1842 children from different communities like the Europeans, Anglo-Indians, upper caste Hindus and Parsees were admitted.[7]

Loreto schools, like other Anglo-Indian schools, were modelled at their inception on the English public schools and aimed at the Victorian ideal of *Mens Sana in Corpore Sano*—a healthy mind in a healthy body.[8] As such, sport as an organized group of activity was projected in the curriculum of both schools and colleges. However, sporting activities in this institution were formalized not before the early twentieth century for a variety of factors. It should be noted that before the 1850s, there is no evidence to suggest that team sports took place in any organized way at the public schools of England.[9] From 1850 onwards, various headmasters brought about organizational and disciplinary reforms in their schools which led to indirect surveillance of the boy's recreational activities and pastimes and thereby limiting field sports like shooting, beagling and ferreting.[10] After the 1860s, the public schools produced a unified and standardized English educational elite through the introduction of team games such as cricket and athletics, which for many became the supreme expression of masculine moral excellence.[11] By the late 1880s, athleticism had become an influential educational movement throughout England, which spread among schools and colleges through downward 'diffusion'.[12] This explains why sports were not included in the school curriculum of Loreto House as early as the 1840s.

Athleticism and games spread from the public schools down to the elementary schools in 1906 when it was formally included in the school curriculum by the Board of Education, according to Peter McIntosh.[13] It is argued that with the inclusion of games and sports in the elementary school curriculum, the proletariat were controlled in the metropolis and following the same process, the natives were to be controlled in the colonies.[14] This argument is partly true and rather a considerable simplification. The following paragraphs will reveal a complete analysis of the role of games in British imperial purpose. The British as an imperial power took with them to the Empire a number of sports for both men and women, ranging from football and cricket to tennis and swimming, indoor and outdoor, played on field track, court and in water, in teams and by individuals.[15] So the British games 'followed the flag' even to colonial India. In the first decades of British rule the one consistent agent of change were the missionaries. They dominated the educational system and their impact on the society was considerable.

In those days outdoor exercise was not visible in the tropical climate of Calcutta. A universal belief of the British in the tropics was that regular exercise was mandatory for maintaining health and morale, as well as personal and public control. Physically energetic games were considered beneficial because they helped Westerners keep fit, build team spirit, form friendships, promote and uphold successful colonial rule, racial superiority and white solidarity, which are an integral part of imperialism.

Arriving in India, the British women found serious competition from the attractive Anglo-Indian women in the marriage market. These Anglo-Indian women had the small bone structure and the general petite physical make-up of the East, to which their colouring imparted vitality and distinctiveness which recalled the beauty of Greece and Syria.[16] In order to eliminate this competition, the British women evolved an insidious, almost viciously malicious, social code. In their capacity for self-preservation, they had drawn a wall of social exclusiveness around the British society. Consequently, a rigid social code was enforced on the British clubs, which grew in numbers during this time. The members of other communities including the Anglo-Indians were squeezed out of these clubs.[17] However, bound to the British by ties of blood, language, dress and habits, the Anglo-

Indian women emulated the British ladies in their leisure activities at the British clubs from the early 1900s. By the end of the nineteenth century, clubs like Royal Calcutta Golf Club, East York Club, Bengal Club, Tollygunge Club, Saturday Club, West Club, Dalhousie Club (in Maidan), Calcutta Cricket and Football Club, and others were used by the European ladies for their leisurely sporting pursuits. A few highly placed Anglo-Indian officials who belonged to the upper middle class of the community were allowed to enter these clubs. The women members of these families used to participate in the sporting activities of these clubs.

The subordinates in the railways, telegraphs and customs, teachers in the lower categories, members working in business firms and embassies in a subordinate capacity, all belonged to the lower middle class of the Anglo-Indian community.[18] The ladies of this class as well emulated the upper middle class and the European women in all respects, particularly in the sporting activities. But they were denied the entry to the European clubs. Thus, they had built a special space for themselves in the field of sport at the Calcutta Rangers Club, Dalhousie Institute, Grails Club, and so on. The second class Britons also had their own clubs and institutes for sports practice. The Anglo-Indian ladies of lower middle-class families used those clubs and institutes for sports practice. Thus, the Anglo-Indian and European ladies together indulged in sports practice in these clubs without any race or colour prejudice.[19] This was a very good example of cultural integration between the two communities through the medium of sports.

In the nineteenth century, the British society was influenced and guided by the Victorian ideal which emphasized the value of sports to develop boyhood, thereby ignoring the issue of women's participation in sports. The sacredness of the home and the dignity and beauty of motherhood were the ideals followed by the Victorians under the guise of convention founded on Christian principles.[20] For a Victorian girl, the idea of life was preparation for marriage followed by the responsibility of motherhood. So, it was believed that feminine participation in athletics will destroy all beauty and charm of women and make her unfit to bear children. Thus physical culture was more detrimental to her than beneficial.[21] However, in the twentieth century, Victorian ideals were condemned and broad-mindedness started spreading far and wide including free thought and its minor offshoots of atheism and communism, free love and free morals.[22] Thus sports became a regular activity for the girls of Loreto institutions. For Western women the freedom to engage in sport was assisted by the advances of the women's movement in their countries of origin, notably in dress reform and women's rights. These achievements were passed on to Asian and Eurasian women, informally with white women as role models and more formally through education.[23] Victorian costumes like ladies crinolines were denounced as unhygienic and not suitable for outdoor exercise in a tropical climate so that they were replaced by well-pleated skirt pants designed to provide freedom of limb and more opportunities for active sports participation.[24] The degree to which physical liberation, including dress reform in relation to sports had progressed by the early twentieth century is clear from photographic evidence. One can compare the picture of Swarnalata Ghose as early as 1866 dressed in a riding habit with a long gown and hat on her head,[25] two slender fingers in a gloved hand held the riding stick, with that of the printed pictures of a basketball team in well-pleated skirts and round-necked, full-sleeved shirts in 1931.[26]

POPULARIZING SPORTS AMONG INDIAN WOMEN

It is important to be reminded that for women, it was essential not to allow any changes in dress or other Western influences to distract them from their essential cultural traits. The contemporary official discourse on femininity emphasized on chastity, obedience, docility,[27] and the 'mother image' was pretentiously projected through the dress code. The 'sari' made her overtly different from the 'Victorian Memsaheb'. In Bengal, the women who were initiated to the world of sports formed a tiny percentage of an elite section of society and their access in most cases was a result of sustained efforts by men to make them literate. Thus literacy mediated between the private world of the *antahpur* and the public world of men, which also included sports, primarily a male domain. The Indian girls with respect to dress were not yet fully liberated because they had to maintain their traditional norms and customs to a certain extent. It is best illustrated through the Girls Guide Rally held on 16 September 1937 at Viceregal Lodge, Darjeeling. Here, the Muslim Company wore white pants and a long white shirt and a blue 'chadar' or shawl from one shoulder. The Hindu Company wore very much the same dress except that they had no shawl but a sash around their waist.[28] Nevertheless, we know that dress was never a serious impediment towards sports participation because the Bethune College girls played quite well in cumbersome saris with the Loreto College girls on various occasions.

The games and activities adopted by the Loreto students were

usually based on the English system of team games, house competitions, leagues and military style drill. In fact, the introduction
of military drills into the curriculum of Board schools/elementary
schools in England dates back to 1871. Peter McIntosh believes that
it was designed mainly as a disciplinary measure, permitted for boys
only.[29] Eventually girls were also permitted to take drill exercises
in schools and colleges. In India, the traditional dress and attitudes
meant mostly gentle drill and callisthenics, and prevented the girls
from engaging in more lively physical exercise and games. This was
evident in Bethune school and college as well, where a company of
Girl Guides was started in 1923, however it did not continue for long.
It was started afresh in 1938-9 but again discontinued from August
1942.[30] In Loreto House, the Girl Guides Company was formed as
early as 1914. It had three patrols, namely—Cornflower, Convolvulus
and Larkspur.[31] YWCA trained the Girl Guides for all the Companies,
both in Bethune as well as Loreto schools and colleges,[32] and regular
inspection rallies were organized to assess the Girl Guides.

Drill followed by sports became an integral feature of the schools
and colleges of Calcutta. In due course it was made compulsory by the
colonial education department. The former was used as an effective
instrument by the British imperialist forces to coerce and control
the natives, which is quite evident from the oath taken by the Girl
Guides—'To be Loyal to God and King Emperor.'[33] In fact, the role
of drill, callisthenics, and games is very significant to understand the
secret of British success in colonization.

Following the Victorian ideals, the Jewish, Brahmo and Hindu
community believed that women were socialized to be docile, gentle,
chaste and nurturing. These attributes were very much opposed to
creating a sportsman because sport involves competition, challenge
and a definite outcome primarily determined by physical skill and
exertion.[34]

Gradually, sports percolated down from the British to other Indian
communities through the system of downward filtration. The British
army in their Indian Empire, as Tony Mason points out, played sport
to maintain their morale and to relieve boredom. Sport was, according
to Richard Cashman, not a colonial priority but simply a way to
maintain British society in an alien environment. However, from
1835 onwards when the British articulated a policy of anglicization,
greater involvement of Indians in the bureaucracy and the army
helped to introduce elite Indians to British sports. Naturally, the Parsis
who were anglicized, frequently imitated Englishman's enthusiasm
for sports. Sports thus gradually became part of the British civilizing

process. However, initially they had certain reservations regarding the capacity of the Indians; particularly they differentiated between the manly Marathas, Rajputs and Sikhs and the effete, unmilitary and cowardly Bengalis.[35] On the contrary, the Parsis, who, considered to be the descendants of a martial race and were socially mobile within the colonial framework, became the pioneers of sport in India.[36]

The Parsis of Calcutta thus took to organized sport and provided a model for other elite Indian groups like the Baghdadi Jews and upper-class Western-educated Bengali elites to follow. Flower Silliman, a Calcutta-based Baghdadi Jew woman recalls how her family used to watch football and hockey on the distant maidans through a pair of field glasses while listening to the commentary in an old fashioned radio.[37] The girls of Parsi families used to study in Loreto House where they played basketball and hockey with upper class British, Anglo-Indian, Armenian, Baghdadi Jews, and aristocratic Bengali girls from early twentieth century. The Loreto College girls, especially those belonging to the Anglo-Indian and Parsi communities, made rapid progress in basketball by winning prizes in the women's senior league and knockout tournaments. Popularity of basketball helped the Indian girls also to learn it enthusiastically and compete in the league matches.[38]

With the influx of non-white athletic talent, Western dominance of the championships was immediately and significantly overturned as Indians proved just how talented they were alongside the Anglo-Indians. This inspired the Indian girls of Loreto House to a greater extent. The Anglo-Indians continued to identify their interests with those of their fatherland Britain, rather than of their motherland, India. Along with the Parsi and the Jewish communities, they maintained distance from the natives. Despite their distinctiveness and distance from the natives they served as role models for the natives, especially the way they emancipated themselves, breaking into the male world of sports.[39] For instance, by practising skating on the roads and playing badminton and the like on the Park Circus maidan, they inspired Muslim girls like Nasima De (nee Banoo) to indulge in such activity. Unfortunately, Nasima could not pursue her sporting career due to family restrictions but was able to take the pressure of work in the capacity of a political activist and teacher in her later life due to her early initiation to the world of sports. She was inspired by Anglo-Indian teachers in the Sakhawat Memorial School for Muslim girls to play basketball, baseball, and track and field games on a competitive basis.[40] Thus, inspired by the European, Anglo-Indian, Parsi and Jewish communities, the upper-class Hindu women also participated in competitive sports both within and outside the Loreto College.

In the 1920s, badminton and cycling were the popular leisure activities of the girls of Bethune school and college. In fact, Ashoka Gupta recapitulates her wonderful experience of cycling with her friends Preeti Datta and Saivalini.[41] But it was almost impossible for the day students (who formed 78 per cent of the entire college) to spend their leisure together because their departure at the end of the college hours was being determined by the necessity of going by one of the college buses. Therefore, in most cases, leisurely sporting activities were confined to the boarders of the college.[42] In due course of time, competitive spirit which is natural and universal to sports was introduced both within and outside the college premises. Following their example, drill and sports thus became a regular feature of Diocesan College, Mission Boarding and Hindu High Schools,[43] Gokhale Memorial Girls School, Brahmo Balika Vidyalaya, and Victoria Institution in the 1920s.[44]

In the 1920s certain socio-political forces like large-scale partici-pation of women in the mainstream Gandhian movement, their active involvement with militant nationalism, emergence of *mahila samities* (women's associations) both in the metropolis and in the districts, and limited female suffrage brought about changes in the sphere of physical education for women. The contemporary journals also highlighted the importance of sports among women and claimed that participation in sports would further stimulate the movement for women's emancipation. For instance, in Calcutta, after one sports programme, the *Deepali Patrika* reported: 'If Bengali women concentrate more on physical exercise than dance and song, then they would be really considered moving towards progress. Only in Bengal, the mothers are called Abala.'[45] This criticism for Bengali mothers could be removed if the Bengali girls follow Bani's footsteps. During this time (1934) Bani Ghosh broke Miss Lucy's (an English woman) record in the national swimming club sports.[46] The average Bengali girls lacked physical stamina because their life did not include any kind of routine physical exercise since their early childhood. They were rather taught to stay indoors and play indoor games. Hence, they entered the domain of sports little later than their anglicized counterpart.

During the 1940s and 1950s various articles were published in contemporary magazines regarding the lower standards among health of Bengali women in comparison to other provinces of India and Western countries. These articles inspired the girls to take up sports seriously.[47] A few articles also highlighted the fact that the girls and women needed physical exercises and sports not just for their own physical fitness but to procure healthy children.[48] It can be argued here that a strange dichotomy existed among the male intelligentsia about women's participation in sports. On the one side they wanted that the women should walk away from traditional gender expectations and challenge the male dominated *status quo* in the field of sports. On the other side, women's quest for equal opportunity, physical empowerment and respect were being resisted by many men and institutional forces. These articles reflected that the future of any nation and its people depended upon the child (progeny) and the bearer of that child, the mother.[49] So the mother through regular exercise should enhance her beauty, strength and power.[50] Thus the Bengali *bhadralok* allowed the women to participate in sports not for their own recreation or enjoyment, but rather for healthy progeny who would be strong enough to fight the might of the white race. It was also specifically mentioned that women need exercise which are not rigorous and strenuous so they are able to retain their femininity.[51] Hence such sports were prescribed for women through which they could display their female characteristics. For instance, *Prabartak* strongly recommended slow-cycling for women because fast cycling was considered harmful for the physical build of women,[52] particularly their reproductive function. However, survey studies from the 1950s and 1960s suggested that the occurrence of major disorders during pregnancy was no greater in athletes than in non-athletes. In short, these surveys demonstrated that strenuous exercise had no detrimental effects on pregnant women.[53]

So, from the 1920s, the Bengali women became conscious of the importance of sports. But physical activities was mostly confined to the so-called feminine sports. Rigorous sporting activity among women was still discouraged by the society. Cricket and soccer both remained a male monopoly because of their more masculine character as envisaged by the colonial male. Perhaps, they believed that involvement in these masculine games would lead to a conscious challenge to their hegemony. Even the educated women as heads of educational institutions were opposed to further such masculine sports in their institutes for its corrupting influence on the students.[54] They were not opposed to women's recreation in the sporting arena but it remained confined to badminton, table tennis, basketball and track and field games in their institutes. Thus women's physical activity was controlled by an ideological system of gender roles and values that dictated what a woman can and cannot do with her physicality.[55]

Moreover, for most Bengali women, the ultimate goal was marriage, which hampered their sporting talents and restricted it within the college premises for a short duration of three years. E.A. Gait had aptly pointed out that 'The degree of B.A. is a very valuable asset in the matrimonial market.'[56]

For women, marriage and motherhood are considered mandatory for fulfilment and identity formation.[57] They are expected to have such qualities like gentleness, caring, nurturance, obedience, co-operation, dependence (on men), passivity, physical frailty and sexual submissiveness, which are treated as womanly virtues.[58] Thus social and cultural inferiority are imposed on them. The process of socialization from her childhood manipulates them towards the traditional ideals of womanhood.[59] Here, one needs to emphasize that a woman's world gets restricted within the confines of household and she is not allowed to seek recreation (which includes sports) elsewhere, rather she is destined to sacrifice her life for the 'others'.[60] Sports did not fall within the purview of defined womanly virtues; rather it was equated with the prevailing model of masculinity, which emphasized aggressiveness, striving for dominance, competition, size, physical strength and phallocentrism. Thus, Bengali girls and women with all their emotions, enthusiasms, aspirations and fantasies were not allowed to participate in sports either as spectators or performers because culture imprints on women the sense of their limits. In fact, due to this socio-cultural restraint, one female player lamented during this time: 'If we play football we will play much better than men. But we don't want them to feel ashamed of that.'[61] Despite gender role stereotyping, many Bengali girls competed with the English, Anglo-Indian, Parsi and Jewish girls for the first time in 1938 at the Girls Inter-School Sports in Calcutta. Even earlier, Purna Ghosh was able to make her presence felt in athletics among the Anglo-Indians in the 1930s.[62]

Amidst such integration and acculturation, one can also visualize a sort of confrontation and struggle between the Anglo-Indian and the Bengali girls. In the late nineteenth and early twentieth centuries when the Bengalis were challenging the might of the British Raj by defeating them in their own game, the Anglo-Indians were doing the same with the Bengalis. The former's feeling of hostility towards Indians, especially the Hindu majority community, was due to the fact that they were against complete Indianization of services. This endangered their service position in the railways, posts and telegraphs. This resentment and rivalry was thus evident in the field of sports where they took on the Bengalis. For instance, at the Kalighat Annual

Sports, in most cases, Bengali girls were not allowed to compete with the Anglo-Indian girls.[63] On the other hand, in the inter-school and inter-college competitions, the Anglo-Indian girls studying in the Loreto schools and college, La-Martinere, St. James, or Dow Hill competed with the Bengali girls studying in Gokhale Memorial Girls School, Bethune Collegiate School, Victoria Institution, Scottish Church and Ashutosh College. In all these competitions, strong anglophilia along with an attitude to challenge the natives was quite evident. This attitude of maintaining distance from the natives was also visible in non-participation in various sporting events. For instance, in the Third Annual Women Sports Meet in 1938, only seven colleges sent their names.[64] Significantly enough, Loreto College consisting mostly of Anglo-Indian girls did not participate in this sporting meet.

In the colonial period, particularly from the 1920s, an interest was thus generated towards sports among women in Bengal. However, the Bengali girls did not involve themselves in sporting activities simply to emulate their British and Anglo-Indian counterparts. In other words, it was not simply an act of mimicry;[65] rather it can be argued that sports acted as mirror in which the female identity assessed itself.[66] It not only promoted women's emancipation but also inculcated the notions of self-cultivation and self-worth among women. For instance, from 1935 to 1942, Ila Sen, a Bengali girl, had established herself as an excellent sports woman, who was equally proficient in athletics, basketball, badminton and tenniquoit.[67] She had even broken the fifty meters run record of an Anglo-Indian girl— Barbara Edward in 1937.[68]

At the same time, women's participation in sport was certainly part of a nationalist enterprise. Mrinalini Sinha has argued that in the second half of the nineteenth century, middle-class Bengalis made several efforts to combat the problem of the emasculation of the Bengali male.[69] There was a revival of the *akhra*, a culture/gymnasium, in order to cultivate and instil a sense of pride in the physical power of the Bengalis. Thus the growth of 'new woman' and her 'womanhood' can be understood under the light of effeminate *babu* of the nineteenth-century Bengal, who was quite weak and fragile; hence the revival of his strength was needed. In this context, thus, womanhood was often equated with motherhood. It is quite evident that feminine motherhood was juxtaposed to the prevalent masculinity of *bhadralok*. The contemporary vernacular journals are full of details with respect to revival of all the powers of women,[70] for inspiring the men to fight against the British.[71]

CONCLUSION

Christian missionaries were integrally involved in European over-seas expansion in ways that went far beyond the preaching of the gospel. They were necessarily deeply committed to change many aspects of the indigenous cultures. In fact, they were said to have brought Christianity, chemistry and cricket in a single package.[72] Coupled with that, Western women's educational work in colonial India played a profound role in bringing physical freedom to Asian, Eurasian and Indian females.[73] In Bengal, the schooling of girls in the early twentieth century provided an expanded space for growth to women but it was essentially embedded in the societal context. It ensured that women remain passive actors in the process of schooling (regarding the curriculum of academics as well as physical education and sports), do not question the patrifocal ideology and do not transgress the social boundaries and work within the accepted system of values. Thus girls were not encouraged to play football or cricket and were expected to play with the swing, hopscotch, etc., both within and outside the school and college premises.

Women's issues are thus often marginalized in all communities. They are accused of being divisive in a time of need, privileging one internal division over the community as a whole. So, for entry into sports, they had to emphasize and wage a collective struggle for identity against male domination—which formed the common cause and at the same time acknowledged difference (in this case, ethnic, religious and cultural differences of all the communities). While women are socialized to use their bodies to please others, their men counterparts are socialized to use their bodies to please themselves.[74] Socialization into sport (i.e. the agents or agencies that have been in-fluential in attracting women towards sports) as well as active sports participation differed from community to community and from time to time. So, in order to understand the inequalities in sports based on gender and race, one has to reject the notion of a fixed female identity because differences existed not only between men and women but between women themselves and also 'within a woman'.

Finally, the power equations between the colonizer and the col-onized had also contributed towards social stratification in sports based on gender and race. The Parsis and the Jews, though had identified with the British ways, never saw themselves as British nor did the British accept them as *British*. The desire of colonial mimicry or resemblance with the colonizer was strong in them as among the Anglo-Indians because they vehemently refused assimilation with the Indian society. They did not see themselves as 'the colonized' nor did they experience the kind of hatred or low self-esteem which was the fate of the most Indians. Besides, they did not face the strictures imposed on most Bengali Muslim women; rather they had more space to carve out a place for themselves within their communities. So they were at an advantageous position while participating in sports, compared to Bengali women.

NOTES

1. Karuna Chanana, 'Female Sexuality and Education of Hindu Girls in India', in Sharmila Rege (ed.), *Sociology of Gender: The Challenge of Feminist Sociological Knowledge*, Delhi: Sage, 2003, p. 295.
2. Austin A. D'Souza, *Anglo-Indian Education: A Study of its Origins and Growth in Bengal up to 1960*, Delhi: Oxford University Press, 1976, p. 5.
3. Ibid., pp. 5-6.
4. Ibid., p. 6.
5. Ibid.
6. Ibid., p. 5.
7. Mother Mary Colmcille, *First the Blade, History of the I.B.V.M.(Loreto) in India, 1841-1962*, Calcutta: Firma KLM, 1968, p. 23.
8. *A Report on Mudaliar Commision on Anglo-Indian Schools in West Bengal*, Calcutta: Orient Longman, 1954, p. 72; Bruce Haley, *The Healthy Body and Victorian Culture*, Cambridge, Massachusetts and London: Harvard University Press, 1978, p. 134.
9. J.A. Mangan (ed.), *Making European Masculinities: Sport, Europe, Gender, The European Sports History Review II*, London: Frank Cass, 2000, p. 63.
10. Ibid., p. 66.
11. Ibid., pp. 66, 71.
12. Ibid., pp. 114-15.
13. J.A. Mangan, *Sport in Europe: Politics, Class, Gender, The European Sports History Review 1*, London: Frank Cass, 1999, pp. 67-9.
14. Ibid., p. 72.
15. J.A. Mangan, and Fan Hong (eds.), *Sport in Asian Society: Past and Present*, London: Frank Cass, 2003, pp. 129, 149, 150.
16. Frank Anthony, *Britain's Betrayal in India: The Study of the Anglo-Indian Community*, Bombay, Delhi: Allied Publishers, 1969, p. 16.
17. Ibid., p. 354.
18. Ibid., p. 352.
19. Ibid., p. 357.
20. Loreto College Magazine, *Palm Leaves*, 1939, p. 63 (henceforth *PL*).
21. Ibid.
22. Ibid., pp. 62-3.
23. Mangan and Hong, *Sport in Asian Society*, pp. 133, 152.
24. Colmcille, *First the Blade*, p. 3; *PL* (1938), p. 20; *PL* (1939), p. 64.
25. *Alumni Journal of Loreto College*.
26. *PL* (1931), p. 92.
27. Aparajita Sengupta, 'From "Nation" to "Gender": Identity "Order" and Women

in Nationalist Thought in Late Nineteenth and Early Twentieth Century Bengal', in Ranjit Kumar Roy (ed.), *Retrieving Bengal's Past: Society and Culture in the Nineteenth and Twentieth Centuries*, Calcutta: Rabindra Bharati University, 1995, p. 63.

28. *PL* (1938), p. 28.
29. Mangan, *Sport in Europe*, pp. 66, 89.
30. K. Nag (ed.), *Bethune School and College*, Centenary Vol. 1, *1849-1949*, Calcutta: S.N. Guha Roy, 1949, p. 117.
31. *PL* (1915), p. 54; *Alumni Journal of Loreto College*.
32. Nag, *Bethune School and College*, p. 117; *PL* (1915-16), p. 41.
33. Kanak Mukhopadhaya, *Samakaler Prekhapate Preetilata Waddadar*, Calcutta: School of Women's Studies, Jadavpur University, 1999, p. 62.
34. E.E Snyder and E.A. Spreitzer, *Social Aspects of Sport*, New Jersey: Prentice Hall, 1978, pp. 17-18.
35. Indira Chowdhury, *The Frail Hero and Virile History: Gender and Politics in Colonial Bengal*, Oxford: Oxford University Press, 1998, p. 5.
36. H.D. Darukhanawala, *Parsees and Sports and Kindred Subjects*, Bombay: the author, 1935, p. 9.
37. Jael Silliman, *Jewish Portraits, Indian Frames: Women's Narratives from a Diaspora of Hope*, Calcutta: Seagull, 2001, pp. 100-1.
38. *PL* (1931), pp. 92-3.
39. President-in-Chief's Address, *The Review*, January 2006-February 2006, p. 3. *The Review* is an Anglo-Indian Journal.
40. An informal interview with Mrs. Nasima De (nee Banoo), active sportswoman in her school and college life.
41. Mira Bhattacharjee and Shanta Sen (eds.), *Bethune College Centenary Volume, 1879-1979*, Calcutta: Bethune College, 1980, p. 117.
42. Nag, *Bethune School and College*, p. 67; Mukhopadhaya, *Samakaler Prekhapate Preetilata Waddadar*, pp. 105-6.
43. W.W. Hornell, *Progress in Education in Bengal, 1912-1913 to 1916-1917, Fifth Quinquennial Review*, Calcutta: Bengal Secretariat Book Depot, 1918, pp. 113.
44. Manoranjan Mitra and K. Zapharah, *Government of Bengal, 1927-1932*, Calcutta: Bengal Secretariat Book Depot, 1933, pp. 124, 113-14.
45. *Deepali Patrika*, Baisakh 1341 BS (1934).
46. *Prabartak*, Poush 1349 BS (1942-43), Bhadra 1348 BS (1941), pp. 445-7.
47. *Nirmalya Vyayam Patrika*, Jaiyastha 1364 BS, pp. 22-4.
48. Shri Mohan Lal Panja, 'Why Women Need Physical Exercise?', *Nirmalya Vyayam Patrika*, Jaiyastha 1364 BS (1957).
49. *Prabartak*, Jaiyastha 1340 BS, p. 185.
50. Ibid., Jaiyasyha 1330 BS, p. 308.
51. *Nirmalya Vyayam Patrika*, Ashwin 1364 BS (1957), p. 66.
52. *Prabartak*, Kartik, Chaitra, 1341 BS (1934), pp. 698-9.
53. Greeta L. Cohen (ed.), *Women in Sport: Issues and Controversies*, Newbury Park, London, Delhi: Sage, 1993, pp. 3, 127-8; *Lady Brabourne College Magazine*, 1953.
54. Boria Majumdar and Kausik Bandyopadhyay, *Goalless: The Story of a Unique Footballing Nation*, Delhi: Penguin Books, 2006, p. 182.
55. Cohen, *Women in Sport*, p. 3.
56. *Lady Brabourne College Magazine*, 1953.
57. Sudhir Kakar, 'Feminine Identity in India', in Rehana Ghadially (ed.), *Women*

in Indian Society, Delhi: Sage, 1998, pp. 44-5. For details see, Homi Bhabha, *The Location of Culture*, London: Routledge, 1994.

58. Sengupta, 'From "Nation" to "Gender"', pp. 63-4.
59. Kamla Bhasin and Nikhat Said Khan, *Some Questions on Feminism and its Relevance in South Asia*, Delhi: Kali for Women, 1986, p. 33; Susan L. Greendorfer, 'Gender Role Stereotypes and Early Childhood Socialisation', in Cohen (ed.), *Women in Sport*, pp. 5-9; Sudhir Kakar, 'Feminine Identity in India', p. 44.
60. Jashodhara Bagchi (ed.), *Indian Women: Myth and Reality*, Delhi: Sangam Books Ltd., 1995, p. 37.
61. *Prabartak*, Chaitra 1346 BS (1939), p. 656. This was the time when girls were playing football in Bengal for a while.
62. *Hindustan Standard* (Calcutta), 16 March 1938.
63. Ibid., 24 January 1938.
64. Ibid., 11 March 1938. The colleges included Ashutosh College, Bethune College, Scottish Church College, City College, Vidyasagar College, Victoria Institution and the post-graduate class of the Calcutta University.
65. For details see, Bhabha, *The Location of Culture*.
66. Mazumdar and Bandyopadhyay, *Goalless*, p. 191.
67. Mukul, *Kheladhulaye Banglar Meye*, Calcutta: Anandadhara Prakashan, 1976, p. 93.
68. Ibid.
69. Mrinalini Sinha, *Colonial Masculinity: The Manly Englishman and the Effeminate Bengali in the Late Nineteenth Century*, Manchester: Manchester University Press, 1995, p. 21. For details on Bengalis' supposed effeminacy, see John Roselli, 'The Self Image of Effeteness: Physical Education and Nationalism in Nineteenth Century Bengal', *Past and Present*, no. 86, February 1980.
70. *Prabartak*, Baisakh 1340 BS (1933), Baisakh 1330 BS (1923), Kartick 1340 BS (1943).
71. Ibid., Kartick 1341 BS (1934).
72. J.E. Goldthorpe, *The Sociology of Post-Colonial Societies, Economic Disparity, Cultural Diversity, and Development*, Cambridge: Cambridge University Press, 1906, p. 56.
73. Inspired by a sense of 'sisterhood' and Christian values, through the English language education, the European women aimed at emancipating the whole person, body and mind of the native women.
74. Cohen, *Women in Sport*, p. 215.

15

Cricket Beats Soaps, Serials and Politics: Cricket and Television in Contemporary India

BORIA MAJUMDAR

INTRODUCTION

The changing relationship between cricket and satellite television in the context of the Indian subcontinent has been a subject of considerable scholarly inquiry. That one nourishes the other is well known. However, what is relatively little known is the degree to which this interdependence has grown in recent times. So much so that cricket tournaments, or rather designated TV tournaments, are being planned with alacrity by the Board of Control for Cricket in India (BCCI). Television rights for these overseas tournaments/ matches from 2006 to 2009 had initially generated $219.5 million for the BCCI.[1] On the other hand, satellite channels too have started planning cricket programming around these tournaments, programming expected to generate millions in advertising revenue.[2] While the organization of such big money events well encapsulates the symbiotic relationship between cricket and satellite television within a burgeoning Indian economy, other local/regional dimensions of this relationship are often no less fascinating. Tele-visual hype generated on the occasion of a regional cricket body election in July 2006 in West Bengal, especially by the multiple 24-hour Bengali news channels, drew attention to the local variant of the story involving big money television and even bigger money sport. This essay, on the basis of two distinct case studies—the implications of the tri-nation one-day series played in Malaysia in September 2006 involving Australia, West Indies and India, and television coverage of the Cricket Association of Bengal elections in July 2006—will comment on the complex and ever changing relationship between cricket and television in India. At the same time it will attempt to question the rationale behind this growing interdependence and probe what this means for the Indian nation at large.

THE DLF CUP, KUALA LUMPUR (12-24 SEPTEMBER 2006)

Even the most ardent of cricket fans will admit that the tournament played at Kuala Lumpur (KL) in September 2006 was not conceived to boost cricket in Malaysia. In fact, a sample survey conducted weeks before the start of the tournament pointed out that three among one hundred people in KL knew that such a tournament involving the world's three leading teams was to start in a matter of days at the Malaysian capital.[3] And in Australia the tournament had hardly evoked any murmur. Perhaps the only times people referred to it was when Glen McGrath and Matthew Hayden made it back to the one-day team and when Adam Gilchrist had announced his unavailability citing possible burn out. Blatantly put, Australia hardly took it seriously. As the Australian selector Andrew Hilditch very aptly put it on the issue of Gilchrist's selection:

Gilchrist is a vital member of the Australian Test and one-day side and performs an extremely demanding role. . . . The best way to prepare him physically and mentally for the upcoming summer of cricket is to allow him to continue his training program at home. We consider this to be an ideal preparation for Adam before the ICC Champions Trophy, the Ashes and the 2007 World Cup.[4]

Even Mahinda Vallipuram, vice-president of the Malaysia Cricket Association had stated in an interview, 'We would certainly like to make it an annual tri-series event, making Malaysia a neutral venue for other teams to come and play. . . . We don't just have the grounds but we have the infrastructure, hotels, an airline hub and a well placed time zone to back us.'[5] Interestingly, not once did he mention in the course of the interview that the tournament would help boost local cricket in Malaysia.

The question that crops up then is why was the BCCI desperate to send the Indian team to play before a paltry crowd of 7,000 Indian expatriates? Even with temporary stands, erected specially for the purposes of the DLF Cup, the Kinara Oval in Pouchong, KL, could only house a little more than 7,000 spectators. More, why did the BCCI spend $4 million to install floodlights at the venue when any stadium in the Indian heartland or in any of India's north-eastern states would have been far better off with such an installation?[6] Was it simply to help the 7,000 odd to view their cricket better? Finally, was such a huge spending for such a small audience justified? Or was there yet another ulterior motive that went far beyond the politically correct argument of trying to boost cricket in Malaysia and thus furthering the timeless objective of trying to globalize cricket? The truth is: the DLF Cup in Malaysia was simply a satellite TV bonanza. It was nothing more than attractive programming organized for the Indian satellite television market by the BCCI. Just like the soaps and the serials, which dominate evening television in India, the DLF Cup helped provide yet another alternative to these in the two weeks between 12-24 September 2006. At the same time, it was an attractive package for the television industry, not only for the broadcaster which had the rights to beam the games live but also for the news channels engaged in what is nothing less than a war for ratings. Nalin Mehta has put it aptly:

Unlike any other country in the world, the Indian television industry has consciously ridden on cricket's shoulders to such an extent that that by 2006, cricket-oriented programming accounted for the greatest expenditure in news gathering across most news channels. So dependent is news television on cricket, for revenues and for viewers; so prominent is cricket in news programming, that it would be fair to call this process the 'cricketization' of Indian television.[7]

It was for these channels that the floodlights were installed; it was for them that Kuala Lumpur was picked ahead of Toronto. Had it been the latter, matches would have started at seven in the evening India time and continued till the wee hours of dawn. And if played under floodlights, they would have consumed the entire night. In contrast, matches at KL started at midday India time and ended by nine in the evening. Television programming around the games easily continued till midnight allowing the broadcasters the opportunity to reap real dividends.

This is not to say, however, that the entire agenda was driven by economic imperatives. While the monetary certainly overshadowed all else, the political too sneaked its way in. It was top-down cricket imperialism at play—host a tournament at a neutral South-East Asian venue; provide them with the necessary funds to build infrastructure; contribute somewhat to promoting cricket in uncharted territories and build on the votes of these associate member countries within the International Cricket Council and also the Asian Cricket Council. Two ancillary points may be made here: cricket once viewed as imperial cement is now perceived as national mortar, and sport, while hardly fundamental to global survival, has been a not insignificant element in imperial and post-imperial nationalistic assertion and denial. Moreover, a strong BCCI is a must to make cricket an attractive proposition for the TV industry. Only if the BCCI is strong enough can it unilaterally decide to sell TV rights for all of India's off-shore games, even if such games involve Pakistan, can it appoint a production house of its choice as host broadcaster and garner returns. It is a form of neo politico-economic imperialism, where the Americanization model of globalization is turned on its head.

This was best exemplified when on 1 May 2006 the subcontinent led by India outwitted Australia and New Zealand in what turned out to be a rather one-sided battle for the rights to host the 2011 World Cup. Aside from the usual exhilaration a successful bid brings forth, the late subcontinental entry culminating in a euphoric triumph in the face of stiff Western resistance drew attention to certain defining truths centering the future of India's most loved passion. The World Cup bid, more persuasively than ever, brought to the fore the political and economic might of Asian cricket, a might acquired largely on the strength of the booming satellite television market.

When the subcontinental delegation led by the BCCI and the PCB landed in Dubai for the ICC meeting to decide the hosts of the 2011 World Cup, they had the necessary financial muscle to take on, and overpower the West. The subcontinental financial might was such that it could easily buy out the West Indians, as was alleged in the media, with a promise to help them monetarily before Cricket World Cup 2007.[8] And in their bank balance, the BCCI-led Asian delegation had elements of aggression that is so historically typical of the West. In fact, the bidding process of the 2011 tournament provides some justification to arguments advanced by globalization champions like Thomas Friedman. Friedman often cites an African folk tale that he feels captures the very essence of the process. The folk goes thus:

Every morning in Africa, a gazelle wakes up. It knows it must run faster than the fastest lion or it will be killed. Every morning a lion wakes up. It knows it must outrun the slowest gazelle or it will starve to death. It doesn't matter whether you are a lion or a gazelle. When the sun comes up, you better start running.[9]

Though the Australasian gazelle had started running way before the Asian lion had even come off its blocks, Asia had the strength to catch up. Thus while cricket has helped India establish a place in the world parliament of nations, the cricket field has also become an instrument to coerce the very global West, lending credence to the saying that globalization continues to be a romantic term with different meanings for different people—success for the powerful and eclipse for the powerless. Only in this case the power centres have been reversed.

And as mentioned earlier, satellite television plays a central role in this role reversal because of its unique relationship with Indian cricket. Why are they such good bed fellows despite the high costs of international cricket coverage? Simply because had television not generated the money it does for cricket, the organization of these tournaments would not be feasible. On the other hand, these tournaments are major attractions for the television industry for wooing prospective advertisers. The whole strategy, as Mehta argues, is to convert a cricket series that would otherwise have been covered as part of the regular sport news into a mega news event like the general election or the annual union budget to tap into the unique Indian passion for cricket.[10]

Given the structure of satellite television in India, in which there is an extreme reliance on advertising in the absence of proper monitoring of households with access to cable, cricket is like the Pied Piper's magic flute, which has a lasting charm on advertisers. In fact, a

TAM study in 2002 found that in comparison to soccer, cricket offered far greater and more effective opportunities for advertisers—in the stadium as well as on television. This partly explains why in 2001 as many as 473 brands advertised on cricket for 16,400 advertising spots on television. . . . For television in general, cricket is a predictable news event, for which advertising can be bought and sold well in advance. For news television, in particular, cricket's centrality to notions of Indian identity offers an opportunity to capture audiences and advertising.[11]

Finally, with the satellite channels starting to target the diaspora with live webcasting, the reliance on cricket is sure to rise in the months to come. This is because cricket, religion at home and a symbolic flexed muscle in the international arena, is India's best-known global brand name. And given that cricket has been crucial in fashioning people's identification with a consumerist ethos within a liberalizing society and economy, it seems that it is destined to be the nation's leading newsmaker in the years to come, making it a darling of the television industry. It is for this reason, besides many others, that modern Indian cricket is enmeshed in politics and this mesh will be pulled tighter in the years and decades ahead. The takeover of the Indian cricket board by the new dispensation under Sharad Pawar in November 2005 is indeed a pointer to what lies ahead. Cricket is now a realm too important politically to be left to cricketers. Such is the power and appeal of cricket today that even when India is not doing too well on the field, interest hardly wanes. In the Victorian era cricket was a political tool of Anglo-Saxon purpose to civilize the world. Today it seems that an Eastern economic imperialism rooted in cricket is about to commence and the link between cricket and satellite television, as mentioned earlier, is central to this commencement.

This is why every match is dissected across many channels in great detail, with the media alternating between baying for a player's blood and praising him to the sky. This media hype explains the large-scale convergence of politicians around the cricket field. While Laloo Prasad Yadav heads the Bihar Cricket Association and Arun Jaitley is the president of the Delhi District Cricket Association (DDCA), Sharad Pawar heads both the Maharastra Cricket Association and the BCCI. By early 2007, he had launched a bid to assume presidency of the International Cricket Council despite having just attended one ICC meeting in his life.[12] A simple math is enough to explain the politician's interest in cricket: as Agriculture Minister Shard Pawar was on television not more than once every fortnight. As BCCI president he was on television more than twice a day.

The question then that begs to be asked is whether this linkage between cricket and television is limited to being a money spinner for both the BCCI and the television industry or does it have a broader significance for the nation both at home and in the diaspora? In other words, are tournaments like the one at Kuala Lumpur examples of simple role reversals of globalization or do they have further complex dimensions that continue to remain ignored?

What these tournaments help accomplish in this age of globaliza-tion is cement enclaves of Indian identity based on cricket. To go a step further, it can be suggested that they help Indianize the global Indian and are examples of what may be called 'glocalization'. Thus when the Indian board seeks to organize a tournament in North America or South-East Asia, what it is in effect doing is drawing attention to a unique variant of globalization by localizing spheres of Indian influence in these regions. Spheres, which are then made known at home by satellite television channels, thus contributing to a strength-ening of an Indian identity. This process is profoundly different from the conventional understanding of globalization as Americanization. When for example American multinationals enter foreign markets and take-over large shares, they are in effect Americanizing the world. With cricket it is different. By organizing tournaments in the West or in South-East Asia, India can never hope to Indianize these regions. This is essentially because the export exponential of cricket is profoundly different from that of Coke or Pepsi and also because the local foundations of these tournaments will continue to be domi-nated by Indians expatriates clinging on to their sport.

While on the one hand this process of Indianization is evidence of India's growing global clout, on the other it helps modify conventional models of globalization based on the developed centre and the under-developed periphery. The unique merger of cricket and satellite television in the Indian case has helped Indianize the global Indian, even if partly, and in so doing has allowed diasporic communities the world over to cling on to their local moorings irrespective of their geographic location.

Thus whether India won at Kuala Lumpur or not was irrelevant, the BCCI and the Indian television industry had already won their matches.

CRICKET ON TELEVISION: THE STORY OF THE CRICKET ASSOCIATION OF BENGAL ELECTIONS

This essay has so far focused on how television has appropriated inter-national cricket for economic gains. In the second part, I intend to turn to how domestic cricket elections were showcased on television, greatly magnifying them into events of national importance. To illustrate this argument, I focus here on Bengali television networks and their blanket coverage of the Cricket Association of Bengal (CAB) elections in July 2006. This event had turned into a lightening conductor for local politics in Bengal and national politics in Delhi. For the Left, the cricket poll became a site for the playing out of factional politics between Chief Minister Buddhadeb Bhattacharjee and his predecessor Jyoti Basu; with Basu backing incumbent CAB president Jagmohan Dalmiya and Bhattacharjee putting up Kolkata's police commissioner as the challenger. Just two months after he delivered the Left Front its greatest ever victory in West Bengal, cricket politics split the chief minister's party to such an extent that he was censured at a specially convened meeting of the CPM's state secretariat for publicly declaring his candidate's eventual defeat as a victory for 'evil' forces over 'good'.[13] For the Congress in Delhi, the election was a chance to cut down alliance partner Sharad Pawar to size. As president of the BCCI, Pawar was openly canvassing support against long-time rival Jagmohan Dalmiya, but in his role as Nationalist Congress Party (NCP) president, he had antagonized Congress leaders in Delhi. Convinced that he was also actively trying to build an alternative coalition at the Centre, Congress leaders saw the cricket election as an opportunity to snub him and dispatched a team, lead by a senior cabinet minister, to Kolkata to campaign against the police commissioner.[14] Hence, the saturation coverage: because cricket in India is more than a game; it is intensely political, has always been so, and is constitutive of 'national' public culture.[15] Television's focus on this election can only be understood in this wider context but television coverage shaped the election as much as it was shaped by it.

The 2006 CAB election was fought between two men: Jagmohan Dalmiya, the incumbent president, and Prasoon Mukherjee, the police commissioner of Kolkata. While Dalmiya had headed this regional cricket body since 1992, Mukherjee was the challenger, personally put up by West Bengal Chief Minister Buddhadeb Bhattacharjee. The chief minister's personal involvement essentially stemmed from two reasons: cricket's immense significance in the political economy and the controversial ouster of West Bengal's Saurav Ganguly from the Indian cricket team in 2005.[16] Both factors were intrinsically linked and the Left Front government's interest in this election can only be understood in this context. To begin with, the Bengal cricket election was an extension of a larger battle for control over cricket administration at the national level. The countdown to the regional CAB election began in November 2005 when Dalmiya lost control of the BCCI, an organization he had controlled since the early 1990s,[17] to Union Agriculture Minister and NCP president Sharad Pawar.[18] The election followed a bitter power struggle and soon thereafter, the BCCI's new dispensation filed a criminal case against Dalmiya, on 16 March 2006, for alleged financial irregularities relating to the financial accounts of the 1996 World Cup.[19] On 9 April 2006, when the Bombay High Court condemned the BCCI for trying to 'frame' Dalmiya,[20] the Maharashtra government, controlled by the Pawar's NCP, approached the Supreme Court of India, which also observed that the case reflected a problem of 'vindictiveness'.[21] As the legal battle intensified, the CAB election provided the next stage for this rivalry.

What did Jagmohan Dalmiya's tussle with Pawar have to do with Left Front and the chief minister of West Bengal? The chief minister stepped into cricket politics because he believed that the rivalry between Dalmiya and the new BCCI bosses would adversely affect Kolkata's cricket economy. Under the new BCCI administration, Kolkata's famous Eden Gardens stadium did not have another international cricket match scheduled for two years and Left Front chairman Biman Bose announced that the Left Front could not remain a spectator as the stadium 'was going out of the orbit of cricket activities'.[22] The second reason was the ouster of former India captain Saurav Ganguly from the Indian team in late-2005.

That decision, just before Dalmiya lost control of the BCCI, caused widespread public protests in West Bengal and even an angry debate in parliament where Bengal MPs, cutting across party lines, registered their anger.[23] Chief Minister Bhattacharjee believed that Ganguly was dropped because of Dalmiya's power politics within the BCCI. Ganguly, widely referred to as 'the Prince of Calcutta',[24] had been closely associated with Jagmohan Dalmiya throughout his captaincy and it was believed that he could not be brought back into the Indian team as long as Dalmiya retained control of the CAB.

Cricket and politics are so enmeshed in each other that when Buddhadeb Bhattacharjee decided to oppose Dalmiya's re-election as CAB president he first asked senior CPI(M) leader and Lok Sabha Speaker Somnath Chatterjee to contest against Dalmiya.[25] When Chatterjee declined, Kolkata's police commissioner, Prasoon Mukherjee was asked to stand. Assured of government backing, Mukherjee announced his formal candidature on 18 June, a decision that immediately split the Left Front. Former Chief Minister Jyoti Basu questioned the prudence of the police commissioner contesting a cricket election and his supporters within the current cabinet formed one side of the divide. On the other side were the current chief minister's supporters—Urban Development Minister Ashok Bhattacharyya, Kolkata Mayor Bikash Bhattacharyya and IT Minister Manab Mukherjee—who welcomed the decision. On 19 June, Chief Minister Buddhadeb Bhattacharjee himself declared that he wanted Dalmiya to quit the CAB.[26] Dalmiya did not back down, however, and received support from the Congress in Delhi. Uncomfortable with Sharad Pawar's political parleys with opposition leaders in Parliament, the Congress decided to use the CAB election as a proxy battle. Union Information and Broadcasting Minister Priyaranjan Dasmunshi was rushed to Kolkata to garner support for Dalmiya.

With the chief minister openly canvassing for Mukherjee, it was inevitable that the CAB elections would be appropriated by television channels and made into a major media event. The West Bengal news channel market is highly competitive with four 24-hour Bengali news channels—STAR Ananda, Kolkata TV, 24 Ghanta and Akash Bangla. Two of these—24 Ghanta and Kolkata TV—were launched in March 2006 and the CAB election became an important platform for gaining ratings and registering their presence by converting the election into a television spectacle. From the last week of June 2006, when there still a month to go for the elections, each of the four Bengali 24-hour news channels created a special segment in their news bulletins that was devoted to the CAB polls. While Star Ananda called its special section *Crossbat*, 24 Ghanta named its section *CAB Singhashan Kar?* (Whose is the CAB throne?). This programming was so prominent that Star Ananda's *Crossbat*, for instance, featured every half an hour on the channel for a full month. It opened with an animation strip of the two contestants as medieval knights in full battle armour. As they galloped towards each other with their swords drawn, the title strip appeared: *Ebare are frontfoot e noy, back foot eo noy, ebare larai cross bat e* (Not on the frontfoot, not on the backfoot, now on *Crossbat*).

Once the fissures within the government became public, the television coverage became even more intense. Following former Chief Minister Jyoti Basu, at least two senior cabinet ministers publicly opposed their chief minister in favour of Dalmiya and in a bid to outdo the other channels, Kolkata TV created a special show on one of these, featuring Sports Minister Subhas Chakrabarty.[27] The programme was titled *Banda Ye Bindaas Hai* (He is a relaxed jolly good fellow). The opening sequence of *Banda Ye Bindaas Hai* showed Chakrabarty in a felt hat waving at his supporters from an open jeep and then cut to the studio where he was interviewed for an hour by two of the channel's resident experts on the issue of the CAB election. This programming was significant because it involved a severe critique of a chief minister who just two months earlier had delivered the Left Front its biggest ever victory in West Bengal and who belonged to a party that had been in power in the state since 1977.[28]

The news segments on the election followed a set pattern. For a full month, political reporters who covered the state legislative assembly were given strict instructions to ask each MLA they met about their loyalties in the election. For example, on 25 June, when Opposition Congress leader and former Kolkata Mayor Subrata Mukherjee attacked the chief minister's intervention on the grounds that a sports body should be allowed to remain autonomous, his statement became the first headline on the prime time 9 p.m. news bulletins on all Bengali channels. Each day's coverage featured a set pattern of statements by politicians from both sides of the Dalmiya divide and every major and minor development figured on all channels as 'Breaking News'. For instance, on 30 June, when the BCCI decided to withhold all subsidies and payments to CAB over the criminal case against Dalmiya, every channel flashed it as a major breakthrough for the anti-Dalmiya combine.

Cricket sucked in a major chunk of news budgets. On 2 July, when Dalmiya convened an emergency general meeting of the CAB to weigh his support and inform members about the chief minister's intervention, multiple OB vans were used for live coverage on all channels. Every time a major player from either camp entered the CAB, the anchors from the newsroom cut across live to reporters on the spot for the latest update. In fact, on occasions, the four channels had more than one reporter at the CAB, with different reporters being assigned different camps. Reporters followed politicians so closely that when on 26 July, Urban Development Minister Ashok Bhattacharyya met Indian Football Association (IFA) Secretary Subrata Dutta at 11.00 p.m. to plead for his support in a private meeting, it was secretly recorded by cameramen from *10 Minuter Khel*, a popular sports show broadcast on Akash Bangla, a Bengali infotainment channel. The telecast of this meeting, recorded by a hidden cameraman, embarrassed the government and allowed Dutta to remain neutral.

It is significant that the channels were not simply reporting the events. Since this election dominated the public discourse in Bengal, it featured prominently on television as well. For instance, when Saurav Ganguly's brother made public an email from the former Indian captain accusing Dalmiya of 'playing with his career' and politicking that cost him his place in the Indian side,[29] Ganguly himself was away playing county cricket in England. His brother released the email in a press conference on 2 July 2006, which was broadcast live by all Bengali channels. The police commissioner's supporters had hoped that Ganguly's attack on Dalmiya would clinch the electoral battle because of his unparalleled iconic status in Bengal. Ganguly's stature in Bengal was such that just six months earlier when he was dropped as Indian captain, a 100,000 crowd at Kolkata's Eden Gardens stadium severely booed his replacement Rahul Dravid during an international game with South Africa. This was wholly unprecedented and Delhi's *Indian Express* described this incident in a sharp editorial entitled 'Serpent in Eden':

Rahul Dravid, his successor, came undone by a late outswinger and began to trudge back to the dressing room, with a dismal contribution of 6. He may, if he stretched his mind back to Eden Gardens's past reactions to prospects of defeat, have expected a rain of plastic bottles. Instead, an applause went round, and the Indian skipper was carried off on a wave of lustily expressed glee. With that malicious gesture, Eden Gardens has strengthened its claims as a dubious host for international matches.[30]

That incident provided a strong flavour of Ganguly's support base in Bengal. After his email against Dalmiya was publicized, however, all four television channels ran SMS polls on whether Ganguly had now turned into a traitor. Discussions on all four channels focused on the close relationship between Ganguly and Dalmiya while he was Indian captain, and whether he was now being ungrateful to his erstwhile benefactor simply to get back into the Indian team. Star Ananda's entire discussion on the topic of 'Ganguly as traitor' was superimposed with a graphic image of Ganguly as the Mughal Emperor Aurangzeb who in the seventeenth century had reversed established Mughal policies of religious tolerance.

The wider sociological implications of equating a 'traitor' with a Muslim emperor are beyond the scope of this essay but there is no doubt that Aurangzeb's religious intolerance has made him a hated figure in the iconography of Indian nationalism.[31] Dalmiya's election managers attributed his eventual victory to the public disclosure of the email and the discussion that surrounded it. They believed it was this that finally turned some fence-sitting voters in their favour.[32]

Television channels also played a major role in publicizing the illegal use of state power as a coercive act during this election. All channels reported how the state diktat over not allowing district sports officials to come and vote had provoked 'mini-rebellions' across West Bengal. This needs explaining. Twenty-six of the CAB's 120 votes belong to district cricket association and universities and for the 2006 election, the government issued orders that instead of local cricket association heads, the districts could only be represented by district magistrates or local superintendent of police. In addition, universities could only be represented by their registrars or vice-chancellors in person.[33] Since they were all government employees, they would have to vote for the government. In some districts, this led to protests and demonstrations by local cricket associations, a fact well covered by the television networks. Some of the university representatives also made their displeasure public. The police commissioner ultimately managed to win only 15 of the 26 votes in the districts and the universities and according to Dalmiya, this was largely due to media coverage. Dalmiya claims that the Intelligence Branch of the Kolkata police compiled a confidential report on election eve that expressed apprehensions over the police commissioner's chances for these reasons but it was ignored.[34] Perhaps the only event that the channels missed during the whole election saga was the meeting between the Union Railway Minister Laloo Prasad Yadav and Dalmiya on the day before the election. The Indian Railways has three votes in the CAB and in this meeting Dalmiya managed to confirm the minister's support, despite an old history of antagonism.[35]

Dalmiya's election managers made good strategic use of television. On election eve, they called television reporters on all channels to float a false rumour that all his supporters were being shifted to a hide-out to protect them from being bought over. All channels carried this news prominently. Its first impact was to raise questions about the money that was being spent on this cricket election but more importantly, from Dalmiya's point of view, the commissioner's managers spent vital hours trying to trace the purported 'hide-out' while Dalmiya continued his last-night political manoeuvring. The next day, on 30 July, Dalmiya assembled his loyalists at the Eden Gardens at 11.00 a.m. and by early afternoon most of his committed voters were in the safe haven of the Eden Gardens club house to start voting.[36]

Television coverage climaxed on election day when all regional channels, and some national broadcasters, dropped *all* other news from the early morning bulletins in favour of the CAB election. Analysts were present in the studios from morning to discuss the election threadbare and dissect each group's strengths and weaknesses. The coverage was more like that of a general election, not an insignificant election to a state cricket body. As the counting was on, minute by minute updates were being shown on some channels. For example, Kolkata TV and 24 Ghanta continuously flashed voter-counts and lead positions through the day. None of these flashes were based on fact because the counting was on in a closed room where only the two rival presidential candidates and the court appointed observer were present.[37] But so intense was the pressure to be different that the channels flashed their versions of the voting counts. Each channel had at least two to three reporters exclusively devoted to the counting. A large number of the 120 voters who came out after casting their votes were interviewed on live television and asked about their preference as well as the mood in the election hall. All channels also conducted multiple SMS polls where viewers were asked to send in their choice for winner through SMS messages, along with the reasons for their answers.

Even after the results were announced, poll analysis went on like it does in the coverage of national elections. The focus on cricket went on till late into the night, except that the graphic element had changed. The Star Ananda animation clip which for a month had showed the two contestants locked in *cross bat* now went a step further and depicted Dalmiya knocking Mukherjee down from his horse with his sword. Another graphic on Kolkata TV showcased a giant Dalmiya dwarfing the chief minister. That all of this had an impact was evident the following day when Buddhadeb Bhattacharjee, in a press conference to announce the signing of a new industrial MOU with a private company, declared his anger at the police commissioner's defeat: 'If you want to call it a jihad, go ahead and write it. . . . It is a victory of evil over good, over right thinking people. This happens at times in history when growth is reversed.'[38]

Although the CPM state secretariat censured him for these comments, television channels exploited them to the fullest. Star Ananda examined the political fall-out for the government through a special hour-long programme titled *Ball e Buddha Bat e Jyoti* (Buddha with the ball and Jyoti with the bat). The main aim of the programme was to discuss the open hostility within the upper echelons of the CPI(M) through a live discussion with former Kolkata Mayor Subrata Mukherjee and RSP leader and minister Nandagopal Bhattacharyya. It was a phone-in-programme where viewers could call in with questions and one Bengali viewer called in from as far as the Andaman and Nicobar Islands to say that he had 'lost respect for the progressive and upright Buddhadeb Bhattacharjee'.[39] That statement culminated the month-long obsession with the CAB elections on Bengali television.

This account of Bengali television in June-July 2006 clearly establishes the pre-eminence of cricket-related programming. Like the national networks in Hindi and English, Bengali language television too has been 'cricketized'.[40] The politics of cricket was so entwined in the politics of the ruling Left Front itself that this was unavoidable. This partly explains television's total focus on the game. Cricket in India is far more than a game and is deeply enmeshed in the wider social and political fabric. Bengali television programming in 2006 reflected this but also played a crucial role in deepening these linkages. By focusing so deeply on cricket, to the detriment of all other news, Bengali television ensured that it remained central to the public discourse. Television's unrelenting focus raised the stakes for Kolkata's politicians and provided a new factor in the political matrix, one that had not even existed a decade ago. Television networks used new technology—graphic animations, SMS polls—to create a new kind of spectacle of cricket.

CONCLUSION

What these two case studies draw attention to is the wedding of satellite television with cricket in India. One possible reason for this wedding was the almost simultaneous opening up of the television and sports market in India. While the BCCI first sold television rights for cricket matches in India in 1993, ESPN, owned by Rupert

Murdoch, entered the Indian market in 1993 as well. In a matter of months ESPN acquired the rights for exclusive broadcast of matches played on Indian soil.[41] And over time the interdependence reached epic proportions, so much so that by 2006, cricket-programming now stretches across into other television genres as well, occupying a pivotal place even across most news channels in India. The other outcome of this interdependence is that the economic well-being of international cricket has come to rely on the strength of the Indian cricket television market. With cricket continuing to be a license to print money for broadcasters in the subcontinent, it is not unnatural that broadcasters like ESPN are looking to earn back 80 per cent of the $1.1 billion spent on buying international cricket telecast rights from the ICC from sales in the Indian subcontinent.[42]

With Indian broadcasters leading the way in terms of global television rights, it also means that India or Pakistan need to play well consistently if the huge amounts invested is to be recovered. If India or Pakistan crash out of major tournaments like the World Cup at the group stage, as in 2007, advertisers' interest in the tournament is certain to nosedive. The near-total dependence on India for revenue generation is a clear indicator of the phenomenal rise of the Indian television industry over the past decade but it raises serious questions about the future of global cricket.

NOTES

1. Zee TV had initially offered the BCCI $219.15 million for the television, radio and Internet rights in non-ICC member countries. The initial media rights tender was for a minimum of 25 games and the venues included Abu Dhabi, Dubai, Holland, the US, the UK, Canada, Hong Kong, Singapore and Kuala Lumpur. Pakistan, Australia, West Indies and England were the four countries that confirmed participation. While the average match bid by Zee was $8.77 million, other companies such as Nimbus offered to pay $8 million per match and Sahara $7.05 million per match. ESPN-Star Sports' bid of $2.86 million per match was disqualified as it was lower than the floor price of $5 million fixed by the board. However, Zee walked out of the contract in June 2007 on grounds of bias. It alleged that the BCCI was unwilling to compensate it for losses in the wake of India's poor showing post-World Cup 2007 and in the light of the new regulations introduced by the government to share broadcast feeds with the national broadcaster. This was something the BCCI had done in the case of Nimbus which holds telecast rights for all matches played on Indian soil until 2010. The Zee vacuum for overseas matches in neutral venues was filled by Nimbus but at a considerably reduced figure.
2. All television news channels in India had exclusive programmes on the DLF Cup in Malaysia. Moreover, each of these programmes had exclusive promos designed and titles assigned. The only channel which did not have a cricket show, Zee,

joined the bandwagon on and from 22 August. This was understandable because Zee had the rights to broadcast the overseas games. It began with a weekly show titled *22 Yards*. The show worked around a short interview and various vignettes that dealt with the week's happenings in world cricket.

3. This sample survey was conducted for the author by three independent South Asian academics and sampled 2000 locals in Kuala Lumpur between 2-8 September 2006.

4. 'Hayden Back in One-Day Squad, Gilchrist Rested', *The Australian*, 22 August 2006, URL: http://www.theaustralian.news.com.au/story/0,20867,20213232-2722,00.html (consulted 11 September 2006).

5. 'Football Crazy Malaysia Keen to Convert to Cricket', *The Hindu*, 6 September 2006, URL: http://www.hindu.com/thehindu/holnus/007200609060343.htm (consulted 8 September 2006).

6. Boria Majumdar, 'The New Discovery of Cricket', *Outlook*, 6 October 2006, URL: http://www.outlookindia.com/full.asp?fodname = 20061006&fname = boria&sid = 1 (consulted 7 October 2006).

7. Nalin Mehta, 'Indianising Television: News, Politics and Globalisation', unpublished Ph.D thesis, La Trobe University, Melbourne, 2007.

8. N.a. 'Asia "Bought" Windies' Vote to Host World Cup—Reports', 3 May 2006, URL: http://www.stuff.co.nz/stuff/0,2106,3655394a10133,00.html (consulted 6 May 2006).

9. This anecdote is frequently referred to by Friedman. For his views on globalization see, Thomas Friedman, *The Lexus and the Olive Tree: Understanding Globalization*, New York: Farrar, Strauss & Giroux, 1999 and *The World is Flat: The Globalized World in the Twenty-First Century*, Camberwell: Penguin Australia, 2006.

10. Mehta, 'Indianising Television'.

11. Ibid.

12. Andrew Miller, 'Worse to Follow', 29 May 2007, URL: http://content-www.cricinfo.com/ci/content/story/296258.html (consulted 30 May 2007).

13. Quoted in Press Trust of India (PTI), 'Dalmiya's Re-Election "Victory of Evil Over Good"' *Outlook Online*, 31 July 2006, URL: http://outlookindia.com/pti_news.asp?id = 402962 (consulted 4 August 2006). For an account of the CPM state secretariat meeting see Press Trust of India (PTI), 'Refrain from Speaking on Dalmiya: Basu to CPM', *The Financial Express*, 5 August 2006, URL: http://www.financialexpress.com/latest_full_story.php?content_id = 136369 (consulted 7 August 2006).

14. For a detailed account of the larger politics of the CAB election, see Boria Majumdar, 'Prasun aur Dalmiya, Prasun aur Dalmiya, Dalmiya', *Ekdin*, 18 August 2006.

15. I am grateful to Nalin Mehta for this analysis, which is part of his recently published monograph, *India on Television*, Delhi: HarperCollins, 2008.

16. Ganguly was dropped after a loss of batting form and a prolonged public tiff with then national coach Greg Chappell.

17. Jagmohan Dalmiya officially served as BCCI president between 2001-4 but controlled the body at least since 1993. In 1993 he spearheaded India's efforts to win the rights to host the 1996 World Cup and served as president of the International Cricket Council between 1997-9. See Boria Majumdar, *Twenty-Two Yards to Freedom: A Social History of Indian Cricket*, Delhi: Penguin/Viking, 2004.

18. On 29 November 2005, Jagmohan Dalmiya's candidate Ranbir Singh Mahendra lost 11-20 to Sharad Pawar in the contest for the BCCI presidency.

19. Prior to filing the First Information Report (FIR) in a Mumbai police station, the BCCI first issued a show-cause notice to Dalmiya for alleged financial mismanagement on 21 February 2006, giving him 7 days to file his reply. Interview with Satish Maneshinde (on phone from Chicago: May 2006), lawyer for Jagmohan Dalmiya.

20. The Bombay High Court in its order held that Dalmiya had been framed by the present BCCI. After the High Court verdict, the State of Maharashtra, in its appeal filed in the Supreme Court, contended that observations of the Bombay High Court were totally uncalled for as the case was still under investigation. The appellant state also contended that the court's order, if not set aside, would cause great prejudice to the state and an adverse effect on the ongoing investigation into the case. Ibid.

21. The State of Maharashtra, which had challenged the anticipatory bail granted to Dalmiya, changed its stance after a Bench comprising Justice S.B. Sinha and Justice P.K. Balasubramanyan observed that 'it was a problem of vindictiveness'. Ibid.

22. 'CAB Polls: Left Front Not to Interfere', The Hindu, 24 June 2006, URL: http://www.hindu.com/2006/06/24/stories/2006062404101300.htm (consulted 30 June 2006).

23. Apart from Left Front MPs, then Defence Minister Pranab Mukherjee (another Bengali MP) from the Congress also demanded that Ganguly should be brought back into the Indian team.

24. First coined by Geoffrey Boycott, this term became widely used in media commentaries on Ganguly.

25. Somnath Chatterjee revealed this to Suman Chattopadhyay, editor of the Bengali daily Ekdin. Interview with Suman Chattopadhyay (Kolkata, on phone from Melbourne: 10 August 2006).

26. 'I Want Dalmiya Out: Buddhadeb', The Hindu, 1 August 2006, URL: http://www.hindu.com/2006/08/01/stories/2006080104981000.htm (consulted 6 August 2006).

27. The other minister to publicly oppose the chief minister was Kshiti Goswami. Their stand reflected the power play within the Left Front government between Jyoti Basu and Buddhadeb Bhattacharjee (Majumdar, 'Prasun aur Dalmiya, Prasun aur Dalmiya, Dalmiya').

28. The Left Front, led by CPI(M), has won every state assembly election in West Bengal since 1977. In June 2006, the alliance won a record 235 of the 293 assembly seats; Election Commission of India (n.d.), URL: http://www.eci.gov. in/database/database.asp (consulted 20 September 2006).

29. PTI, 'Ganguly Accuses Dalmiya of Playing with His Career', 2 July 2006, URL: http://www.outlookindia.com/pti_news.asp?id = 400722 (consulted 5 July 2006).

30. 'Serpent in Eden: Saurav Ganguly's Home Crowd Shows that it can Match its Hero in Churlishness', The Indian Express, 26 November 2005, URL: http://www.indianexpress.com/res/web/pIe/archive_full_story.php?content_ id = 82686 (consulted 19 August 2006).

31. For a detailed and sympathetic account of Aurangzeb's life see Abraham Eraly, The Mughal Throne: The Saga of India's Great Emperors, London: Phoenix, 2004, 2nd edn., pp. 331-429.

32. Majumdar, 'Prasun aur Dalmiya, Prasun aur Dalmiya, Dalmiya'.
33. Interview with Jagmohan Dalmiya (telephonic conversation from Melbourne, 25 July 2006), then president, CAB.
34. Interview with Jagmohan Dalmiya (telephonic conversation from Melbourne: 28 July 2006).
35. Eastern, South-eastern and Bengal Nagpur Railway each have one vote in the CAB.
36. Interview with Jagmohan Dalmiya (telephonic conversation from Melbourne, 1 August 2006).
37. Ibid.
38. PTI, 'Dalmiya's Re-Election "Victory of Evil Over Good"'.
39. The programme was first broadcast between 5-6 p.m. on 2 August 2006. It was telecast again between 12.00 a.m. and 1 a.m. on 3 August.
40. Mehta, 'Indianising Television'.
41. Majumdar, *Twenty-Two Yards to Freedom*, 2004.
42. Boria Majumdar, 'The Precarious Cricket Economy', 13 February 2007, URL: http://news.bbc.co.uk/2/hi/south_asia/6286295.stm (consulted 14 February 2007).

16

Science for Whom? Popular Perception of Science and the Politics of Science Movements in Bengal

SABYASACHI CHATTERJEE

INTRODUCTION: SCIENCE IN BENGALI CULTURE

This essay attempts to explore popular perceptions of science and also intends to address the politics of science movements in West Bengal. To do this it is necessary to give an idea of what the term 'science movement' means at the very outset. The term 'science movement' refers to a process through which scientific awareness in human mind can be developed. Science movements have so far worked in three ways: popularization of science, spread of scientific temper and the use of science and technology for the welfare of the common people.

What is the perception of the people about the term 'science'? What do they mean by it? For a clear understanding of its working domain, the real meaning of the term needs to be analysed in the linguistic perspective. Here, we should also mention the Bengali term for science, i.e. *bijnan*. So let us first think whether there is any difference between the terms 'science' and *bijnan*? Does the difference in language result in any difference of meaning?

From our childhood, we are taught that *bijnan* means *bishesh jnan* or 'specialized knowledge'. Dictionaries generally define *bijnan* as *bastusamuher bishesh jnan* (specialized knowledge about matters) or 'to know something as special',[1] or specialized knowledge.[2] One or two dictionaries define science as knowledge derived from experiments, proof and rational ideas, etc., or even that derived from observation and research.[3] In other dictionaries, it was simply 'knowledge' derived from the root *logos* meaning information.[4] According to the *D.K. Illustrated Oxford Dictionary*, science means a branch of knowledge involving the systematized observation of, and experiments with, phenomena. It further says that science is a systematic and formulated knowledge, especially of a specified type or on a specified subject.[5] The *Cambridge International Dictionary of English* says that science is a knowledge obtained from the systematic structure and behaviour of the physical world, involving experimentation and measurement and the development of theories to describe the results of these activities.[6] Likewise, the *Concise Oxford Dictionary* of Current English opines that science is a branch of knowledge conducted on objective principles involving the systematized observation of and experiment with phenomena.[7] Clearly, there is a difference in prioritization; the Bengali dictionaries primarily term 'science' as a special knowledge while the English dictionaries emphasized on two obvious factors, i.e. experimentation and observation, which are essential to be regarded as science. So the definition of *bijnan* (or science) is wrought with complexities.

Likewise, in Bengali culture, we have a certain *stereotype* of a scientist. We may cite the example of Professor Nani in Parashuram's *Birinchibaba*.[8] The author has satirized the persona of a scientist in the following description of Professor Nani: 'Professor Nani did not profess in any educational institution but he had passed a number of examinations. He pursued different scientific experiments in his home. For that reason, his friends called him "professor". He had no anxiety about earning because he had some ancestral properties.'[9] The visual impression of a scientist this description leaves behind is that of a person in an apron, with dishevelled hair, busy, at the same time self-forgetful and absent-minded. Professor Nani used to impatiently supervise various activities, keeping aloof from all earthly attachments. Persons like Professor Nani, insensitive to their immediate needs and yet very much busy with their so-called scientific activism, is the archetype of a scientist in the Bengali society. But the fact is that science is oriented towards societal needs. So the society should decide how science should be used. Then the question arises: is science used for each and every member of the society? In reality, however, only a handful of influential members generally dictate the manner in which science could be used in a society.

DEVELOPMENT OF SCIENCE: FROM COLONIAL TO
POST-COLONIAL INDIA

The question of patronage in the sphere of scientific research and livelihood of the scientists is a known reality. In earlier eras, royal patronage was crucial to the pursuit of science and technology in

India as elsewhere. In the colonial period, two types of science can be said to have developed: colonial science and national science. On the one hand, colonial science was developed under the patronage of the British rulers, where result-oriented applied science was emphasized mainly to serve the purposes of the colonial state. The aim of that research was to protect the interests of the empire. In 1786, Robert Kyd (an army Major in the East India Company Service), while pleading for a botanical garden in Calcutta, defined 'policy' as the 'common sense of government'. According to Antonio Gramsci, 'common sense is the folklore of philosophy, and is always half-way between folklore properly speaking and philosophy, science and economics of the specialists'.[10] What did 'common sense' mean to a trading company like the East India Company? It was obviously profit. For this profit-making initiative, the colonial power used science and technology. The British rulers rightly realized the importance of science and technology in empire-building.[11] The British did not want to change the social scenario of India, but many traditional ideas had to encounter the challenge of the modern scientific temperament.

National science, led by a band of exceptionally gifted Indian scientists, developed along a parallel line. It stressed, along with a result-oriented experimental approach, the importance of indigenous pursuit of knowledge reflected in curiosity-oriented basic and theoretical research. While various misconceptions of the society did not quite wither away by this development at one stroke, those were questioned by the notion of the scientific thinking of the rational mind. More significantly, however, science was not confined to a single space.

Before Independence, the slogan of 'science for the society' was not spelt out. In 1927, Gandhi told the students of the Indian Institute of Science in Bangalore that he was not an opponent of science but he wanted to put certain restrictions upon scientific research and upon the uses of science in general.[12] And the components of those restrictions would be non-violence, humanity and morality. Gandhi himself seldom used the term 'science' or 'technology', he spoke of the binary opposites: traditional science and industrial civilization. He was in favour of a simple village economy which would not follow the model of scientific and technological developments of the West. In his speech at the Indian Institute of Science, Gandhi had said:

How will you infect [infuse?] the people of the villages with your scientific knowledge? Are you then learning science in terms of the villages and will you be so handy and so practical that the knowledge that you derive in a college so magnificently put and I believe equally magnificently equipped—you will be able to use for the benefit of the villagers.[13]

But after Independence, the state policy did not follow the Gandhian model; on the contrary, the government engaged itself with big development planning. The role of Western science and technology was emphasized in that project.

The question of the relevance of basic research, whose result is not required to meet the immediate demands of the people, is naturally raised. The intention to use the products of science for specific interests is contextualized here. In fact, this context is crucial for understanding the commercial culture of the capitalist society, where all values are judged by investment and income. For that reason, the socially concerned intellectuals like Steven and Hilary Rose even questioned whether there was any need to pursue research on basic matters with a huge expenditure or not. In the case of commercial culture, it is useless to talk about the freedom of thinking and works of human beings if there is no so-called immediate social necessity.[14]

But this opinion is not acceptable on grounds of social justice. The government patronizes scientists with public money, which comes through the taxes collected from the people. One can ask about how that money would be spent—for the freedom of thought and freedom of work or for social necessity only. Would it be possible to combine these two? When science is applied to any developmental project, do the concerned scientists and technologists keep these concerns in their minds?

Anil Sadgopal argues that the developmental concerns were not present in the scientific projects. He narrates his own experience testifying otherwise. He was invited to review the science and technology (S&T) component of education in the context of the Sixth Five Year Plan in 1980. The purpose of the meeting was to make recommendations to the Planning Commission to make S&T education more relevant to the socio-economic needs of Indian society. The chairman of the meeting began by inviting the experts to make their recommendations. Then one after another, the experts started reeling off their views on various schemes and ideas which needed to be implemented. Then a couple of members inquired whether a critique of the S&T component of education in earlier Five Year Plans was available. They then suggested that the meeting should first attempt to find out how the earlier plans had failed to relate S&T education to the needs of society. Truly, the search for the reasons of failure would be the scientific basis of future plans. But our planners did not believe in the necessity of following the method of analysing previous experiences while taking any further step. So they had not followed the proper dictum of science.[15]

This is only a mere instance of the trend that holds good for various other projects as well. If we review the scenario of developmental projects, the same conclusion is reached. All of these were dictated and imposed on the people from above. An instance of a movement can be referred to here. The movement took place in South 24-Parganas of West Bengal where the common people protested against the establishment of a chemical fertilizer company.[16] That was an environmental movement against the so-called 'greater common good'. The entire movement raised an important question, i.e. are oppositional mass-movements the only possible way to make science socially oriented?

The notion of development, as used above, was directed by specialists and middle-class professionals. In the case of a colonial state, Deepak Kumar argues, the entire 'development' discourse was run by experts, middle-class professionals who stood for the state, and by extension, for the nation. Politicians and bureaucrats added their own flavours. All that was done in the name of the masses, who 'entered the picture only as the somewhat abstract ultimate beneficiary'.[17]

The scenario did not change even after Independence. While exploring the Scientific Policy Resolution of 1958, science was viewed to be an important factor which would lead to the democratization of comforts and amenities. It was felt in the resolution that it would not only change the material environment but would go still deeper. It was realized that the idea of a welfare state could be translated into reality specifically with the help of science.[18] In general, the objective of the resolution was to secure for the people of the country all the benefits that could be accrued from the acquisition and application of scientific knowledge.

But how far was the scientific method followed in the application of scientific theories? According to Sadgopal, some major obstacles in the process of spreading scientific method are information gap, the tendency to follow traditions, fatalism and fear of reprisals by the vested interests and inability for abstraction. As he argues:

if we can learn to overcome these obstacles to the educational process, we can see a powerful and growing process of education emerging. If the methods of science can thus be made part of people's thinking, there is hope that the domination of the educated elite and of the vested interests in the field of planning and development can then be challenged by the common people. . . . People's organizations built up through scientific processes, hopefully, will not limit their struggles to demands for merely better wages or land, but would instead struggle for ways of creating and sustaining a society relatively free of hierarchies, and other mechanisms of socio-political backwardness.[19]

It is possible to analyse society's perception regarding science using some Bengali television commercials. One advertisement, for instance, shows a woman asking a scientist what to do about her hair-fall problem. The scientist, who is found reading the *Science Reporter*, a science magazine for the teenagers, comes up with a prompt answer: 'simple solution, vitamin H'.[20] In another commercial, it can be seen that a so-called 'professor' of nutrition is saying that a 'complete planned food' has calcium that strengthens the bones.[21] Both these advertisements indicate the commercialization of the scientist himself. The commercials make use of the society's perception of science in a straightforward manner. Another fact to be noted is that a number of English words and scientific terminologies are used even when the commercials are in the regional languages.

Similar characteristics are evident elsewhere: in computer astrology, fortune-telling machine in fairs, electronic equipment for measuring height and weight with free predictions about the person's life, and 'metal tablets' for changing the fate.[22] All these are the attempts to sell a-science in the packet of science. This endeavour is not new. In 1930, Rajsekhar Basu, in his article 'Apabijnan', noted that as a result of the spread of science old superstitions are gradually disappearing.[23] *Apadharma* (a-religion) has developed in the garb of religion; likewise *apabijnan* (a-science) has developed in the garb of science. In the twenty-first century also, science remains a distant object for the majority of the population.

The roots of this phenomenon may be traced back to the process of learning science in our schools. For instance, in the practical curriculum of life science, a student in school reads like this: 'A beaker is taken. It is filled with water. Then a piece of wood is taken. Three seeds are attached with pins on it. That piece of wood is poured into the beaker.' The experiment itself is seldom actually performed. So a student never gets the opportunity to witness the so-called experiment. Thus science has been learnt through memorization of some facts. On the other hand, science clubs provide students with the actual opportunity of pursuing experiments. It is needless to say that very few learners can get this opportunity. Children's guardians also do not encourage them to take part in the activities of science clubs. They think that those activities may harm the career of their children. Due to excessive load of science teaching in schools, science in practice is ignored. So, in the greater domain, a learner notes down his/her's inference without doing any experiment or observation.

Naturally, in practical life, it is not surprising to notice that these students cannot have a scientific mind. Among them, those who are meritorious, hard working and those who can fulfil the required opportunities, later become scientists. A recent tendency is to study engineering and technology rather than pursuing research in basic sciences. These students are detached from the common people. The daily life of a school-going student is divided into various slots. Along with spending a long hour in school, he/she has to learn different subjects like drawing, singing and swimming. But no concern has been shown to make the students aware of the society.

Though the Scientific Policy Resolution of 1958 of the Government of India spells out that the state will encourage scientific research, yet in fact the government has been spending a huge amount of money on the defence sector.[24] The main thrust area of scientific research lies in defence research. The exhibition of technology is easy in this sector. There is also a doubt about the works of governmental research organizations, which are supposed to pursue research for the people's welfare.

Some governmental departments often advise people to depend upon godly power, even in the course of applying science. The buses of Delhi Parivahan Nigam (Delhi Transport Corporation) bear inscriptions inside the coaches like 'Let us work, let god adjudge the result', while the Uttar Pradesh State Transport Authority is more spiritual in declaring 'During journey, go on praying to God'. Along with that, in many programmes sponsored by the central and/or state government and even in government's own programmes, Hindu religious rituals like breaking of coconuts and lighting of lamps are followed. The leaders often consult almanacs and astrologers to determine the auspicious time for taking oath for the office of ministers or filing nomination papers for elections.

So it is very hard in this scenario of unscientific temper to make the society scientific and to make science social. However, the journey to fulfil this goal has started. Popular science movements have begun with the aim of achieving this goal. That brings us to the development of the concept of popular science in Bengal to which the next section of this essay turns attention.

DEVELOPMENT OF POPULAR SCIENCE IN BENGAL

Since the era of Enlightenment in Europe, science is commonly assumed to advance the cause of human civilization. But this notion was never fully realized in the colonial period. The early years of post-colonial Bengal were also influenced by the colonial attitude towards science. Though there were some endeavours on the part of scientists and social workers in the course of national science, yet these were mostly exceptions. It was only from 1960 onwards, when ideas like people's history, popular culture, people's ideologies were coming into the discursive practices of historians, that the notion of a popular science movement gained currency among the Bengali intelligentsia. It was only in the 1980s that the popular science movement managed to stand on its own.

What does the term 'popular science' mean? Why the adjective 'popular' has been used to determine the nature of science? Is science not relevant for the people? Is the adjective necessary for reminding us that it should be used for the people? Thus the concept of popular science needs thorough examination to understand the full implications of the term.

The first pamphlet raising the issue of popular science was published in January 1982. That pamphlet of twenty pages was written by Manindra Narayan Majumder and was published by Amulya Mondal. Titled *Gana-bijnan Andolon—Ki O Keno* (Popular Science Movement—What and Why?),[25] its cover page clearly mentioned there was certainly scope for further conceptual development and that the booklet was only 'a primary draft'. On the cover, the publication stressed on the role of science in social revolution. Meanwhile, in October 1983, a special number of the *Pragatibarta* on popular science was published.[26] In 1984, another 'primary outline' was published from Lokbijnan Prokashoni. It was again a pamphlet of twenty pages entitled *Ganabijnan Andoloner Disha: Ekti Prathamik Ruparekha* (The Direction of Popular Science Movement: A Primary Outline).[27] In 1985, Bhaskar Gupta and Srijnan Halder wrote *A Report on Popular Science movement in West Bengal: A Brief History and Present Situation*.[28] In 1987, a booklet on *Manuser Janya Bijnan* (Science for the People) was published from the Paschimbanga Bijnan Mancha (PBBM).[29]

Like PBBM, some other organizations also tried to define the nature of popular science in their own ways. In 1989, a souvenir was published on the occasion of a gathering of the *Utsa Manus*, where the focal theme was Popular Science Movement (PSM).[30] In that souvenir, Manindra Narayan Majumder, Smarajit Jana, Srijan Sen, Ashok Bandyopadhyay and others introduced the issue in different ways. Similarly, in the souvenir of the Naihati Institute of Science and Culture (1990), Pradip Basu wrote an article entitled 'Paschimbanger Ganabijnan Andoloner Itihaser Prathamik Ruparekha' (Primary

Outline of the History of PSM in West Bengal).[31] In 1994-5, Birbhum
Branch of the PBBM published a two-volume book on popular
science: *Janabijnan Parichay* (Introduction to the Popular science).[32]
There were also some other articles on the PSM, published in science
as well as in general magazines. In 1999, two important books on
popular science were published. The first book was published from
the Centre for Social Work and Research, Tripura, and the other from
the Halisahar Bijnan Parishad.[33] Thus from the vast writings on these
issues, one may notice the process of development of popular science
and side by side the growth of popular science as a discipline. That
is why in recent times, three magazines—*Mukhapatra Chetana, Jnan
Bichitra* and *Nandan*—have published special issues on the theory
and practice of popular science.[34]

Let us now distinguish between *science* and *popular science*. Theo-
retically, science is meant for the welfare of the people. But in practice
there was a shift from this theory. A prominent scientific-worker
once remarked that the activities centering round science separate
itself from life. On the contrary, science and technology are closely
associated with society, economy and governance of the state. So it is
expected that science should solve the problems of human society.[35]
But that expectation was not fulfilled as science has also been
applied within a definitive power structure. Science has developed a
hegemony of its own and has shown a marked tendency to become
authoritarian.

Popular science, by contrast, purports to promote the cause of
science from below. It aims to free science from the laboratories
and the coterie of bureaucracy. Another objective is to create public
opinion for the practice of science oriented towards the people,
instead of using science as a weapon of governance, exploitation and
making profit. Moreover, popular science emphasizes mostly on the
spread of scientific temper and rationalism. In a nutshell, it can be
said that the popular science's main objective is to bring science from
the upper echelons to the level of the downtrodden people. Both the
theorists and the activists are of the opinion that science is intimately
related with the socio-economic condition of any nation.

Science can be said to have two dimensions. On the one hand,
there is a capitalist science that promotes the interest of capitalism. It
is true that in Europe during the period of the Scientific Revolution,
the development of science was helped by capitalism. Later on, the
capitalists virtually appropriated the benefits of this science. As a
reaction against that, the concept of popular science was developed.
As Mao Tse Tung had said with respect to the Cultural Revolution,

' "Peoples" means both of the people and by the people.' How and to what extent these two meanings are appropriate to popular science is a different question and deserves further discussion.

The journey from science to popular science was initiated to remove the distance between science and the common people. When science was confined to the question papers of examinations, research works at laboratories, dominance of the experts and technological complexities, the common people generally keep a safe distance from it. So the aim of the popular science is to make a close bond between science and the common people.[36] In popular science, therefore, the adjective 'popular' has given a stress on the thought of social consciousness in science.

What should be the Bengali term for *popular science*? There are two terms in general use in Bengali—*Janabijnan* and *Ganabijnan*, but their usage is controversial. The activists are sharply divided on this issue.[37] A section of activists, instead of using these two terms, prefer *Lokbijnan*. With some exceptions, the term *Janabijnan* has been used by the PBBM and other similar-minded organizations. On the other hand, the Ganabijnan Samanway Kendra, Paschimbanga (People's Science Coordination Centre, West Bengal) and its affiliated sister organizations prefer *Ganabijnan*. The difference in name has become a bone of contention between the leftists who are in government and the radical lefts who are not in the government. But while making his own comments, Dr. Sankar Chakraborty, the president of PBBM said that there is little need to give so much importance to the Bengali translations as both these terms are more or less the same. He even admitted that the scientific workers who belonged to the idea of *Ganabijnan* did some good job. According to him, this term was used by some ultra-radicals like the Naxalites. However, the implications are the same.[38]

But some thinkers differ. One of them, Dhrubajyoti Dey, an experienced scientific worker, has said that the believers in *Janabijnan* had never organized any movement against any unscientific project of the establishment; they never stood against the irrationality of the established order. So, to him, *Janabijnan* is nothing but the abridged form of *Janapriya Bijnan* or popular science.[39]

One may question the essential features of the popular science concept of these two groups. According to the *Janabijnan* group, the aims of popular science are to give the benefits of science to every people, to fight against superstitions and para-sciences, to make people conscious about the problems and solutions of health and promote scientific temperament among commoners, peasants-workers and even illiterates along with the educated class. Undoubtedly, the *Janabijnan* movement emphasizes on science-popularization programmes. But along with this, the PSM also organizes movements that are relevant to the socio-economic and political contexts. On such occasions, it campaigns either for or against any particular project for the sake of people's interest. For the same purpose, it acts as a pressure group to play a major role in determining the policy decision of the government. This is evident in various environmental movements like the anti-nuclear movement, the anti big-dam movement, and so on. A movement which gained much importance in the newspapers and became a major headline in Kerala was an environmental movement called the 'Silent Valley Movement', organized by the Kerala Shastra Sahitya Parishad (KSSP).[40] So the popular science activists of Bengal have a respectful attitude towards their Keralan counterpart.

For the convenience of determining the nature of popular science, the declared aims of both *Jana* and *Gana* groups can be compared. The PBBM, the believers in *Jana*, declare their aims to be:

1. To make people conscious about the uses of natural resources for social interest.
2. To encourage the uses of science in daily life.
3. To develop consciousness among the people regarding environment and people's health. To educate the people regarding the ill-effects of various drugs made by multinational companies.
4. To help scientific enquiry and activities.
5. To struggle for science education through the mother tongue.
6. To struggle against superstition and unscientific concepts.
7. To oppose any application of technology which are not in favour of the people.
8. To struggle for making appropriate policy and programmes so that the people can get the fruits of science.
9. To publish popular magazines and booklets regularly for the spread of science among the people.
10. To adopt necessary programmes for fighting against any attempt of using science in destructive war.[41]

In contrast, the aims and objectives of Ganabijnan Samanway Kendra, Paschimbanga, as laid down in its official documents, are:

1. To spread science in simple language and through the vernacular so that the common people can understand it. To make every person literate, scientifically rational and a believer in humanity.
2. End the dependence on foreign states for development of science

and technology, since it is necessary for the progress of indigenous agriculture and industry. It emphasizes on the all round welfare of the greater part of the society. It should be used to solve the basic problems of society on the basis of primary needs.

3. To oppose the production and import of those goods which are adverse to the interest of greater society. On the other hand natural resources should be utilized on the basis of real needs of the people.

4. To oppose that S&T which acts as a tool of the consumerist culture of the elite or the privileged class.

5. For the sake of the people, it demands for the implementation of pro-people health policy, expansion of scientific treatment facility and to oppose all kind of unscientific treatments.

6. To trace the pollutants that destroy the environment in any particular project based on S&T. To eliminate these pollutants, it stresses on environmental awareness among the common people.

7. To oppose the uses of science for making weapons (i.e. nuclear weapons), to oppose research, production, experiments and application of nuclear weapons.

8. To engage scientists and technologists in the work of scientific and technological research and to apply these for the sake of the real greater common good.

9. To inform the common people about the facts regarding S&T-related planning and their applications.[42]

After discussing the aims and objectives of two major PSM organizations of Bengal in a comparative perspective, one may get an idea about the concept of popular science as it is practised in West Bengal. However, to what extent these aims have been followed and realized is a different issue altogether.

The movement and conceptual development of popular science are twin processes. Nowadays, the approaches of governmental schemes or established institutions are also rapidly changing with new notions of globalization and commercialization of markets. The minds of the common people are also being gradually influenced by the growing impact of the media and the consumerist world. Thus both the developments of concepts and movements are now related with the global phenomenon. With scientific and technological advancement like computer and internet there is again a possibility of confining science within the elite or privileged class. To combat this tendency, the need for the development of popular science is getting more importance than before.

SCIENCE AND THE PARTY: POLITICS OF
SCIENCE MOVEMENT IN WEST BENGAL

The feeling that science should be popularized among the people was the key factor behind all science movements. From this popular perception, some individuals and organizations undertook the noble task of popularizing science. They were of the opinion that the government should take some measures which would help the common people directly or indirectly. They favoured the use of people-friendly technology, but were afraid that such technology might not be adopted in the normal run of things. Pressure had to be exerted from within and outside, which would persuade the government to adopt a people-friendly science-and-technology policy. Here a theoretical contradiction between the attitude of the union and the state government needs to be addressed. There was a criticism over the union government's developmental policy that was initiated and developed by Jawaharlal Nehru and led by the Congress government. It was a departure from the focus on cottage, small-scale and rural development. With the defeat of the Congress in 1977 Lok Sabha or parliamentary election, the Janata Party government triggered criticism of these developmental processes conducted by Nehru and the Congress government. Jayaprakash Narayan, who spearheaded the Janata wave in 1977, was himself a strong advocate of the Gandhian perspective on development.[43] Besides, there was a general criticism of the science and technology policy. The opposition argued that this policy had failed to give the benefits of the science and technology project to the general people.

At this time, the Left Front government came to power in West Bengal. Immediately after that, the CPI(M), the major constituent of the Left Front government, did not play any definite role in the realm of science movements between 1977 and 1986. But in 1986, the party was attracted to the science movement because of its growing popularity and future prospects. In that year, the state committee of the CPI(M) issued a letter to the party members entitled 'Primary Discussion on the Importance of Spreading Scientific Outlook'.[44] In it the committee clearly stated that the party was not taking any initiative for the growth of science movements in West Bengal. It was said that the science movement in the state was dominated by other political outfits rather than the party itself. There were various political ideologues who were giving leadership to that movement. The state secretariat felt in 1986 that it was high time for the party to play a major role. This letter of the party emphatically argued that their intention to enter into the science movement was to drive out the divergent political ideologies and give the movement a unity of purpose and approach.[45] For the establishment of a science organization of their own, the party leaders convened a meeting on 17 August 1986 at the CITU Hall. They asked the party members who were associated with the science movements to be present there. The state secretariat of the CPI(M) issued a draft resolution for the consideration of the interested party members.[46] Then a 'Preparation Committee for the Science Movement' in West Bengal was formed. That committee convened a convention in the Moulali Youth Centre on 14 November 1986. During that convention, the Paschimbanga Bijnan Mancha was formed.[47] In the draft resolution, the state secretariat of the CPI(M) explained science as a means through which people's living standard could be improved. It hoped that through science, people would become rationalists. It complained that in a capitalist society, science had been used for the interest of a handful of capitalist groups. On the other hand, in a socialist society, science and technology could be deployed for the betterment of the whole society. So a rational approach was needed to use science in a proper manner.[48]

The state committee of the CPI(M) alleged that in India science and technology had been used for the commercial interest of the capitalist class. In the name of modernization, science and technology had aggravated the problem of unemployment, the people had been deprived of the benefits of scientific and technological advancement.[49] They alleged that the central government was reluctant to support scientific and technological research and development. In the educational sector, a very small percentage of students could get higher education along scientific lines owing to the policy of the contemporary central government. Even scientific temperament, considered crucial to address the problems of superstition, religious fundamentalism, communalism, and regionalism, did not develop among students. In this context, the CPI(M) argued that only a strong science movement could develop a scientific outlook among the people. They said that the aim of the party was to develop a state-wide science movement.[50] But along with that, as it was clearly stated in the draft resolution, one of the major aims of the science movements would be to oppose the industrial and educational policy of the central government. It was also stated that the party-sponsored science movement would support the positive role of the central government if the latter took any scientific and technological policy for social interest. The aim of the party was to show the alternative way through which science and technology could be used for society.[51]

The party also felt that the Left Front government could play the role of a collaborator in this movement. Some of the departments of the state government could take necessary initiatives to popularize science and to bring scientific outlook among the people. At the same time, the established political party faced some regular problems in popularizing science. These problems arose from the ideal of adjustment with the state machinery, accommodation with a federal government's policies and corruption within the party.

Thus the science movement was dominated by the political ideologies of the Left, with the main aim of opposing the hierarchical union government. But despite this domination, all the existing Left-oriented science activists were not brought together under the banner of Paschimbanga Bijnan Mancha. The members of the People Science Coordination Centre, West Bengal, a major coordinating organization of the people's science movement in the state, were not incorporated into it. Some of the members of that organization alleged that as they were neither members nor supporters of the CPI(M), they were not taken into confidence by the Paschimbanga Bijnan Mancha.[52] The argument that the state government only could help the science movement buried the possibility of establishing a broad-based science movement even before the emergence of the science organization itself. The science activists, who were outsiders to the party, could not identify them with the last line of the party letter where it was clearly mentioned: 'those science clubs and science-minded persons, who support our aims and objectives, can join the movement'.[53] Here the implication of the term 'our' was very clear—it implied that allegiance to the party was an essential prerequisite for joining the movement. By this, the non-party science activists were alienated naturally from the Paschimbanga Bijnan Mancha.

In the same letter, it was also stated that more or less four hundred science clubs were working in the state. But most of these had no specific activities. Only a handful of clubs' activities were regular and continuous. Such allegations, however, ignore the process of forming various science clubs in different parts of the state from the early 1980s. It should be pointed out that the process of coordinating endeavours of the science clubs of the state started long before the emergence of Paschimbanga Bijnan Mancha; Eastern India Science Club Association (EISCA) was formed in 1981 and Ganabijnan Samanway Kendra, Paschimbanga started functioning from 1982.[54]

Undoubtedly, the Paschimbanga Bijnan Mancha has played a great role in the arena of popularization of science. Its effort to make people conscious about the total solar eclipse in 1995 was noteworthy.[55] But the popularization of science has mostly been unable to address the issue of social customs and superstitions as a theme of the science movement. That is why the Left-oriented intellectuals have indirectly accepted different modes of patriarchy and feudal hierarchy, reflected on social occasions or through religious rituals related to marriage or death.

The Paschimbanga Bijnan Mancha does not acknowledge its connection with the party. As the president of the organization Sankar Chakraborty said, 'it is the malice propaganda of a vested interest group'.[56] But the record suggests otherwise. A careful look into the political-organizational report, resolutions and reports of the different fronts of the CPI(M), published on the occasion of the party's nineteenth state conference clearly reveals that the party had its dominance over the Bijnan Mancha.[57] It was clearly stated in the organizational documents that the work to develop the science movement all over the state was started in 1986 (with the establishment of the Bijnan Mancha). It was further observed that the decision of forming a science movement in an organized manner was taken by the party. The party had a special role in the process of the formation and development of the movement.[58] So it is needless to say that Bijnan Mancha was dominated by the ideology of the ruling group.

More importantly, the aims of the organization, as written in its constitution, and the proposed aims written in the party letter, were found to be identical. It clearly exposed the established Left orientation in the formation of the Bijnan Mancha.[59] On the one hand, it caused harm to the movement by alienating other science activists; on the other the cadre-base of the organization lacked the necessary quality. Even the leadership of the organization expressed its worry about the quality of the science workers.[60] On the part of the members of the Bijnan Mancha, the science popularization programme was motivated by the party line with the goal of opposing the central government's policy. Thus the broad front with the representation of every block of science activists could not emerge.

The Paschimbanga Bijnan Mancha had a great organizational network. From its inception, it had a three-tier federal organization (State Committee–State Secretariat–District Committee).[61] It gradually expanded even at the block level of the state. Thus it had a great potential; but partial outlook and factionalism debarred it from opposing each and every anti-people measure of the establishment. If one analyses the draft resolutions of the first state conference of the Paschimbanga Bijnan Mancha, one finds that nearly four out of every five resolutions were directed against the central government for political interest of the party. Hence, the other and more important issue, i.e. spread of scientific temper, was neglected.[62] From the party letter and some other organizational documents of the Bijnan Mancha, we also find that the leadership was interested in projecting the science worker as the 'ideal human being'.[63] But this aim was not fulfilled. Quantitative increase in the number could not solve the problem. As the politics of numbers became the most important thing to consider, many people joined the Bijnan Mancha who did not have a scientific attitude towards life and those who failed to keep parity between theory and practice. The strong presence of such people at the rank and file of the organization conveyed a faulty impression of quality to outsiders, who did not want to join the movement. Thus the science movement of the state suffered.

The case of the Bijnan Mancha needs to be understood in the wider perspective of the hegemonic attitude of the political party/established order to capture the people's mind. The great potentiality of the science movement attracted the political party in power.[64] It tried to appropriate the opportunity provided by the science movement to gain political mileage. No doubt, the science movement could not be detached from politics. The science workers would like to take part in the movement to reform the interrelationship between science and the society. This work is definitely political, and in a broader sense the science movement must also be considered a political movement.[65] But when that politics is directed only to serve the interest of the party, problems will follow.

Along with the CPI(M), other political parties also tried to use the opportunity to work through science organizations. The 'radical humanists' played a pivotal role in the first phase. Later in 1991 they formed the Bijnan Prasar Parishad. In 1994, the Bijnan O Yuktibadi Mancha was formed which had relations with the CPI. There was another organization named the Break-through Science Society (founded in 1995), which was close to the Socialist Unity Centre of India (SUCI).[66]

CONCLUSION

It should be noted that the notion of 'science for the society' is the driving force behind mobilization of public opinion against life-threatening science and technology policy. Here political actors, along with various professionals and social activists, have a great role to play. The popular science movement is a part of this effort of mobilization. Though largely influenced by a leftist ideology, this movement operated outside the platform of the left party politics in the 1970s.[67] It was with the establishment of the Paschimbanga Bijnan Mancha in 1986 that the science movements were connected to the 'platform of Left party politics' in West Bengal. With active cooperation from the party and the state government, the Paschimbanga Bijnan Mancha succeeded to an extent in mobilizing public opinion against the central government. Herein lies the importance of the Bijnan Mancha. However, the success of this trend is limited and there is much that remains to be done by the popular science movement.

NOTES

1. Subal Chandra Mitra (ed.), *Saral Bangala Abhidhan*, 8th edn., Kolkata: New Bengal Press, 1984, p. 948.
2. Rajsekhar Basu (ed.), *Chalantika*, Kolkata: M.C. Sarkar & Sons, 12th edn., 1385 BS (1978), p. 510.
3. Ibid. Also see Shailendra Biswas, (ed.), *Samsad Bangala Abhidhan*, 2nd edn., Kolkata: Sahitya Samsad, 1961, and Jnanendra Mohan Das, (ed.), *Bangala Bhasar Abhidhan*, 2nd edn., Kolkata: Sahitya Samsad, 1986, vol. 2, p. 1569.
4. Mitra, *Saral Bangala Abhidhan*, p. 948.
5. *The D.K. Illustrated Oxford Dictionary*, Oxford: Oxford University Press, 1998, p. 738.
6. *The Cambridge International Dictionary of English*, Cambridge: Cambridge University Press, 1995, p. 1266.
7. *The Concise Oxford Dictionary of Current English*, 8th edn., Oxford: Oxford University Press, 1996, p. 1081.
8. Parashuram (Rajsekhar Basu), 'Birinchibaba', *Parashuram Rachanabali*, vol. II, Kolkata: M.C. Sarkar & Sons Private Ltd., 1969, cited edition 1974, pp. 3-26. Translated from Bengali by the author.
9. Ibid., p. 9, translation by the author.
10. Q. Hoare and G.N. Smith (ed.), *Selections from Prison Notebooks of Antonio Gramsci*, New York: International Publishers, 1971, pp. 323-6, quoted in Deepak Kumar, 'Science and Society in Colonial India: Exploring an Agenda', *Proceedings of the Indian History Congress: Diamond Jubilee Session* (held in Calicut, 1999), Aligarh: Indian History Congress, 2000, p. 451.
11. Deepak Kumar, 'Science and Society in Colonial India', pp. 434-55. In another article Deepak Kumar remarked: 'Colonial Science is a dependent science wherein the result-oriented research in applied science supersedes the curiosity-oriented research of pure science.' Deepak Kumar, 'Colonial Science: A Look at the Indian Perspective', in Deepak Kumar (ed.), *Science and Empire*, Delhi: Anamika, 1991, p. 6.
12. *The Hindu*, 19 March 1925, quoted in Raghvan Iyer (ed.), *The Moral and Political Writings of Mahatma Gandhi*, vol. 1, Oxford: Clarendon Press, 1986, pp. 310-15, cited in Deepak Kumar, 'Science and Society in Colonial India', pp. 444-5.
13. Ibid.

14. Steven and Hilary Rose, *Science and Society*, Pelican Books, quoted in Pratul Bandyopadhyay, *Bijnaner Ruparekha* (Outline of Science, in Bengali), Kolkata: Pratikshan Publications, 1995, p. 68.
15. Anil Sadgopal, 'Between Question and Clarity', *Science Today*, October 1981, p. 23.
16. Sabyasachi Chatterjee, 'An Environmental Movement Against the "Greater Common Good"', in Biswajit Mukherjee and Rahul Ray (eds.), *Environmental Awakening*, Kolkata: Sikha Books, 2005, pp. 180-9.
17. Deepak Kumar, 'Science and Society in Colonial India', p. 446.
18. Najma Heptulla, *India's Progress in Science and Technology: Continuity and Change*, Delhi: Oxford and IBH Publishing Company, 1986, p. 24. Also see G.H.Keswani, 'Jawaharlal Nehru and Science', in B.R. Nanda (ed.), *Science and Technology in India*, Delhi: Vikas, 1977, pp. 1-20.
19. Anil Sadgopal, 'Between Question and Clarity', pp. 29-31.
20. An advertisement of 'Keo Karpin Hair Vitalizer', developed by Dey's Research Centre, a product of the Dey's Medical Stores Pvt. Ltd., Kolkata.
21. An advertisement of 'Complan', a product of Heinz India (P) Ltd., Mumbai.
22. Swapnamay Chakraborty, 'Bijnan Noy, E Tar Mukhosh' (This is not science, but a mask of it), *Ananda Bazar Patrika*, 22 March 1998.
23. Rajsekhar Basu, 'Apabijnan' (1929), in *Prabandhabali* by Rajsekhar Basu, ed. Dipankar Basu, Kolkata: Mitra and Ghosh, 2001, p. 35.
24. *What We Need is a New Science Movement*, Kolkata: Breakthrough Science Society, 1997, p. 8.
25. Manindra Narayan Majumder (ed.), *'Samaj Biplabe Bijnan' Ganabijnan Andolan Ki O Keno? Ekti Prathamik Khasra* ('Science in Social Revolution', Popular Science Movement—What and Why? A Primary Draft: in Bengali), Kalyani, Nadia: Pragati Trust, January 1982.
26. *Pragatibarta*, Bishes Jana Bijnan Sankhya (Special number on Popular science) 7, nos. 9-10 (1-16 October 1983).
27. *Ganabijnan Andoloner Disha: Ekti Prathamik Ruparekha* (Traces of Popular Science Movement: A Primary Outline), Kashinagar, South 24-Parganas: Lokbijnan Prakashani, June 1984.
28. Bhaskar Gupta and Srijnan Halder, 'A Report on Popular Science Movement in West Bengal: A Brief History and the Present Situation', undated and unpublished.
29. *Jibaner Janya Bijnan*, (Science For Life; in Bengali), Kolkata: Paschimbanga Bijnan Mancha, 1987.
30. *Souvenir published on the occasion of 1st adda of Utsa Manus*, Kolkata, 1987.
31. Pradip Basu, 'Paschimbange Ganabijnan Andoloner Itihaaser Prathamik Ruparekha' (Primary Outline of the History of Popular Science Movement in West Bengal; in Bengali), in *Souvenir of 'Naihati Institute of Science and Culture'*, June 1990
32. Sanat Kumar Sutradhar, *Janabijnan Parichay* (Knowing Popular Science; in Bengali), vols. 1-2, Birbhum: Paschimbanga Bijnan Mancha, 1994.
33. Mihirlal Ray, *Janabijnan Andolon* (Popular Science Movement; in Bengali), Agartala: Centre for Social Work and Research, 1999; Samir Sen, Sudip Kanti Dastidar and Sandip Ray (eds.), *Ganabijnan Bhabna* (Thinking Popular Science; in Bengali), Halisahar: Halisahar Bijnan Parishad, 1999.
34. 'Bijnan Andolon: Samasya O Sambhabana' (Science Movement: Problems & Prospects; in Bengali), in *Mukhapatra Chetana* 10, no. 1 (June-August 2000);

Jnan Bichitra, Jana Bijnan Bishes Sankhya (Special number on Popular science) 24, no. 7 (January 2000) and *Nandan, Bijnan O Bijnan Andolon* (special number on Science & Science Movement) 36, no. 12 (December 2000).

35. Rabin Chakraborty, 'Ganabijnan Andolon—Ekti Bhabna O Kichhu Avijnata' (PSM—A Thought and Some Experiences; in Bengali), *Bijnan O Bijnankarmi*, March-April 1984.

36. Ashok Bandyopadhyay, 'Ganabijnan, Dharma O Rajniti—Andolon' (Popular Science, Religion and Politics—Movement; in Bengali), unpublished.

37. Diptendra Roychoudhury, 'Jana-Gane Ladai' (Struggle Between *Jana* and *Gana;* in Bengali), *Anandabazar Patrika*, 6 May 1989.

38. Conversation with Sankar Chakraborty, Kolkata, 21 March 2000.

39. Dhrubajyoti Dey, 'Ganabijnan: Rajniti: Dharma' (Popular Science: Politics and Religion), *Ananda Bazar Patrika*, 26 May 1989.

40. *Science for Social Revolution*, Trivandrum, Kerala: Kerala Sastra Sahitya Parishat, n.d.

41. *Constitution of Paschimbanga Bijnan Mancha* (PBBM), p. 10.

42. *Proceedings of the first Conference of 'Ganabijnan Samanway Kendra, Paschimbanga'*, held at Kalyani, on 22-3 March 1989, published in October 1989.

43. V.V. Krishna, 'Science, Technology and Counter Hegemony—Some Reflections on the Contemporary Science Movements in India', in Terry Shinn, Jack Spaapen and Venni Krishna (eds.), *Science and Technology in a Developing World, Sociology of the Science Yearbook 1995*, Dordrecht: Kluwer Academic Publishers, p. 379.

44. *Party Letter No. 6 of the C.P.I. (M)*. West Bengal State Committee, 20 July 1986.

45. Ibid., p. 2.

46. That draft resolution of 11 July 1986 was included in the party letter of 20 July 1986.

47. Shankar Chakraborty, *Paschimbanga Bijnan Mancha*, Kolkata, n.d., p. 1.

48. *Party Letter No. 6*, p. 3.

49. Ibid., p. 4.

50. Ibid., p. 5.

51. Ibid., p. 6

52. Aniruddha Dutta, *Prasanga: Gana Bijnan Andolon* (Regarding the Popular Science Movement; in Bengali), *Manabman* 35, no. 4 (October-December 1996), p. 299.

53. *Party Letter No. 6*, p. 8.

54. Sabyasachi Chatterjee, 'Paschimbange Bijnanchetanar Itihaas' (History of the Scientific Temper in West Bengal; in Bengali), *Itihaas Anusandhan-12*, ed. Gautam Chattopadhyay, Kolkata: Firma KLM, 1998, pp. 589-99.

55. Sabuj Mukhopadhyay, 'Ganabijnan Andoloner Pathe Paschimbanga—Suryagrahaner Pariprekshite Ekti Paryalochana' (West Bengal in the Path of Popular Science Movement—A Review in Respect of the Solar Eclipse; in Bengali), unpublished Study Paper of the Department of Mass Communication, Jadavpur University, 1996, p. 7.

56. Sabuj Mukhopadhyay, 'Ganabijnaner Pathe Paschimbanga—Ekti Samkshipta Paryalochana' (West Bengal in the Direction of Popular Science—A Brief Review; in Bengali), *Mukhapatra Ganadarpan* 8, no. 6 (February 1996), p. 19.

57. *Political-Organizational Reports*, Proposal and Reports of Different Fronts of the CPI(M)'s 19th West Bengal State Conference, 27-30 August 1998.

58. Ibid., p. 180.
59. Ibid., p. 183.
60. *Party Letter No. 6*, and *Paschimbanga Bijnan Mancha—Gathantantra*, (Constitution of Paschimbanga Bijnan Mancha; in Bengali), Kolkata, November 1987.
61. *Resolutions of the Second State Conference of Paschimbanga Bijnan Mancha*, held at Yuvabharati Krirangan (Salt Lake Stadium), Kolkata, 8-10 March 1991.
62. *Paschimbanga Bijnan Mancha—Gathantantra*, p. 13. First State Conference was held on 19-20 March 1989 at Yuvabharati Krirangan (Salt Lake Stadium), Kolkata.
63. Report of the State Committee of Paschimbanga Bijnan Mancha, placed at its first state Conference.
64. It was frequently suggested that politicians could benefit from a more scientific frame of mind. See Jonathan Harwood, 'Scientific Knowledge as Political Authority', in M. Gibbons and P. Gummett (eds.), *Science, Technology and Society Today*, Manchester: Manchester University Press, 1984, p. 49.
65. Bankim Dutta, 'Bijnan Andolone Raajniti' (Politics in Science Movement; in Bengali), *Manabjamin*, January 2001.
66. Sabyasachi Chatterjee, 'A Historical Study of the Science Club Movement in Bengal', *The Quarterly Review of Historical Studies* 39, nos. 1 & 2 (April-September 1999), pp. 72-87.
67. Krishna, 'Science, Technology and Counter Hegemony', p. 381.

17

Constituent Assembly Election in Nepal: From Monarchy to a Republic— A Political-Cultural Transition

AMIYA K. CHAUDHURI

Nepal has been a hotbed of political turmoil in the last one and half decades as the political uncertainties in the domestic sphere have adversely affected Nepal's credibility as a democratic state. While democracy has faced multi-pronged challenges in Nepal, the country's progress in the realm of development too has suffered from related strains. In such a context, the present essay argues that the overthrow of the monarchy and the Constituent Assembly election of April 2008 in Nepal can be regarded as landmarks in the country's contemporary history. At the vortex of an irreversible process of globalization, the new political system evolving in Nepal since the elections has to negotiate with the new realities of liberalization, privatization and global forms of popular culture. The essay, in the light of the popular euphoria over the last election, enquires whether the state and the civil society in Nepal, languishing from the want of good governance for long, would be able to reprioritize its democratic institutions and adapt the challenges of global commercial culture into its traditional cultural milieu. It also suggests that political transition and electoral politics in a conflict-ridden country like Nepal is frequently embedded in the suppressed or entangled ethos and practices of popular culture.

INTRODUCTION: THE SOCIO-POLITICAL CONTEXT OF
CONTEMPORARY REALITIES IN NEPAL

Nepal is arguably on its way to a genuine democratic transition. The political and social turbulence ended with the election in April 2008, and the perspective of the constitution making and the election thereafter will determine the nature of the regime and the new culture it would unfold. The nature of the three distinct political formations with various socio-cultural moorings and imbibed political cultures deserve redefinition because of the multicultural scenario and ambience that have been apparent during the last three decades or so as also the type of democracy they profess to establish. But it entails a host of emerging socio-political and cultural problems that the new government in Nepal would have to confront. The people of Nepal cannot be taken for granted as they have been by the Maoist cadres and their People's Liberation Front during the ten years from mid-1990s to 2006. During this period the Maoist guerrillas had a field day in entire Nepal from the forest areas of Terai to the higher ridges of the mountain. As a result, people had always to live in fear. Extortion, kidnapping and abductions for money were the *modus operandi* of the Maoist party and its cadres to run the maoist establishment throughout the territory. The farming communities, ordinary small farmers, regular agricultural labourers in the villages had to meet the financial demands of the Maoists. The same fate befell on the salaried people—serving both government or non-government sector. School and college teachers, ordinary government employees and others had to encounter the same problems. It was, as it happened, a redefinition of cultural priorities. During this period of more than a decade and a half the long cherished popular cultural heritage of the people was thrown into utter confusion.

The April 2008 election marked a watershed in the electoral history of Nepal. Already a process of political-cultural transformation had started in the early 1990s. The political culture that was brewing had several ramifications in its popular manifestations. The lifestyle of the people, even possibly gender equations and workplace attitudes, had gradually begun to change. The moorings of change found reflection in many an arena of the everyday life of the Nepali people. The values, beliefs and customs that had once been regarded as sacrosanct were in the melting pot. Some of the remarkable changes became perceptible in the Nepali media—both print and visual—and in the performing arts—cinema, theatre, music, and even street shows. A visibly poor Nepali adaptation of other cultural signs around myth, slogan and symbol seemed to be around the country, which used to be so unvitiated and original once. All these changes did not come about all of a sudden. What hastened the process of political transition in Nepal since the 1980s was a mix of fear and curiosity consequent upon the influence of the political ideology of western liberalism on the one hand and 'progressive' perspective of Marxism and Maoism[1] on the other. Immediately before and during the elections in Nepal, popular perceptions indicated that the people were enormously uncertain, agonized and often afraid to speak out. But in a psychologically confused state of mind they expressed the possibility of the Maoists' prospect of being saddled in power.[2] If it were so, varied changes in political culture, popular ideas of institutions, and perceptions of social interaction through different media would take place. But how 'it is too early to predict', rightly opined Lokraj Baral.[3] Nepal had to undergo a tortuous time since the mid-1990s due to the Maoist movement and the resultant chaos. For instance, before the Maoist onslaught Hindi films, drama and cultural shows depicting Indian mythology and even Maithili and Hindi language enjoyed enormous attraction and influence not only in the Terai region but also in the hill and mountain areas. But the situation began to change quite perceptibly thereafter.[4]

However, there are contradictions among the three regions themselves, among it the Terai adjacent to India, the hill (the middle) and the mountain (higher ridges) areas. From the historical point of view the Terai was less important, as the focus was on the Ganga, the 'holy' river. There were 'oral traditions' of religious and popular culture both among the Hindus and the Muslims as recorded by travellers at that point of time.[5] Their ancestors moved into the areas about 200 years ago around the time the *Gorkhali* conquest took place in the Kathmandu Valley. The area had been affected by intermittent waves of invaders in the past, but the cultural ambience did not alter much because the Muslims in and around the territory were the descendants of Hindu converts rather than Turks, Afghans or Arabs.[6] Their bonding together, although as separate religious communities, arose out of their cultural heritage and living side by side as neighbours for ages. The Terai region, the largest and most populous, shares many of the cultural attributes that are found mostly in the adjoining Bihar and north-eastern Uttar Pradesh in India. Most of the Indian goods and other cultural exchanges are routed through the Terai region to Kathmandu.

It was expected during the Jana-Andolan-II,[7] from early 2005 till the formation of the transitional government led by the Nepali Congress (NC) leader Girija Prasad Koirala, that a new political scenario was going to unfold. However, the situation in Nepal became almost uncontrollable. The people's anger was focussed solely on King Gyanendra, rather than on corruption, poverty, unemployment and lack of development.[8] These were genuine grievances but they could be put on backburner until the king was deprived of his entitlement.

The people wanted the king to be shorn of his power as the ruler. He must be shifted from the palace to the museum. The general public in Nepal liked to believe in the myth that the king of Nepal is Vishnu incarnate. The popular slogan raised by the CPI Maoist in Kathmandu and elsewhere in Nepal as well was, 'Ram naam satyo ho Gyanendra ko hatya ho'[9] (God is true but Gyanendra is to be killed). A new political culture was going to evolve in the context of the emergence of a new and stronger political formation other than the Nepali Congress and the mainstream Communist Party of Nepal.

Having captured majority seats in Constituent Assembly, the Communist Party of Nepal (Maoist) was supposed to stay in power much longer unless the people of Nepal thought and voted otherwise in the next election for a democratic republican parliament as per the provisions of the constitution to be drafted by the recently elected Constituent Assembly. After the palace massacre King Gyanendra took over but he was extremely unpopular. A few political parties of course supported the institution of monarchy even then. Ultimately, when the Jana Andolan-II came to fruition with the decision of the political parties to converge on certain basic issues of the future governance of the country, the Election Commission was empowered to draft an interim constitution. The king was compelled to resurrect the parliament he himself had dissolved during the people's movement and invite Girija Prasad Koirala to head the government. The old government in a new garb, in the process, suspended the king politically and emasculated him till the final decision of the Constituent Assembly.

While this tumultuous course of events was taking place, people throughout Nepal were full of excitement and expectations. Yet none in the country, particularly in the valley, was exception to a sense of uncertainty about the emerging political scenario. From the *pan* (betel leaf) shop owner, rickshaw-puller, taxi driver and housewife to the white-collar executive, administrator, artist, teacher and university professor, everybody began to share the same popular sentiments and perceive political churning for the better.[10] During the election, an array of foreign and Nepali journalists, election observers as also UN observers were present in Kathmandu. Anything that appeared to go wrong before and during the electoral process was brought to the notice of the Chief Election Commissioner who tried immediately to take necessary actions. The chairman of the Election Commission of Nepal and other officials were ever ready to keep an eye to the electioneering by the political parties.[11] The daily press meet at the Media Centre, Kathmandu, by the Chief Election Commissioner and four other members of the commission was a routine affair. All this was part of the daily concerns for not only the journalists and intelligentsia but the people on the pavements as well.[12]

The Communist Party of Nepal, Maoist (CPN-Maoist) emerged as the largest single political formation after 10 April 2008 election, held under an interim Constitution in a very difficult and volatile political situation in the state. It looked like it was time to bid adieu to the liberal democratic system that began to operate after the monarchy had almost been compelled to accept a party-dominated democratic parliamentary form of governance with a constitutionally limited monarchy at the head. Let us briefly look at the history of parliamentary democracy in Nepal. In the early 1990s, due to social upheaval and political demand by most of the major political parties, King Birendra had to abandon the partyless Panchayat system of governance prevailing in Nepal. A new constitution embodying provisions that are essential to run a liberal democratic system with a constitutionally limited monarchy at the head was drafted. Accordingly, the Election Commission, set up by the provision of the constitution, under its 'supervision, direction and guidance' held the first democratic parliamentary election in 1991. All the political parties registered under the provisions of the constitution fought the election with their party symbols. A new political regime under a competitive political party system came to prevail in a country that was still under the influence of a feudal political culture. Possibly the new phase in Nepali politics was still adapting to a coalition-making political culture. A majority-party-dominant government along with factional squabbles in the dominant party or a predominant party with other supporting parties remained the trend in Nepali politics. Occasionally, the politics of coalition-making appeared to be the better option under the fragmented and multi-party system in Nepal. But a political culture of coalition governance was yet to evolve, as the political parties were still learning the basic lessons of coalition politics. It is necessary for a country like Nepal to initiate this step in view of the fact that Nepal's polity is socially very fractured, thanks to numerous caste and ethnic identities.

Political coalition may help to mobilize people to feel the advantage of being socially coalesced. This would also help ensure a stable polity. But this did not happen during the 1990s. There is another constitutional mechanism, that of adopting some variants of proportional representation. But proportional representation may sometimes become unworkable. To test its efficacy in Nepalese polity, the interim constitution of Nepal has adopted certain provisions for a partial proportional representation to frame the final constitution of the country.

It entails a gamut of change—change of the mindset, accepting or gradually adapting to a set of political principles, beliefs, motivations, values, practices and above all a sense of accommodation. This cannot happen overnight. It presupposes patience that helps formulate guidelines for political action and social mobilization. In this context, the critical questions all how will political parties like the NC, a mass-based party, and the Communist Party of Nepal Unified Marxist Leninist [CPN (UML)] contain the largest ruling party, the Maoists, and get it to become a part of the parliamentary system. It will also be interesting to watch as to how the CPN (Maoist) with its avowed Maoist ideology of 'People's War'[13] adjust to the parliamentary ethos and the economic scenario of Nepal in the age of global economic transition dominated by big business and industrial houses. The future of this adjustment will perhaps determine the structure and process of politics in Nepal.

NEPAL UNDER THE SHAH DYNASTY[14]

Nepal emerged as a unified state over a period of nearly 240 years. The institution of monarchy, the state machinery and the administration were centred at the Kathmandu Valley with its more than two thousand years of urban existence. The autocratic Rana regime, the overarching prime ministerial rule and the Rana family were overthrown in Nepal in 1950-1. Before the take-over of Nepal by Prithvi Narayan Shah, the founding father of the Shah dynasty, Nepal actually comprised the detached territories of many kingdoms under different kings and vassals with various cultural orientations. In the past, these kings and vassals enjoyed tremendous influence over the people in their area of hegemony. The Buddhist religious and cultural influence, too, was overlapping across the ethnic identities. The monarchical objectives apparently were to establish Hindu religious ethos to bring the warring ethnic and caste groups together, thereby making them conscious that although they were different from one another in their cultural moorings they were Hindus by birth. While Buddhism was actually a protest movement of the under-privileged against Hinduism, it was not totally antithetical to Hinduism as such. It represented a new religio-cultural manifestation against the rigid rituals and practices of Vedic Hinduism. As the political authority calculated, this would help the monarchs to reign in the manner they liked. On the other hand, factitious groups would not be able to come together to challenge the authorities of the regime. Under the hegemonic rule of the king even the sibling political parties were made out to be enemies, helping indirectly the king and institution of the monarchy to be more secure.

King Tribhuvan in the early 1950s and King Birendra after the death of Tribhuvan improvised the Panchayat parliamentary system of governance. It was like a non-party political process. The candidates were not allowed to contest on political party tickets. The leaders were unhappy with this system and organized popular movements. The Nepali Congress was particularly in the forefront getting indirect support from the leaders of Indian National Congress and the Praja Socialist Party (PSP) of India. But the movements could not gain in momentum. The popular cultural effects of the democratic cravings were not more than marginal till the late 1980s, and this trend continued up to the early 1990s. However, like his predecessor, King Birendra also perpetuated the same policy of depriving the people of their basic political rights. The political parties were till then not prepared to redeem their freedom of democratic choice and functioning.

From the very beginning of the monarchical establishment in Nepal the Hindu kings attempted to keep aside as far as possible the Buddhist religious influences from the country. But the monarchical regime did not do away with Buddhist relics in different places in Kathmandu and elsewhere in the state. In some areas, particularly in the Terai region, Buddhist religious teachings and cultural ethos continued to be manifested in local popular cultural forms such as literature, music and drama. The Buddhist architectural designs in the royal palaces, particularly in the Narayanhiti Palace, are remarkable pieces of art. Some great monasteries are still to be found in important places like Dhulikhel and Bhaktipur. The place where the sleeping Buddha-Nilkanth (Burha Nilkanth, as in Nepali pronunciation) image was installed in a squarish pond is of immense popular interest cutting across religious divides. In fact, Buddhist religious influences are still perceptible in the life of the people in areas like Sambhunath Mandir or Balaji Park in Kathmandu and Kapilavastu in farthest north of Terai.

A well laid-out highway was constructed with the help of the Chinese government that has connected Nepal with Tibet. This is the road the Buddhist Tibetan refugees would use to come over to Nepal and India. Many buildings and palaces were built after the designs of Buddhist monasteries and even the making of the statues and images of Hindu gods were sculpted in the image of Buddha and

Buddhist culture in many places in Nepal. It is really an attempt to synthesize the Buddhist and Hindu religious ethos and to some extent the prevailing societal culture. The Buddha-Nilkanth in its sleeping posture may be designated as a cultural synthesis of Hinduism and Buddhism in Nepal.

The evolution of a new relationship among the people irrespective of their caste and ethnic origins in a unified Nepal was one of the enduring contributions of the Shah regime. The socio-religious and cultural ambience, environmental uniqueness, political institutions, political culture and societal differences with a medley of numerous ethnic and caste compositions have made Nepali culture a most interesting melting pot in contemporary South Asia.[15] Yet the country presents an extraordinary contrast. Nepal, as John Whelpton has argued,

has been constantly buffeted through history by its neighbors, the two Asian giants, China and India. Economic and political turmoil over the last fifty years (since early 1950s) came to a head first in the Jana Andolan-I in the late 1980s for democracy and then climaxed in the massacre of the royal family in 2001 by a member of the same family. The people believed it to be a despicable conspiracy hatched by the second inline of inheritance in monarchic hierarchy. All this gave rise to an eruption of the Jana Andolan-II of really a civil war within the next few years.[16]

LOCATION AND DEMOGRAPHY:
A DEVELOPMENT PERSPECTIVE

It is pertinent to look at the geographical location and demographic pattern of a country to understand its society and politics. Situationally, Nepal is a buffer state between India on the south and south-west and China on the north and north-west. Geo-strategically, the state is very important to both India and China. Till recently Nepal was very close to India for maintaining its defense establishments and conducting foreign relations as also ensuring domestic trading interest through a series of agreements and the treaty of 1950s.

Nepal comprises an area of 147,181 sq. km with a total population of 2.89 crore (as estimated in July 2007) with a growth rate of 2.13 per cent per year. Literacy rate is as low as 45.20 per cent, the male being 62.70 per cent and the female 27.60 per cent. Table 1 shows the regional distribution of population and importantly the density of population in the sub-regions of the three distinct regions, namely the Terai adjoining Bihar and Uttar Pradesh in India, the hill areas of middle Nepal and the far western part, the mountain areas of the

TABLE 1: REGIONAL DISTRIBUTION OF POPULATION IN NEPAL

(in lakhs)

Area (Geographical Division)	Total	Male	Female	Total (%)	No. of house-holds	Average house-holds (%)	Population Density per sq. km
Nepal	231.51	115.64	115.88	100.00	42.53	5.44	157
Mountain	16.88	8.37	8.51	7.29	3.20	5.28	33
Hill	102.51	50.17	52.34	44.29	19.83	5.27	167
Terai	112.12	57.10	55.02	48.43	19.51	5.75	330
East Terai Area (Adminis-trative Division)	32.9	16.65	16.34	14.25	6.17	5.28	454
Central Terai	39.34	20.34	19.00	16.99	6.71	5.87	422
Western Terai	17.53	8.87	8.66	7.51	2.89	6.06	333
Mid-western Terai	12.31	6.20	6.11	5.32	2.09	5.88	168
Far-eastern Terai	9.95	5.04	4.90	4.30	1.55	6.43	205

Source: *Central Bureau of Statistics, Kathmandu*, 2001, as quoted by B.C. Upreti, in *Nepali Journal of Contemporary Studies* VII, no. 1 (2007) (percentage marginally corrected and figures are taken in terms of lakhs).

Note: During the intervening period till July 2007 the population increased considerably. But the share of percentage points of population in each of the region and sub-region remained more or less the same.

state as also the distribution of the same in the sub-regions of the Terai region. A close consideration of the population distribution is an important component in tracking the political orientations of the people living in different societal, cultural and political environments as seen in the perspective of political objectives and activities of the important political parties in Nepal.

Table 1 clearly points to the importance of the Terai region as a whole and its impact on the politics and popular culture of Nepal. In the context of its constant interaction with the mid-hill region of the state in respect of its nearness with India, economic activities, politico-social and cultural discourse, its natural environment and wide forest cover, the population density played a dominant role in moulding the social attitudes of the people at large. The strategies of most of the important political parties of this region in Nepal did appear to be devised accordingly.

Nepal is a landlocked country and mostly agricultural. The valley is quite developed in agriculture, agro-industries, and small industries including garments production and handicrafts. It has to depend to a large extent on the imports from India and China but tourism as an industry, particularly incoming tourism has been booming as always. Women play a significant role in Nepalese society and economy. The society is not as closed as its two other South Asian neighbours like Bangladesh and Pakistan are. Through the Sino-Nepal and Indo-Nepal porous borders, the drug mafias carry on their clandestine activities. An illegal but booming underworld drug business grew up and possibly there might be an invisible financial arrangement between the Maoist activists and the drug mafias during the hey-days of the Maoist guerrillas in the 1990s. While this surmise was always difficult to substantiate, it was a fact that drug addiction made a worsening impact on the younger generation of people in the state. In areas like Thamel as elsewhere in Kathmandu Valley, constant interaction amongst young foreign tourists and local boys and girls gave birth to a kind of 'rock and punk' culture, discernible in their lifestyle, habits, dresses and taste in vocal and musical instruments (mainly on Spanish guitar and other string musical instruments). Even the younger members of the royal family were not immune to this trend.

Since the 1990s the political economy of Nepal has been in dol-drums. But the situation was not as irretrievable as it became after the palace massacre in 2001. As a result of intense pressure by the evolving people's movements mounted by the Nepali Congress, the Communist Party (undivided) in Kathmandu and other Madeshi Parties largely in Terai, King Birendra had to loosen his autocratic monarchical grip and introduce a democratic constitution in 1991. The period from 1991 after the parliamentary election to early 2007 was characterized by political instability and the rise of the Maoist movements that had fully engulfed 25 districts and partially another 26 districts out of the total 75 districts of Nepal. As Whelpton has noted, 'The Maoists stepped up their extortion scheme and began targeting in particular the country's private schools, whose abolition was one of their 40 demands they presented in February 1996.'[17] In their strongholds, the Maoists had been demanding cuts from the salaries of government school teachers and by the end of 2000, as claimed by the teachers, nearly 90 per cent of the schools in the valley had to offer 'protection money' to the Maoist activists. They 'prevented the school authorities from teaching Sanskrit and the singing of the national anthem, which expressed loyalty to the king'.[18] The political establishments during this period, particularly from 1999 till date, failed to tackle the situation. The economy also seemed to be in the midst of a crisis at this point of time. However, compared to the period between 1951 and 1990 and more specifically during the Panchayat system, the condition was not as bad. Rather some tangible progress was made. Whelpton gives the impression of a modest development in Nepal post-1990:

The road network which expanded from 276 to 7330 kilometers between 1951 and 1990 had reached 15308 kilometers by 2000. The number of telephone lines 25 in 1951 and 63293 at the end of *Panchayat* period stood at 255800 by the end of the century, while the corresponding figures for hectares under irrigation were 6200, 550467 and 716000. Literacy rate rose from 39 % to 58 %. Unfortunately, at the same time the main weaknesses of the pre-1990 economy were also perpetuated. Although 1993-4 did see agricultural production increase by 7.60 % and GDP by 7.90 % this was an exceptional year and agriculture remained on the whole stagnant. The twenty-two year Agricultural Perspective Plan endorsed in 1995 by the major parties, aimed to boost the long-term annual increase from 3 % to 5 %, but it offered no immediate relief. At the end of 1990s, 500,000 youngsters were coming in to the job market. Of these, 100,000 had completed their secondary education but failed the school Leaving Certificate examinations and thus had no prospect of obtaining the white-collared employment that their schooling had prepared them for.[19]

As per the data estimated in 2005, Nepal's GDP amounting to a purchasing power parity is 39.90 US dollar and the GDP real growth rate amounts to 2.70 per cent and inflation rate 7.80 per cent. During the 1990s Nepal's trade with countries other than India was stable at around 70 per cent. Nepal usually exported readymade garments and other manufactured items. Nepali industries were heavily dependent on the US and German markets. The external debt amounted to USD 3.34 billion.[20] During the last 10-15 years an attempt was made to build-up infrastructure and feedback channels in and around Kathmandu, which were much less than necessary for the developmental objectives for different underdeveloped areas of the state. The poverty index was abysmal and inflationary potential unchecked. The disaggregated data in Table 2 significantly testifies to this contention.

Nepal has traditionally been an agrarian society. It is very difficult to make a quick changeover to an industrial or at least semi-industrial state by structural adjustment only. Even substantial amounts of foreign aid to the tune of US $5.20 billion to break the grip of poverty was still below the needs and expectations of the people. Under such circumstances the expectation levels of the people are high but they are skeptical whether a new regime under the leadership of a Maoist party and a supreme leader taking over a liberal democratic system would be able to deliver.[21]

TABLE 2: HUMAN DEVELOPMENT INDEX: 2004

Region	Life Expect- ancy at Birth	Adult Literacy	Mean Year of Schooling	GDP per capita (US$)	Life Expect- ancy Index	Per Capita Income Index	HDI	Ratio to National HDI
Nepal	60.98	48.6	2.75	1310	0.600	0.429	0.471	100.0
Terai Eastern	63.95	46.1	2.54	1235	0.649	0.420	0.478	101.3
Terai Central	63.65	50.7	3.03	1266	0.644	0.425	0.491	104.2
Terai Western	61.70	38.7	3.01	1222	0.612	0.418	0.451	95.8
Terai Mid-western	64.70	50.2	2.60	1277	0.663	0.425	0.484	104.7
Terai Far-western	64.80	48.6	2.42	1130	0.538	0.455	0.440	93.4
Terai	57.30	49.2	2.34	1244	0.548	0.421	0.450	95.4

Source: Human Development Report, 2004, Nepal.

ELECTORAL POLITICS IN CONTEMPORARY NEPAL: THE RISE OF THE CPN (MAOIST)

After the failure of Panchayat system, King Birendra had to enact a new constitution in 1990. The constitution, except in some emergency situation, granted the king limited power. A genuine liberal parliamentary democratic mode of governance was adopted. The political parties were allowed to go in for competitive politics and real democratic political process was expected to start. Accordingly, a general election was held in 1991, which brought the NC, with the majority of seats in the parliament, to power. But it could not hold on due to factional feud between Girija Prasad Koirala and his party rivals. The mid-term poll in 1994 brought back a hung parliament. The Communist Party of Nepal (CPN) or the UML as the largest party formed a minority government that could not sustain for long and was succeeded by a series of coalitions. In 1996, the Communist Party of Nepal [CPN (Maoist)] under the leadership of Pushpa Kamal Dahal alias Prachanda began a nationwide movement, called the 'People's War', with his band of Maoist activists, which was called the People's Liberation Army (PLA) in Maoist vocabulary. Another government under NC took over after the parliamentary election of 1999 (Table 3). Table 3 shows the number of parties (quite a number belonging to different regions) and the total and percentage distribution of votes polled and seat shares among the parties.

TABLE 3: TOTAL VOTES GAINED, PERCENTAGE OF VOTE SHARE AND
PERCENTAGE OF SEAT SHARE IN NEPALI PARLIAMENT 1999

Party	Votes	% of votes	Seats	% of seats
Nepali Congress	3,214,068	37.29	111	54.15
Communist Party of Nepal (UML)	2,728,725	31.66	71	34.63
Rashtriya Prajatantra Party (Thapa)	899,511	10.44	11	5.37
Nepal Sadbhavana Party	277,239	3.22	5	2.44
Rashtriya Jana Morcha	121,394	1.41	5	2.44
Samyukta Janmorcha Nepal	70,119	0.81	1	0.49
Nepal Workers and Peasants Party	48,015	0.56	1	0.49
Communist Party of Nepal (ML)	567,987	6.59	0	0
Rashtriya Prajatantra Party (Chand)	293,952	3.41	0	0
Rashtriya Janamukti Party	92,567	1.07	0	0
Nepali Janta Dal	11,175	0.13	0	0
Janamukti Party Nepal	9,528	0.11	0	0
Communist Party of Nepal (Marxist)	7,654	0.09	0	0
Nepal Dalit Shramik Morcha	6,852	0.08	0	0
Hariyali Nepal Party	6,638	0.08	0	0
Mongol National Organisation	6,329	0.08	0	0
Nepali Janta Party Rashtriya Sambriddhibad	4,835	0.06	0	0
Communist Party of Nepal (United)	4,715	0.05	0	0
Rashtriya Janata Parishad	3,434	0.04	0	0
Jana Congress	1,906	0.02	0	0
Shivsena Nepal	1,727	0.02	0	0
Nepal Socialist Party	950	0.01	0	0
Bahujan Samaj Party, Nepal	835	0.01	0	0
Nepal Praja Parishad	773	0.01	0	0
Samyukta Prajatantra Party Nepal	297	0.00	0	0
Nepal Samyabadi Party (MLM)	190	0.00	0	0
Save the Nation Movement	161	0.00	0	0
Pragati Upayogoto, Nepal	155	0.00	0	0
Nepal Janabhavana Party	120	0.00	0	0
Rashtrabadi Janata Party	105	0.00	0	0
Social Democratic Party	97	0.00	0	0
Samajbadi Garib Party	81	0.00	0	0
Nepal Janahit Party	68	0.00	0	0
Nepal Suraksha Party	56	0.00	0	0
Nepal Rashtrabadi Dal	55	0.00	0	0
Mechi-Mahakali Jana Samanwaya Dal	35	0.00	0	0
Independents	236,548	2.74	0	0

Source: Nepal Election wikipaedia.

In the 1999 election, more than three-dozen parties contested but only a few among them—the Nepali Congress, CPN (UML), Nepal Sadbhavana Party, and Rashtriya Janamorcha—won considerable number of seats. The Nepali Congress won absolute majority, but thanks to bitter internal feuds, the leadership of the NC changed thrice during this period. The NC finally was split and the faction led by Sher Bahadur Deuba could not rise to the occasion and the parliament had to be dissolved. A minority coalition under Deuba took over till the parliament was dissolved again.

It was a period of extreme political instability and uncertainty. Two negotiations between the CPN (Maoist) and the respective governments in power in 2001 and 2003 failed and the clashes between the opposing sides intensified. Under such tense situation and disturbed societal cohesion, King Gyanendra brought the country under a state of emergency. The government could not order any election due to severe insurgency carried on in all the three major parts of the country. Gyanendra took over power after the massacre of the royal family including King Birendra and his line of successors in June 2002. He dismissed the Deuba government and constituted a fact-finding committee. However, the report of the committee, if any, never came to light. The people of Nepal—possibly all categories— were shocked and never forgave Gyanendra and his son Paras for such a drastic step and the manner in which the king thenceforth conducted the state of affairs in the country.

Through a royal proclamation in February, Gyanendra usurped absolute power and took up the post of chairman of the Council of Ministers. In the context of political uncertainty and social unrest, the king restricted political freedom, muzzled the media, blocked all communication channels in and without, and detained the political figures all around the state.[22]

In April 2006 the NC initiated a people's movement (Janandolon-II) and six other parties including the CPN and CPN(UML) party as also some parties based in Terai regions joined the movement. Subsequently, the two factions of the NC closed their ranks and with few other communist factions merged themselves with the CPN (UML). The king was forced by the circumstances to resurrect the dissolved parliament and instal Girija Prasad Koirala as the prime minister. The CPN (Maoist) joined the front after a prolonged peace negotiation process with the Koirala government.

In January 2007 the resurrected parliament with the participation of the Maoists enacted an interim constitution. The king was deprived of his executive power. To be more correct, he was suspended so that he could neither interfere in matters of governance nor in the electoral process. The political sphere and constitutional functionaries were made immune from monarchical authorities. In December 2007, on the basis of a 23-point programme between the six main parties and the Maoists, the amended interim Constitution was finally accepted. The government under the leadership of Girija Prasad Koirala declared the parliamentary election on the date to be fixed by the Election Commission. Nepal was declared as a Republican State subject to the ratification of the Constituent Assembly. The interim constitution would retain a mixed system of electing 40 per cent representatives by the First Past The Post (FPTP) system, 56 per cent by a List System of Proportional Representation (PR) and another 4 per cent by nomination by the newly elected prime minister. Later on it was found that some of the ethnic groups went unrepresented in the Constituent Assembly. It was decided without any hitch among the political parties that the ethnic and caste groups that did not get any seats in the newly elected Assembly (Table 4) were to be included as far as possible.[23]

As Figure 1 based on Table 4 indicates, three major political formations—Communist Party of Nepal (M), NC and the CPN (UML)—won most of the seats both in direct and proportional representation systems. These three parties bagged the major share of seats in both the systems of the election. Under the circumstances without a coalition or alliance between the two or three parties, government formation was not possible. Ideologically, though the CPN(M) and CPN(UML) are closer to each other, they went apart on the question of office sharing. Here in this case the other four parties belonging to the Terai region, except the Rashtriya Janamorcha, which was believed to have sympathy with the monarchical insti-tution, played a crucial role in selecting the first president of the New Regime. Accordingly, the NC won the presidential post as it was quite obvious that the largest party CPN(M), coming out very successfully in both the systems of elections, would be getting the post of the prime minister. The supremo of the CPN(M) Prachanda would naturally lead the new government. The CPN(UML) got the post of vice-president and again the candidate from the NC, with the support of the Terai-based parties, was voted as the chairman of the Constituent Assembly. The Madhesi Jana Forum (MJF) bagging 30 and 22 seats in the direct and proportional systems respectively along with three other smaller parties—Terai Madhes Democratic Party (9 and 10 members, see Table 4) Sadbhavana Party (Mahato) (4 and 5 members), Nepal Mazdur Kisan Party (2 and 2 members),

TABLE 4: TOTAL NUMBER OF FPTP SEATS AND PR SEATS AND PERCENTAGE
SHARE OF SEATS WON BY THE PARTIES

Parties	Total	FPTP [240]		PR [335]	
		Seat Won	Vote Share (%)	Seat Won	Vote Share (%)
Communist Party of Nepal (Maoist)	220	120	50.0	100	29.9
Nepali Congress	110	37	15.4	73	21.8
Communist Party of Nepal (UML)	103	33	13.8	70	20.9
MJF	52	30	12.5	22	6.6
Terai Madesh Democratic Party	20	9	3.8	11	3.3
Sadbhavana Party (Mahato)	9	4	1.7	5	1.5
Rashtriya Prajatantra Party	8	0	0.0	8	2.4
Communist Party of Nepal (ML)	8	0	0.0	8	2.4
Janamorcha Nepal	7	2	0.8	5	1.5
Communist Party of Nepal (United)	5	0	0.0	5	1.5
Rastra Prajatantra Party Nepal	4	0	0.0	4	1.2
Rashtriya Janamorcha	4	1	0.4	3	0.9
Nepal Majdoor Kishan Party	4	2	0.8	2	0.6
Rashtriya Janashakti Party	3	0	0.0	3	0.9
Rashtriya Janamukti Party	2	0	0.0	2	0.6
Communist Party of Nepal (Unified)	2	0	0.0	2	0.6
Nepal Sadbhavana Party (Anandi Devi)	2	0	0.0	2	0.6
Nepali Janata Dal	2	0	0.0	2	0.6
Sanghiya Loktantrik Rashtriya Manch	2	0	0.0	2	0.6
Samajbadi Prajatantrik Janata Party Nepal	1	0	0.0	1	0.3
Dalit Janajati Party	1	0	0.0	1	0.3
Nepal Pariwar Dal	1	0	0.0	1	0.3
Nepal Rashtriya Party	1	0	0.0	1	0.3
Nepal Loktantrik Samajbadi Dal	1	0	0.0	1	0.3
Chune Bhawar Rashtriya Ekata Party Nepal	1	0	0.0	1	0.3
Independents	2	2	0.8	0	0.0
TOTAL	575	240	100.0	335	100.0

Source: *Election Commission*, Constituent Assembly Election, 2008 (as published
finally on 25 April 2008).

and Rashtriya Janamorcha (1 and 3 members)—played a very significant role in the process of electing the president, vice-president
and the chairman of the Constituent Assembly that would play the
dual function of making the New Constitution and a parliamentary
government.

The April 2008 elections of the Constituent Assembly (CA) is a
watershed in history of electoral politics in Nepal. It appears to be

CA poll results

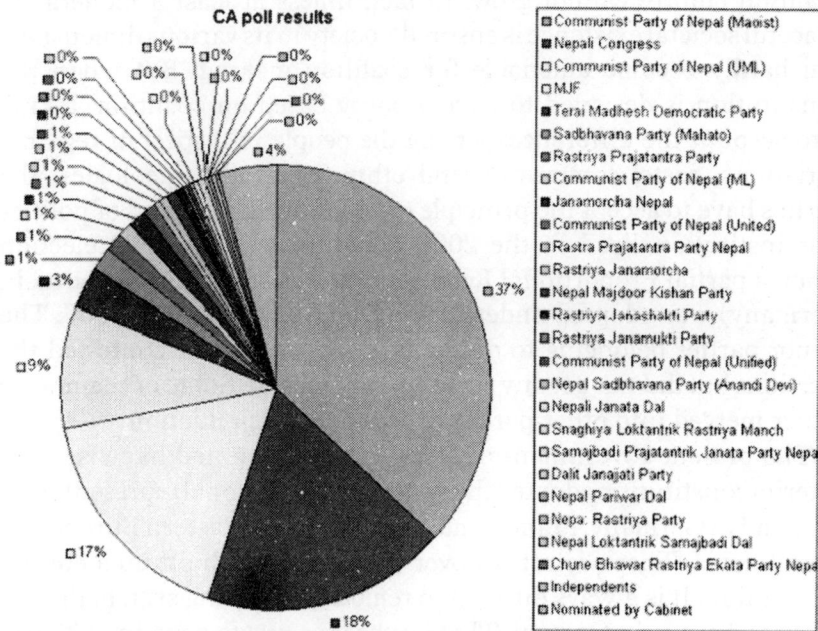

Legend:
- □ Communist Party of Nepal (Maoist)
- ■ Nepali Congress
- □ Communist Party of Nepal (UML)
- □ MJF
- ■ Terai Madhesh Democratic Party
- □ Sadbhavana Party (Mahato)
- ■ Rastriya Prajatantra Party
- □ Communist Party of Nepal (ML)
- ■ Janamorcha Nepal
- ■ Communist Party of Nepal (United)
- □ Rastra Prajatantra Party Nepal
- □ Rastriya Janamorcha
- ■ Nepal Majdoor Kishan Party
- ■ Rastriya Janashakti Party
- ■ Rastriya Janamukti Party
- ■ Communist Party of Nepal (Unified)
- □ Nepal Sadbhavana Party (Anandi Devi)
- □ Nepali Janata Dal
- □ Snaghiya Loktantrik Rastriya Manch
- □ Samajbadi Prajatantrik Janata Party Nepa
- □ Dalit Janajati Party
- □ Nepal Pariwar Dal
- □ Nepa: Rastriya Party
- □ Nepal Loktantrik Samajbadi Dal
- ■ Chune Bhawar Rastriya Ekata Party Nepa
- □ Independents
- □ Nominated by Cabinet

Figure 1: Scoreboard

successful at least as at present to rope in the CPN(Maoist) in the parliamentary democratic culture as well as in the electoral process. Secondly, the party after 10 years of armed insurrections in different areas of the state surrendered the arms possessed by the People's Revolutionary Army (PLA) of the Party to the United Nation's Monitoring Body and began living in tents in and around the military cantonment areas. Third, they really participated in the CA elections in a peaceful manner. Although the Young Communist League (YCL) attempted to distort the electoral process in some selected areas, they more or less appeared to be peaceable and maintained apparent calm before and during the crucial election. The supervision and conduct of the election by the Election Commission under the Chief Election Commissioner Bhoj Raj Pokharel was bold and absolutely fair. It was not a mean achievement, thanks to the pre-election understanding among the seven main political parties of Nepal during the people's movements in 2006, culminating in the Janandolon-II in 2006-7.

In fact, it was the split in the political parties—first in the CPN after 1996 and then in the NC after 1999—which clearly drove Nepal to coalition politics. But politics of coalition is a complex process and has its own ethos. Unless political parties imbibe certain socio-political values and a sense of common objectives of responsive governance, coalition culture cannot grow. In fact, unless at least a moderately peaceful societal existence is ensured, society in its various dimensions can hardly become amenable for coalition making. But when the constitution is designed to have a polity based on coalition, taking into account the differences among the people in respect of regional variations, caste, community and ethnicity as also ideologies, the parties have to accept the principle of coalition. This brand of politics was institutionalized in the 2008 Constituency Assembly election when a partial Proportional Representation System (List as found in Germany) was adopted under the interim Constitution of 2007. The minor parties belonging to different parts of the state contested the elections but did not get any seat shares (Table 3). Some of them were either merged into other parties or went out of circulation.

The present government of Nepal has been elected likewise. The interim constitution adopted the system of proportional representation as found in Germany, France, and countries of the Eastern Europe and Scandinavia. These countries over the years have built-up a culture of coalition. It is always difficult to remodel a working system than to adapt to an existing system. That is what is going to happen in Nepal. In the meanwhile the possibility arises that the political parties—quite large in number—are to practice the art of accommodation, if to survive in the unfolding political process in Nepal. More importantly, it is yet to be observed as to how Prime Minister Prachanda and his presently fractionally divided Maoists colleagues conduct themselves in the new coalition government to frame finally a new constitution, the newly elected popular government mandated for. There might be more challenges Prachanda will have to confront once the serious business of constitution-making proceeds.

THE CONSTITUENT ASSEMBLY ELECTION OF 2008 AND THE FUTURE OF POLITICAL CULTURE IN NEPAL

As already noted, the 2008 Constituent Assembly Election in Nepal appears to unfold a new political culture of parliamentary democracy. The adoption of a proportional system of representation, wholly or partially, is a new experiment that other South Asian countries shun for reasons of their own political survival. To institutionalize the fragmentations of society may not be a desirable step or sometimes may indicate a dangerous portent. It may be possible only in some economically developed West European and Scandinavian countries for their advanced social life and political ideology.

Nepal in comparison with its big neighbours is smaller in population structure and composition. Therefore what augers well in a country of Nepal's size may not fit in elsewhere in bigger South Asian countries. The CA of Nepal has been elected partially by the PR structure to frame a new and final constitution of the country. But in the light of past experience, the representatives of the country may not follow the same course of action. The ongoing politics among the political parties and the evolving perspectives of each may determine the provisions of the constitution.

The people of Nepal are quiet, tolerant and peace loving. Every political observer of Nepal has to reckon with two incidents that have left indelible imprints in their minds. The massacre of the royal family in 2002 and subsequent usurpation of power by King Gyanendra were horrifying experiences for a peace-loving people of Nepal. The palace massacre of an entire royal family was ever palpable. But Gyanendra taking over the mantle could not absolve himself of the responsibility and his son Paras appeared to be involved in the 'conspiracy' (if any) in people's perceptions. The people also did not like Gyanendra's forcible imposition of emergency on the nation, gagging political voices and the instructed opinion of the civil society. More importantly, the ordinary men on the street as well as others belonging to different strata of society suffered a lot in terms of life and property during the Maoist movements in many of the districts across the country since 1996. From 1996 to 2005, the Maoists gunned down some 13,000 men and women. With the popular upsurge of February 2005, the expectations of the people for a democratic changeover rose to a new height. In that context, the ideas and actions of the 'Seven Party Coalition' took deep root in people's psyche. However, till the signing of a 12-point second agreement in December 2007 the CPN(M) did not show enough interest to participate in the government.

According to the agreement, all the parties decided that monarchy as an institution would be abolished and the State of Nepal would become a Republic. Taking into view the three important regions and within it five administrative units, a federal structure was envisaged. The interim constitution made a provision that a total of 575 members were to be elected in the Constituent Assembly Legislature and 26 people would be nominated according to their contribution to the socio-economic and cultural life of the state. But the 12-point agreement decided that 240 members were to be elected directly from 240 territorial constituencies. Provision for proportional representations was made on the basis of ethnic and caste groups and communities belonging to the three major regions—Terai, Hill and Mountain areas and the undeveloped sub-regions. The reservation for women in the PR list would be 50 per cent. Although the interim constitution was framed in early 2007, the election date was deferred twice because of the Maoists' intransigence. People apprehended that the election might not be held at all.

The Maoists and their leader Prachanda were affiliated to the Revolutionary Internationalist Movement (RIM)—a Trotskyite out-fit located in the US. It was doubtful whether these revolutionaries would surrender their arms and would take shelter in tents around the military cantonment. The Maoists who participated in the CA election in a big way removed the apprehension. But the YCL, as already noted, did not always observe the rule of the game particularly in some of the booths during the election. The total number of booths that were marked sensitive was not more than 95 out of 22,000.[24] It is really an achievement for the Nepalese masses to bring back the Maoists and their Supremo Prachanda to the mainstream political activities and the politico-electoral process. If the interactions between the liberal democratic parties and the communists could survive the test of time, that might harbinger a new tradition of mixed political culture with salutary impact on the popular culture in Nepal.

The CPN (Maoist) got 240 of the 575 seats, securing 29.90 per cent of PR vote and exactly 50 per cent of the seats as per the territorial constituency vote share. The next place was occupied by the NC bagging 110, while the results of other important parties were: CPN (UML) 103, MJF 52, Terai Madhesh Democratic Party (TMDP) 20, Sadbhavana Party (Mahato) 9 and Rashtriya Prajatantra Party (RPP) 8 seats. There were a number of other smaller or split-away parties in the fray. Many of them got 1 to 7 seats. But the surprising element was that most of them won 1 or 2 seats in the PR election but then got trounced out in the constituency system (Table 4). Here in lay the importance of introducing some sort of PR electoral system where the population and for that matter the voters were not as large as in India. The number of voters in Nepal was 1.76 crore. It is matter of debate whether the parliament that took all the executive decisions and helped the constitutionally independent Election Commission to conduct the CA election was really constitutional. Actually this was the argument of the purists.[25] In this connection, it is to be kept in mind that Nepal had to undergo a very difficult time socially, economically and particularly politically from February 2005 till the seven parties after a long drawn movement came to an agreement that a secular Nepal without a monarchical system should be rebuilt. In this respect, the people of Nepal at large overwhelmingly endorsed the activities and policies of these seven parties coalition. Possibly, this was one of the main reasons that brought the Maoists and their ideologue Prachanda to the mainstream democratic politics. It seems to be a cultural transformation for a revolutionary party. If it subsists even after the framing of the new constitution afterwards, it will have a tremendous impact on the popular culture among the people. According to the election results, the CPN (Maoist) with Prachanda as the leader will have the first claim to form the government provided other parties including the parties dominating the Terai region follow the rules of parliamentary game (Figure 1 and Table 4).²⁶ If it does not so happen and Prachanda chooses to sit in the opposition,²⁷ that would be a betrayal to the system itself.

For the concerned political parties, the election of the CA is a transitional step. However, the mandate of the CA, acting also as the Nepal Legislature, is limited. It will formulate the final constitution within a period of two years and, if necessary, with a grace period of another six months, exercising both the constituent and legislative power during this period. After the constitution is adopted this body will call for a general election to constitute the Nepali Parliament.

The Nepali society is essentially fractured in terms of ethnic, caste and sub-caste divisions almost like that of India and her states. Internecine rivalries are germane and numerous conflicts among them are found to be prolific in the past. The Maoists during their People's War appropriated these conflicts to the most. Table 5 shows the numerous ethnic and caste divisions and their corresponding percentages that have been prevailing in Nepali society. It is difficult with a liberal democratic mindset to agree to institutionalize the caste- and community-wise social fragmentation but perhaps circumstances of a particular country may demand such provision to politically empower the neglected lot.

POSTSCRIPT

The immediate aftermath of the April 2008 election in Nepal was characterized by unusual political confusion as the three most important political parties were almost at loggerheads with each other regarding the selection of the three most important executive and parliamentary functionaries. After a lot of hassles, the Maoist leader Prachanda in coalition with the CPN (UML) finally formed the government. However, ultimately, the question that baffles the minds of the liberals in and without is whether a liberal democracy under the leadership of the NC in coalition with other political parties or a Maoist and Communist monolith would come up. This trans-

TABLE 5: MAJOR ETHNIC AND CASTE DIVISIONS IN NEPAL (%)

Parbatiya (Nepali-speaking) 40.30% Twice-born	Brahmin	12.90
	Thakur	1.60
	Chetris	16.10
Denouncers	Dasami sanyasis and Kanphata Yogis	1.00
Untouchables	Kamis (metal workers)	5.20
	Damais (tailors)	2.00
	Sarkis (cobblers)	1.50
Newars (Newar or Nepali speaking) 5.60% entitled to religious initiation	Brahmins	0.10
	Vajrachariyas	0.60
	Shresthas	1.10
	Uray (tuladhars, etc.)	0.40
Other Pure Caste	Maharjans	2.30
	Ekthariyas and other smaller groups	0.70
Impure castes	Khadgis (Kasis), Dyahls (podes), etc.	0.40
Other hill or mountain ethnic groups (tribes) Speaking Tibet-Burman Languages or Nepali	Magars	7.20
	Tamangs	5.50
	Rais	2.80
	Chepangs	0.20
	Thamis	0.10
	Gurungs	2.40
	Sunuwars	0.20
	Limbus	1.60
	Bhotiyas	0.10
	Sherpas	0.60
	Thakalis	0.10
Madheshis (speaking north Indian dialects, Awadhi, Bhojpuri, Maithili) 32.00%	Castes	16.10
	Brahmins	1.00
	Kshatriyas:	
	Rajputs	0.30
	Kayasthas	0.30
	Rajbhats	0.20
	Baniyas (Vaisas)	0.50
Other Pure Caste	Yadavs/Ahir (herdsman)	4.10
	Khushawahas (vegetable growers)	1.10
	Kurmis (cultivators)	0.90
	Mallahs (fishermen)	0.60
	Kewarts (fishermen)	0.50
	Kumhars (potters)	0.30
	Halwais (confectioners)	0.20
Impure but Touchable	Kalwars (brewers/merchants)	0.90
	Dhobis (washermen)	0.40
	Telis (oilseed pressers)	0.40

Untouchable	Chamars (leather workers)	1.10
	Dushads (basket makers)	0.50
	Khatawes (labourers)	0.40
	Musahars (labourers)	0.80
Ethnic groups (9.00%)	Kumals	0.40
Inner Terai	Majhis	0.30
	Dhanuwars	0.10
	Darais	–
Terai proper	Tharus	6.50
	Dhanukas	0.70
	Rajbanshis	0.40
	Gangais	0.10
	Dhimals	010
	Marwaris	0.20
Other than Hindus	Sikhs	0.10
	Muslims	3.30

Source: Compiled from John Whelpton, *A History of Nepal*, Cambridge: Cambridge University Press, 2005.

pired from the attitude of the Maoist Prime Minister Prachanda who 'derided publicly at the parliamentary system of democracy'.[28] The Nepali Congress felt that a conspiracy had been in progress against the exiting democratic system in the country. As Ram Chandra Poudel, the vice-president of the NC, has argued: 'The Maoist-led government is yet to act upon the past agreements—which may force the Nepali Congress to wage a revolt against the Maoists.'[29] If this sort of controversy and distrust continues among the important political actors, it might impact upon the people at large. Of course, there is a distinct possibility that the representation of social fragments in the political arena will help grow a mixed popular culture in Nepal. However, it is still uncertain whether the new constitution, which is being framed by the CA, would retain a parliamentary system or a presidential one. The Maoists and the Communists of all hues were successful in abolishing the 240-year-old monarchical institution. This will possibly impact upon the popular culture in its various ramifications. It is difficult but agreed upon by the parties in ethnically divided nation to bring under a federal system. It is to early to predict that the Maoists led by Prachanda would avoid adapting to liberal democratic parliamentary system. After taking over the charge of the nation, Prachanda, to the dismay of the concerned parties, declared that he would like to revise the Indo-Nepal Treaty of 1950. He has already begun his policy to maintain equi-distance from and equal relations with China and India. What the portents would be are yet to be seen. Till date the prime minister appears to run the politics of the nation on some sort of the politics of accommodation. The remarkable step that might have far-reaching influence and consequences on the everyday culture of the state is the change of Nepal's calendar. According to Vikramvat calendar, Nepal is 57 years ahead of the Julian Calendar followed all over the world. But recently, the Nepal government has decided to relinquish its progressive status by going 879 years back, i.e. to dig out the prevailing date scale lost in 1179. The adoption of the Nepal Sambat calendar is considered to be a significant step of the present government, pointing to the importance of popular cultural tradition as useful instrument of political mobilization. This might also have some resemblance to the Indian variety of vote-bank politics as the adoption of the Sambat by the government reflected the sentiments and demands of the Newar community, which is the oldest and most powerful original community of Nepal. With such tactical politically instrumental cultural manoeuvre already in place, the world around is looking in keen expectation for the shape of things yet to take in Nepali society and polity, which is still in a fluid state.

NOTES

1. Interview with Madhav Nepal (CPN-ULM), 8 April 2008, with Prachanda (Maoist supremo), 11 April 2008, and with Girija Prasad Koirala (Nepali Congress), the then prime minister, 11 April 2008.
2. Interviews from 7–13 April 2008 with a cross-section of ordinary citizens— cab drivers, rickshaw pullers and many others revealed this. But intellectuals like Lokraj Baral, Krishna Hatechhechu and other members of NCCS, a few professors of Tribhuvan University, a few littérateurs and music composers were firm in their opinion that seeing the Maoists' terror for more than a decade, possibly the Nepali Congress would get the majority to be followed by the CPN-UML (unified Marxist-Leninist).
3. Interview with Lokraj Baral, former Professor of Political Science at Tribhuvan University, Nepal and Director of Nepal Center of Contemporary Studies (NCCS), 12 April 2008.
4. Interview with Professor Krishna Hari Baral, Professor of Music, Tribhuvan University, Kathmandu, Nepal, 8 April 2008. We visited Nepal during 7-13 April 2008. University departments were declared closed for the ensuing elections. On the eve of the elections, Professor Baral, an expert in Hindi and Urdu *ghazals*, began to compose mostly in Nepali language, choosing themes from contemporary Nepali society and its changed politico-linguististic idiom.
5. John Whelpton, *A History of Nepal*, Cambridge: Cambridge University Press, 2005.
6. Ibid., p. 15.
7. Jana Andolan-II or the seven-party movement started in Nepal in 2005 culminating in the suspension of the king and overthrow of the monarchy in 2008.

8. Sheela Bhatt, 'Nepal: A People's Movement Grows with Fury', 24 April 2006, available at http://www.rediff.com/news/2006/24nepal .

9. Ibid.

10. During our visit to Nepal before and during the election of 2008, I met a number of journalists belonging to *The Nepali Times, The Spotlight, The Himalayan Times, The Independent* (Nepal), *The Kathmandu Post, The Telegraph* (Kathmandu) and *The People's Review*, all of whom expressed the same opinion in personal interviews as well as in the newspapers, 7-13 April 2008.

11. Interview with Bhoj Raj Pokrel, the Chief Election Commissioner, Nepal, 7, 9, 10 and 12 April 2008.

12. As I was not a member of a team of observers from India, I was not provided with any conveyance to oversee the election in different constituencies on 10 April. But the Election Commissioner was kind enough to permit me to be present at the media centre at any time of the press-meet along with the local and foreign journalists including those from India and Bangladesh.

13. Interview with Prasant (not the real name), Secretary of the Party and the most important man in the central party office of the Maoist Communist Party in Kathmandu, 11 April 2008.

14. The genealogy of the Shah dynasty is as follows: Prithvi Narayan Shah (1743-75) > Pratap Singh (1775-7) > Rana Bahadur (1777-99) > Girvana Yuddha (1799-1816) > Rajendra (1816-47) > Surendra (1847-81) > Prithvi (1881-1911) > Tribhuvan (1911-55) > Mahendra (1955-72) > Birendra (1972-2001) > Gyanendra (2001-8).

15. There are a number of important studies that have dealt with these various aspects of Nepali history. See for example: *Nepali Journal of Contemporary Studies*, a bi-annual publication, Nepal Centre for Contemporary Studies; Krishna B. Bhattachan, 'Possible Ethnic Revolution or Insurgency in a Predatory Unitary State Hindu State, Nepal', in Dhruba Kumar (ed.), *Domestic Conflicts and Crisis of Governability*, Kathmandu: Centre for Nepal and Asian Studies, 2000; H. Federick Gaige, *Regionalism and National Unity of Nepal*, Berkeley: University of California, 1975; Tulsi Ram Baidya, *Prithvi Narayan Shah: The Founder of Modern Nepal*, Delhi: Anmol, 1993; Siddika Shamina, *Muslims of Nepal*, Kathmandu: Nurun Nahar, 1993.

16. Editor's note, Whelpton, *A History of Nepal*.

17. Ibid., p. 209.

18. Ibid.

19. Ibid., pp. 200-1.

20. Derek O'Brien, *The Penguin CNBC_TV 18 Business, Year Book 2006-07*, Delhi: Penguin Books, 2007.

21. The results of the Constituency Elections held on 10 April 2008 were declared on 25 April. It indicated that the CPN (Maoist) under Pushpa Kamal Dahal alias Prachanda would be able to hold the rein of the nation. See Krishna Hachhethu (author and coordinator of the Democracy Project at Nepal), *Nepal in Transition: A Study on the State of Democracy*, Stockholm: International Institute of Democracy and Electoral Assistance (IDEA), 2008.

22. Hachhethu, *Nepal in Transition*.

23. *The Himalayan Times* (Kathmandu), 20 May 2008.

24. Press-release of the Chief Election Commissioner at the Media Centre, Kathmandu, 6.30 p.m., 10 April 2008.

25. A number of articles appeared just before the April election in *The Himalayan Times* (7-9 April 2008) and *The Kathmandu Post* (9 April 2008).
26. Ibid.
27. *Nepali Times*, 25 April 2008.
28. *The Telegraph* (Nepal), 21 October 2008.
29. *Constituent Assembly Debate*, Nepal, 19 October 2008, quoted in ibid.

Review Article

18

Bollywood, Popular Culture and Cultural Diffusion

SREEMATI GANGULI

Mihir Bose, *Bollywood: A History*, London: Roli Books, 2007.
Sudha Rajagopalan, *Leave Disco Dancer Alone: Indian Cinema and Soviet Movie—Going after Stalin*, Delhi: Yoda Press, 2008.

Popular culture is conceived to be what is popular within a given social context. These books trace the story of Indian popular culture through the study of that particular segment which arguably attracts the maximum media attention, whether in India or abroad. Both the books have undertaken Hindi popular cinema as the focus of their study. While Mihir Bose tells the story of the evolution of Hindi cinema in India, Sudha Rajagopalan analyses the impact of this genre of Indian cinema on the Soviet audience between the period 1954, when the first Indian film festival was held in the USSR, and 1991, when the disintegration of the USSR took place.

The mainstream Hindi cinema industry based in Mumbai (erstwhile Bombay) is termed as 'Bollywood', again a popular term (meaning a poor man's Hollywood) but not a worthy one as it robs it of its uniqueness. The first book is not a hardcore academic endeavour, but a refreshing narrative that is built upon stories and anecdotes. It has extensively used interviews, newspaper reports, film magazines and a wide array of published as well as web-materials. But all these have not burdened the narrative; rather have helped the story to traverse some 110 years, starting from 1896 when the Indian audience were shown, for the first time, six short films at Watson's Hotel, Bombay, by the Lumiere Brothers.

The book is divided in five parts, each part having several sub-sections. Bose is fascinated by the reach as well as the sheer might of Bollywood which produces more than a 1,000 feature films annually and has a daily audience of 14 million. And in comparison with Hollywood, Bose argues, in the Prologue 'Bollywood is the first and only instance of a non-Western society taking a Western product and so changing it that it can now claim to have created a new genre, one that reaches audiences that the original cannot' (p. 27).

The first part, 'In Step with the World', traces the beginning of the journey for Indian cinema. It meticulously depicts each step of movie-making in India, starting from the first use of motion picture camera by Harischandra Sakharam Bhatvadekar to capture a wrestling scene in the late 1890s as well as the films by Sen brothers, Hiralal and Motilal, that started the Bengali chapter of the Indian film industry, to the achievements of the three stalwarts of the earliest period of Indian cinema—Dadasaheb Phalke, Jamsetji Framji Madan and Dhirendranath Gangopadhyay. Bose has also drawn attention to the recommendations by the 1928 Census Committee, which brushed aside the exaggerated fears of the government about the demoralizing effects of films on Indian youth and challenged the idea of imperial preference by observing that 'If too much exhibition of American films in the country is a danger to the national interest, too much of other Western films is as much a danger' (p. 84). In such a context, Bose argues, notwithstanding the British warnings about the evils of Hollywood, Indian cinema still followed the Hollywood model for quite some time.

In the second part, 'When Bollywood was like Hollywood: The Studio Era', the story focuses on the second-generation mavericks of Indian cinema. It depicts the roles of B.N. Sircar, Devaki Kumar Bose and Pramathesh C. Barua as well as that of the New Theatres, which made Kolkata the centre of Indian cinema. Bose has also discussed the rise of alternative centres like Pune and Mumbai under stalwarts like V. Shantaram and Himangshu Rai and the introduction of the star system in Bollywood. The first such star was Ashok Kumar, and later, there were 'the Big Three of Bollywood'—Dilip Kumar, Raj Kapoor and Dev Anand. Bose notes a very interesting point that the film-makers of that era had to do a very difficult task of nation-building through films in a country of so many languages and a number of regional movie centres. As he remarks: 'films were an agent of a much wider social change, of making a new country from a very old one' (p. 127).

The third part, 'Minting Film Gold in Bombay' talks of the post-

Partition scenario, when the three big stars of Bollywood and directors like Bimal Roy, Guru Dutt and K. Asif were at their best and Bollywood was searching for the right ingredients or 'masalas' to prepare the right kind of curry that would suit and satisfy the tastes of the Indian audience. The fourth part, 'A Laugh, a Song and a Tear', on the other hand, deals with the twin themes of music and comedy as essential parts of Bollywood culture. This section has mostly concentrated on the singers and comedians. However, a more detailed discussion on the wide diversity (as this music equally borrows from both Indian and Western classical as well as folk sources) and patterns of application of music in Hindi films might have been attempted as this sort of music already has a specific niche audience. The last part, 'Anger and After', discusses the phenomenon called Amitabh Bachchan in Bollywood and some of his next-generation stars, particularly Aamir Khan, who certainly deserves special mention for the different kind of movies he promotes.

Interestingly, Bose has concentrated only on the mainstream of this Bollywood phenomenon, leaving aside the so-called 'art-film' and even the 'middle-of-the-road' genre of cinema. While it may not be necessary to talk of the 'new wave' cinema in a book on popular cinema, but it is a fact that experimental movies by Mani Kaul, Kumar Sahni, Shyam Benegal, Govind Nihalani, and Sayeed Mirza have definitely added a new dimension to the film culture of India. Therefore, a discussion on the decline of this genre of cinema and the all-pervasive reign of popular Bollywood cinema with the onset of economic globalization that transformed the concept of popular culture in India would have enriched the work immensely. It is also quite inexplicable that directors like Hrishikesh Mukherjee, Basu Chatterjee or Basu Bhattacharya, whose movies reflected the aspirations and struggles of the Indian middle class during the 1960s and 1970s have not found their deserved place in this book. These comparatively low-budget (and not always star-studded) movies set another angle to Bollywood culture, a trend that lost its appeal and market in the 1990s as the definition and characteristics of the Indian middle-class underwent radical transformation with the advent of the LPG (Liberalization, Privatization, Globalization) phenomenon. Bose has also carefully avoided such sensitive issues like the shoddy financing of movies or the crime-finance nexus in Bollywood.

The book by Sudha Rajagopalan, based on her doctoral research, is a serious academic study on Bollywood and its cultural diffusion. The context of the study is the relative relaxation of rigid governmental policies in the former Soviet Union, affecting the cultural habits of the Soviet audience. Based on oral history methodology and archival research in the Soviet Union, Rajagopalan analyses the responses, interpretations and debates on Indian cinema as carried out among the circles of Soviet audience of Indian movies—policy makers, critics and sociologists. In other words, she tries to address a moot question in 'Introduction': what can the import and reception of Indian films in the Soviet Union express "about the interaction between official cultural prescriptions and popular tastes, between dominant ideas and alternative preferences?' (p. 17).

Rajagopalan begins by narrating different traits of Indian cinema that caught the imagination of the Soviet people in 'Indian Films in the Soviet Past: Memories Articulated'. For the Soviet audience, the expressive and highly emotional themes, melodramatic treatment, 'magnificent songs' and 'stunningly beautiful dances' in films that display the Indian culture, 'the iconization' of glamour and the sentimentality of the film stars were in stark contrast with the Soviet 'monochrome' and 'grey' realities. The 'exoticism', particularly the 'visual ostentation and wide colour palette' of Indian films always offered an image of festivity and *skazka* or fairytale-like treatment of *byt* or everyday reality.

The second chapter of the book, 'Import/Facilitation', deals with the policies of the Goskino and Sovesportfil'm that dictated the choice of Indian films to be imported and the process of reconciling strategic interests, audience needs and the assumed role of these institutions as mentors of global progressive cinema. The third chapter, entitled 'Cultural Mediation and Disengagement', focuses on a very interesting facet of the cultural experience—the interactions among the Soviet viewers, movie critics and sociologists on the extent of the preponderance and popularity of Indian films. Critics took it upon themselves as vanguards of 'Socialist realist arts' and demanded raising of consciousness on social realities from films, and very few so-called Indian art films like *Chhinnamul*, *Interview* or *Nishant* satisfied them. Their total indifference to, and, at times, bitter criticism of Indian popular cinema showed their disengagement from the tastes and expectations of the common Soviet people. The role of the sociologists in this entire play was to intervene and mediate between the aesthetic tastes of the cultural intelligentsia and the mass audience, and, for Rajagopalan, the 'ambivalence' of the sociologists regarding their mediative tasks made contradictory tendencies more pronounced.

Rajagopalan also describes the popular responses towards Indian popular cinema in 'Public Voices' as expressed in letters to journals and film magazines like *Isskustvo Kino, Sovetskii Ekran,* and *Goskino* as well as the debates on the aesthetic tastes of the audience and critics around four very popular Hindi films—*Love in Simla, Sangam, Bobby* and *Disco Dancer.*

She aptly explains the emergence of a 'lively cultural space' in the post-Stalinist Soviet society through the enthusiasm of the audience as well as the 'contestation' of this by the 'indifference, ineffectiveness and indulgence of mediators'.

The book thus opens up a new vista in the study of Indo-Soviet relations. It is not a typical history of Indo-Soviet cultural relations but an unusual and a very significant analysis of Soviet domestic cultural scenario through the prism of the responses and repercussions that Indian popular films excited in the post-Stalin period. Indian popular films received various characteristic adjectives from different quarters—'Otherworldly, cathartic, aesthetically spectacular, morally edifying, politically expedient, commercially lucrative, banal and corrupting'. The author concludes that through the debates and interactions among the sections who tolerated it, who defended it and who despised it, Indian films got the 'meaning and significance' of a cultural product and this comment provides a unique dimension to this genre of movies.

While the book provides a unique case-study of Bollywood going global even before the onset of globalization of the 1990s, a few points, though, could have been better explained. First, there should have been a more detailed discussion of the so-called 'grey Soviet realities' as Indian films were accepted as more colourful by the Soviet audience against that perspective. Second, an elaboration of the film export policy of the Indian government would have been useful in understanding the context of the cultural diffusion of Hindi movies in the former Soviet Union. Last but not the least, given the impact of Indian films on the Soviet audience and their learning experiences through these films, a more-layered discussion on Indian cultural diplomacy and the use of this type of *soft* power would surely have enriched the perspective of the work.

The most certain trait of popular culture is that it changes constantly and through this constant process, it generates new ideas and currents and represents a complex web of interdependent and interconnected views that have a direct appeal for, and influence on the society at large. The first book, in search of a history of Bollywood, has presented a story of Indian society and culture and the changes these have encountered over all these years through the lens of cinema. For example, his comment that while Dilip Kumar had to change his name (Yusuf Khan) to gain popular acceptance, actors like Aamir Khan or Salman or Shahrukh Khan have become immensely successful even with their Muslim names is a good observation. In turn, it provides an interesting story of the evolution and development of entertainment industry of India. The second one has showed the dominant and alternative cinematic preferences of the various sections of Soviet society, through which the on-going churnings in the cultural scenario of the USSR are evaluated. And so it has become a very innovative way of analysing the particularities and peculiarities of Indian cinema as well.

Research Notes

19

My Journey Through Myanmar: Culture, People and History

SWAPNA BHATTACHARYA (CHAKRABORTI)

My first academic journey to Myanmar (former Burma) started rather accidentally; it was not exactly a direct journey with clear-cut aim to know the country and her people. When I was studying the history of South and South-East Asia at the South Asia Institute of the University of Heidelberg in the late 1970s and early 1980s, I had the privilege to listen to Professor Hermann Kulke's lectures on early trade, art and architecture, and civilization of South-East Asia. Those lectures gave me enough food to rethink the old trade and religious linkages between eastern and southern India on the one hand and South-East Asia on the other. Yet South-East Asia remained somewhat a distant region for me. It was a copper-plate inscription from early medieval Bengal, granting of land to a temple situated in Pattikeravisaya of Samatata Mandala of Pundravardhana Bhukti, which excited my imagination about the connection between Bengal alias India and Burma. Pattikera was an old Buddhist kingdom situated somewhere between Bengal and Arakan. Though my knowledge about Buddhist Arakan was at a nascent stage in those days, yet I could clearly see the passage between Buddhist Bengal and Buddhist Arakan, along which pilgrims passed by and entered into the Buddhist heartland of eastern India centred in Bodhgaya and to the Bay of Bengal region as a whole. The old Buddhist civilization of early south-eastern Bengal, Samatata-Harikela region as it was known, was an extension of the old Buddhist civilization centred in Arakan. Besides other works, two important books by B. Morrsion, *Political Centres and Culture Regions of Early Bengal* and *Lalamai: A Cultural Centre in Early Bengal* made my understanding of the region considerably mature. Those who are familiar with my works on Myanmar and Bengal, written over the last two decades, may see the continuity of my 'obsession' with the Bengal-Myanmar connection from those days of the early 1980s. Today, when the scholars of Bangladesh speak of their 'Look East Policy', this region, where Bengal and Myanmar meet (Chittagong-Arakan region), comes with a special attention: for Bangladesh the region is a gateway to South-East Asia, just as for India the four states of Manipur, Nagaland, Arunachal Pradesh and Mizoram are.

My desire to make myself further acquainted with Myanmar made a significant progress in the mid-1980s when I started learning the Myanmar language, sitting at the feet of my respected *Saya* (teacher), U Tin Htway, at the South Asia Institute, University of Heidelberg. It was a great privilege to listen to my teacher's words as he was well-versed in Pali and Buddhism. He not only taught me the Myanmar language and its grammar but also gave me a historical profile of the development of this fascinating language in the context of the rich cultural heritage of the Myanmar people. First and foremost, what attracted me were the rich vocabulary of the language and the presence of a large number of Pali and Sanskrit words. In cases where those words entered into Myanmar language with phonetic changes, it is very hard to recognize unless explained to the learners. There are loan words from various other languages as well. It speaks for the rich cultural history of the people of Myanmar, to which so many scholars have referred. In recent years, Thant Myaint U's book *The River of Lost Footsteps: Histories of Burma* describes brilliantly this process of fusion and integration. Myanmar accommodated outsiders into the fold of her civilization—people from a large number of affiliations. Centres of power shifted with the shifting of concentration of power from one group of people to the other: Pyus, Mons, Rakhines, Burmans, Shans. The process of indigenization was as fascinating as it happened to be the case with India.

Myanmar is situated at the most important highways which connected China with India, Tibet and Nepal with South-East Asia on the one hand and Central Asia on the other. Burma's state-building process started in the early years of the Christian Era, when contact with Buddhist India (south India) appeared to be extremely significant. Lower Myanmar was actively engaged in trade, which was partly dominated by the early people of modern Malaysia and Indonesia. Coastal Burma, Pegu and Martaban regions were involved in the maritime trade activities prevalent between the Coromandal coast of India and the Mediterranean world. Thaton, the flourishing port in ancient Lower Myanmar, was dominated by the Mons. The region between Sittang and Salween rivers was known as the Mon kingdom of Ramannadesa. Thaton (Sudhamma) was also known as

Suvaranabhumi or the Golden Land, a term widely known to Indians. To this general terminology, we should better bring a number of regions around the Bay of Bengal which now belong to various countries of South and South-East Asia. Those who want to be especially engaged with the Mons may refer to Michael Aung Thwin's recent work *The Mists of Ramanna: The Legend that was Lower Burma* (2005). And, obviously, to understand the extreme significance of old Arakan, Pamela Gutman's book *Burma's Lost Kingdoms: Splendours of Arakan* remains the source of most convincing archaeological facts, connecting the region with the old Buddhist civilization of India.

Also, as Thant Myiant U has pointed out, Myanmar became extremely important for the trade between China and Rome. How important was the Mon culture and history for understanding the Mranma people, who were centred more in the middle and upper parts of the country, became clearer to me when I learnt that it was from the Mons (also called Talaings) that the Mranma people borrowed their script. One, however, has to go back earlier, as High Roop has shown in his work *An Introduction to the Burmese Writing System*, to the time of the Pyus, who, being already present in the fifth century AD, used a script for a Pali inscription, which had a similar script to that of Kadamba used in the third century in North Canara, near Goa on the west coast (Roop). Tha Tun Oo's work *Myanmar Culture* pays a good deal of attention to the south Indian origin of the Pyu script. A significant item is a Buddhist Pali manuscript on gold-leaf, written in Vengi-Kadamba script of South India. Roop argues that the language of the Tibeto-Burman Pyus later also used a script resembling the Pallava script used in the Theravada centre of Conjeeveram in Madras. We often think that the Pyus left no sign or were somehow lost. But it seems that in later periods they remained and got mingled with other races living in various parts of Myanmar. They got assimilated with the Mons and Mranmas, and if we accept the opinion that Pagan is derived from the word *Pyu* and *Grama*—village of the Pyus—then there is no doubt that besides the Mranma and the Mon people, the Pyus had their share too, in making Pagan civilization, as it was.

In contrast to Indo-Aryan (to which Sanskrit belongs) languages, Myanmar language is a Tibeto-Burman language. It belongs to the great Sino-Tibetan language family. The most important mark for Sino-Tibetan language is that it is a tonal language. The same word with a different tone makes a difference in meaning. There are three tones: short, level and heavy. Another important feature is that Myanmar (Burmese) is an agglutinative language, which means that there is no conjugation of verbs. Instead, verbs get additional suffixes to carry the sense. The third feature of Myanmar language is that it is monosyllabic; words have a single syllable. For someone like me, coming from a Sanskrit and Bengali background, at the first stage, the Myanmar language appeared very different, and even difficult. In course of time, however, leaning the Myanmar language became extremely exciting. The more I went through the textbook, the more commonalities I saw between the two cultures: Indian and Myanmar. Stories from the *Jataka*s and other literatures from India wandered around the regions, particularly in what we have just identified as *Suvarnabhumi*, and Myanmar was the heartland of *Suvarnabhumi*. By reading pieces of texts, I realized the people of both Myanmar and India belonged to the same cultural milieu, with same values, social practices and philosophy of life. Both the people believe in wisdom, morality and sacrifice. How animism and Hinduism found their places in the Theravada Buddhist world of Myanmar people has been lucidly elaborated in Khin Maung Nyunt's seminal work *Myanmar Traditional Monthly Festival* (2005). This mood of tolerance and assimilation of Myanmar people finds expression in all spheres of cultural life: performing arts like marionette theatre, music, drama, dance, and various works of art like lacquer ware and wood carving.

But what is Myanmar culture? To clarify this point, I should write something about the history of the Pagan Empire (*c.* 849-1287), and about my visit to the archaeological sites at Pagan preceded by a short visit to Mandalay, both in 1995. The Pagan archaeological site, the largest in the whole of Myanmar, is situated on the left bank of the Irrawaddy River. It covers an area of 16 square miles, and its location signifies that it controlled the rice fields of Kyaukse in the heartland. Though Pagan was of earlier origin, the authentic history of the Pagan dynasty starts with the ascendance of King Anawrahta (Aniruddha) during 1044-77. He is seen as the unifier of Myanmar. After conquering the Mon kingdom of Lower Myanmar, with Thaton as the centre, he tried to prove his legitimacy as a Buddhist king by attempting to acquire the Pali scriptures which King Manuha, the Mon king, refused to submit. With the help of Shin Arahan, Anawrahta converted his people into Theravada Buddhism. Nevertheless, he needed the Mons who helped him build the city of Pagan, for the Mons were highly talented people with the knowledge of art and architecture. As much as one gets impressed by Anawrahta's might and spirit, I personally find in Kyanazittha (Sanskrit: Jnanasiddha) a very impressive king. He was married to a Bengali Mahayanist named Abeyadana. This marriage brought Kyanzittha closer to Buddhist Bengal. And one should not forget that there is a temple in Pagan dedicated to this Pagan queen from Bengal. It was thus quite natural, mentions Tun Shwe Khin Mrau in his work *Mrauuk-U* that when Minraibaya, the Rakhine king of the Pyinsa dynasty, was in distress as his father Minbeeloo got dethroned and murdered, he took refuge in Kyanzittha's kingdom. My present engagement with the Rakhine state (Arakan) gives more attention to the twentieth century and the present day. Yet old stories of linkages helped me understand the present with a vision forward. I therefore understand why the recently concluded (formalized) Kaladan project linking India's landlocked north-east with the Rakhine state (Arakan) generates so much satisfaction and fulfilment for both the people. The cultural regions, which were closely linked with each other over thousands of years, suffered unnatural isolation due to the British policy of 'Divide and Rule'. Some reflections on this can be found in one of my earlier article, 'Some Observations on Political Systems, Religion and Culture of Western Myanmar, Northeastern India and Southeastern Bangladesh in the Context of Present Trends in India-Myanmar Relations' (*Asia Annual*, 2006).

What appeared most imposing to me, however, was the unprecedented structure: the Ananda temple built again by King Kyanazittha (1084-1112). Everywhere—in all the temples and other architectures—one witnesses how the Pagan kings adjusted to the prevailing political and religious mood in the entire region, stretching from their centre down to the Bay of Bengal and beyond, in Sri Lanka on the one hand, and in the Bengal-Bihar region on the other. Buddhist Palas (eighth to thirteenth century AD), struggling as they were in the face of rising power of Islam and declining trade, must have got their inspiration for their cultural and political survival from the powerful kings of Pagan. Indeed, the Pagan kings maintained their contact with Bodhgaya. Mahayana Buddhism, Naga cult, worships of Indian gods and goddesses like Brahma, Shiva, Indra, Vishnu, Ganesha are visible everywhere. Going through the archaeological site was an unprecedented experience for me. Going inside the two temples—Nandamannya (*anantapunya*: eternal wisdom) and Payathonzu—was most exciting for me. Mahayana influence is clear in one of the murals showing a standing Buddha in the *varada-mudra* accompanied by Tara, which was the symbol of female power in the Mahayana domain. In one of my earlier writings, published in the *Journal of Ancient Indian History* (1997), I tried to link the 'three temples' (the word Payathonzu means three temples) with not only the three refugees, Buddha, Dhamma and Sangha, but with the Trinatha cult widely practised in Nepal, Tibet, Bengal and such areas influenced by Mahayana school. These three Naths (Lords) were Min Nath, Matsyendranath and Goraksa Nath. The Tibetan version of Matsyendranath was Luipa, who was born in the Sandvipa Island in the Bay of Bengal area, which was famous for its Tantric-Mahayana tradition, while the same Matsyendranath is deified in Nepal as Avalokiteshvara, the Bodhisattva. Buddhists of Nepal worship him as an exponent of the Natha cult. Thus, one can see how closely linked was old Pagan with eastern India, Nepal and Tibet.

While sitting in my hotel in a quiet afternoon, looking at the waters of Irrawaddy flowing through, I was paying my homage to Michael Symes, John Crawfurd, Sir Henry Yule, Dr. Emil Forchammer, Duroislle, Taw Sein Ko, Gordon Luce, Niharranjan Ray and such other scholars and statesmen who made Pagan known to the outside world. It may be interesting to mention that Lord Curzon, the Viceroy of British India and British Burma, while stopping at Pagan in the year 1902, ordered the construction of the original Ananda Museum, and in the same year the 'Burma Circle' of the Archaeological Survey of India was set up with Taw Sein Ko as the director.

My journey to Myanmar in 1995 brought me also to Mandalay, the capital of the last royal dynasty of Myanmar. King Mindon Min of the Alaungapaya (also known as Konbaung) dynasty shifted his capital to Mandalay in 1857, the year of the Indian Mutiny. Myanmar was then confronting the severest challenge from British imperialism since a large part of the country had already been under the British occupation. Arakan and Tenasserim were annexed in the First Anglo-Burmese War of 1826 while the Second War (1852) resulted in the annexation of Pegu. In my recently published book, *India-Myanmar Relations 1886-1948* (2007), I have shown how important Mandalay remains for the Indians. Mahatma Gandhi described Mandalay as the real place of pilgrimage for every Indian. Balgangadhar Tilak wrote his *Gitarahasya* while interned in the Mandalay jail. Subhas Chandra Bose also drew his inspiration from Myanmar Buddhism while spending his days in Mandalay jail. I was interested to see the palace which witnessed so many events of colonial history, which bound Myanmar with India and vice versa. In recent years, the capital of Myanmar has been shifted to Nay Pyi Taw, which is not very far from Mandalay. In many ways, thus, Mandalay remains to be a destination of pilgrimage for Indians. It carries memories of a common history of the freedom struggle. Mandalay also houses the great image of the Mahamuni, once the symbol of independent Buddhist kingdom of Arakan. With the annexation of Arakan by the Burman king Bodawpaya in 1784, it was brought to Mandalay, the capital of the powerful Alaungpaya dynasty, which controlled much of what we call today South and South-East Asia. I tried to sum up the most revealing information regarding this story of the spreading of Mahamuni tradition in Assam and such places in my recent article 'Religion and Colonial Politics: Assam, Myanmar and Buddhism'. It is most inspiring that new economic movements along the India-Myanmar border will make it increasingly possible for travellers, business people, pilgrims and others to go to Mandalay from Manipur in the near future. Quite some time back, Mandalay got its due share: the Government of India opened its consulate in this historic city. Opening of all the north-eastern states is urgently needed not only for the economic development of the region, but also for better understanding of a common history.

In 2005 an invitation came again from Myanmar, a country which I love so much for its unique cultural heritage and individuality. The invitation was from Myanmar Historical Commission to participate in their Diamond Jubilee celebration. The conference was held in Yangon University, a place which was already familiar to me since my first visit in 1995. The names of Indian scholars like W.S. Desai and Niharranjan Ray are still remembered with great respect here. I chose to present a paper on how Myanmar Buddhism provided inspiration for Buddhist resurgence of what we call neo-Buddhism in India. Had I not taken up my present project at the Maulana Abul Kalam Azad Institute of Asian Studies, I would never have perhaps come across the little known fact of Dr. Ambedkar's Myanmar connection, and his love for the country, where Buddhism has a unique tradition of continuity. Between the busy days spent in Yangon, it was possible for me to undertake a trip to Pegu, which is called Bago in Myanmar language. Pegu is renowned for the Shwemawdaw pagoda, for Kalyani inscription, for the sixteenth-century powerful king Bayinnaung, and last but not the least, for the largest Buddhist image called Shwethalyaung. According to Aung Thaw's *Archaeological Sites in Burma* (p. 104), among the early Indian settlers of Pegu, a certain section might have been from Orissa. Pegu was also known as Hanthawaddy, connecting the place with *hamsa*, duck. In this region, in later days, the Burmese (Burman) supremacy replaced that of the Mons'. Yet the Buddhist tradition went on without any break. I was amazed to see the very famous and the largest reclining image of Buddha, called Shwethalyaung, built in AD 994. This coastal region of Myanmar is also famous for its close link with Buddhist Sri Lanka. King Dhammaceti, whose another name was Ramadhapati, undertook a vigorous attempt to reform Buddhism along the line of Sri Lanka. The famous fifteenth-century Kalyani Inscription of Dhammaceti, which I had the chance to see, tells the story of this pious mission of Dhammaceti, and also Pegu's relation with Sri Lanka and south India.

In December 2006, on an invitation from the Myanmar Institute of Strategic and International Studies (MISIS), Ministry of Foreign Affairs of Myanmar, the Maulana Abul Kalam Azad Institute of Asian Studies sent a delegation to Yangon to meet the colleagues there for discussion on various aspects of cooperation in the field of India-Myanmar relations. It was altogether a new experience for me. The delegation, led by the chairman of institute, Prof. Jayanta Kumar Ray, included four Fellows from the institute including me. The Myanmar Consulate in Kolkata, especially Consul General U Soe Paing and Consul U Khin Htun, played a large role in facilitating the trip. In Myanmar, we discussed a wide range of subjects with our hosts (MISIS), and were also invited to deliberate on the trends of current developments in the economic, cultural and political relations between our countries. We visited the important monuments and places in Yangon, especially those bearing memories of a common past, like the *mazahr* (graveyard) of the last Mughal emperor Bahadur Shah Zafar, in the quiet corner of Yangon. The MISIS also organized a meeting with the Union of Myanmar Chamber of Commerce and Industry (UMCCI) and the Yangon University. The Swe Dagon Pagoda, the spiritual soul of Yangon, could be seen from hotel Summit Parkview where we stayed. It was this pagoda, which made Rabindranath Tagore 'unwilling' to leave the golden land when he was en route to Japan. Tagore's Buddhist mind wanted to experience eternal peace, sitting under the cool shadow of this pagoda. Indians living in Myanmar and those on visit to the country go in large numbers to the pagoda to offer their prayers.

Myanmar called me again in 2008 as I undertook a field trip to the country in October. My work with the relevant archival materials on the Rakhine State (Arakan) preserved in the National Archives Department under the Ministry of National Planning and Economic Development, Government of Myanmar, was one of my major academic programmes. It went very well. My previous visits had already made me familiar with the city of Yangon—a city which bears so many evidences of her close contact with India. The Botatung area, where I was staying this time, itself is a place where the great novelist Sarat Chandra Chattopadhyay lived for some time during his long sojourn in British Burma during the early years of the twentieth century. In the evenings, after a busy day's schedule,

I allowed myself the pleasure of leisurely looking at the Rangoon River as well as the Botataung Pagoda from my balcony at YMCA. Government institutions and organizations that I visited included MISIS, Union of Myanmar Federation of Chambers of Commerce and Industry (UMFCCI), National Archives Department, Department of International Relations of the Yangon University, University Central Library, Yangon, and the National Museum. I was delighted and much impressed to see the enormous interest for India among all the members of the said institutions. Interest for Indian music, dance and cinema is visible among a large number of common people in the city of Yangon. Equally inspiring for me was the knowledge of the common people in Myanmar about India's progress in the Information Technology sector.

My visit to Prome (Pyay) has left with me some lasting memories which I want to share here with my readers. I have already mentioned the contribution of the Pyu people in the making of Myanmar culture. Besides the archaeological site called Sriksetra (meaning in Sanskrit beautiful place), the museum with a rich collection on Pyu civilization is worth visiting. Pyus, though Tibeto-Burman, were bearers of a civilization very closely related with various parts of India! The impact of various schools of Indian art, like Gupta art or Pala-Sena school of art, is visible in the objects displayed in the museum that I visited. Another unique experience was meeting a very renowned writer of Myanmar named Saya Paragu while visiting his Shantiniketan library. He is such a great admirer of Rabindranth Tagore that he not only named his house and library 'Shantiniketan', but also dedicated himself to translating a large number of Tagore's works into Myanmar language. Paragu's writings in general including his translated works are extremely popular among Myanmar people. His huge collection includes books in Myanmar, Sanskrit, Pali, English and Japanese languages. The last day of my last visit to Myanmar was spent in visiting some old edifices bearing memories of what I have already referred to as the 'common past'. The Gandhi Memorial Hall is one of them. Durgabari, which I also visited, remains as always an important centre for not only Bengalis, but all Indians living in Yangon. Also Kaba Aye, the World Peace Pagoda, built in 1954 during the Sixth Buddhist Council held in Yangon, stands witness to a past when Myanmar and India were very close partners in the mission of preaching the message of peace pronounced by Lord Buddha. Standing there remembering such figures as Dr. Ambedkar, Jawaharlal Nehru, General Aung San, and U Nu, I also paid homage to figures like U Wisara and U Ottama, who became great inspirations for Indian nationalists and who fought against British colonialism, sharing the same ideological platform.

Myanmar, though a Buddhist-majority state, is a country where a large number of other religious communities including Muslims, Christians, and Hindus, and races like Shans, Karens, Kachins, Mons, Chins, and Rakhines live peacefully with the Buddhist population. Mixed marriages and other avenues of social interaction are common. People mix with each other in a natural and spontaneous way. I cherish to visit the rest of this beautiful country, where, in recent times India is increasingly coming up as a natural partner for future development and prosperity to be shared by both the countries.

ACKNOWLEDGEMENTS

I am indebted to the following persons for their constant inspiration and valuable support in my academic engagement with Myanmar: Prof. Jayanta Kumar Ray, Chairman, and Prof. Hari Shankar Vasudevan, Director, MAKAIAS, U Soe Paing, former Consul General of the Union of Myanmar, U Khin Htun, former Consul, Consulate General of the Union of Myanmar, Kolkata, and U Soe Win, Deputy Director General, Protocol Department, Ministry of Foreign Affairs, Union of Myanmar. I also thank Dr. Kausik Bandyopadhyay, my colleague at MAKAIAS, for inspiring me to write this paper.

20

Media Reconstruction and the Popular 'Hindi Serial' Culture in Contemporary Afghanistan

ARPITA BASU ROY

Culture and cultural differences have been at the heart of human behaviour throughout history. Hence the significance of culture remains crucial in the rethinking of world politics that stemmed from the end of the Cold War. The increasing pace of globalization and the shrinking of the globe has brought different cultures into closer contact and presented a challenge to traditional patterns of culture and social order. Cultural change has created friction where people of one culture perceive those of another not just as alien but also threatening.[1] Cultural counter-reactions and suspicions particularly to the culture of the West have created significant cleavages. The cultural context of post-9/11 Afghanistan—a nation in political transition—seems to face similar dilemmas and cleavages in relation to media reconstruction. A study of how the reconstruction of its erstwhile devastated media and its current projections actually pose a threat to the elements of continuity entrenched in the society and how counter-reactions to it from other sections are actually manifestations of subconscious changes that a society may aspire, make for an interesting study. For this purpose, I attempt to explore the reactions to the dubbed versions of Hindi soaps, telecast through a private channel in Afghanistan. This I consider to be part of the popular culture in contemporary Afghanistan because of its extensive social currency among the masses.

MEDIA IN STABILIZATION AND RECONSTRUCTION

The development of an independent, pluralistic and sustainable media, it is believed, is critical to fostering long-term peace and stability, particularly for the communities that are conflict-ridden and are in their reconstruction phase. Media are explored as models to envision, to design, to formalize and to implement platforms for communities. However, in the process, media tend to be criticized by skeptics who mistrust it, because they are accustomed to platforms that are controlled either by the state or by political groups looking to further their political agenda. It is generally believed that the creation of a robust media culture would allow citizens to begin holding their government accountable for its actions and ensuring its commitment to democracy.[2] Media can be used for reconciliation by exposing diverse views instead of dividing ethnic groups. For this to happen, attempts have to be made to avoid partisan coverage with a multiethnic approach to report social tensions.[3]

During decades of civil war and instability, particularly during the Taliban regime, the country's mass media agencies and journalists were reduced to little but memories of a time when the print media was widely available and radio broadcasts were thriving. The loss of skilled individuals, institutional capacity and technical equipment, coupled with severe censorship, nearly destroyed what remained of the country's mass media. In a society that closed down television broadcasting, forbade music and sports programmes on radio and banned pictures from appearing in newspapers, no media assessment can ignore Afghanistan's recent history. Yet since 2001 the Afghan media has made a great deal of progress. There has been tremendous growth in private and state media; in television, radio and newspapers; with national, regional provincial and metropolitan coverage.[4]

Media experts believe that sustainability is the key challenge facing the nascent Afghan media sector. As one international media consultant points out, 'We not only had to create media outlets, we also have to create a media market.' Compared to neighbouring countries, press freedom in Afghanistan has improved, but much more needs to be done to provide a lasting enabling environment to the media sector. Although international journalists often face little intimidation, scores of Afghan journalists have been threatened and victimized by various warlords and militia commanders. According to a young Afghan journalist Muhammad Nabi Tadbeer, compared to the Taliban era, the Afghan media has undergone momentous growth but its ultimate success hinges on political stability. 'Over the past century we have had cycles of relative stability and development, but any development has always been destroyed by conflict and turmoil.'[5]

The politics of media support and development in Afghanistan are microcosms of the larger politics of reconstruction and development in the country. The developing media landscape, including the legislative and regulatory context, is critical to the development of community broadcasting and has been marked by both positive developments and setbacks. There are a variety of centres of influence in the current reconstruction and development context, which include the Afghan government, UN agencies and development organizations, the International Security Assistance Force (ISAF), regional political-military powers (often referred to as 'warlords'), the US-led Coalition Forces, and emerging Afghan civil society organizations, including an independent media. There are many positive initiatives at the national level and in major cities, but little attention is paid to community-based media and rural areas. The picture that emerges illustrates the sensitive nature of media in Afghanistan and hints at the complexities of the policy-making process in the current environment.[6]

There is a significant presence of international actors in the post-war media development. The international media development organization, Internews, has helped establish an FM radio station. Around 300 publications are registered with the Ministry of Culture, a large part of which operates from Kabul. Most Afghan cities and towns have modest publications—dailies, weeklies, bi-weeklies, monthlies and quarterlies, and some happen to be the mouthpieces of political parties and military factions like Payam-e-Mujahid and Afghan Millat.[7] Afghans are still steeped in radio culture as the majority of the population, particularly in the remote rural regions, depend on the radio for news and information. The British Broadcasting Corporation (BBC), the Voice of America (VOA), Radio Free Europe/Radio Liberty (RFE/RL) and many other international stations broadcasting in Afghan languages provide the only reliable sources of news and information. In addition to the projected 45 Internews community stations, the state-run Radio Afghanistan has 17 stations. Owned and managed by the business-savvy young Australian-Afghan Mohsini brothers, Arman FM is the country's most successful commercial pop station. Starting in late 2003, the station soon captured the imagination of Kabul's four million people. Attracting around 80 per cent of the city's listenership, it's still the most popular radio station in the capital.

By contrast, the development of television in Afghanistan has been slow. According to most estimates, one-third of the Afghan population has access to television and all attempts at reforming the state-owned Afghan television have been abandoned. Many in the Ministry of Culture and Information believe that privatization might be the last resort for white elephants such as Afghan TV and the Bakhtar News Agency, another subsidiary of the information ministry. With USAID funding, Arman FM had started Afghanistan's first independent commercial TV channel, Tolo TV, in early October 2004. Nevertheless, television has been extremely popular, particularly in the urban areas. Politics in democracies, it is said, relies to a large extent on mass media, especially television, and on communicative strategies borrowed from entertainment and advertisements. The importance of culture, then, increases as areas of life previously thought to be independent of it begin to fall under its influence. As the next section of this discussion will show, television, movies and other forms of popular culture tend to replace traditional authority figures in the society.[8]

INDIAN SOAPS IN AFGHAN MEDIA:
REACTIONS AND COUNTER-REACTIONS

Afghanistan's television is the most visible symbol of the country's transformation since Taliban's downfall in 2001. Television generally plays an important role in shaping the beliefs and attitudes of younger people as well as offering them behavioural role models. Hence traditional 'guardians' of culture perceive change not just as alien but also as threatening. Cultural counter-reactions and suspicions, particularly towards Indian soaps aired by private channels, have created significant cleavages in contemporary Afghan society and politics.

These Indian soap operas, with their tales of family drama and trysts among the rich and beautiful, have transfixed Afghans brought up on turgid state broadcasts and under a Taliban prohibition on television.[9] In the six years following the fall of the Taliban, Afghanistan has around 13 stations,[10] a very popular channel being Tolo TV which airs a few Indian soaps dubbed in the local language and which dominates the peak time and gets around 10 million viewers.[11] Moreover, significant Afghans have been returning from exile, bringing back new ideas. A large youthful population, particularly in the cities, has been eager for new ways. Afghanistan has its own pop stars who sing ballads and folk songs, and even a rap star. The Afghan version of the *American Idol* talent show, put out by Tolo, was a sensation, but it also raised criticism, especially when a woman finished third in the competition.

Reactions

Despite a wave of unprecedented freedom since the overthrow of the puritanical Taliban, Afghanistan remains a deeply conservative Islamic society. Conservative Muslim clerics and some politicians are outraged by these soaps. Branding the programmes immoral and against Islamic culture, the critics started a campaign to press the private channels to pull the plug on the soaps. At Friday prayers at Kabul's largest mosque, Enayatullah Balegh, an influential cleric and university teacher said that he and his followers were adamant. 'We are 6,000 people in this mosque,' he said in front of his congregation, and his intention 'is to go and blow up all the TV antennas if they do not stop it.' The congregation chanted in response: 'God is greatest, we are ready.'

The clerics' campaign gained traction in April 2008 when some members of the parliament, supported by the Ministry of Information and Culture, issued a declaration to the private TV channels to stop broadcasting five Indian soaps. Conservatives object to the Indian soaps because they show men and women together, women dressed 'immodestly' and the worship of Hindu idols. The channels have made concessions, cutting scenes of Hindu worship and blurring areas of bare flesh. But that hasn't appeased the critics.[12]

President Hamid Karzai, who has a reputation as a liberal but has been under pressure from conservative forces over several issues including television, has stepped gingerly into the fray. Trying to keep both sides happy in the run-up to a presidential election in 2009, Karzai has insisted that media freedom will be upheld, but added that unsuitable material should not be broadcast. 'There will never be interference with media freedom but media freedom should be compatible with the culture of the Afghan people,' Karzai said at a news conference. 'We wish television to stop them,' he said, referring to programmes 'in contradiction with daily life.' Karzai insisted, 'Like rest of the countries in the world, our TV broadcasting should be in line with our culture, based on society's moral standards.'[13]

Defiant voices

Various sections of the society, however, show defiance to such conservative pronouncements. The National Union of Journalists is seriously concerned about the anti-media propaganda. The Union also criticized national and international organizations including the UN and the EU, for failing to speak out against what it called the government's attempt to curb freedom of speech. Some members of the Union also said that it would affect Afghanistan's relations with India that plays a large part in rebuilding the country.[14]

Most viewers do not see any contradiction. The attraction towards these soaps is such that the lead characters of the serials are held in high esteem among viewers, particularly the women. 'I like Tulsi a lot, my children like her a lot,' said Dell Jan, a mother of six, referring to the main character in one of the most popular Indian soaps. 'When the serial starts on TV, we stop all work, even eating, and watch it,' she said. 'We love it—it's entertainment for the children.' People resent the fact that the government is trying to ban their favourite soaps and say that they won't let that happen.[15] The defiance of the television stations appears prominent. 'It is against the media law,' Masoud Qiam, a senior presenter for Tolo TV, said in an interview, referring to the declaration. 'We will not stop the airing of the soap operas. The government should be concentrating on more weighty matters, such as corruption, poppy eradication, rule of law, how to attract investment and other important matters.' Media rights activists suggest President Hamid Karzai, who has expressed support for the ban, was trying to put pressure on the media to please conservative elements ahead of elections in August 2009. 'His popularity has suffered huge damage due to his failures in recent years, exposed by the free media,' says Fahim Dashti, editor of the prominent *Kabul Weekly* and a spokesman for Afghanistan's National Journalists Union. 'I think he wants to stop media telling the people about his failures during the sensitive election campaign,' he says. 'It also seems the President uses this to reflect himself as a good Muslim in an attempt to attract support from conservative circles and communities ahead of the elections.'

REGENERATION OR DEGENERATION?

Whether such soaps on television lead to a degeneration of cultural ethics and norms of a society or whether these actually help re-generate a new and bigger concept of culture encompassing popular aspirations are matters of debate. Many argue that the content of such dramas affect people's behaviour and ways of thinking within and about their immediate and extended families by portraying an illusive and unreal picture of a lavish way of life for many poor Afghan families. It is also argued that inappropriate behaviour by women, incongruent to Afghan culture, telecast through the serials is likely to have a polluting effect on this puritanical Islamic society. The media, both private and government, *should* be able to deliver to people what is most needed in the current context rather than just projecting a commercial product.

However, the inevitability of a culture being affected by that of others is an inescapable reality in today's age of globalization, particularly in a context where Afghanistan is being integrated into the community of nations. Yet whether this can be studied in the context of 'cultural globalization' or more appropriately cultural imperialism is doubtful. Indian soaps cannot be perceived as agents of cultural imperialism because of the immense popularity they enjoy and because India as a regional power is generally regarded as a friendly country where Bollywood remains an epitome of entertainment. It will be appropriate to conceive such recreational telecasts as a mental space for relaxation of a war-weary and psychologically torn population. The phenomenon of popular Hindi serials is most unlikely to degenerate the Islamic ethos or *Pashtunwali* (the code of conduct of the majority ethnic group, the Pashtuns) that is traditionally practised. Yet there may be a tendency of a section of the population, particularly the urban youth and women, to adopt certain nuances from these television telecast and help regenerate newer concepts of cultural life.

While divisions of opinion keep the society alienated on such issues, one needs to reiterate that the media in a war-torn society should be used more for reconciliation by exposing diverse views instead of dividing groups. Attention should be paid to exploring mutual understanding through the co-production of television news and public documentary programmes between different ethnic communities.[16] However, the space for entertainment for the war-weary Afghans in the form of films and soaps should not be restricted. Media programmes should have a dual aim to entertain within social norms and at the same time improve cross-ethnic understanding by covering all communities and groups in society as part of the social rehabilitation strategy of peace building.

NOTES

1. Simon Murden, 'Culture in world affairs', in John Baylis and Steve Smith (eds.), *The Globalization of World Politics*, 2nd edn., Oxford: Oxford University Press, 2001.
2. Yll Bajraktari and Emily Hsu, 'Developing Media in Stabilization and Reconstruction Operations', *Stabilization and Reconstruction Series*, no. 7, United States Institute of Peace (USIP), October 2007.

3. Ho-Won Jeong, *Peacebuilding in Postconflict Societies: Strategies and Processes*, Delhi: Viva Books Private Limited (in arrangement with Lynne Rienner Publishers), 2006, p. 181.
4. *Afghan Media Commission Report*, Final Report of the Afghan Media Commission, 2005, available at www.jemb.org/pdf/JEMBS_LGL_MC_Final_Report_2005-11-18_Eng.pdf.
5. Abubaker Saddique, 'Afghanistan's Media Renaissance', *Newsline*, January 2005, available at www.newsline.com.pk/NewJan2005/newsbeatjan2005.htm.
6. Bruce Girard, 'The Potential for Community Radio in Afghanistan', report of a fact-finding mission, 5-22 October 2002, available at www.comunica.org/afghanistan.
7. Ibid.
8. Biswarup Sen, *Of the People: Essays on Indian Popular Culture*, Delhi: Chronicle Books, 2006, p. 3.
9. Jonathan Burch, 'Indian Soap Operas Cause a Stir in Afghanistan', *International Herald Tribune*, 17 April 2008.
10. Some major TV channels are RTA (government), Tolo, ATN, Ariana, Lemar, Samshad, Noorin and AINA.
11. David Blair, 'What Afghanistan Wants to See on Television', *Telegraph* (London), 31 March 2008.
12. Sardar Ahmed, 'Afghanistan's Indian Soaps Provoke Cultural Debate', *Kuwait Times*, 4 June 2008, available at http://www.kuwaittimes.net/read_news.php?newsid = NzI1MTU3MjI0.
13. Ibid.
14. 'Afghan Leader Says He Backs Ban on Hit Indian Soaps', *AFP*, Kabul, 22 April 2008.
15. The author got this perception while conversing with the Afghans in Kabul, 1 June 2008.
16. Jeong, *Peacebuilding in Postconflict Societies*, no. 3, p. 181.

21

Encounters: Reflections on Culture and Identity in Post-Soviet Uzbekistan

ANITA SENGUPTA

For a few *kopecks* she was willing to swing a smoking bowl of herbs before you and drive away the evil spirits. This encounter, a common enough experience for an Indian in India, occurred at the central Amir Timur Square in Tashkent dominated by a towering statue of Timur atop a horse. It has been chosen not because it is unusual but precisely because this is a normal encounter for any 'outsider', something that adds to the exotic character that is so central to most

Figure 1: Amir Timur's Statue at the Amir Timur Square, Tashkent.

descriptions of the region. However, this exotic encounter leaves behind questions about popular cultural traditions in a classic 'zone of contact' as it points to the survival of traditions older than Islam. Shamanistic traditions have always been a part of Central Asian tradition, and ethnographers like V.N. Basilov have remarked that while this may seem strange at first, the fact that shamanism became a part of Islam in the region actually resulted in its continued significance. In their outlook, shamans did not differ from other orthodox Muslims and while beginning rituals shamans regularly appeal first to Allah, then to various Muslim saints and only afterwards to their helping spirits. Islam also influenced shamanism in other ways by abolishing shamanic ritual costume, and by influencing a change of the traditional drum with rosary beads. Many Uzbek and Tajik shamans deem it necessary to obtain the blessings of a clergyman for ordination to be a shaman. Shamanism in turn is said to have influenced the activities of unofficial Muslim clergy. The residents of Bukhara, for instance, thought that certain *ishans* possessed a special ability to 'cure' the sick, because they had a protector spirit.

Such encounters raise questions about the nature of popular culture and identity in post-Soviet Uzbekistan. The construction of an identity is said to assume importance when problems of social dislocation emerge within social structures. In the contemporary Central Asian situation, this dislocation is being identified primarily in terms of dislocation of cultural authenticity and tradition. What is seen as having been dislocated are the structures of Islamic culture and language. The process of identification then necessarily involves a reidentification with the lost heritage. The common practice is to identity a generic understanding of Islam as the 'lost heritage' and then attempt to come to an understanding of what re-identification would mean. This necessity of re-identification is based on the supposed fact that Islam forms an important part of the sense of community of such Central Asian groups as the Uzbeks. This in turn implies the political potential that it carries with it in the region. The closeness of the attributes of power and of the sacred has traditionally been recognized by political anthropologists, examining the process of the formation of states, and it was the recognition of this potential that leads to the interest in the role that Islam could play in the process of state formation in the region in the current scenario. Since this was also my area of interest, generic understandings of the relationship seemed useful.

However, one soon realized that in the Central Asian situation, one would have to begin with the recognition of the fact that 'an Islam' was never a reality in the region. Islam in Central Asia does not have a monolithic structure, and various other trends like Sufism or even pre-Islamic faiths like shamanism, and other religions particularly Buddhism and Zoroastrianism exerted influence and wielded power. In fact, the Uzbek state itself recognizes *Navroz*, the festival symbolizing the arrival of spring and a remnant of Zoroastrian tradition, as an 'Uzbek' national tradition with a national holiday on the day. It is also important to remember that Islam itself is not monolithic. Apart from the major split between the Sunnis and the Shias, there always existed different doctrinal tendencies—traditionalist, fundamentalist, and in the nineteenth and twentieth centuries, modernist. There is also the interplay in the region between dogmatic religion, Sufism and popular piety, 'official' Islam and 'popular' Islam. All these streams share one faith, but the social structures in which their common Islamic sentiment developed, differed, as did their political experiences. In fact, it was interesting to learn that there are also regional differences in the practice of Islam even among the so-called 'settled' peoples with an acquaintance pointing out that the continuation of Islamic practices were more visible in Bukhara, their city of origin, than in Tashkent. Of course, what they included within the practices of Islam, regular visits to *mazars* for instance, imbibed within itself practices with much older traditions. There was also a case of sub-regional identity coming into play in representations of popular culture, creating further complexities.

This leads to the realization that in most scholarship on religion in the Central Asian region, the emphasis on the crucial role of 'an Islam' probably resulted primarily from the supposed Soviet era emphasis on the identification of a structure that was to become the principal focus of anti-religious propaganda. As a result, it was pointed out that the current structure of Islam in the region is said to owe much of its organizational and academic existence to Soviet efforts. This, however, ignored the fact that there was recognition of this diversity in Soviet ethnographic literature, which mapped the contours of these beliefs in detail. Examination of Soviet research on the religious and cultural traditions of the region points to the fact that there was detailed examination of other religious traditions, albeit as *perezhitki* or survivals of older traditions that the socialist system would replace. This assumes importance in the light of the fact that official Soviet Islam was recognized as having remained a link in the chain of the modernist *Jadidist* version of Islam. Among the early forms of religion, totemism had attracted the attention of Soviet scholarship; attention had also been focused on magic, mythology and folklore. Soviet ethnography had also focused attention on syncretism, for example, on the syncretic character of 'everyday Islam' with the survivals of pre-Islamic 'cults', which, having been absorbed by Islam, created distinctive everyday religious phenomena among different Muslim peoples. Basilov cites the works of O.A. Sukhareva, G. Snesareav, T. Bayalieva and L. Lavrov to show extensive studies of pre-Islamic relics among the Uzbeks. He also pointed to literature that shows that besides mainstream Islamic thoughts and beliefs, Sufism in its popular forms had absorbed certain pre-Islamic traditions of the region. Current studies on everyday life in the region point to a similar syncretism with the coexistence of *'namaz* and wishing trees' signifying the diversity of everyday religious life.

Figure 2: Entrance to the *Ark* in Bukhara.

Similarly, language is considered a vital component of identity. Yet my personal encounter with linguistic traditions and one that left the most lasting impression was in a city whose bilingual identity brings into question the entire corpus of literature about language as the basis of the 'imagined community'. During a cultural extravaganza organized on the occasion of the 2,500th year celebrations of the city of Bukhara, at the *Ark* in Bukhara, I happened to start a conversation with the man on my right. I was then embarking on my doctoral thesis on the formation of the Uzbek state and was interested in linguistic identity as a prerequisite for the formation of the modern state. 'What is your language', I asked in the course of a conversation being conducted in Russian, only to be met by a confused stare. 'Is it Uzbek or Tajik', I persisted, convinced that the ethnic origin of the man would soon be clear. The closest I got to the answer, which was a complex one reflecting a long history of the intermingling of Turkic and Persian peoples and resulting common cultural and linguistic tradition, brought into question the entire thesis that 'print capitalism' leads to the construction of an imagined community. What is immediately brought to the forefront is the fact that this is a generalization and it fails to take into account the specificities of certain historical experiences.

One such experience is that of the formation of the Uzbek nation state. Here, the acceleration in the pace of development of a pre-existing dialect of a language that was then designated as 'the' Uzbek language led to the creation of an 'Uzbek' identity, and eventually to the formation of the independent Uzbek state. Since the Uzbek experience is unique, its specificities need to be taken into account. In the Uzbek case, the importance of an examination of the role of language and linguistic identity arises from the fact that language was the guiding principle for the 'creation' of the national republics in the years immediately after the Revolution. On the other hand, once the republics came into existence, linguistic issues and a linguistic identity acquired political significance. However, any examination of this crucial role of language would necessarily have to take into account the fact that linguistic identity in pre-Soviet Central Asia was not actually a crucial element of identity as most people were multilingual by norm. Bilinguality or multilinguality was the reality against which the 'one nation one language' norm, now propagated by nationalizing states as their crucial component, developed. In most situations, diglossia was a way of life, and hegemonizing states could not do much to change it all of a sudden. Modern state formation often requires that multiplicities be ironed out with uniformities. Yet the coercive demand that each person must have one language has been hard to reconcile with the trajectories of an Uzbek's linguistic past. The problem of determining the true boundaries of the language is indeed difficult to determine.

Most examinations of linguistic issues conducted in Uzbekistan today point to the growing recognition among the non-titular groups of the necessity for learning Uzbek. A case study conducted among women in the city of Tashkent in October 1991, which covered 208 women of Russian, Korean and Greek ethnic groups, found that there was a growing understanding among the women of these groups for learning the Uzbek language. This shift was particularly evident among Russian women who would have previously considered the study of Uzbek unnecessary. A somewhat different survey was conducted by the present author among the students of the *Tashkent Davlat Sharkshunoslik Institut*, during February-March 1998—students who were interested in Indian languages and were then being taught Bengali by a colleague and the author. In fact, encounters with people with some knowledge of Hindi are not uncommon in Tashkent. This, of course, is partly because of the Soviet era connections with India but mostly due to the popularity of the Hindi film industry. In fact, negotiating everyday life in Tashkent becomes easier once one is identified as an Indian and therefore somehow connected to popular cinematic idols. This ranges from a simple *Namaste* on being identified as one to being stopped for a impromptu rendition of *Mera Joota Hai Japani*, which, strangely enough, happens even today.

The respondents for the survey were students of the age group of 16-20 years. The principal question that was asked was framed as 'Should Uzbek be the only state language in Uzbekistan?'. This question was asked since one of the predominant issues being debated and discussed in post-independent Uzbekistan was 'Uzbekization'—the transition to the use of the Uzbek language in all spheres of life. However, since most Uzbeks were generally found to be diglossic, it was considered to be important to make an assessment of this reportedly widespread significance of the use of the Uzbek language. A correspondence was sought between the answer to this question and various independent variables like age, sex, residence, education, ethnic group, religion, language spoken at home, language used with friends, at work, preferred language for reading newspaper/for TV and radio programmes. This meant that while on the one hand language used in daily intercourse was sought to be determined (in language spoken at home and language used with friends), on the other, language/languages used at work, for reading newspapers and for TV/radio programme was also sought to be determined. The survey also sought to record the intergenerational change in the use of language and, accordingly, respondents were asked about language/s spoken by their parents and grandparents. As students of a language institute, the respondents themselves were generally multilingual. However, for the purpose of the study, bilinguality in Uzbek and Russian or monolinguality in either Uzbek or Russian has been considered.

The sample for the survey was drawn from young undergraduate students of a language institute, where most of the students were residents of Tashkent. The students themselves were in nearly all the cases multilingual. Since the respondents all belonged to a uniform age group, were all residents of Tashkent (though some said that they were residents of Uzbekistan) and their educational backgrounds were similar this did not significantly affect the pattern of their answers. It was found that while all the Uzbek respondents were conversant in both Uzbek and Russian, Osset, Tatar and Russian respondents were bilingual in

Russian and in most cases English. Respondents with mixed parentage (Russian father and Uzbek mother or even vise versa—evident from the language spoken by parents) show an interesting combination of Russian as the language spoken at home and Islam as the religion. As with the respondents themselves, the parents and grandparents of Uzbek respondents were recorded as conversant in both Uzbek and Russian, while parents and grandparents of non-Uzbek respondents are bilingual in Russian and their mother tongue, in this case Tatar or Osset. Also while the parents of Uzbek respondents were recorded as bilingual in Uzbek and Russian, the grandparents were in some cases unilingual in Uzbek, possibly pointing to a change in linguistic preference in the recent past.

Given the fact that the sample consisted principally of young Uzbeks (about 77 per cent of the respondents), it could well have been surmised that this potentially 'nationalist' group would opt for Uzbek being declared as the language of the state. The results showed otherwise. It was found that 64 per cent of the students said no when asked whether Uzbek should be the only language of the state. Of those who said 'no', 76 per cent were Uzbeks. Further correspondence showed that this answer could not be directly correlated with ethnic group status. Nor could it be correlated with the language spoken at home. It is more closely related to the language that has been recorded to be the one in use at work, and the language in which the respondent reads newspapers and watches TV/radio, etc. Of those who said 'no', 28 per cent use only Russian for the above-mentioned cases and 60 per cent use both Russian and Uzbek. However, most of the respondents pointed to their mother tongue as the language spoken at home. The results of the survey points to linguistic preferences of a diglossic society. It also points to the fact that linguistic changes do not occur all of a sudden and, therefore, to the compromises that each 'new' state has to make in the course of determining its linguistic policy. In fact, this becomes evident from an examination of legislation on language in Uzbekistan today, which takes note of this. It is interesting that in the course of a conversation that the author had with the-then First Secretary of the People's Democratic Party, Abdulhafiz M. Jalolov pointed out that language is important principally as a means of transmission of ideas. Members of a nation may speak in many languages but still think of themselves as one people. In any case, a significant part of the younger population now wish to be part of a single globalized community and are keenly interested in learning English.

Such encounters are not just illustrative of a shifting historical phase easily encapsulated within definitions of transition. They embody the reality of a region that has negotiated numerous 'pasts' with legacies that remain significant even today. Here, the 'popular' often redefines formal structures. It is, therefore, in the course of reflections on such encounters with 'legacies' that the true essence of the cultural traditions in the region becomes apparent.

REFERENCES

Basilov, V.N., 'The Study of Religions in Soviet Ethnography', in Ernest Gellner (ed.), *Soviet and Western Anthropology*, London: Duckworth, 1980.

———. *'Izbranniki Dukhov'*, in Majorie Mandelstam Balzer (ed.), *Shamanic Worlds: Rituals and Lore of Siberia and Central Asia*, New York and London: North Castle Book, 1997.

Savelieva, Tatiana, 'The Role of Education in Formation and Development of Language Competence of Women in Uzbekistan Under Conditions of Poly Ethnicity', *Contemporary Central Asia*, 1, no. 1, 1997.

Shahadeo, Jeff and Russell Zanka (eds.), *Everyday Life in Central Asia Past and Present*, Bloomington and Indianapolis: Indiana University Press, 2007.

Sukhareva, O.A. 'Perezhitki Demonologii i Shamanstva u Pavninnekh Tadjikov', in G.P. Snesareyev and V.N. Basilov (eds.), *Domusulmanskiye Verovaniya i Obriyadi v Srednei Azii*, Moscow: Nayuka, 1975.

22

Orbiting the Steppe

SUCHANDANA CHATTERJEE

The image of the Eurasian steppe as Russia's turbulent Turko-Mongol frontier is passé. Fringe areas lying to the east and the south of the Urals, east of Vladivostok and north of Kazakhstan are being re-examined as grand connectors of a Turko-Mongol interactive space and having the potentiality of 'societies in motion'. While the focus continues to be on the spatial arenas called Eurasian borderlands, there seems to be a noticeable u-turn from the Russia-centric image of imperial control and resistance to the interactive phenomena represented by environment and ecology, human relationships, migratory movements of traders, pilgrims, intellectuals, exiles and convicts.[1] Such perspectives about human history have influenced generations of writers, post-colonial and post-socialist, and the attention shifts to cultural units, regional groupings and group identities. This brings back Owen Lattimore's view of dissociating oneself from fixed points of history.[2] Lattimore's disciples have continued the tradition of their mentor by not only challenging the methodological assumptions of dominant narratives about the Eurasian frontier but also representing it as a world space. Their focus is on the multitude of cultures that dominate this space and the emphasis shifts to insider's perspectives about value-based tradition, heritage moments, customary law, lifeways and indigeneity.[3] Frontier studies have been refashioned as 'regionology'[4] that includes a spectrum of ideas about regional dialectics and addresses questions like 'identity manipulation' (as in the case of the Sarts and the Uzbeks),[5] takes into account time frames and community identities that are hardly noticed and questions the premises of several debates. For example, the paradigmatic notion of binaries stressing differences between the steppe nomad (Kazakhs, Kyrgyz) and their sedentary neighbours (the Uyghurs), Inner and Outer Asia, the empire-builder (Chingiz Khan) and the empire-hackers (the post-Chingizid generation) is critiqued. The issue in question is not the sordid tale of disintegration, but the saga of integration or order, bequeathed to the autochthonous people of Eurasia by the *zhuz*[6] of the Golden Horde, the *yasa* (law or order) of the Mongols,[7] the spiritualism of the Buryats and the Buddhists, the White Tsar mythology of the Altaians[8] or the Kazakhs' *aul* (nomad's encampment) lifestyle. The tangled histories of the steppe have acquired more attention than in the past—there is as much interest in the Turko-Mongol lineage as in the Chinese legacy linking the nomads' world with the Chinese economic dominion in the Yenisei region. The steppe ecumene also extends to the west including the Volga-Ural historical and cultural domain, the Tatar spiritual and institutional links, the Tatar-dominated group identities in Muslim Russia and to the east that refer to varieties of Islamization in Inner Asia,[9] peripheral Islam in Siberia and Kazakhstan, oral history tradition among the Kyrgyz, local heroes and their eulogies (Kuchum Khan, Kenesary Kasymov), syncretism of scholar-enlighteners (Chokan Valikhanov) whose influence was underrated in *jadid*[10] writings. There is an overarching zeal about Eurasianism and its antecedents, reflected in Olzhas Suleimanov's *Az i Ya* doctrine[11] comparable to President Nazarbayev's visions about a Eurasian ethos with Kazakhstan emerging as Eurasia's new tomorrow. Nazarbayev's 'Kazakhstan-2030' banner highlighting the steppe's regional potential is the rhetorical guidebook for visionaries. But the regional aspirations are also thwarted by inconsistencies and ambiguities that their regimes represent. These are some of my impressions of the steppe locales of Almaty, Bishkek and Novosibirsk which I visited last year as a member of the Institute's delegation that participated in a seminar-series in collaboration with some of the premier institutions in the region.

BISHKEK-ALMATY-NOVOSIBIRSK

Talking about Bishkek's academic circuit, it is the Kyrgyz-Turkish Manas University (housed in the spacious Jal Campus and facing the Ala Tau mountains) that engages in a networking of scholars and institutions dealing with the Turkic world. The Turkic World Congress is a major event of the University that focused on Turkish lineage, metaphorical representations of the past, nomad economy, oral history traditions among the Kyrgyz, historical sources tracing early contacts between the cultural citadels and political capitals. The Third International Congress on Turkic Civilization: Globalization and Turkic Civilization (Bishkek, 28-31 May 2007) in which the Maulana Azad Institute's delegation participated was a mega-event about history, culture and interconnectedness of the Turkic world. The academia's image-building rhetoric is pretty much obvious as one moves towards the independence square or the main street crossings in Bishkek. The billboards advertise the Turkic identity of the Kyrgyz. But the cultural barometer is starkly missing in the shops and stores that advertise only material comfort of western living and reflecting a crude understanding of Western modernity. Bishkek sways to the tune of the Western media but unlike Almaty or Astana, fails to impress as the hub of foreign investment. It is a beauty hub and the beauty of the Issyk Kol resort, is the traveller's delight. Bishkek, showcased as Asia's Switzerland, is like a model in a beauty show that fades from memory as soon as the show is over. The serenity of the blue mountains (the snow-capped Ala Tau where the Issyk Kol is located), is a reminder of that beauty-speak, so are the forefathers' blessings and *tengri* culture about which Bishkek's taxi-drivers and escorts speak so often. But the residents are also aware of the odds of urban living as the rich and the gorgeous prance around in the swanky plazas while the morose vendors on the bustling streets try to sell every possible item they display.

Astana, the new Kazakh capital is still like a baby in its cradle though it is trying desperately to thrive on its image as an administrative capital. Almaty on the other hand is the financial capital, the powerhouse of industrial and financial magnates and the hotseat of intellectual deliberations. The scholar environment of Almaty's Academy of Sciences is awesome. The city is a magnificent spectacle of memorials and monuments that are dedicated to their poets and writers like Abai Kunanbayev and Olzhas Suleimanov. The austerity of nomadic living is not what the city represents. Almaty is a city that experiments with every opportunity that comes its way. Kazakhstan's grandiose plans of emerging as the energy hub of Central Asia were conveyed by Institute for World Economy and Politics (IWEP), the Presidential think-tank of Kazakhstan. There is considerable optimism among policy experts about the fact that Kazakhstan is trying to create a space for development. Development also means adaptation and Kazakhstan's ability to adapt to the changing situation has kept the country ahead of its Central Asian counterparts. The impulse to move on has silenced Nazarbayev's critics. The cultural experts in Almaty are enthusiastic about Kazakhstan's 'heritage plans'. The country's legal experts are trying to set a moral standard by re-evaluating their judicial practices and legal institutions and it is in this context that the *biy* (rich landowner) judicial precedent is discussed more often. The Kazakhs believe that the nomadic legacy has been like a lifeline and a source of sustenance for inhabitants of the steppe. As we crossed the Bishkek-Almaty highway in less than four hours, a sharp breeze swept across the highlands and semi-arid grassy steppe which reminded me of the gutsy horse riders who braved this rugged terrain centuries ago.

The trip also included a short visit to a section of the steppe territory in the north, which straddles the forest zone of South Siberia. This horizontal stretch of land is not the nomads' terrain but a settler's enclave—which represents Russia's zoom and boom zone that is crisscrossed by the Trans-Siberian Railway and is connected with the Buddhist centres in Buryatiya and Kazakhstan's nanocentre Ust Kamen. The historical significance of merchant centres like Tomsk and Barnaul is undisputed. South Siberia is a part of this steppe ecumene and represents a paradise which is so different from the wilderness of the far north. In their emotional walk-the-talk interviews on the picturesque spot of the Ob 'sanatorium' called *Bukhta* (which was a three hours' drive from the science hub Akademgorodok), scholars of the Institute of History, Novosibirsk expressed their feelings for Siberia's Russian and Asian identities. *Oblastnichestvo* (regionalism) based on the regional aspirations of Siberian patriots Nikolai Yadrintsev (1842-94) and Grigorii Potanin (1834-1920) is very popular in Siberia today.

Emotions about Akademgorodok, the Siberian city of science, have not waned. A dream project of the Soviet era, the place is stunning right from the word go. Nestled in a corner of the city, Akademgorodok looked like a poster in a science magazine, an eye-catching institution where specialized centres of learning and scientific laboratories are housed and which has become a symbol of professionalism, research motivation and scientific commitment.

JAPAN AND EUROPE: THE ACADEMIC REACH

In the past year, there were good occasions to talk about personal experiences and get professional feedback and scholarly inputs about the region's identity and history. The Slavic Research Centre (Hokkaido) and Max Planck Institute for Social Anthropology (Halle) are highly rated as repositories and 'fieldhouses'. In Max Planck Institute, research is about the plurality of lifestyles, dialectics of the present and an attempt to re-examine social transformation as a phenomenon, recounting past experiences and comparing them with the current situation. The scholars affiliated to the Siberian Research Centre work on projects like environment and land use, generational perspectives, lifestyles, public and private space of House of Culture for which they also collaborate with German universities.

In Tokyo and Hokkaido too, short-term projects are popular and scholars and university students work either as teams or on individual basis. Projects like Islamic Area Studies of the University of Tokyo, the critical bibliography and epistemology framework of Central Eurasian studies of the Centre of Turkic-Ottoman Studies in Paris have involved a new breed of researchers. Allen Frank's manuscript analysis is an eye-opener about Muslim religious and educational institutions and Islamic scholars' teachings that have been seldom appreciated as educative guidelines. Kazakh spirituality and religious learning in Tajikistan should not in any way be confused with 're-Islamization'—this is a revelation of a generation of scholars that have addressed previous gaps in Central Asian historiography, pointing to the urgency of transmission of local texts that have not seen the light of the day because they have been guarded by families who have been wary of suspicion by the authorities. The evidence of family networks and connections with spiritual leaders in Tajikistan is a reflection of cultural diffusion too. There are indications about the ambiguities of relationship between the religious intellectuals and political authority, the devout and the impious. Now, these are crucial differences that can be ascertained by deconstructing historical moments and relearning texts which require sufficient skill and expertise. The expert lineage includes scholars like Stephane Dudoignon, Allen Frank and Uyama Tomohiko who have addressed innocuous questions about spirituality, religious practice and intellectualism in the steppe and Central Asia. In their research, they have highlighted engagements of pre-revolutionary and post-revolutionary generations and their strong local influence as disseminators of religious learning in Central Asia, Russia and China.

Max Planck's Social Anthropology groups, distinct because of their engagement in the field, also complements the perspectives of other disciplines. The foreign scholars' lecture programme arranged by Siberian Studies Centre was a unique opportunity to exchange views about history and historiography, methodology and perspectives. There was a book discussion programme in which discussants reviewed a few chapters of the new book *Natsionalzmy v Srednei Azii: v poiskakh identichnosti* (2007), authored by Sergei Abashin, the Moscow-based ethnographer. The discussion was about the author's critique of the methodology of Soviet anthropology and the Uzbek-Tajik discourse about contested histories and identities. The theme of my paper was living histories of the region and the idea of a Turko-Mongol heritage and vibrant nomadic ecumene that was also connected to a Russian past. The discussions that followed indicated the consensus among scholars about disengaging oneself from stereotypical representations of history and getting more involved in the life frames that represent living history. As Siberia's fate is linked with the steppe, there were many living histories that had to be narrated and which were beyond the scope of a dominant historiography.

These interactive meets were educative and were a shade different from the unwieldy panel discussions of international conferences like ESCAS X Conference in Ankara and the Central Eurasian Studies Conference in University of Tsukuba, which were attended by academicians of different hues who largely expressed their commitment to the disciplines they belong, NGO activists who were advocating their own agendas of sustainability and civil society, anthropologists who professed micro-region analysis, area programme directors and institutional heads who decided on patterns of academic networking dealing with pertinent questions about managing Central Asian research in Europe through a careful handling of resources that were available and the educational programmes that could be offered. Quite evidently, international research would be structured along the lines of availability as well as allocation of funds. So, Central Asian studies worldwide were also hardcore economics and management issues. These were clearly 'command lectures' to which the audience could neither comment on nor engage in serious deliberations. More interesting were parallel sessions that posited research questions about historical interludes taking into account specific cases like the Alash Orda phenomenon or rendering useful archival data about food and water policy during the East Bukharan insurgency movement or even questioning the methodological assumptions of Eurasianism and projecting the Altai case as the anti-thesis of Eurasianism, gauging the milestones in Inner Asia's intellectual history and trying to situate Mongol historiography in that particular context of intellectual tradition. Pondering over these and other historical subjects e.g. the tribal past and miscalculated socialist enterprises *korenizatsiya* (indigenization) and collectivization scholars immersed themselves in rapid-fire rounds about timelessness, transition and development, seeking to redefine methodological terminologies and several theoretical assumptions. So, it was a myriad of concepts, ideas and terminologies that were addressed in every alternate panel on history, society and politics. The kinship, ethnicity and identity-related panels were field-based that discussed the working of kin and clan-based identities, religious legacies (Sufi and *khwaja* lineage). The surprise element was the discourse about the nomads and their history, reference to Mongol memory and Ottoman integration. Central Asian public space got a fair treatment in audio-visual representations like art and architecture, music and theatre. Yet, the biggest show of all was the international relations' panel, bringing within its fold a range of discourses about the geopolitical space of the Central Asians, the game of naming, and every odd paper that was a tirade against dominant discourses. The papers reflected multi-layered interest ranging from energy and oil politics to the games played by actors and non-actors in the region.

The Central Asian Studies conference in Tsukuba (14-16 December 2007) addressed the important issue of approaches to the *study* of Central Asia, dealing with hybrid opinions about politics, history, society and international relations. The conference was a meeting point and breeding ground of interpretative arguments about history and history-writing and transition debates relating to Central Asia. Prof. Hisao Komatsu's keynote presentation on the evolution of Central Asian studies in Japan was a clear indication of the emphasis on source-based research that had already become established as a tradition in Japan and the University of Tokyo's Area Studies Projects like Slavic Research Centre of Hokkaido took the principal initiative in that direction with support from the Ministry of Education of Japan. Sons of the soil (viz., Farkhod Tolipov) made candid statements about their post-socialist disillusionments, ethnologists (viz., Sergei Abashin) pointed to the omnipresence of individual and collective memories, historians (Uyama Tomohiko, Mara Gubaidullina) reconsidered sources in history to counter celebrated notions and theories about orientalism and modernity, scholars re-examining the world of Islam (Stephane Dudoignon, Allen Frank, Bakhtiyar Babajanov) detailed every evidence about spiritual authority, dissemination of Islamic literature and the religious and literary agendas of the *jadid* newspaper *Haqiqat*. The Tsukuba platform was also an occasion to defend my paper on a silenced phase of Bukharan history, i.e. the transfer of power during 1920-4 reiterating the approach that silences in Central Asian history were not few but many.

The Tsukuba chapter was followed by a visit to Hokkaido on the pretext of an invited talk about Indian perspectives about Central Asia and Siberia that largely reflected on the format of 'studies' and musings about India-Central Asia historical links. Post-lecture, I surveyed the source-stock of the Slavic Research Centre Library which has, in tune with its research thrust on Eurasian borderlands like the Kalmyk republic, Chuvash and Orenburg has refashioned frontier discourse as regionology. For quite some time the centre has been focussing on Central Eurasia and its regional components and themes that are very relevant to my research on Siberia and Kazakhstan. The Western academia has been responsive to the inter-disciplinary nature of area studies conducted at the SRC but there has been scarce Indian understanding about the profound scholarship or research possibilities that exist there. What I found interesting is the Japanese academia's contemplations about Slavic Eurasia, structuring it as a discipline to extend the scope of Central Eurasian area studies. International summer and winter symposia, fellowship programmes, guest lectures, academic exchanges and student visits are major components of this comprehensive academic programme which also nurtures young researchers' Central Asian projects that are sponsored by the Ministry of Science and Education in Japan. The thrust areas of these sponsored projects are pedagogy, history and religion in the Central Eurasian region. The working of the Orenburg-Omsk governor generalate, the concord with the *muftiyats* and spiritual assemblies in Central Asia, the imagined communities of the Chuvash and the Marris, which are so distinct from the Kazan domain strike a different chord from the structure of Central Asian studies that are pet projects of core groups associated with centres like Indiana, Harvard, Carnegie Endowment or cater to the worldwide network like the CESS and ESCAS. The SRC's library is tempting and is filled with primary documents of the imperial government in the steppe and Turkestan, military historical records (Red Army journals), statistical surveys (*sborniks*) and Norman Ross microfiche collections on the Steppe Commission. The Centre's cartographic collections, collections on historical geography and periodicals on the Russian revolutionary movements as well as War archival materials are treasure troves.

Orbiting the steppe has been an unforgettable experience. The region, once shrouded in obscurity is now a happening place. The steppe phenomenon is the new global agenda for scholars, activists, business groups and institution-builders.

NOTES

1. Andreas Kappeler, 'Yuzhniy I vostochnyi frontir Rossii', *Ab Imperio*, no. 1, 2003; Alfred Rieber, 'Changing Concepts and Constructions of Frontiers: A Comparative Historical Approach', in *Ab Imperio*, no. 1, 2003.
2. Owen Lattimore, *Inner Asian Frontiers of China*, Hongkong: Oxford University Press, 1988.

3. Lattimore's ideas about interactive zones of China were revived by another Sinologist David Christian. David Christian, *A History of Russia, Central Asia and Mongolia: Inner Eurasia from Prehistory to the Mongol Empire*, vol. I, Oxford: Blackwell Publishers Ltd, 1998.

4. Kimitaka Matsuzato (ed.), *Regions: A Prism to View the Slavic-Eurasian World, Towards a Discipline of 'Regionology'*, Sapporo: Slavic Research Center, 2000.

5. Sergei Abashin, *Natsionalizmy v Srednei Azii-v poiskakh identichnosti*, St. Petersburg: Aleteiya, 2007.

6. *Zhuz* literally means hundred in Kazakh and is believed to be a confederation of Kazakh tribes.

7. David Morgan, 'The "Great *Yasa* of Chinggis Khan" Revisited', in Reuven Amitai and Michael Biran (ed.), *Mongols, Turks and Others, Eurasian Nomads and the Sedentary World*, Leiden: Brill, 2005.

8. Andrei Znamenski, 'Power of Myth: Popular Ethnonationalism and Nationality Building in Mountain Altai, 1904-22', *Acta Slavica Iaponica*, no. 22, 2005; Marlene Laruelle, 'The White Tsar: Romantic Imperialism in Russia's legitimizing of conquering the Far East', *Acta Slavica Iaponica*, vol. 25, 2008.

9. Allen J. Frank, 'Varieties of Islamization in Inner Asia: The Case of the Baraba Tatars, 1740-1917', *Cahiers du Monde Russe*, 41, 2/3, April-September 2000.

10. The Arabic term *jadid* means new and is became associated with the new method of learning that was introduced in the sphere of school education in the Central Asian region in the eighteenth and nineteenth centuries.

11. *Az* is the old Slavic word for the first person singular pronoun, 'I', *I* means the conjunction 'and', *Ya* is the modern Russian equivalent of 'I', the same first person singular pronoun. *Az I Ya* is interpreted as the varying 'I's, or selves whose identities differ but are brought together as one. See Harsha Ram, 'Imagining Eurasia: The Poetics and Ideology of Olzhas Suleimanov's Az I Ya', *Slavic Review*, vol. 60, no. 2, Summer 2001.

Book Reviews

Fighting Like a Guerrilla: The Indian Army and Counterinsurgency

Rajesh Rajagopalan
London: Routledge, 2008

KRISHNAN SRINIVASAN

The book's theme is straightforward enough—why, usually but not invariably, do states stronger than their adversaries lose guerrilla wars whereas they triumph in conventional warfare? This question is responded to by a case-study, that of the Indian Army's Peacekeeping Force in Sri Lanka in the late 1980s.

The question posed by the book is not really as rhetorical as the author seems to suppose. The proposition that the stronger party usually loses in guerrilla war has to be treated as highly contestable. And is it so easy to determine who the winner is in conventional warfare? Quintus Fabius Maximus and Phyrrus put paid to such hypotheses in very early history. Is it easy to determine a 'winner' in guerrilla warfare? The common supposition is that if insurgents are not crushed convincingly, they win, and that if the counter-insurgents do not win overwhelmingly, they lose. And is there such a clear-cut difference between conventional and guerrilla war? Most all-out conflicts are a combination of both.

This book is the text of a Ph.D. thesis, and it shows. It is packed with footnotes and seventeen pages of references, which could and should have been spared for the general reader. The use of the personal pronoun and rhetorical questions could have done with editing out. The first eighty-one pages have nothing to do with the title of the book, but comprise a disquisition on theoretical propositions and what other authors have written on the subject. There is a 'summary' after every chapter, rather like a school textbook, and in the section dealing with the case-study, there is an excess of alphabet soup; it is not uncommon to find up to 14 acronyms a page, which is an avoidable annoyance.

The book becomes far more interesting when it finally arrives at dealing with the Indian Peace Keeping Force (IPKF) in Sri Lanka. Rajagopalan claims it failed to win because of the 'conventional war bias' in its counter-insurgency doctrine. But perhaps the more basic problem was that the Indian Army had no clear directives or mandates or criteria for success—'ambiguous', as the author says himself, adding that it was 'not surprising that the Indo-Sri Lankan Agreement (ISLA) unraveled'. In other words, does this case-study fit the mould of the stronger army succumbing to a guerrilla force? Neither side wanted peace, so the peace-keeping operation was obviously rendered useless. Rajagopalan seems to mistake the effect for the cause, and also makes nothing of the egregious failures of diplomacy, and even common sense, on the part of Rajiv Gandhi, his immediate circle of advisers in and outside the Prime Minister's Office, the Research and Analysis Wing (RAW), and J.N. Dixit, the High Commissioner in Colombo.

The ISLA was a shoddy agreement, full of holes and waiting to fall apart. It did not provide for the fool-proof disarmament of the Tamil Tigers (LTTE). The IPKF was the main instrument of implementation; it was supposed to enforce the ceasefire, to collect weapons handed over by the Tigers, and dismantle the Sri Lankan army camps set up after May 1987. When the ceasefire inevitably collapsed, the IPKF was asked to use force against the LTTE. The author draws attention to the lack of numbers, lack of intelligence, and poor Indian Army 'doctrine' that was in any case never explicitly stated. Hardly surprising therefore that he concludes that 'the LTTE performed well partly because the IPKF performed so badly'.

The taking of Jaffna in 1987 by the IPKF was 'despite immense blunders'. The LTTE learned fast that there must be no more set-piece battles and so it proved till 1990 and the IPKF's withdrawal. The record of the Indian Army was by no means fully tarnished; it established control in urban areas, and provincial and national elections were held. But the Tigers were not defeated, and never accepted the ISLA, and the battle for hearts and minds was far from won since the support for the Tigers among the Tamils, for reasons including mortal fear, did not diminish. There was opposition to the IPKF operation both in Sri Lanka and in India. The Tamils who saw the Indian Army as assisting the cause of Eelam were disillusioned, and Tamil Nadu allowed the LTTE to function clandestinely from that state.

Despite these obvious disadvantages, Rajagopalan prefers to point in particular to what he claims is the erroneous Indian Army's counterinsurgency doctrine which has a strong conventional war bias that continues even after the IPKF experience and that with the Mizos and Nagas—though Kashmir is not mentioned. This doctrine reflects the obsession with external threats and the threat perception from Pakistan and China. Another factor cited by the author is the extent to which Indian cultural values shape state behaviour, including that of the Army. Unlike the US, Russia, Pakistan and Sri Lanka, asserts Rajagopalan, the Indian Army sees insurgents as people with legitimate grievances that need to be settled politically and not by military solutions that will not suffice; therefore minimum force needs to be used. Here is an interesting and novel proposition, highly contestable, but also highly worth developing. Let us hope Rajagopalan is induced to consider that as his next project.

Reading Orientalism: Said and the Unsaid

Daniel Martin Varisco
Washington: University of Washington Press, 2007

KRISHNAN SRINIVASAN

This book concerns itself with a deconstruction of Edward Said's 1978 book *Orientalism* and provides an exhaustive commentary on the intellectual debates that Said's book spawned—though the book was proclaimed so dense that it was almost impossible to read. So this is a briefcase-size *vade mecum*, a book about a book, and the author describes it a light-hearted approach, a 'judicious satirical criticism'.

One book should not define a man, but in the case of the late Palestinian Arab-American Christian Edward Said, that is precisely what has happened. Said's view in essence was that previous writing about the space east of Europe revealed more about the writers than the people written about in a very Occidental framework, which was part of a generic Western complicity of imperial ambition and colonial expansion. Said was the first to advocate that colonialism operated not only as a form of military rule but also as a discourse of domination that severed an imaginary East from a dominating West.

The argument in *Orientalism* is that a pervasive and endemic Western discourse, 'the magic wand of Western domination of the Orient', has constructed 'the Orient' which is false and prevents the perception of real authenticity, even by the Orientals themselves. Therefore the study of Islam and the Middle East is through a sieve that divides a superior West from an inferior East. So the question arises: does the Orient, as myriad Western travellers, writers or theologians considered it, really exist or not?

Daniel Varisco is an anthropologist who was working in rural Yemen when he encountered *Orientalism,* and agreed this was an issue that had to be dragged out of the closet to expose what he calls 'National Geographic exoticism'. Such is his dedication to dissect Said's work that as many as three pages are devoted to an analysis of the cover illustration of *Orientalism*'s 1979 paperback. The author is in full agreement with most of Said's political positions on the overbearing and condescending West but tempers his praise of Said's achievement by alleging that Said was frequently inconsistent, both in theory and execution, and also points out that Said's thesis paradoxically received scant attention among the constituents he wanted to protect, namely Muslims and the Arab world.

Varisco deals with the critical reaction to Said, the faults in his historical hindsight, and the absent self-critique of Orientalist authors and the self-representation of Orientals capable of representing themselves. He poses the question whether the 'real Orient' can ever emerge from the binary thinking that opposes East and West. He identifies what is missing in Said's approach as being any systematic sense of what the real Orient was and is. This criticism is not new, however. Said himself wrote: 'I have avoided taking stands on such matters as the real, true or authentic Islamic or Arab world.' Said seemed to have dodged the real issue, so no blueprint was provided on how to proceed or avoid the Orientalism pitfalls. If Said accused the West of creating a false essence, his critics in turn accused Said of creating an equally false essence of the Orient, and this has become a theological going-nowhere argument. Also, at which point do colonialism and neo-colonialism become post-colonialism and the attitudes they engender?

This book has mention of persons of Indian origin like Partha Chatterjee, Homi Bhabha and Gyatri Spivak. There is the now obligatory reference to Huntington but happily not to Fukuyama. Varisco concludes that moving beyond a West-East binary vision requires the recognition of an inevitable ethnocentricity in ourselves and a measure of intellectual tolerance. If half the US population still believe in a literal Adam and Eve story despite Watson and Crick and the human genome, how, he asks, can we fault Orientalist scholars for ongoing stereotypes perpetuated in the media and popular culture? The 'Orient' was perhaps invented, but it continues to be perpetually re-invented.

Shridath Ramphal: The Commonwealth and the World

Richard Bourne (ed.)
London: Hansib Publications, 2008

KRISHNAN SRINIVASAN

This slim book, comprising 12 essays, an introduction and a poem, is a tribute to Shridath Surendranath Ramphal, the Guyana-born statesman, on his eightieth birthday. Few great men are of the calibre of Oliver Cromwell who is reported as saying to the painter Peter Lely, 'Paint me, Master Lely, as I am, warts and all'. So those readers looking for a penetrating investigation or analytical critique of Ramphal's legacy are not likely to find them here. It is observed in the editorial note that there has not been any proper biography of Ramphal so far, and it may be asked therefore why the authorized biography route was not taken at this juncture rather than this compilation of short essays; the latter is clearly no substitute for the former.

Be that as it may, Ramphal was the executive head of the Commonwealth, a multilateral organization of which India is a prominent member, from 1975 to 1990, and as such the book will be of importance to Indian scholars of international relations, and the general public as well—the more so since Ramphal is by way of being a highly successful person of Indian origin, who achieved prominence in the milieu of multilateral diplomacy.

The editor, Richard Bourne, sets out the conspectus and Ramphal's priorities and achievements with admirable clarity, sensitivity and perception in the introduction, and it is to be regretted that Bourne did not allow himself the liberty of a much longer treatment of the subject. Ramphal's major involvements were directed towards the removal of racism from South Africa, the need for fairer trade and socio-economic development for those living in poverty, the problems of a depleting environment and the imperative of closer cooperation between nations.

Commonwealth history during the years of Ramphal's stewardship is extensively recorded elsewhere, and the reader will encounter little that is new in the various contributions. The Commonwealth Secretariat's strength was at its peak during the Ramphal years and was able to impact favourably on the eleven expert group papers and the four international commissions on critical transnational issues that Ramphal either sponsored or in which he played a leading part.

Indian readers will pay special attention to the two essays by Indian contributors, Moni Malhoutra and Siripurapu Kesava Rao, both of whom had worked with Ramphal in the Commonwealth Secretariat, and the essay on the Commonwealth and South Asia by James Manor. Malhoutra's piece has some amusing anecdotage, and interesting information on Ramphal's role in the London conference that led to Zimbabwe's independence. Mugabe's ignorance of electoral procedures on the eve of the elections leading to independence is particularly revealing. Siripurapu Rao's article, as befits a man whose precise hand has drafted all the major Commonwealth pronouncements from 1990 to 2002, has gravitas, is better written, and deals with Ramphal's attempts to bring about peaceful change in apartheid South Africa. Malhoutra draws attention to Ramphal's initiative in setting up the Commonwealth of Learning with its Open University concept; while Rao refers to Ramphal's work leading to the Southern African Development Cooperation Conference and the eventual admission of Portuguese-speaking Mozambique as an exceptional anomaly in the Commonwealth.

James Manor's is, by and large, an unsympathetic portrayal of South Asia between 1975 and 1990. It is not productive to make a retrospective assessment of what Ramphal may or may not have done with the post-Harare mechanisms—presumably a reference to the Commonwealth Ministerial Action Group set up to monitor and, where necessary, penalize member states that are delinquent in democracy and human rights. Ramphal as secretary-general did not have 'to deal with' the troubled and troublesome regimes as is implied by Manor. Ramphal was not inhibited in working with the governments then in power in the same way that he did with equally deficient or worse regimes elsewhere in the Commonwealth, including in the country of his birth.

It is curious that neither of the Indian contributors nor Manor give any indication that Ramphal was partial to upholding Indian interests; he was considered by New Delhi to be supportive of the Indian position, and the Indian endorsement to his candidature was regarded in New Delhi as being crucial to his obtaining a third term. Perhaps Indians deceived themselves, and the truth lies in the fact that Shridath Ramphal was capable of being all things to all men.

Ramphal was a visionary man and a great innovator. He was a pioneer environmentalist. From the most pedestrian of contributions, there yet emerges the picture of a restless far-seeing activist who was not discountenanced by the possibility of failure. Scattered though the pages are his countless offspring: the Iwokrama Project in Guyana, new emphasis on the problems of small and micro states, the creation of the Caribbean Community and the African-Caribbean-Pacific dialogue with the European Community, the South Commission and the International Institute for Democracy and Electoral Assistance— though the last-named finds no mention in the book.

Richard Bourne's task to edit this selection of essays was no easy one. Inevitably, the essays cover a wide variety of styles, idioms, and literary and scholarly capacity. There are repetitions and clichés. But some valuable nuggets of historical footnotes and interpretation are to be found: how the vexatious land question in Rhodesia was papered over at the London conference; how Nyerere obstinately opposed the economic reforms mooted at the South Commission. The essays are in varying degrees of adulation of the Ramphal reputation, and one contribution, by Guy Arnold, makes no mention of Ramphal at all and is surely out of place in this volume.

There is a great deal about the United Kingdom and the Commonwealth in this book, and emphasis on Africa and the West Indies. We can accept this as part of the provenance of the book and the preoccupations of its subject. There is no examination as to whether fifteen years was too long for anyone to hold such a high international post. Nor any mention as to why Ramphal overreached himself in his losing attempt to be elected as United Nations secretary-general. How did he come to be so misguided? Ramphal's nine years as a high official in Forbes Burnham's cabinet in Guyana is covered, but without enquiry as to whether Ramphal found it distasteful to work for a leader who was autocratic, rigged elections and discriminated against the Indian community, sowing the seeds of racial hostility in that country which remain to this day.

Some titles are given; others are not. Even 'Mr' and 'Mrs' are not used consistently. There does not seem to be any reason for polite or honorific forms of address in a book like this. One name is spelled in different versions on different pages. It is not clear why only S.K. Rao's name is not printed in upper case in the inside back cover. While these objections may seem like carping, small matters give cause for irritation. But they do not distract from the profile of Shridath Ramphal as a major international figure, with bravado and eloquence and that indefinable but much valued asset, charisma. Not all Ramphal's initiatives bore fruit, and he had his setbacks. Certainly the warts were there, since he is human, and they are well hidden in this volume. Nevertheless this volume of essays about Ramphal has redirected our attention to this considerable innovator and fashioner

of some of the international architecture that endures and operates
in our times, and we owe a debt of gratitude to Richard Bourne for
this.

History of Ancient and Medieval India: From the Stone Age to the 12th Century

Upinder Singh
New Delhi: Pearson Education, 2008

KRISHNAN SRINIVASAN

Encouraged by the claim of the author and the publisher that this
book is not only for the specialist historian but the general reader,
a generalist review may be acceptable. To begin with, this is a
monumental work, but its very table-top physical dimensions make
it very hard to read. There is no doubt, however, that for any scholar
dealing with early Indian history, this book should be a must read.

Did Indians lack curiosity about the world around them? Did they
have any concern for historical narrative and the collection of data?
Did their interests go beyond the religious and philosophical to the
worldly? While Upinder Singh makes no attempt to explain why
such basic questions should arise, it is extraordinary to what extent
she has to rely on indigenous religious texts and foreigners' (mainly
Greek and Chinese) accounts. The former is as reliable as using the
Old Testament as a historical document. Why were the 'Indians' so
uncurious about themselves and even about the East and South-East
Asia over which they held so much influence?

Therefore, up to page 350, we are still in the pre-Christian era and
with little documentation other than religious and quasi-religious.
Accordingly, the work offers more a history of literature and art
and artefacts than history of society, especially for the first couple
of hundred pages. Perversely almost, the author prefers to adopt the
reverse of the 'great man' view of history. So there is no mention of the
battle of Hedaspes between Alexander and Porus, or the war between
Ashoka and the Kalingas that led to Ashoka's fervent adoption of
Buddhism. There is also no mention of St. Thomas the apostle in
India, which may be of doubtful historicity, but no mention either of
the arrival of Christianity in India, which is more surprising.

There is inadequate cross-referencing between the several illustrations and the text as well as a wholly unsatisfactory index. There is no clarity why some items are in the index and others in the glossary and vice versa. Some subjects of interest to the general reader like the *ashvameda* horse sacrifice in the Vedas and the non-existence of a Pali script do not receive any attention.

Yet Upinder Singh's book fills a need: to close the gap between archeology, art and early history, especially when few other writings from such a perspective actually exist. Her work certainly leaves other gaps, which will have to filled by scholars coming after her.